THE
SHAHNAMEH
VOLUME V

THE
SHAHNAMEH
VOLUME V

Hakim Abul-Ghassem Ferdowsi

Translated by Josiane Cohanim

GIROUETTE BOOKS

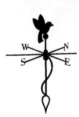

Girouette Books

New English translation copyright © 2023 Josiane Cohanim
Published in the United States of America
By Girouette Books
Santa Monica, California

Paperback ISBN 978-1-7349661-8-3
Ebook ISBN 978-1-7349661-9-0

girouettebooks.com

Cover art by ZariNaz Mottahedan
Cover design by Talia Cohanim
Typesetting and layout design by Sepehr Aziz

"The ancient book detailing the words
And the actions of good men has grown old.
I take upon myself to reintroduce it to the world,
To renew the memory of prominent and proud men.
It will be composed of six times ten thousand couplets,
And consist of beautiful lyrics able to cast aside grief."

CONTENTS
VOLUME FIVE

PREFACE

PART TWENTY-EIGHT

The Twelve-Year Reign of Hormozd

PART TWENTY-NINE

THE SASSANIAN EMPIRE CONTINUED

The Thirty-Eight-Year Reign of Khosrow Parviz

PART THIRTY

The Thirty-Eight-Year Reign of Khosrow Parviz (continued)

PART THIRTY-ONE

The Thirty-Eight-Year Reign of Khosrow Parviz (continued)

The Adventure of Khosrow and Shirin

PART THIRTY-TWO

The Seven-Month Reign of Ghobaad, Known as Shirooy

PART THIRTY-THREE

I. The Six-Month Reign of Ardeshir, Son of Shirooy

II. The Fifty-Day Reign of Goraaz, Called Faraaeen

III.   The Six-Month Reign of Boorandokht

IV.   The Four-Month Reign of Azarmdokht

V.   The One-Month Reign of Farrokhzaad

VI.   The Twenty-Year Reign of Yazdegerd

Appendix:

PREFACE

"If Wisdom is acquired from a source of knowledge,
Learning will never be wasted, not for a single moment.
You will realize it is all one with infinite expression.
When you face the true branch on the tree of learning,
Your knowledge will grow to be unlimited.
Then your turn will come,
And your purpose will be to reveal the path to others." (Volume I)

The fifth volume resumes during Sassanian times and opens with the reign of Khosrow Parviz. This fickle and feeble king is confronting a brutal challenge from the leader of the royal armies, Bahraam Choobineh, who has accused him of lacking a link to the royal line.

As in Volume Four, kings are inferior characters, exhibiting cruelty and corruption, while it is the wise counsellors who are the most honorable, noble, and valiant. During his struggle with his throne, Khosrow Parviz seeks the aid of the Rumi Caesar, while the army leader, Bahraam Choobineh, strategizes a way to win the good graces of the Chini Emperor. Here we see the territorial struggle for Iran-Zamin that involves both the west, the land of Rum, and the east, the lands of Tooran and Chin. This sort of struggle dates to the beginning of the poem to the reign of the sixth ruler, King Fereydoon, and to the allocation of various parts of the empire to his three sons, Salm, Toor, and Iraj. Later, during the reigns of Kay Kaavoos and Kay Khosrow, the clashes were mainly between the rulers of Iran and Tooran. During the reign of Lohraasp, we see more interactions with the land of Rum. During the Ashkanian and Sassanian times, the action alternates between Iran and its eastern neighbors, and Iran and its western neighbors. Now, with Bahraam Choobineh waging war on the King of Iran, we see for the first time an Iranian leader rising against his own ruler. And he will not be the only one. The fight is no longer with Ahriman or deevs, neither is it with another empire; Iranian leaders rise to oppose their own king.

After the death of Khosrow Parviz, there follows a succession of kings and queens whose reigns are short-lived. Throughout *The Shahnameh*, Ferdowsi calls attention to the necessary attributes for prosperous leadership. An example is evident in the words of the last Sassanian ruler, King Yazdegerd,

"This is the way a man acquires immortality
After his body has been buried in the dust.
The most important thing for a king
Is to proceed and rule with justice and faith.
Everyone praises his name and his person.
I wish to remain alive long enough to eradicate
The roots of evil proliferating in the world."

The stories repeatedly posit that a person who slays a prince or a king is doomed to be pursued and to suffer a miserable end. This is evident in the case of Zahaak with King Jamsheed, in the princes Salm's and Toor's cases with their brother Iraj, with Afraasiyaab with both King Nozar and Siaavoosh, and perhaps even Rostam after he is forced to save himself by killing Prince Esfandiar. When Tous kills the King of Mokran in the war against Afraasiyaab and a warrior attempts to cut off the dead king's head, Kay Khosrow asks for a dignified and proper burial for him:

"Let us hold back acts of cruelty.
One should never sever the head of a king or else
He will be deemed inferior to the lineage of Ahriman."

In the present volume, the legitimacy of King Yazdegerd is questioned by Maahooy Soori, whose greedy advances are not unlike Bahraam Choobineh's attempts to usurp the throne. Toward the end, the noble Iranian leaders warn Maahooy Soori about the perils of executing his own ruler:

"O man of criminal intentions, the deev has blinded you.
Know that kingship and prophecy are two pearls
Implanted in the same ring. To break one of them
Is to trample wisdom and life beneath one's feet.
Observe what you are about to do, and put an end to it.
Do not offend the World Creator,

For you will be the first to be punished.
You will leave behind for your sons a harvest
That will produce bloody leaves and bitter fruit."

Later, his children do collect the bitter fruit of their father's actions.
Still, in the case of the death of the last Sassanian king, there is no
Kay Khosrow to rise for retribution and restore the monarchy. We
are steeped in history, and there is no turning back to kingship. *The
Shahnameh* closes with a rather brief account of the Arab invasion of
Iran and the death of its last ruler. Ferdowsi concludes his epic saga
by telling us that the caliphate "brings a new religion and replaces the
throne with the pulpit."

The Shahnameh is a text about long ago kings, some thousands of years
old. It was written over one thousand years ago, and yet it still speaks
to us in ways that help us make sense of our modern world. Legends
and myths reflect our common dreams, according to both Carl Jung
and Joseph Campbell. Legends and myths provide insight into our
world by revealing a perspective beyond the obvious, the familiar,
and the physical, and by awakening dormant pathways deep within.

Ferdowsi did not imagine the stories on his own. He compiled them
from the sources he had, both oral and written. Since then, many
poets, writers, and translators have built on his book to create their
own works, as has been done in the present translation. Beyond the
original, I am grateful for two important editions I leaned upon over
the years: the original Persian text by Dr. Seyed Mohammad Dabir
Siaghi (2007) and the excellent French translation by Jules Mohl, *Le
livre des rois* (1878). This translation began as an exploration into a
work of literature to gain more clarity into the stories and the history
of an ancient, glorious civilization. Ultimately, it unfolded into a
deeper understanding of the human odyssey.

What I thought would be a simple art project turned out to be a
sixteen-year journey into translating twenty-five hundred pages of
verse, more than fifty thousand couplets. It opened the door to my
own quest into who I am and the mysteries of life. At first I intended
to complete the project at the point when Rostam's adventures
come to an end. But I found great value in reading and translating
to the very end of the poem. I was fortunate to have started the first
volume with my friend ZariNaz Motahedan, and I am grateful for
the continued partnership with Soudabeh Araghi to the very end,
the very last word on the last page of Volume Five. Her wise reading

of the Persian text deepened my appreciation. Furthermore, we are lucky to have educators everywhere teaching in Persian, in English, and in other languages to guide interested readers and to bridge the connection between past and future generations.

Ferdowsi opens his poem with the verse: "In the name of the Creator of Soul and Eternal Wisdom," a powerful though abstract idea. Soul and Eternal Wisdom (or *Kherrad*) are concepts interwoven throughout the poem as the warp and weft of human existence. He tells us that before the creation of sun and moon, earth, planets, animals and man, came the first creation: *Kherrad*, which is most difficult to translate but is an ancient ever-expanding knowing, equivalent to absolute pure consciousness or an infinite intelligence encompassing all of consciousness. Ferdowsi returns to this theme again and again. We, as human beings, have access to this Wisdom, though our ability to absorb and to retain varies from one person to another. Wisdom is "the king of language," the author tells us, and we must seek to express ourselves with it. In the second segment of the Prelude, "In Praise of Eternal Wisdom," Ferdowsi elaborates on *Kherrad*:

"Eternal Wisdom is both breath of life and initial vibration.
Eternal Wisdom is both inner eye and source of life.
Without inner vision, joy may not flourish,
For this guardian of life, precious Eternal Wisdom,
Is the first thing we learn about and the first creation."

Ferdowsi's foundational idea is of an infinite, ever-expanding source that we can tap into. Throughout, he periodically reiterates this point and reminds us of the importance of seeking, investigating, inquiring into and acquiring as much of this inner knowing as we possibly can. Living in an age where information is readily available at the touch of our fingertips, we often fool ourselves into thinking that education is meant to further our knowledge. Ferdowsi invites us to rise above the mere acquisition of knowledge, to explore the mystical qualities of life on earth, and to use our free will and, with compassion, lead our own battles against ignorance. We must deny the deev access to our minds, to conquer and overcome darkness to lift ourselves and come to a level of clarity through acting with and in *Kherrad*. Successfully binding the deev and living in wisdom will allow us to reach sovereignty and raise ourselves to the level of King Fereydoon:

"Follow the path you live, follow justice and give to others,
And in this way, you will be like Fereydoon.

Seek the things Fereydoon revered so that you may
One day crown yourself and make claims to royalty."

Ferdowsi achieved his dream of immortality, his legacy leaving an indelible mark on Persian culture and literature. He speaks to us through his stories and through his everlasting poetic expression. He is our connection to the past and our inspiration to lower the crown of sovereignty onto our heads and to rule over our individual kingdoms with love, justice, and generosity. We can re-create the present with an eye fixed on the glorious world Ferdowsi portrayed to the reader over a millennium ago.

About This Translation

This translation is based on two editions of *The Shahnameh*: the original Persian text edited by Dr. Seyed Mohammad Dabir Siaghi (2007), and a French edition, *Le livre des rois*, translated by Mr. Jules Mohl (1878).

Although Ferdowsi uses the past tense for his stories, it seemed more natural to narrate the English translation in the present tense. This provides a sense of continuity and permanence, as if the values he upholds cannot be constricted into a specific time frame.

Spelling and Pronunciation

In order to transfer text from Persian to English, we have used a simple form of transliteration. While it may vary from the more common methods, it makes sense to us and, we hope, will to the reader. In this approach, names of characters and places are spelled based on their pronunciation in Persian, rather than on their Romanized equivalent. For example, Zoroaster is *Zartosht*, Alexander is *Eskandar*, China is *Chin*, and Rome is *Rum*.

Most of the sounds for long syllables are pronounced as in English:
1. Aah sounds, as in "fall," are spelled *aa*, as in *Zaal* or *Rudaabeh*, except when a word ends in *ah*, as in *shah*, or *an*, as in *Iran*, *Tooran*, or *Nariman*. Some exceptions include *Baarmaan* and *Hoomaan*. One phonetic exception is in the second syllable of *Ghaaran* which has the *a* sound as in "fan."

2. Oo sounds as in "fool" are most often spelled *oo*, as in *Tooran* or *Fereydoon*. A few exceptions are *Zu* and *Tous*.

3. Ee sounds, as in "feel," are spelled *ee* as in *beed* and *deev*. At times we revert to -*i*- as in *Giv*.

Persian Words

The Persian language offers a unique perspective that requires careful consideration when translating into English. Finding an accurate English equivalent is often a daunting task. A number of words, such as *farr, kherrad,* and *ayeen*, are almost impossible to translate accurately. We have attempted to provide corresponding English words in footnotes and in the glossary; however, these may not completely capture the essence of the original words.

The absence of pronouns in Persian can lead to the use of vague terms such as "it", "this", or "that" to refer to a person or an object. This translation avoids pronouns when it comes to Yazdan, the divine Creator, and Sooroosh, the archangel. In the case of Simorgh, the mystical bird, we chose feminine pronouns to convey nurturing and maternal qualities.

VOLUME FIVE

The Sassanian Empire:
From Hormozd, Son of Kesra Anushiravan,
to the last ruler, King Yazdegerd

PART TWENTY-EIGHT

The Twelve-Year Reign of Hormozd

1 | The Beginning of the Story

The month of Tammuz[1] looks down at red apples
With a smile and quarrels with the apple tree
Over its leaves and its fruits:
"During spring, drunk with joy, you garnished
Your chest with a bouquet of blossoms.
Its colors exhaled a breath of modesty
And its stems a breath of tenderness.
What did you do with your flowers?
Where did you find such a bargain, at the marketplace?
Who gave you these chrysoprase and carnelians,
Heavy fruits that weigh down on your branches?
You might have asked a price for your blossoms.
You might have adorned your cheeks with lovely colors.
Your neck is tinted with the color of shame,
Your robe exudes the scent of musk.
Have you borrowed your stole from Jupiter?
Have you stained your pearls with blood?
Your chest is made of chrysoprase,
Your skin radiates with hints of purple,
Your head rises above the Kaaviani banner.
At the sight of your yellow, red, and white attire,
I surrender all my hope on the leaves of roses."

O spring, my idol, where have you gone?
You are hiding beneath garden ornaments.
Your breeze continues to perfume Mehregan,[2]
And I shall celebrate you again with a cup of wine.
I shall still sing your praises when your mantle turns
Yellow and adorns you like Hormozd's crown.
Though today fortune spins in my favor,
The imprint of my skills will not endure after I am gone.

◇◇◇◇◇◇◇◇◇◇◇◇

1 Tammuz: Tenth month of the Hebrew calendar and the modern Assyrian calendar;
corresponds to July on the Gregorian calendar.
2 Mehregan: Iranian fall festival in the month of Mehr, or October.

2 | King Hormozd Climbs on the Throne and Addresses the Army Leaders

There lives a border guard from Herat,[3]
An old, experienced, amiable man
Who knows many things and whose name is Maakh.
He is eloquent, noble, and prosperous.
I asked him what he knows on the subject of Hormozd
And his ascent on the throne of justice.

The old chief of Khorasan recounted to me
That Hormozd, upon climbing on the illustrious seat,
First pays homage to the almighty Creator,
Master of fate, then he proclaims,
"I shall bring glory to the throne and honor noblemen.
I shall shelter the world beneath my wings,
Following in my father's example,
Always in line with royal custom and royal majesty.
I shall make wrongdoers tremble in fear.
I shall return peace and tranquility to the oppressed.
If someone commits a crime, I shall be patient.
If someone is subject to suffering, I shall come to his aid.

"The qualities that support greatness are patience,
Kindness, generosity, justice, and dignity.
Know that nothing, neither good nor bad,
Remains hidden from the World Creator.
My ancestors, who bear their era's crown
And who were praised for their sense of justice,
Sought only integrity, affection, power,
Courage, propriety, their inferiors' submission,
The favor of noblemen, and the demise of their enemies.

"I am master in all the earth's nations.
I command with power, authority, and intention.
A pure man will revere a king elected by Yazdan.
The first quality of a king is liberality:
Through it, the world fills with beautiful things.
I shall tend to the poor with affection

◇◇◇◇◇◇◇◇◇◇◇◇◇
3 Herat: Or Hari, city in ancient Iran and in today's western Afghanistan.

And be the protector of the wealthy.
As confident as a man can be with his own means,
It is only at my side that he may prosper.
Do not hide from my benevolent heart your most
Cherished desires, and, if you fear something,
It will be easy enough for me to rectify it.
May any of you who is favored by fate
Be happy in the shelter of crown and throne.
I shall attain glory only when I am kind, just, and generous.

"Allow yourselves to grow more affectionate.
Distance hatred and greed from your hearts,
For the eyes of the one who abstains from these
Two vices will never witness a day of misfortune.
Whether you are great or small,
Make every effort to satisfy the World Creator,
And may the sensible man never submit to ingratitude.

"If providence favors a certain person,
Do not seize what belongs to him.
Do not frequent men who utter crooked words,
For speech is only for appearances.
If you are blessed with a just king,
Do not accuse him of a weak mind.
You may reproach him for negligence, though
He may be studying the words of ancient kings.
When a ruler spreads kindness, you must not
Scatter the seeds of perversity in the world.
Anyone who disregards my counsel
Is sure to reject the favors of the revolving dome.
When the king is pleased with you, all is well.
When you disobey or defy him,
Your place is at the door of perdition.
Your servitude has aspects of gentleness
And aspects of harshness, but if the king
Has reason to grow furious with you, even
A single time, he will disdain your subjugation.

"Never abstain from acts of kindness
Because they cost you some effort and pain.
Do abstain from rejoicing at the sight
Of an act of injustice or a cache of wealth.

Once you attain the object of your desires,
You have reached your destination, and
You may place seventy crowns upon your head.
You will then leave behind everything
You have worked for to your enemy.

"I take to heart what touches the poor,
And I shall never turn my thoughts away.
I ask our pure Foster Parent to grant me the joy
To bring happiness to the poor with my treasure
And to never afflict the heart of a pure man.
Those who pose in the world as kings
Possessed with the yearning for a treasury
Think of nothing else but the money.
I shall make them renounce their power.
I wish not for anyone to be the master of another.
Here is how I begin and how I shall end.
This is the content of what I say in public
As well as the substance of my private thoughts.
May the Creator bless you!
May the dome of sky be like another earth for you!"

The assembly listens to the words and thinks deeply.
The heads of the rich fill with fear,
The hearts of oppressors split in two,
But the souls of intelligent men and poor men
Beat with a sense of joy and happiness.

3 | Hormozd Kills Izad Goshasp and Poisons Zartosht, the Grand Wise Master

Hormozd governs in this way
Until his power is well established
And he is the master in every way, acting to his will.
He then changes, displays an evil nature,
And distances himself from the path of rules and faith.

He sentences to death those who stood by his father,
Men honored, happy, and perfectly secure.
He sentences them to death though they are innocent.
Such are to be the customs and the path of the king.

There are three scribes who worked for Anushiravan.
One is an old, learned man, and two are young:
One is named Izad Goshasp, the other Borzmehr,
Both wise, glorious, and full of affection; the third one,
Maah Azar, is a wise man whose heart is content.

The three stood before Anushiravan's throne
In the function of ministers and viziers.
Now Hormozd intends to sentence them to death,
For he fears that they may one day show ingratitude.

He begins by imprisoning Izad Goshasp,
Binding him with iron links for no reason at all.
The heart of the grand wise master, Zartosht,
Is troubled, and his grief renders his cheeks pale,
For he is a good-natured, insightful man.
The captivity of Izad Goshasp wounds his heart,
And he feels as if he has been stricken by an arrow.

One day passes. Izad Goshasp is deprived
Of servant, food, clothing, and a consoling companion.
He sends a message to his friend, the grand wise master:
"O wise man, you are for me like the marrow to my skin.
I am in the royal prisons without anyone to tend to me.
I am famished and wish to eat. My distress is vast.
Bring me some suitable fare. If I die,
Send cloth and someone to sew my shroud."

His heart deeply troubled, the wise man replies,
"Do not lament of chains if your life is not in danger."

He is afflicted by the message and pales with worry.
He says, "This unkind, unseemly man will find out
That his wise master has sent something to prison,
At which time my life will be worth an obolus.
Some calamity will befall me at the hand of the master,
And his face will pale with anger."
He despairs with a sense of pity for Izad Goshasp.

Zartosht commands his cook to send food to prison,
Then he climbs on his Taazian horse
And gallops to the side of Izad Goshasp.
At the sight of him, the prison guard is stricken

With such terror that color drains from his face.
Yet he dares not tell him to refrain from entering,
For he has to deal with a new king.

The old man sets foot to the ground weeping
And enters the cell of Izad Goshasp.
They embrace, hearts full of sorrow,
Lashes akin to a spring cloud.
They speak about the king's wicked nature
Until they have nothing more to say.

A table is set before Izad Goshasp.
They silently take the barsom in hand,
Then Izad Goshasp utters his last wishes,
Murmuring them as if in prayer.
The wise master listens to him speak about his wealth,
His palace, audience hall, and all that is precious to him.

Then Izad Goshasp says to the wise master,
"O fame seeker, speak to Hormozd in my name:
        'O King, even if you were to refuse to hear me,
        Think of the work and the labors I have endured
        In service to your father, raised in my arms.
        Now you reward my years of pain with prison?
        Beyond that I should fear for my life?
        On the day of judgment, I shall uncover
        My innocent heart before the Creator,
        A heart full of the grief inflicted by the king.
        If you wish to show mercy to a man
        Who has never committed a single crime,
        It would be a most righteous act,
        For a generous nature well suits a king.'"

As the wise master makes his way to his palace,
One of the king's agents runs at the same time
To report to Hormozd all that he has seen and heard.
His heart immediately hardens toward Izad Goshasp.
He sends someone to prison to execute him.

The king receives reports of the wise master's words,
But he never makes a show of his displeasure.
He reflects on all the ways he could kill Zartosht.
In the end, he commands his cook to secretly poison him.

When the wise master arrives at the hour of the audience,
To take his orders from the illustrious king,
The king says to him, "Do not walk away today,
For I have engaged a new cook."

The wise master sits, a table is set, and immediately
His face pales, as he understands that this spread
Is undoubtedly meant to plunge him to his death.
The cooks bring the dishes, and the king eats.
But upon receiving the poisoned plate,
The wise master observes it attentively, knowing
In his pure heart that the food has been contaminated.

Hormozd observes him in silence
And reaches his hand toward the dish
In a polite gesture to flatter the servants.
He reaches for a bone with marrow
And says to the grand wise master,
"O man of pure mind, here is a delicious
And delicate morsel that I wish you to taste.
Open your mouth; this is the way you are to eat."

The wise master says, "I implore you by your life!
May your head and diadem live forever!
Do not command me to eat this treat.
I am quite full; do not push me further."

Hormozd says, "I swear by the Sun and the Moon,
By the pure soul of the king, world master,
That you will take this piece from my hand
And not humiliate me by refusing."

The wise master says,
"The king commands, and I shall obey."

He eats the morsel, rises from the table
Moaning and twisting, runs to his palace,
And tells no one about the poisoned food.
Once his bed is made, he reclines screaming in agony.

He asks for bezoar, which they find in his treasury,
But the antidote does not work on this poison.
The wise master bitterly invokes Yazdan

To help him against Hormozd.

The king sends a trusted man to assess the situation
Of the wise master and see if the poison is working.

The wise man's eyes fall on the emissary,
And tears flow down his cheeks as he says,
"Go to Hormozd and tell him,
          'Your fortune is on the decline.
          I shall complain to the Supreme Judge.
          From now on, you will not sleep soundly,
          For you will be abandoned to divine justice.
          I take leave of you, O evil man.
          Your wicked deeds will bring you misfortune,
          And your enemies will triumph.
          You will not remain here on earth for long,
          And you will leave behind a cursed name.
          We shall appear before the Creator on equal footing.
          You have lost the privilege of a peaceful sleep.
          Since you have committed malicious crimes,
          Expect severe punishment to follow.'"

The trusted servant returns weeping
And reports the reply to King Hormozd.
The king regrets his actions,
He twists and writhes with their consequences.
He expels deep sighs, unable to imagine
A way of escaping the coming grief.

The grand wise master dies,
And sensible men shed copious tears for him.
Such is the world, full of pain and suffering.
Why should you take pride in a crown?
Why should you extend a hand toward a treasure?
This moment of pleasure will pass,
As time counts each of our breaths.

4 | Hormozd Sentences Simah Borzeen and Bahraam Azarmahan to Death

Once the affair of the wise master sadly ends,
The entire nation is shaken by grief.
The bloodthirsty and unworthy world master
Does not reflect on the misfortune of fate.
He prepares himself to shed more blood,
Making use of Bahraam Azarmahan to that end.

One evening, as night deepens, he summons him,
Seats him crouching before him, and says to him,
"Do you wish to obtain security
And be preserved from mistreatment and petulance?
When the sun shines in the dome of sky
And the mountain crest is like the back of an armor,
You will come to my court with Iran's noblemen,
And you will take your positions before my throne.
I shall question you on Simah Borzeen,
And you will not hesitate in your replies.
I shall ask you what kind of a man is your friend,
Whether he is an evil worshipper or a Yazdan worshipper,
And you will answer me that he is a wicked man,
Malevolent in every way, and of the race of Ahriman.
Then you can ask me anything you desire:
Slaves, seal, throne, or diadem."

Bahraam replies, "I shall do so and will criticize him
One hundred times more than you request."

In this way, the king seeks a pretext to deprive
Simah, light of the world, from any sympathy,
Though he came from an illustrious family
And was his father's favorite.
He strays from the righteous path
And flings himself into deceit and tricks,
Weaving the sad pattern of his dim fortune.

When the pearl-colored veil is ushered in,
And the sun reveals itself in the house of Gemini,
The world master sits on his ivory throne
And hangs the precious crown above.

33

Iran's noblemen assemble at the door
In two rows until a crowd arrives.
The chamberlain raises the curtain,
And they enter the audience hall.

Bahraam Azarmahan enters first,
Then Simah Borzeen and noblemen of the new court.
Each takes his position on his assigned seat,
And the crowd remains standing.

The king addresses Bahraam Azarmahan and asks,
"Does Simah Borzeen, who is present at court,
Deserve treasure, or is he an unworthy, wicked man?"

Bahraam Azarmahan understands the origin
And the reason for the world king's question.
He knows that they would all have cause to weep
And that in the end they will be buried without a shroud.

Bahraam replies, "O noble King,
Do not speak of Simah Borzeen, for he is the one
Who converted the land of Iran into a desert.
He has neither brain in his head nor skin on his body!
He speaks always of the worst things
And measures his decisions on them."

At these words, Simah Borzeen exclaims,
"O my dear, longtime friend, why give a false testimony?
Do not associate yourself with the deev!
What actions and words worthy of Ahriman
Have you witnessed in me since we became friends?"

Bahraam Azarmahan replies, "You have sown seeds
In this world for which you will collect the fruits.
From the fire you have lit, you will collect its black smoke.
Kesra had called us, you and me, and made us crouch
Before the royal throne in the presence of wise men,
Borzmehr, Izad Goshasp, high-ranking and fair-faced.
He asked who is the most worthy of the imperial throne
And who is endowed with natural majesty.
He would give kingship to the most worthy,
Whether he is the eldest or the youngest.
We all stood up and unanimously replied that

The son of a Turk woman is not worthy of kingship,
That no one wished to have him rule
Since he is of the family of the Emperor of Chin
And displays an ill nature, not to mention the fact
That he resembles his mother in stature and demeanor.
You alone declared that Hormozd was worthy,
And now you are well rewarded for your action.
It is for that reason that I have given testimony
Against you and my mouth utters curses."

Hormozd pales with shame at these words.
He banishes them both to the darkest prison
And does not speak of them for two nights.
On the third night, as the moon appears
Over the mountain crest, he gets rid of Simah Borzeen:
He has him killed in prison like one executes a thief.
But he draws from this act only curses and sorrow.

When Bahraam Azarmahan learns that
The pure-hearted man has disappeared,
He sends the king a message in which he says,
"O King whose crown is above the moon's sphere,
You know how much effort I have exerted
To keep your secrets hidden and how,
Before your father, glorious king,
I always acted in your favor.
If you wish to summon me and seat me
Near the royal throne, I shall advise you usefully.
Do not let me remain bound in a cell.
Iran will gain from my freedom, and sensible men
Will be free from concern and worry."

Hormozd receives the message
And selects a trusted man among his servants
To lead Bahraam to his illustrious court.
He summons him in the dark night,
Speaks gentle words to him, and says:
"Tell me something that will bring joy to my fate."

Bahraam replies, "I have seen in the king's treasury
A simple black box in which is placed a case that contains
A piece of writing in Persian traced on white silk.
Upon it rests the hope of Iranians and the land of Iran.

35

You must study this writing from your father,
Glorious king and world master."

Hormozd sends for his vizier, always ready to serve,
And says to him, "Search the old treasures
For a simple box, secured with Anushiravan's seal.
May his soul always remain young!
Bring it to me right away at night,
And do not waste a moment searching for it."

The treasurer makes haste, looks for the box,
Finds it with the seal still intact, and takes it to the king.

The world master opens the box invoking
The name of his father, Kesra Anushiravan.
He finds in it a case fixed with a seal.
He swiftly draws a sheaf of silk from it
And examines the writing traced by Anushiravan.

The letter says: "Hormozd will be a king
Without equal for the duration of ten and two years.
Later, the world will fill with trouble,
And the name and fame of the king will be lost.
Enemies will appear from every corner,
Specifically a man of ill race, akin to Ahriman.
The king's army will scatter on every side,
And the enemy will sweep him off the throne.
The evil man, a relative of his wife,
Will burn his eyes and deprive him of his life."

Hormozd looks at the letter written by his father.
He is seized by terror and tears the piece of silk.
His eyes fill with blood, his face pales.
He says to Bahraam, "You scoundrel,
What did you seek in this writing?
Do you wish to bring an ax to my head?"

Bahraam replies, "O son of a Turkish woman,
When will you grow weary of bloodshed?
You are of the race of the Emperor of Chin
And not from the lineage of Kay Ghobaad,
Yet Kesra placed the crown upon your head."

Hormozd understands that, were this man
To remain alive, he would raise a bloody hand on him.
With these sharp words, he returns Bahraam to prison.

The following night, as the moon raises its head,
The executioner kills Bahraam in his cell.
No man of reason, neither guide nor wise man,
Is left at court to advise and counsel the king.

All evil comes from a wicked nature.
Guard yourself from giving into poor inclinations.

5 | Hormozd Returns to the Practice of Justice

From then on, pleasure disappears from
Hormozd's life as worry pierces his heart.

He sojourns in Estakhr for three months every year
When the nights are shorter, with no desire to leave,
For the city is beautiful and the air is transparent.

He dwells in Isfahan for the three autumn months.
Isfahan, where noblemen dwell and the air is fresh.
In the winter, he resides in Ctesiphon
With his host, his wise men, and his advisors,
And in spring, he retreats to the plains of Arvand.

Some time passes in this way.
His heart continues to be terrified by the letter.
He prays three times a night,
His mind no longer fixed on evil,
His hand no longer engaged in bloodshed,
As he abstains from committing unjust acts.

Every day, as soon as the indigo veil of night disappears
And the mountain of yellow topaz breaks through,
A herald proclaims: "O illustrious, glorious,
Intelligent men, if a sprouting seed is trampled upon
And the farmer is afflicted by its loss,
Or if a horse enters a cornfield or if a man raids
An orchard, the horse's tail and ear must be cut off
And the thief's head hung at the gallows."

The king travels the world for months and years.
Nothing escapes him, neither good nor bad.
He performs acts of justice in all the lands,
Where grateful farmers praise and bless him.

He has a cherished son akin to the moon.
The father gives him the name of Parviz
And at times calls him Khosrow the joyous.
Never does the son leave his father's sight,
And the father feels unsettled in the absence of his son.
One day a horse that serves as a mount
To Prince Parviz escapes from the stables.
The young horse gallops toward the sown fields
With his groom chasing after him.

The field master appears and bitterly complains
To the groom: "Whose horse is this?
One must mourn for his tail and his ears!"

The groom says, "It is the horse of Parviz Shah,
Who cares and tends to his subjects."
He reports to the king the actions of the farmer.

Hormozd replies, "Go quickly, calm yourself,
And immediately cut off the horse's ears and tail.
Next, we must estimate the damage caused
On the field and have Khosrow pay for it.
Whether it is one hundred or seven hundred dirhams,
He must give it to the master of the field."

Parviz hears of the sentence and engages noblemen
To visit his father to ask forgiveness
And to beg him to leave the horse's tail and ears intact.
But the king, vexed at the affair of the horse,
Poorly receives these worldly men.

The groom, terrified of the king,
Rushes to the young horse, and with his dagger
Cuts off the ears and tail of the guilty beast.
Then, according to the king's command,
Khosrow pays the farmer who demanded justice.

The king departs for the hunt with an escort,

And they return with much game.
A rider, son of a leader, a man of high fortune,
Finds a vineyard full of abundance,
Plentifully bestrewn with sour, unripe grapes.
He commands his servant to pluck some grapes
And take them to the palace master and to the cook.

The vineyard owner arrives and says to the rider,
"O evil man, you did not endure the effort it takes
To raise these vines, and you did not duly pay for them.
Why do you deprive me of the fruit that I alone grew
While you had nothing to do with its production?
I shall go and complain to the king."

The valiant cavalier, for fear of calamity,
Instantly removes his richly bejeweled golden belt
And presents it to the farmer.

At the sight of the belt, the vineyard owner says,
"How you wish to hide your evil actions!
Guard yourself from meeting with the king.
You will not find a merchant in me,
So therefore do not attempt to bargain.
I am the one who obliges you by accepting the belt.
If the king hears of this affair, you are a dead man."

King Hormozd is celebrated for his victories
And his courage, having never lost a battle.
He is equally ready to ask and demand justice
And raise his Kianian diadem to the moon.

Brave and glorious, he never remains long in Mada'in.
This hero, vanquisher of lions, never rests,
Neither in spring nor in summer,
Neither in winter nor in autumn.
He crosses the world constantly in an attempt
To acquit himself of the profession of king.

6 | King Saaveh Drives an Army Against Hormozd

After ten years of royal prosperity,
Enemy voices begin to rise on all sides.
On the road to Herat advances King Saaveh,
With timpani, elephants, treasure, and army.

If you wish to know the number of troops,
Multiply four hundred by one thousand.
In addition, there are one thousand
Two hundred war elephants.
The world appears too narrow for their passage.

This host weaves like the warp and weft
Through the land from the desert of Heart
To the edge of the River Marv.[4]
Saaveh leads his army to Marv,
And the earth disappears beneath the dust.

He writes a letter to Hormozd saying,
"Recall your troops, repair bridges and roads,
Prepare fodder, and think of our swords.
I wish to travel through your kingdom.
My host journeys through seas, mountains, and plains."

The king reads the letter and pales
At the idea of the vast army approaching.

On the other side advances the Rumi Caesar,
Filling the land with one hundred thousand
Valiant and illustrious Rumi riders.
He captures and occupies with his sword
All the lands once seized by Anushiravan,
Whose name alone still stirs up his heart.
Reconquered, the people of these regions
Profess their loyalty to the Caesar's authority.
In every nation advances an army commanded
By a powerful and celebrated leader.

On the road to the land of the Khazars

◇◇◇◇◇◇◇◇◇◇◇◇◇
4 River Marv: Perhaps a reference to the Murghab River.

PART TWENTY-EIGHT

Arrive troops rendering the region black.
An experienced chief commands them
With his own treasury occupying the stretch
From Armenia to the gates of Ardabil.

On the side of the desert of spear-striking riders[5]
Advances an innumerable host under the command
Of young and proud leaders such as Abbas and Amr.
By their devastations they convert to flatlands
All the nations from which Hormozd draws tribute.
This army lands on the banks of the Euphrates River
And takes up space barring the growth of a blade of grass.

As his fortune begins to dim, Hormozd receives news.
He listens to his agents' reports, and the world king,
Once so happy, now withers, repenting for his actions,
For depriving his court of sensible advisors, all dead now.
Unable to single out men of sound counsel around him,
He finds cause to tremble deep in his soul.

He summons the Iranians and fills the hall
With men whom he seats before the throne.
He reveals the secret he held to the noblemen
About the armies coming their way,
So vast that no one can recollect such an occurrence.

All the border guards gather around.
They emit all sorts of opinions and say,
"O King, full of care and caution,
Listen to us for once in this circumstance.
You are an insightful ruler, and we are your subjects,
Yet we do not consider ourselves worthy wise men.
You have sentenced to death sages and scribes
In violation of the laws and the rules of religion.
Think and find a solution, someone to protect our land."

The wise man who serves as vizier says,
"O sensible King, you embrace wisdom.
If the Khazar army invites us to battle,
Your valiant troops will not hesitate.

◇◇◇◇◇◇◇◇◇◇◇◇◇
5 Land of spear-riders: Refers to the Arabian desert.

41

We shall deal with the Rumis!
We shall destroy the Arabs, pluck out their roots!
It is King Saaveh who squeezes you the tightest.
It is him who obscures our bright days.
Threats are rushing in from Khorasan
That may destroy our land and our treasure.
We must take action, launch an attack without delay
As soon as the Turks cross the Jayhoon.

The king, yearning for advice, says to the wise man,
"What action can we take against Saaveh Shah?"

The wise man replies, "Prepare an army.
By leaning on his host, a king raises his head.
Call the review inspector so that he may
Evaluate the number of people able to serve."

The review inspector arrives with his roll
To call the number needed for the army,
A number estimated at one hundred thousand men,
Including many riders and many infantrymen.

The wise man says, "With such an army,
We are ready to face King Saaveh in battle.
But if you wish to conduct yourself with courage
And righteousness, if you wish to renounce
Tortuous paths that lead to perversity,
You can save your subjects from a great calamity,
As is the duty of the King of Kings.
You have heard the significant story of Arjaasp,
The old destroyer wolf, and how he caused
Such harm with his Chini riders to Goshtaasp
And Lohraasp, all because of their religion;
How much misery did the city of Balkh endure
And how difficult life became in the land
Until Esfandiar was set free and was able
To engage in battle, as he so desired.
If the world king wishes not to listen to me,
The Turks from Chin will cause him much grief.
It is true that I am above the king in age,
But I shall never surpass him in wisdom."

The king replies to the wise man,

42

"The Caesar will not attack us. I shall return
To him the cities seized by Anushiravan,
And he will return to his home in Rum."

He selects a valiant, learned, and able writer as envoy,
A good observer, to relate to the Caesar
His intention to reinstitute the Rumi cities,
Adding the following message:
"On your side, guard yourself from stepping
Foot into the land of Iran if you wish to maintain
Your power and the favors of good fortune."

The envoy travels to the Caesar and acquits
Himself of the message from the King of Iran.
The Rumi ruler immediately returns
Without trampling the bordering region of the land.

Hormozd, King of Kings, selects a host that makes
The day disappear beneath the dust it stirs.
He sends it to the land of Khazaria to occupy
The mountains and scorch the properties.
The army chief, named Khorraad,
Is an illustrious, glorious, and just man.
Once he reaches Armenia with his troops,
The Khazars bar the road, but the Persians kill
Many of theirs and capture a sizable booty.

Upon hearing of Khorraad's triumphs over the enemy,
The Arabs return to their lands disappointed.

At the news of the victory, King Hormozd understands
That his next action is to fight against King Saaveh.
He sits deep in contemplation, delving into wisdom.

7 | Hormozd Summons Bahraam Choobineh

The king has a servant named Nastooh,
A happy man, intelligent and foreseeing.
He says to the world king, "May you live eternally!
May the evil eye never find its way to you!
My father is an old, learned sage named Mehran Setaad,

Whose wisdom finds no equal in the world.
He holds himself in a corner with the *Zand Avesta*,
Having renounced dreams and ambitions
Because of his advanced age and his fatigue.

"I just visited him for one day and one night.
I have spoken to him of King Saaveh,
His war elephants, and his vast host.
He said to me,
          'The events long ago forecast
          Are now coming to fruition.'
I questioned the old Mehran Setaad
On his knowledge of these affairs,
And he replied,
          'If the world king enquires,
          I shall reveal to him the secret.'"

The King of Kings immediately sends
One of his noblemen to fetch the aging man,
To place him in a litter, and swiftly travel with him.
The old Mehran Setaad arrives at court,
Heart full of wisdom, head full of words.

The king asks him,
"What do you know of ancient times?"

The old man replies, "O King,
You know how to speak and how to remember!
At the time before the Emperor of Chin agreed
To send your mother to the land of Iran,
I was commanded to travel to Chin leading
One hundred and sixty young, valiant lords
To ask for her hand in marriage.
Your father, a king full of wisdom and virtue,
Did not wish to receive from the emperor
The daughter of a slave as a spouse
And commanded me to ask
For the hand of only a queen's daughter,
Since it does not suit a king to wed a slave.

"As we entered the emperor's illustrious court,
We offered him the homage due royal kings.
He allowed me to visit the women's apartments,

Where he held five daughters, fresh as spring,
All beautiful and worthy of the royal throne,
Full of color, grace, and fragrance.
Holders of heather gait, the young ladies' faces
Were adorned, their curls garlanded with roses.
Your mother was the only one among them
Who was humbly attired without diadem,
Bracelet, necklace, or jewels.
She was seated, head lowered in silence,
Her face timidly veiled by her sleeve.

"She was the only full royal daughter,
And my acumen guided me to her.
Her mother was the daughter of a Chini ruler
And, by her pure nature, above bad inclinations.
The mother felt wistful at the thought
Of her daughter's absence from court.
Still, I selected her from among the maidens,
Keeping my gaze away from the others.
The emperor said to me,
        'Do set your sights on another daughter.
        All five of them are beautiful and glorious.'
But I replied,
        'I only desire this one for the king.
        If I were to select another,
        Misfortune would ensue.'

"He then summoned his advisers,
Sat them crouching before the royal throne,
And addressed them questions on the future
Of his daughter and the rotation of her star.
One of the astrologers said,
        'May you witness only days of happiness!
        May you always hear truthful words!
        Your daughter and the King of Iran
        Will produce a child akin to a fierce lion,
        Tall of stature, strong of arm, valiant,
        And as generous as a cloud.
        He will have black eyes and little patience.
        His father will die, and he will succeed him.
        He will spend a great part of his inheritance,
        Perform evil acts for some time, and then stop.

45

'An audacious king will appear
With a vast host of Turks with the intention
Of seizing the lands of Iran and Yemen.
The King of Iran will be concerned
And will fear the powerful and fortunate man.
But he will have a subject, who lives far away,
A renowned rider, completely devoted to his majesty,
Tall of stature, head covered in musk-black curls.
He will be hulking, bear strong bones,
A powerful nose, and a dark complexion.
This ambitious world seeker is Choobineh.
He will come from a family of warrior heroes.
He will travel from his residence to the royal court,
And, followed by his countless troops,
He will surprise and overcome the hostile Turk
And destroy his army from end to end.'

"Never did I see a man happier than the emperor
Upon hearing this discourse.
He offered Anushiravan his daughter,
Who was the diadem of all maidens.
I accepted her in the king's name,
And my mission complete, I returned.
The emperor drew so many jewels from his treasury
That transporting them became a challenge.
He escorted us with a retinue
To the shores of the River Jayhoon,
Placed his cherished daughter in the boat,
And returned from the river sorrowful.
The loss of his daughter filled his soul with grief.

"Now that I have recounted to you all that I saw,
O King, search for the man I have spoken of.
Tell the envoy to make haste in finding him,
For the king's victory is in his hands.
Do not share this matter with either friend or enemy."

After these words, his soul abandons his body,
And the assembly sheds bitter tears.
The King of Kings is deeply confounded,
And his lashes release his heart's blood.

He says to the Iranians,

46

PART TWENTY-EIGHT

"Mehran Setaad remembered this story,
And having related it from beginning to end,
He passed away and returned his soul to Yazdan.
Thanks be to the Creator for this old man
Who transmitted to us what we needed to know.
We must now search all the provinces
For the hero he has described to us,
Whether he dwells among noblemen or not.
Search tirelessly until you find him
And are able to bring him to me."

There lives an illustrious lord, head of
The royal stables, whose name is Farrokhzaad
And whose sole concern is to please the king.
He presents himself at court and says,
"The description given by the blessed man
Exactly matches Bahraam Choobineh, son of Goshasp,
An illustrious rider, according to me,
Most skillful in the handling of a horse.
If the description does not apply to him,
We have no other resource.
You entrusted the governance
Of Bardah and Ardabil to him,
And he has become border guard there,
With timpani and elephants."

The king sends an emissary mounted on a camel
Of speed, with the order to tell Bahraam
To ride from Ardabil to the royal court
Without stopping for anything,
Not even to scratch his head,
And to arrive without timpani or escort.

The envoy takes the command to Bahraam
And repeats to him what Mehran revealed.

8 | Bahraam Choobineh Arrives at the Court of King Hormozd

The ambitious Bahraam rushes from Bardah
Without calling army warriors to his side.
Once at court, the king invites him in promptly.
This man, full of experience, showers
The illustrious ruler with blessings and praise.

The king observes him at length
And forms a good opinion of him.
Recognizing in him the signs
Indicated by Mehran Setaad before his death,
He smiles, and his face regains its serene composure.
He receives Bahraam graciously,
Addresses him the customary questions,
And assigns him a sumptuous dwelling.

As the dark night casts its musk-scented veil
And the sun reveals its face, Bahraam attends court.
Noblemen open the way for him to pass.

The world master calls him, seats him above others,
And speaks to him about the nation's affairs
And Mehran Setaad's words: "What do you think?
Must I make peace with Saaveh Shah
Or should I send an army to fight him?"

Bahraam, the battle seeker, replies,
"If Saaveh wishes to engage in war,
It would be a defeat for us to ask for peace.
Furthermore, you would embolden the enemy,
Should they see you weakly surrender.
If you engage in feast at the time of battle,
Your rule would concede to submission."

Hormozd tells him, "What shall I do?
Shall I wait or take the road?"

He replies, "If the enemy turns away from justice,
We must fight and destroy him.
A powerful, wise man once said,

'A man who is in the wrong
Will not win against the law.'
Attack an enemy who seeks to harm you.
I shall combine water and fire in the same riverbed.
If we act any other way, the ancient celestial dome
Will search and replace you with a new king.
But if we employ the strength of our arms
And our skills, we shall be exempt
From blame before Yazdan, the pure.
We are ten thousand undefeated Iranians.
If we reject the troubles of battle,
The malevolent ones who seek only to blame
Will accuse you of flight at the time of war.

"But if we send a shower of shots over the enemy,
If we turn our bows into dense spring clouds,
If one hundred thousand swords and maces
Are raised against us on the field of battle
In a way that we cannot overcome
And we are forced to reject good fortune,
Only then shall we be coerced into accepting
The enemy's command, and only
After life, strength, and body will have failed us.
Let us fight to see what the sky's rotations
Will bring us of good and bad fortune."

The king smiles at Bahraam's words
As they bring radiance back to the throne.
The worldly noblemen exit the hall, hearts swollen,
And say to Bahraam, "When he questions you,
Do not speak so boldly, for Saaveh's troops
Are so numerous that they leave no space
For ants and flies to pass through.
Who would dare take command of the army
After what you have told Hormozd?"

Bahraam replies, "O illustrious and valiant men,
If the glorious king commands me,
I am ready to take on the post of army leader."

Talebearers immediately repeat Bahraam's arguments
To the king, adding ten words to each word he uttered.

9 | Hormozd Names Bahraam Choobineh Army Leader

The King of Iran feels relieved from the worry
The marching army of King Saaveh had caused him.
He gives Bahraam the command of his troops
And elevates his valiant head to the clouds.
Fame-seeking warriors salute Bahraam as their leader.

The new army chief presents himself before the king,
Covered in battle gear and armor, and says,
"Would the king allow me to review the troops
To assess their numbers and to see who
Among them is well suited for war
And who will pause at a time of acquiring glory?"

The king says to him, "You are the army commander,
On you depends our fortune, good and bad."

The leader departs for the site of the review
And asks the troops to parade before him.
He forms an army of Iranians fighters,
For which he selects the best cavaliers.
Ten plus two thousand of them are named,
Dressed in mail and riding horses of golden covers.
The group comprises forty-year-old men only:
Anyone younger or older is rejected and dismissed.

Bahraam Choobineh is commander in chief,
Celebrated for his astounding courage.
He places a vengeful man named Yalan Sineh
To march at the front of the illustrious troops.
His chest is full of ardor for battle.
He is to make his horse fly about,
Remind the brave men of their births,
And awaken in their hearts the urge to battle.

Next he selects Azar Goshasp, who, in an impulse,
Does not turn his horse from a blazing fire,
And charges him with the protection of the loads
And securing the two army wings on the same line.

In the rearguard, he places Konda Goshasp,
A man who seizes lions by the tail from atop his steed.

Then the army cavalcades before the shah.
The warrior hero addresses the troops:
"O illustrious men of penetrating minds,
If you wish for Yazdan to come to your aid
And dissipate the gloom of our dark position,
Do not oppress anyone or cause any harm.
Do not make use of weapons to inflict pain.
As soon as the sound of trumpets resounds
In the night, quickly rise and find your chargers
In a way as to fill the darkness with terror.
As soon as it is time for battle,
Neither horse nor soldier must lend a thought
To the extent of his strength or to the need to rest."

King Hormozd is thrilled to hear of Bahraam's
Wise preparations, his words, and his actions.
He opens his treasury and pays the fees.
He hands over to Bahraam his stores of weapons,
Calls on the treasurer, and opens the doors.
He brings to town a few teams of war horses
Wandering in pastures and commands the leader
To ask for anything else he may need, adding,
"You have seen all sorts of battles and have
Heard of the quantity of weapons and troops
In the possession of the illustrious Saaveh Shah.
You know that the Turks will rattle the arena
On battle day, yet you have selected only ten plus
Two thousand riders dressed in coats of mail.
I do not comprehend how you can function with so few,
All the more since instead of young warriors ready
To strike, you singled out forty-year-old men."

The commander replies "O King of blessed star
And sweet words, you know the stories
Of noblemen, world rulers of eras past.
If his majesty, my master, wishes to listen to them,
I shall prove that, when one has the support of
A winning fortune, the number of troops matters little.
Kaavoos found himself captive in Haamaavaran,

An innumerable host watching over him.
Rostam selected ten plus two thousand riders,
Among the most able and most courageous,
And liberated Kaavoos from his bonds
Without enduring any harm or injury.

"Similarly, the noble leader Goodarz, son of Kashvaad,
Took an escort of ten plus two thousand cavaliers
Riding horses in caparisons to avenge Siaavoosh.
Another time, the noble Esfandiar
Drove twelve thousand brave men against Arjaasp
And found a way to accomplish his feat
And destroy the fortress and the army of Turks.
If a host is more vast, it loses its courage and sense,
And the leader who leads innumerable troops to battle
Will end up drowning in humiliation over the outcome.

"Furthermore, you say that forty-year-old men
Will not fight better than young warriors,
But a forty-year-old man has experience
And more courage than others.
He remembers with tenderness
The salt and bread he owes you.
He has seen the many fluctuations of fate,
He fears the speech of malevolent people as much
As he feels shame and does not retreat in battle.

"Finally, the soul of a man who has served
Does not get easily discouraged,
For he thinks of his wife, children, and family.
A young man sees a bait and falls into an ambush.
He displays little patience at the time
When one must proceed unhurriedly.
He has neither wife nor children, nor sown fields.
He cannot distinguish the valuable from the worthless.
Since one may acquire wisdom without experience,
He cannot perceive what is crucial in a venture.
If he wins in battle, he is happy, rejoices, and stops.
If vanquished, he flees, exposing his back to the enemy."

The king's face blossoms like a spring rose,
And he says to him, "Leave the palace,

Go to the square dressed in battle armor."

The leader departs to asks for his belt,
His coat of mail, and his Rumi helmet.
He flings the caparison on his dun charger
And attaches his rolled-up noose on the saddle knob.

The world owner marches to the square with his vizier,
Armed with ball, mallet, and arrows.
The leader arrives with armor, mace, and Rumi helmet.
The king praises him, and Bahraam kisses the ground.

Bahraam exhibits his might and his skills
With mace, mallet, bow and arrow.
The king brandishes the imperial banner
Illustrated with the figure of a purple dragon,
The same banner that was carried proudly
At the lead of Rostam in times of battle.

The King of Iran holds the banner, strokes it,
And hands it to Bahraam with many blessings.
He adds, "The one from whom you hold
This banner is the man my ancestors referred to
As the leader of the people, the hero Rostam,
World conqueror, victorious and insightful.
May you always triumph in your devotion to the king!
I imagine you as another Rostam,
Equal to him in courage, valor, and dedication."

The warrior blesses him and says,
"May you remain victorious
And always maintain a state of serenity!"

King Hormozd returns to his palace, and
His warriors disperse as army leader Bahraam
Clutches Rostam's banner in a state of elation.

10 | Bahraam Choobineh Departs to Fight King Saaveh

As dawn raises its head over the mountain
And the dazzling shield of sun appears in the distance,
Commander Bahraam presents himself to the King of Iran.
He bows low to the ground in the presence of a crowd
And says, "I was a man without pretense.
By your grace, I am considered the diadem of the world.
I have a favor to ask of his majesty: that he sends with me
A trusted man so that he may write in his letters
The names of the warriors who fight bravely
And fling enemy heads into the dust, so that
Each may be rewarded with the object of his desires."

The king replies, "Mehran, the scribe, is a young man
Who knows how to speak and observe."

He commands Mehran to accompany the leader,
They leave the palace in haste, and march off to war
Under the leadership of Bahraam.
The army marches out of Ctesiphon,
An army of intelligent, brave, and valiant men,
With a leader who, lion-like, holds his head high.

Bahraam departs, and the king enters the palace
And secretly confers with his grand wise master.
Hormozd says, "This man will be happy on battle day.
But what do you think will happen after?
We must reflect on the possible outcome."

The wise man replies, "May you live eternally,
For you deserve a life without end!
It is indeed unimaginable that, with his strength
And stature, with his harsh and insightful speech,
This warrior would fail to reach victory
And return prosperity to our sterile world.
I only fear that in the end he rebels against the king
Who raised him, for he spoke boldly and displayed
His lion nature when he addressed his majesty."

Hormozd replies, "Do not spoil the bezoar

By mixing in it the poison of fate's malevolence.
If he gains victory over Saaveh Shah, he will be worthy
Of receiving the crown and throne from me.
May he remain as he is and never change,
For he will make a glorious king!"

The wise man pales at the king's words and bites his lips,
But the king does not forget this exchange.
After a little time, he selects in his court
One of his confidants, for he wishes to learn the truth.
He says to him, "Go in haste to the commander
And report back to me everything you witness."

The emissary departs instantly on Bahraam's trail,
Keeping his mission secret.
He is an expert guide able to interpret the future
And predict the outcome of a venture to the king.

It so happens that Bahraam, outside the gates of Ctesiphon,
Marching at the head of the army, spear in hand,
Encounters on the road a merchant.
Still at a distance from the army chief,
He holds an open basket made of willow stalks
Containing a heap of sheep heads.

The leader launches his horse and picks up
One of the heads with the tip of his spear.
He dashes about, then throws the head onto the ground.
As he walks, he predicts: "This is exactly the way
I shall seize Saaveh's head and fling it on the road
In plain sight of his troops, and thereby destroy his army."

The king's emissary observes these actions
And draws a prediction: "This man of auspicious fortune
Will one day be master of a throne with all his labors,
Then when he has obtained the object of his desires,
He will disengage from court, relinquish
His royal duties, and rebel against the king."

He returns and recounts what happened
To the world master, who is seized by pain and worry.
He finds the prophecy more bitter than death.
He withers, and this green leaf blackens.

He selects a young man from court as messenger
To travel in haste to the commander warrior
And say to him, "Do not advance beyond this point.
Return early in the morning, and come to me.
I shall dismiss all the visitors from the hall,
For I wish to give you all the advice you need,
And I have thought of many valuable strategies."

The young envoy repeats the words to Bahraam,
Who sends the reply to the king: "O wise monarch,
One does not summon back an army on the go.
A retreat would be a bad omen, and the enemies,
Upon hearing the news, would regain courage.
Once I gain victory, I shall return to your side,
Having glorified your land and your army."

The envoy returns and reports the response
Of the king's most loyal servant.
Hormozd Shah is delighted, and the pains
Taken by the envoy are wasted.

The next morning, the commander sets his army
In motion and summons Yazdan's blessings.
He marches to the province of Khuzestan
Without anyone suffering during the passage.

Once there, a woman charged with a sack full of straw
Wanders through the troops.
A rider approaches her and takes the sack from her
Without making a gesture to pay her for it.
The woman rushes to Bahraam, crying:
"I was robbed by one of your raiders,
His head covered in an iron helmet.
He snatched from me a pack of hay,
A pack on which my livelihood depends."

They search for the man and drag him in haste
To the valiant Bahraam, who says to the thief,
"Did you think this is an affair of little significance?"

They transport him running out of the tent enclosure,
Break his head, feet, and hands, split his waist in two
With a sword, and fill with fear the hearts of evildoers.

Then a proclamation resounds at the tent pavilion,
"O illustrious men full of good intentions,
Anyone who grabs a bit of straw will not find a defender.
I shall have him cut in half with the sword.
Purchase anything you may need with silver coins."

The army continues its march harmlessly toward Damghan,
And all the sites, whether on the road or further away,
Fall under its protection.

11 | Hormozd Sends Khorraad Borzeen to Saaveh Shah With a Perfidious Message

Hormozd is plagued by concern for his host,
The elephants, and the treasures of Saaveh.
His heart is full of doubt,
And Bahraam fills it with further distress.
His mind worried, his heart broken,
He falls prey to fear and terror.

As the dark night reveals itself in the moon's sphere,
The king says to Khorraad Borzeen,
"Prepare to travel to the enemy.
Make every effort without coiling from fatigue.
Assess the number and the caliber of their troops,
Who is their leader and who are the warriors.

He prepares a letter full of advice addressed
To the wicked king and includes countless gifts
Worthy of royalty. He says to his messenger,
"Travel to Herat, and when you come across an army,
Know that it belongs to the valiant Bahraam.
Do not believe that it may be any other host.
Present yourself to Bahraam to communicate
The message I have told you, and tell him
Many times how much I hope for his victory.
Tell him that, by means of good messages and good news,
I wish to prepare an excellent trap for Saaveh,
But the latter must not discover Bahraam's secret
Or learn his name and how renowned he is.
Tell him that I shall make King Saaveh fall in his nets

By means of lengthy, flowery speech."

Khorraad Borzeen prepares for the road
And travels in the direction indicated by the king.
When he encounters Bahraam, he tells him
All the secrets that he was entrusted with.
Then he goes to Saaveh Shah, at the location
Of his elephants, treasures, and troops.
He sees him, covers him with praise,
Pays him homage, and secretly conveys to him
The message he has been charged with.
He goes even further than the king
To persuade Saaveh to drive his army to Herat.

The illustrious Bahraam enters the plain of Herat
And sets up camp at the side of a spring.
A round of Turk sentinels exits camp
And spots Bahraam and his army.
At the sight of the valiant warriors,
The Turks return in haste to King Saaveh
And announce the presence
Of a corps of troops on the plain of Herat
Under the command of an illustrious leader.

King Saaveh hears the news, and this man,
So uncertain on the path to follow, grows concerned.
He summons Hormozd's envoy
And, furious, speaks to him at length:
"Evil deceiver, have you not seen the precipice?
Have you come from the court of Hormozd Shah
With the design of setting a trap for me?
How dare you bring a Persian army to fight me!
How dare you raise your tents in the meadows of Herat!"

Khorraad Borzeen replies to Saaveh Shah,
"If a small cavalry appears before your vast host,
You need not suspect any form of treachery.
It is simply a border guard passing through
Or a powerful man hoping to find shelter
Who has left his land to come to you;
Or perhaps it is a merchant with an escort for security.
Who can reach your land when the mountains

And rivers are replete with the threat of war?
I shall send someone toward the camp
To assess the nature of this man wandering here."

King Saaveh is pleased and says,
"It is all very well; such an action is satisfactory.
We shall send someone to assess
Whether this person has good or bad intentions."

When Khorraad Borzeen returns to his tent,
Night rapidly descends to cling to the mountain.
He makes preparations to take the road of flight
And escape death and destruction.

Saaveh instructs the Emperor of Chin,
His young, intelligent son, to advance with an escort
From his father's camp to the warrior's side.

The son appears before the Iranian army
And sends a cavalier to ask who are the armed men
And what is the goal of their expedition.

A Turk rider departs as swift as dust and cries,
"O illustrious warrior, who is your leader?
Who is your commander and your champion in battle?
The Chini ruler, who is the king's eyes and heart,
Wishes to see him, but without an escort."

One of the army warriors reports the message
Of the Turk to Bahraam, and the leader
Exits the tent enclosure and plants at his feet
A shining banner rising above his head.

The Emperor of Chin notices it, rushes over,
Covering his bounding horse with sweat,
And interrogates Bahraam: "Where are you from?
Why have you camped here? I heard that you fled Pars
For having been abused and having committed murder."

Bahraam replies, "Heaven forbid that my thoughts
Reflect solely a desire of vengeance on Hormozd.
I come here with an army to engage in battle.
I come from Baghdad on the order of the king.

Once we received news at court of the advance
Of King Saaveh's army, Hormozd said to me,
    'Go and block the road for them
    With mace, spear, sword, and arrow!'"

The Emperor of Chin rushes to his father to relate the news.
King Saaveh listens to him, grows suspicious,
And instantly asks to see Hormozd's envoy.
They tell him that Khorraad Borzeen has fled,
Weeping and regretful to have come in the first place.

King Saaveh says to his son, "How did this evil man
Find his way in the dark night with such a vast host?
How could our spies be so negligent and ineffective?"

12 | Saaveh Shah Sends a Message to Bahraam Choobineh

Saaveh sends an eloquent old man to Bahraam,
To whom he says, "Go and tell the Persian:
    'Do not foolishly abandon your honor here.
    You should understand that the king, your ruler,
    Sought only your death when he sent you
    To fight a man who has no equal in the world.
    He told you, "Go and bar the way for him."
    These words should not have charmed you.
    If a mountain wished to oppose my passage,
    I would surely trample it beneath the feet
    Of my mighty elephants and my troops.'"

Bahraam smiles at the dim strategies of this man:
"If the world king secretly meditates my death, I must,
If such is his pleasure, surrender my body to the dust."

The envoy returns to Saaveh Shah
And repeats to him what the eager warrior said.
Saaveh tells him, "Return to the Persian and say,
    'Why are you in such need of speech?
    Since you have come to the battlefield,
    Demand from us what you wish to acquire.'"

The envoy tells Bahraam, "Reveal your secret.
My ruler is a man of good fortune,
And he wishes to acquire a servant like you."

Bahraam replies, "Tell him,
       'If you wish to act justly, do not employ subterfuge.
       If you truly wish to coexist in peace with the king,
       I shall receive you as my guest in this land.
       I shall follow all your instructions.
       I shall give your army gold and silver
       As well as diadems and crowns to the worthy.
       I shall send a cavalier to my king
       So that he can travel halfway to greet you.
       He will provide you with provisions
       As one does with his equal.
       He will receive you amicably
       Should you wish to be his friend.
       But if you intend to fight,
       You will be tossed into a turbulent sea.
       You will expose yourself to the whale's jaws
       And be forced to return to the plains of Herat
       In a state that will make noblemen
       Bitterly weep for you in pity.
       I shall return you with scorn,
       Not allow you to remain here.
       May you find a trench at your door upon your return!
       May the storm follow you and rain be your escort!
       Your ill fortune plunged you into your demise.'"

The envoy departs, running as swift as wind,
And recounts the message of the ambitious man
To the king, from beginning to end.

The King of Turks enters into a fit of rage
Toward this man of lion heart, avid for war.
He calls for the preparation of timpani and elephants.
Then he says to the envoy,
"Return to the deev-man with another message:
       'There is no glory in fighting with you,
       And I have no desire to kill you.
       Just as your king is my inferior,
       You rank below my court's noblemen.

But if you seek protection from me,
I shall raise your head above the assembly.
You will receive from me much wealth,
And your host will be furnished by me.
An ambitious man like you does not seek
To gain valor in vain and foolish words.'"

The illustrious envoy returns to Bahraam
And repeats to him the words he holds at heart.

Bahraam listens to the unworthy message and says,
"We must not hide my reply from your king. Tell him,
      'If I am so unimportant that my insignificance
      Covers me in shame, the King of Kings,
      On his side, despises you too much
      To grow furious and to fight with you.
      It is I, because of my smallness, who has come
      With an army to destroy the tribe of Saaveh Shah.
      I shall sever his head and send it to my king,
      For it is not even worthy of carrying at spear tip.
      It would be a great humiliation for me
      To be your protégé, who,
      Despite his insignificance, comes to attack you.
      You will only see me on battle day,
      A banner the color of lapis lazuli behind me,
      And the sight of this dragon will be your death.
      Your head and your helmet will be
      The scabbard for the steel of my spear.'"

13 | Saaveh Shah and Bahraam Choobineh Draw the Lines of Battle

The king's envoy listens to the brusque words
And turns his back on Bahraam Choobineh.
He reports it to the King of Turks, whose wrath explodes.
He asks for the drawing of timpani
And drives majestic elephants to the plain.
The land dims with dust stirred by the horses' hooves,
And the blare of trumpets resounds.

When Bahraam learns that the army nears,

That the valley and plain are littered
With yellow, red, and black banners,
He tells his troops to climb on horseback and advance,
Covered in coats of mail and with heavy maces in hand.

Behind him stands the city of Herat,
Before him a sword-wielding army ready to strike.
He lines up the left and the right wings,
United as a single heart and a single body.
It is as if the world is made of armor,
As if stars borrow their gleam from the blades of steel.

Saaveh Shah observes the lineup on the field,
He notices the elaborate war apparatus
And the skills of the commander.
He sees that Bahraam has all of Herat behind him
While his own remaining terrain
Is rather confined and puts him at a disadvantage.

He says to his skilled, worldly companions,
"This Persian king sent a deceiver to me
Who remained until his army seized the city,
Leaving us nothing but a field full of brush."

He forms his army ranks in the constricted space.
The air is obscured, and the earth disappears from sight.
He has forty thousand men on the right wing,
Javelin-throwing and spear-holding cavaliers.
On the left wing, there are forty thousand as well,
Ready to strike with spears and swords.
In addition, he places forty thousand more
Behind the line of battle, having to exclude
Many soldiers because of the restricted space.

Finally, they form a wall of elephants
In front of the troops to bar the way.
But the heart of Saaveh Shah is worried
That his army may not be fully deployed.
It is as if fortune is announcing to him
That his throne will soon be vacant.

14 | Saaveh Shah Sends Another Message to Bahraam Choobineh

Once again, an eloquent and cunning emissary
From Herat arrives at Bahraam's side with a message:
"The fortune granted by the sky is not favorable to you,
For you wish not to listen to my repeated advice.
Befriend wisdom and open your heart's eye.
You encounter two men like no other
Among the royal races of the world.
They shine like the dazzling sun in the sky.
They are braced in armor throughout the year
In service to their immense valor.
I am one of them, the true world master;
The other is my son Parmoodeh, of illustrious birth.

"My army is more vast than leaves on trees
And consists of many blessed warriors!
If I were to count my elephants and troops,
The mere number of raindrops in spring clouds
Would be laughable in comparison.
I own weapons, tents, and tent enclosures
Beyond the conception of your imagination.
Were we to enumerate my horses, my men,
My plains, my mountains, you would grow weary.
All other rulers fall beneath my status,
Though they may not even be worthy of lower rank.
Even if the waters of the sea were to flood the earth
Or mountains were to grow feet to move,
They could never seize either my vast treasure
Or my war apparatus, the fruits of all my efforts.
All the illustrious world leaders consider me
And call me King, except for the Persian ruler.

"As for your fate, it is clear in my mind
That it falls into my hands.
If I were to advance with my host,
We would block passage to ants and flies.
Furthermore, I have one thousand
Elephants enclosed in armor,
Whose odor provokes riders to flee.

64

PART TWENTY-EIGHT

Who in Tooran or Iran would dare approach me?
Who would dare contend with me to cause me harm?
My army occupies all the land from here
To the gates of Ctesiphon and will always
Occupy this region, for I can add more land to it.
Who, O my dear enemy, has deceived you?
Or perhaps such a man is rather confused or mad.
Have you no pity for yourself? It appears not,
For your sight refuses to distinguish
Between good and bad.
How could a wise man yield to such frivolous talk?

"Renounce this battle and come to me.
I shall not leave you standing alone for long.
I shall give you power, offer you my daughter,
Along with unlimited prestige and a royal diadem.
You will find grandeur at my side,
And you will be above the miseries
Ensured by a state of subjection.
When the King of Iran is killed in battle,
His crown and throne will fall into my hands.
I shall then give you his throne and crown,
His diadem, his treasury, and his royal robe.
I shall leave the land of Iran for the land of Rum,
Abandoning to you army, treasury, and nation.

"I tell you this as I have taken a liking to you.
You have gloriously begun this affair
And know how to manage an army.
You are acquainted with the strategies of war.
Your father and your grandfather were army leaders.
There is no duplicity in my intentions.
I only wish to be kind to you.
You bring forth a small host to contend with me.
You will not receive further messages from me
Should you refuse to accept my offers."

65

15 | Bahraam Choobineh's Reply to King Saaveh

The envoy speaks, and Bahraam listens to him.
His reply is rather dim as he says,
"You stand out of favor in the midst of noblemen.
You are a worthless ruler in the world
Who lavishes us with worthless words.
No one respects you anymore.
I recognize by your first and last messages that
Your strength relies on your speech, not your actions.
But any man whose end approaches
Attempts to display his courage in his dialogue.
I heard your wicked words, and my heart failed
To tremble at the thought of your threats.

"First you declare that you will kill the king
And offer me his land and throne.
Such a thing reminds me of the words of a powerful man
Who said that when one expels a beggar from his village,
He will spread the word that he had been village chief,
That everyone was his slave while he was the master.
The sun will not shine upon the world for two days
Before I send your head to the king on my spear tip.

"Furthermore, you say that I will have cause
To be grateful for your daughter, your treasure,
Your army, and your land and that I will greet
You as a king who knows the ways of the world
Because you have offered me your daughter's hand,
That you will not keep the throne of Iran for yourself,
That you will send, from your beautiful palace,
Your daughter and your wealth to me, and that
You would have a friend such as me in Iran
And the heroes would no longer seek to fight you.
Today my spear is positioned at your ear.
I shall cut off your head with my dagger,
And once you are dead, your head, crown,
And treasury will be mine; mine will be your daughter
And everything you have amassed with much effort.

"Moreover, you claim to have crowns and thrones,
Elephants and innumerable horses.

An illustrious man who stirred on the battlefield
Said that a dog runs more keenly
When the water is farther from its cup.
The deevs diverted your heart when you declared
War on the king, and you now shudder faced with divine
Retribution and the awareness of your wrongdoings.

"Then you declare that all the noblemen,
Owners of crowns and diadems, are your subjects,
That all the great cities on earth are yours
And the entire world trusts your words;
The roads to the cities are open,
Subjects and rulers are free to cross the border.
But if you knock at their door, you could just as well
Obtain a kingdom for a thicket full of thorns.

"Also you mention forgiving me,
But you are far from taking into account
My courage, and when you see my spear,
You will not be speaking to me of pardon
And will not be begging me to be your subject.
When I form my army ranks,
I will hold for nothing your troops and your court,
Your war elephants and your throne.
I shall weigh your host for the mere price of an obolus.
When a king utters so many falsehoods,
He does not acquire honor in the world.
You tell me you cultivate affection for me
And will single me out as army leader.
But what is significant to me is the fact
That my own sovereign treats me with great honor.
I offer you three days of rest, but when
The crown of the world-illuminating sun appears,
We shall transport your head to the people of Iran,
Firmly planted on a spear tip to be proudly
Displayed at the door of Hormozd's hall."

The envoy departs, cheeks as yellow as curcumin.
His young and fertile fortune quickly aging.
With this message, Saaveh's face instantly dims.

Parmoodeh, the emperor's son, says to Saaveh,

"What is weakness in the face of an army
So insignificant one must find its fate deplorable?"

He marches to the royal pavilion's opening and gives
The command for cymbals, Indian bells, war elephants,
And timpani, wishing to paint the skies in hues of ebony.

The illustrious emperor is worried about
His valiant son's preparations for battle.
He greatly fears a fight with Bahraam,
And the fresh leaves of his tree wither.
He says to his son, "O army favorite,
Do not engage in war before the morning."

The two hosts return to their camps,
Troops depart from the leaders' tent enclosures,
Fires are ignited on both sides,
And the army fills with rumor and chatter.

16 | Bahraam Choobineh Has a Dream and Lays Out His Army

Bahraam remains alone in his tent.
He summons the Iranian warriors
And discusses the battle plan with them
Until the world is drenched in darkness.

The Turks and the Persians recline to sleep, and those
Who desire world conquest relinquish their dreams.

Bahraam sleeps in his tent, restless with worry.
This lion-man has a dream in which the Turks
Fight him bravely and defeat his entire army,
Cutting off the road back to the royal court.
He implores his warriors to help him.
He is on foot, and no one comes to his aid.
He is shaken awake, deeply disturbed by the dream,
His valiant head bursting with a sense of dread.
The rest of the night he obsesses with worry and grief,
Then he dresses, sharing his dream with no one.

At that moment, Khorraad Borzeen arrives,
Having run away from Shah Saaveh's court.
He says to Bahraam, "How can you be so trusting?
Look at the trap set for you by Ahriman.
Do not abandon the Iranians' lives to the wind.
Have some consideration for our illustrious men.
I implore you by your courage, have pity on your life,
For you have never been responsible for such a task."

Bahraam says to him, "You could not
Have acquired more valor in your land.
They sell fish from the summer season to the time of frost.
Your work is to set up traps; you reside near water basins.
You are not a man of spear, mace, and arrow.
As soon as the sun climbs over the dark mountains,
I shall show you how to fight kings and armies,
And you will witness his corpse lying on the ground
Amid wounded men and elephants."

As the sun rises in the house of Leo
And the world is as white as a Rumi complexion,
The blare of trumpets resounds.
The earth trembles with the commotion
And with the pounding of horses' hooves.
Bahraam orders his troops and mounts his steed,
Wielding a mace that has witnessed many a fight.

One can count three thousand mail-shielded,
Skilled, and tested cavaliers on the right wing.
Bahraam sends the same number of valiant riders
To the left wing. On his right is Izad Goshasp,
Who is able to cross the water's flows on his horse.
On his left is Konda Goshasp,
A worshipper of the temple of Aazargoshasp.
At the rearguard is Yalan Sineh, with an experienced corps.
In the vanguard is Hamdan Goshasp, whose charger
Sets ablaze reeds with the metal of its horseshoes.
Each one leads a group of one thousand warriors,
Valiant, stone-hearted riders.

A proclamation is announced to the troops:
"O men armed with spear and golden helmets,

I swear by Yazdan that I shall cut off the head
And fling into burning flames
The worthless body of anyone who opts to flee,
Even if he were faced by a lion or a leopard."

There are two paths leading to camp
By means of which one can easily escape.
Bahraam raises a barricade on each road, ten spans high,
Then he takes position in the center of his troops.

The master scribe of the world king
Approaches the army leader and says to him,
"You are not strong enough for such a venture.
It is not a sensible course of action.
Observe the armies on this battlefield.
We are like a strand of white hair on black buffalo skin.
One can distinguish neither land nor mountain or sea,
So numerous are the Tooranians armed with swords."

Bahraam cries out brusquely,
"O coward of dim fortune,
Your business is with ink and paper.
Who, in this army, considers you a man?"

The scribe approaches Khorraad Borzeen and says,
"Bahraam has become the companion of a deev."

The two old men seek a path of escape
To evade death and destruction.
The two scribes bite their lips,
On one side for fear of the King of Kings,
On the other side for fear of a shower of shots.

Now there is a steep incline, away from
The battlefield and the road taken by the Tooranians.
The two fearful scribes climb to the top,
And, from their high observation point,
They fix their eyes on the Turks and on Bahraam
To see their actions and behavior during the fight.

After organizing his troops,
Bahraam leaves the site of battle, emotional
And rolling in the dust before Yazdan, saying,

"O pure Supreme Judge, if you find this war unfair,
If you prefer Saaveh to me, give him self-control
In battle and victory over the Iranians.
But if I am to defend your cause,
If for that reason I endanger myself and my head,
Grant fortune to me and my army
And return prosperity to the world."

He leaves the site in a state of deep emotion
And climbs on his horse, bull-headed mace in hand,
Like Rostam in the war against Kaamoos,
The hearts of all the lion-men fill with terror,
For they see in him this era's Rostam going to war,
A panther beneath him, a whale in his hand.

17 | Bahraam Choobineh's Battle With King Saaveh

On his side, Saaveh Shah addresses his troops:
"Conjure up magic spells to send tremors of fear
Through the hearts and eyes of the Iranians
And to preserve you from acts of evil."

Those skilled in the practice of spells toss fire into the air.
One of the lion-like sorcerers, a tall and hulking man,
Sits on his horse, one hand holding a large serpent,
The other gripping a colossal dragon.
He rushes forth on the battlefield
And sets ablaze horses, men, and troops.
A fierce windstorm and a black cloud rise,
And a shower of shots falls on the Persians.

Bahraam cries, "O powerful leaders and warriors,
Discount the spells you are subjected to
And lead the army into battle with greater fury.
This is nothing but deception and black magic,
And one must pity those who resort to such methods."

The Iranians shout and seize their weapons,
Ready and willing to spill blood.

Saaveh Shah, on his side of the battlefield,

Notices the inefficacy of the spells
And the relentless forward motion of his enemy,
With Bahraam charging at the head of troops.
Saaveh drives his host against the left wing
And flings himself upon it like a wolf on a herd of sheep.
He breaks the Persians on this side,
Then assails the army center.

Bahraam observes the proceedings,
Notices his troops fleeing before the Turks,
Rushes forth, and, with his spear, flings
Three men off their horses and into the ground.
He says, "This is the way one must fight,
A representation of our glorious custom.
Have you no shame before the World Master
And before our brave and illustrious men?"

He rushes to the right wing like a fierce lion
Urged by hunger, and he breaks a large faction,
Forcing its leader's banner to fall into oblivion.

From there he approaches the army chief
In the center unit and says, "This affair is cursed!
If this battle is prolonged, our troops will scatter.
Look and see how the road appears."

They search the surroundings, unable to find an exit,
For they had built a hill over the passable road.
Bahraam says to his mightiest warriors,
"A wall of steel stands before us, and only those
Able to create a breach to cross this wall will find
Safety and return to Iran and to the king alive.
Bravely spill blood, cover your heads
With your shields, and strike hard with your daggers.
If the fortune watching over us is in our favor,
It will reward our efforts with throne and diadem.
No one must give up hope on Yazdan, so that
Our brilliant day does not convert to darkness."

On the other side, King Saaveh says to his noblemen,
"Bring the elephants to the army front.
Advance the troops en masse for the fight.
Narrow the world for the enemy."

At the sight of the elephants from afar,
Bahraam grows concerned, draws his sword,
And says to his leaders, "O illustrious, bold warriors,
Bind your Chaadji bows and don your helmets.
By the life and the head of the world king,
The elected leader of noblemen
And the crown of righteous men,
I implore all those who carry bows
To prepare them instantly and to plant
Arrows of poplar wood into elephant trunks.
Then you must seize your maces,
Rush to battle, and eliminate the enemy."

The leader binds his bow, dons his helmet of steel,
And sends a shower of shots through the air,
Using his bow to simulate a spring cloud.

His troops advance behind him.
Stars are obscured by arrow tips
And fletches that pierce elephant trunks.
Valleys and plains ripple with a sea of blood.

The wounded elephants trample
Their own troops beneath their feet.
They turn their backs to evade the blows
And cross the entire field of battle.
The army follows them, and the world becomes
As unsettled as the waters of the River Nile.
The army is in a great state of confusion.
Many men are killed, and misfortune
Fully triumphs over their brutal end.

In the region, beyond the routed army,
At the top of a beautiful hill,
They had placed a golden throne
On which sits the belligerent King Saaveh.
His host is like a mountain of steel in motion.
Heads are covered with dust, souls are dim.
Behind the men come the war elephants,
Crushing the warriors with their front legs.

Saaveh Shah's eyes fill with tears.
He attempts to understand his army's defeat.

He hurries to climb on a Taazian charger
And takes off in fear of a grave calamity.

Bahraam rushes after him like an elephant in heat,
A noose hanging on his arm, a bow in his hand.
He says to his troops, "O renowned warriors,
Ill fortune has made its mark on them.
This is neither the time to tell secrets nor to speak.
Send a rain of shots over their heads.
Make the effort to act as suits bold cavaliers."

He climbs on the hill where Saaveh Shah
Had sat on his throne with his golden headdress.
He sees a Taazian steed resembling a lion
And leaping toward the plain like a tiger.
He selects an arrow of poplar wood
Garnished with four eagle feathers,
Its tip sharp and as shining as gleaming water.
He rubs his bow from Chaadj, places the ring
On the deerskin, extends his left hand,
And bends the bow with his right hand.
The curvature of the bow makes a crackling sound.
The arrow brushes Bahraam's finger as it
Flies out into the air to pierce Saaveh's backbone.

Saaveh Shah drops into the dust, head first.
A pool of blood spreads beneath him.
Thus falls this ruler, master of a vast host,
Master of a golden throne and a golden diadem.

Such is the action of the revolving dome of sky:
Never will you find its face merciful.
Take care not to boast about a powerful post,
And no matter how certain you may be
Of your present state of peace and comfort,
It is wise to dread potential hardships.

The combative Bahraam approaches him,
Drags him through the dust, and separates his royal head
From his body in the absence of aid and of his men.

When the Turks arrive at the side of their emperor,
They encounter a cast out, bleeding, headless corpse.

They wail a common cry and weep bitter tears.
The earth is tumultuous and the air is simmering.

Saaveh's son says, "This is the work of the Creator,
And fate has watched over Bahraam."

The road taken by the army of Turks is so narrow
That many men perish in the march.
Many others are trampled beneath elephant feet,
And not one in ten survives or is free to return home.
All the others have either been crushed
By elephants or decapitated on the battlefield.

18 | Bahraam Choobineh Executes a Sorcerer

After nine hours have passed on this day of misfortune,
The Iranians cannot find a single enemy alive
Except for those who are bound to captivity,
Their souls pierced by grief, their bodies pained by wounds.

The road is covered with strappings, Indian swords,
Bows and arrows, and fallen helmets
That did not protect heads against death.
The earth is a sea of blood,
And in every corner one finds empty-saddled horses.

Bahraam makes the army rounds
To determine the number of perished Iranians.
He comes across Khorraad Borzeen and says,
"Spend the day to take part in our efforts.
Look for who among the Iranians is deceased
And over whose death we must weep."

Khorraad Borzeen surveys the battlefield,
Visits all the tents, great and small.
An illustrious army man is missing, one full of merit,
Named Bahraam, he is of the race of Siaavoosh.
Son of a great leader, he is an important Iranian chief.
Khorraad looks everywhere for him,
Running around like an insane person,
Hoping to find some hints of his whereabouts.

He examines all the wounded and the corpses
But finds no trace of Bahraam.

The army leader is deeply afflicted and repeats:
"Alas, this hero full of caution!"

Bahraam remains absent for some time,
Then reappears like the lost key of a locked door.
He brings a redheaded Turk with cat eyes
Whose heart appears ulcerated by anger.

At the sight of Bahraam, Bahraam Choobineh exclaims:
"May you never be the companion of dust!"
Then he interrogates the evil Turk:
"O hellish-looking man, exiled from paradise,
Who are you? What is your birth, what is your race?
Your mother will have cause to weep for you!"

The Turk replies, "I was a sorcerer, and my life
Was nothing like the life of an honest man.
Every time my leader goes to war
And the circumstances grow challenging,
I conjure up, in the middle of the night,
Dreams to stir and stimulate slow-moving men.
I am the source of your nightmare,
Hoping to cause you harm.
But I must search for a more powerful means,
Since my spells have no effect,
Since the star of misfortune turned against us,
And all my efforts drifted away into the wind.
If you can show mercy for my life,
You will acquire in me a resourceful friend."

Bahraam listens to him and reflects,
His heart anxious and his cheeks pale.
First, he thinks, "This man can serve me well
On battle day and in threatening times."
Later, he thinks, "What profit did Saaveh Shah
Draw from this sorcerer of dark paths?
Know that all good things come from Yazdan
To those who express gratitude."

He commands his head to be severed

And separates his vile soul from his vile body.

Once the sorcerer has been executed, Bahraam says,
"O Supreme Master of justice, virtue, power,
Victory, majesty, glory, and the royal crown,
Joy and sorrow, all come from you,
And the one who chooses the path is eternal."

The noble scribe arrives and says, "O bold warrior,
No king has ever come across an army warrior
Of your standing, neither Fereydoon nor Bahraam
Nor Anushiravan! You are equal in strength to a lion.
You are glorious and of sound counsel.
At times you protect; at times you destroy.
The entire land of Iran subsists thanks to you.
All the hero warriors are your slaves.
The throne of power gained its strength from you.
Our subjects have been saved by you.
You are a leader and the son of a leader.
Happy is the mother who bore you!
Your birth is illustrious; your roots are illustrious;
You stand above all men in glory and wisdom."

At this point, the noble warriors of the king disperse.

19 | Bahraam Choobineh Sends Saaveh's Head to Hormozd With a Letter of Victory

As dark night twists its black curls
And the veil of ebony descends,
Men's eyes succumb to a deep sleep,
And the world rests from the beat of timpani.
The wheel of sky continues to turn,
Finding the night dark and prolonged.

In the end, the yellow vessel of sun climbs
To emerge out of the water.
Men resume their labors,
And their slumber dissipates.

The leader appears, sends for his companions,

And asks them to cut off the heads of all
The deceased noblemen, chiefs, and leaders,
And all those who led the Turks in battle.
He commands a dazzling banner
To be planted behind each head.
He gathers all the heads and the prisoners
And removes them from the battlefield.

Then he summons his scribe and discusses
Various subjects with him at length:
The illustrious and innumerable host,
The motions of the revolving dome of sky,
The means employed against the battalion,
The struggle led by the Iranians
And how not a single cavalier shed his armor
For the duration of one day.

The scribe writes a letter to the king,
And Bahraam selects an emissary from among his men.
He places the head of Saaveh on a spear.
Then his battle banner, the heads of Tooran's leaders,
And the banners of the Chini riders are placed
On a race camel to be rushed to the King of Iran.

He sends the prisoners and the booty gathered
Without touching it to Herat and awaits the king's orders.
He also sends with the heads an expert in affairs
To obtain permission from the king to attack
The army of Parmoodeh, son of Saaveh.
The race camel departs toward the world ruler,
Along with effusive salutations
And a guide preceded by a rider.

On the other side, the Turk and Chini riders withdraw,
Stripped of gear and weapons, horses and loads.
Together they return to the land of Tooran.

Upon hearing the news, Parmoodeh removes
The crown of royalty from his head.
The Turks cry out in distress.
Life appears bitter to their noblemen.
Their heads are covered with dust,
Their eyes are full of tears, and no one can eat or sleep.

Parmoodeh summons the heroes,
His eyes shedding his heart's tears of blood.
He asks how this vast host lost on battle day.

One of his advisors says,
"We underestimated the Persian army.
Never will anyone find in the world
A cavalier as mighty and bold as Bahraam.
His army was not even one hundredth of ours,
Yet not a single one of his warriors was injured.
Yazdan, the World Master, guided him.
I could speak more, but you may not wish to listen."

Parmoodeh reflects on how to proceed.
He boils with fury, his cheeks pale,
And he decides in his pain to continue the war.
His army is composed of one hundred thousand
Illustrious men skilled in the art of battle.
Parmoodeh drives them from his residence to the plain
And to the edge of the River Jayhoon,
Ready to avenge his father's death
At the hands of Bahraam Choobineh.

Meanwhile, Hormozd, son of Anushiravan,
Sits with his noblemen and says despairingly,
"O army leaders, for two weeks now,
No news of Bahraam has reached our royal court!
What do you say? What has happened?
What will happen?
We must spend some time in deliberations."

While the king speaks, the master of ceremonies
Enters to communicate some excellent news:
"May the world master live eternally in joy!
Bahraam has vanquished Saaveh and has
Brought light into the world with his victory!"

The king summons Bahraam's envoy,
Offers him a seat above the noblemen,
And questions him. He replies,
"O illustrious King, everything unfolded
Just as you wished on the battlefield.
May you live always in peace and joy,

For your enemy's fortune has faded!
The heads of Saaveh and his youngest son,
To whom the father gave the title of Faghfoor,
Are at your door, pricked on the tips of spears
For the entire nation to see."

The King of Kings stands up to engage in prayer:
"O guiding Judge, you have annihilated my enemies.
O Creator of Sun and Moon, I was in such distress,
Hopeless for my fortune,
That I convinced myself I would be overthrown.
It is neither my valiant army nor my leader
Who brought about a victory but Yazdan,
Who wished to reward a devoted servant."

He asks for one hundred thousand royal dirhams
From his treasury, his inheritance from his father.
He distributes one-third to the poor,
Giving the larger portion to his servants.
He sends another third to the fire temple,
Where Nowruz and the feast of Saddeh are celebrated,
To hand out to the priests for the fire sanctuary.
Finally, he allocates the third share to active men
Who are to restore the destroyed caravansaries
In order to appease the travelers' fatigue.
Then he grants a tax remission of four years
To the poor as well as to owners of crowns and thrones.

A letter is written on the part of the king to relate
To all the renowned rulers of provinces
That Bahraam has vanquished the enemy host
And has severed the head of Saaveh with his dagger.

For seven days, the king holds a stance of prayer.
Then, on the eighth day, when
The world-illuminating sun rises in the sky,
He summons the leader's envoy and happily
Seats him in the assembly of noblemen.
He quickly writes a response to Bahraam's letter
And plants a tree in the garden of splendor.
He sends him a silver throne, golden slippers,
And other precious and valuable objects.

He names the bold leader governor of the land,
From the border with the Hephthalites
To the River Jayhoon, entrusting him with the deed.

Then he says to Bahraam Choobineh,
"Distribute all the wealth you have amassed
On the road to your troops,
Except for the personal riches of Saaveh Shah,
Which must be sent to my court.
Then you will battle Parmoodeh
For as long as he insists on independence."

He gives alms to the people of Iran, confirmed
With letters patent that he sends to all the regions.
Next he dresses the messenger in a robe of honor,
And the servants of the king bring him a horse,
A signal of his impending departure.

Bahraam is quite thrilled with his envoy's return.
He distributes all the booty to his troops,
Except for the impure King Saaveh's treasure,
Which he sends to the king's court,
Carried by illustrious and worldly riders from his family.
Then Bahraam departs with his army to engage in war.

20 | Bahraam Choobineh's Battle With Parmoodeh

As soon as Parmoodeh is apprised of Bahraam's
Attempts to seize the imperial throne,
He places all that he has in terms of gold and silver,
Jewels, and other wealth in one of his castles,
Named Aavaazeh, a place where he feels safe
And where he can enjoy the pleasures of life.

He crosses the Jayhoon with his host and advances
In pomp and circumstance toward the battleground.
The two armies close in on each other,
Not taking time to pause and eager for battle.
They select a suitable place to camp,
Two travel days from Balkh,
Leaving between them a space of two farsangs

Occupied by a large plain fitting for a battlefield.

The next morning, the warring Bahraam
Departs in haste to survey enemy troops.

Parmoodeh spots him and selects a steep hill
Where he settles his army,
Leaving no empty space on the plain.
From there he observes the Iranian troops,
The sight of which makes the desert tremble.
He sees Bahraam towering over the forces.
He is stunned by his stature and his limbs
And invokes the name of Yazdan many times.

With a deep sense of disquiet, he addresses his escort:
"This leader is the companion of a lion.
One cannot estimate the number of his troops.
No one will dare attack them,
For their leader is a proud and wrathful man.
The black dust beneath his feet
Will transform into a sea of blood.
But when darkness descends,
We shall execute a night assault
To banish fear and worry from our hearts."

Parmoodeh enters his tent enclosure
To hold a war council and to declare,
"This is one of the greatest ventures,
For, even though the army is rather small,
The riders and their mounts appear mighty.
They occupy the first rank among proud warriors.
They are armed with Choobineh as their leader,
To whom the tips of spears are mere thorns or weeds.
He is full of pride for having vanquished Saaveh
And rather drunk on blood, but if the Creator
Comes to my aid, I shall avenge my father's death,
Even if my enemy were a massive mountain."

At the time when Bahraam entered the campaign
And left Iran, marching against the Turks,
An astrologer had told him,
"Abstain from undertaking a venture on Wednesday.
If you do not pay attention to my advice,

PART TWENTY-EIGHT

A great calamity will befall you
And your affairs will turn to your disadvantage."

Now, between the two armies is a garden
In the middle of the battlefield, and Bahraam
Marches there on Wednesday and claims,
"We are going to have a wonderful time today!"

Rich carpets, wine, and food are brought,
Musicians are summoned,
And Bahraam settles in to drink wine in the garden.

Once the first part of the night passes,
A sentinel enters Parmoodeh's pavilion
And recounts to him that Bahraam
Is wasting his time with cup and wine.

The army leader selects among his troops
Six thousand valiant, illustrious cavaliers
And sends them over to surround the garden
Without a display of light.

The leader Bahraam is informed of their movement,
Their intentions, and the prince's plan.
He commands Yalan Sineh
To dig a hole in the garden wall.

Then Bahraam and Izad Goshasp climb on their steeds
With their boldest companions
And exit the garden through the hole.
One finds the execution of this plan
By the proud riders indeed most astounding.

At the garden door rises the sound of trumpets,
And Bahraam rushes into the brawl.
A second hole is dug up quickly,
And the Persians overturn the corps of Turks.

Bahraam, javelin in hand, leaps like a half-drunken man.
Few Turks escape his might.
His head holds an insatiable thirst for bloodshed.

The crash of blows administered by leaders reverberates

Like pounding steel hammers on a blacksmith's anvil.
From the garden to Parmoodeh's camp,
The road is littered with bodies deprived of heads.

As soon as the proud Bahraam returns
To his encampment, he contemplates a night attack.
With half the night passing, he dresses in armor
And drives his troops to the other side of the plain
Without being spotted by a patrol.

He arrives at the enemy camp,
And the sound of clarions rises to the moon.
With the echo of trumpets' blare in the middle
Of the night, the Turk riders rise suddenly,
Between the clatter of war and the obscurity.
They are quite unable to recognize each other.

Flames erupt from swords, burning air and ground.
Few valiant Turks remain alive,
And blood tints the stones the color of coral.

King Parmoodeh takes flight, as swift as dust,
His mouth dry, his lips blue.
He runs until dawn's radiance spreads
And the dark night withdraws its cloak's hem.

The Iranian leader reaches the Turks
And shouts a cry as fierce as a sparring lion.
He says to Parmoodeh, "O King who runs away,
Do not mingle with warriors.
You are not yet a man, O my son, you are a child,
And you are better off suckling your mother's breast."

Parmoodeh replies, "O destroyer lion,
Until when do you intend to spill blood?
On this day of battle, the crocodiles in the river
And the leopards on land are weary of the blood
Of noblemen. Have you not grown tired yet?
I believe you are a ferocious beast.
You have cut off the head of King Saaveh,
Whom the revolving dome of sky treated with tenderness.
You have destroyed his army in such a way
That the Sun and Moon have taken pity on him.

I am the heir of this valiant king.
Pretend that you have defeated me miserably.

"Our mothers give birth to us to die,
Whether we are Persians or Turks.
I find myself in flight as you rush after me,
But you will seize me only at the time of my death.
Allow me to live a little while longer so that I may
Come to represent an Iranian soldier to you.
Perhaps I will perish; perhaps you will.
Do not bother yourself; do not ignite your mind.
It is not a suitable behavior for an army leader.
I withdraw to my tent, attempt to retrace my steps.
I shall write a beautiful letter to the king
As is necessary under such circumstances,
Hoping that he will receive it favorably
And will save me from this invasion.
I declare myself his throne's devoted slave
And renounce all notions of sovereignty.
Distance from your heart any thoughts of war,
Be in good spirits and abandon yourself to feast."

Bahraam listens and returns to his camp,
In complete agreement with Parmoodeh's every point.
After having rested from the battle,
He marches to the Chini encampment.
He makes the rounds of the battlefield
And cuts of the heads of the deceased chiefs.
The heads are gathered to form a large mass.
Bahraam asks for stones to be piled up.
The warriors name this site Mount Bahraam.

He asks for all the booty and the armor
Of the riders to be brought up the hill.
Then he writes a letter to the king
On the subject of Parmoodeh and his vast host.
He recounts all that occurred with the Turks
And their king avid to avenge his father,
Who, in fear of the sword, resorted to ruse
And left this place in utter defeat.

On his side, Parmoodeh, the Emperor of Chin,

Closes the door to Fort Aavaazeh
And sits in contemplation, deeply worried.
Many troops gather around the castle,
But no one knows his plans for war.

Bahraam says, "It is an expression of weakness
To postpone battle when one is in the countryside."
He commands Yalan Sineh to select three thousand
Cavaliers from his camp and Izad Goshasp
To order four warriors to mount their steeds
And to strike, without delay, the necks of the Hephthalites.
By this action, he hopes to incite the king to exit his fortress
Once he sees the plain transformed into a river of blood.

21 | Parmoodeh Sends a Message to Bahraam

Bahraam Choobineh remains in this way
For three days at the castle gate.
On the fourth day, when the world-illuminating sun
Appears in all its splendor, he sends a message
To Parmoodeh, leader of the land and of the tribe:
"O brave ruler of the lands of the Turks and Chin,
Why do you prefer this castle over the others?
What became of Saaveh's drive to conquer the world?
Where are his treasures, where is his power?
Where are his elephants braced in coverings of steel?
Where are his wise men of lucid mind?
Where are his magic spells and incantations,
For you to hold yourself in this manner locked up?
Was the land of Tooran not sufficient for you?
Never did a man of your father's standing exist,
Yet here you are, hiding in the castle like a woman,
Striking your head with your bloody hands.
Open the fortress gates, ask forgiveness,
Call me your protector at the side of the king.
Send out your crates of gold and silver to the plain.
If you desire to retain your treasures, you will
Give up your land, for a king must despise gold.

"I am your intermediary at the royal court,
For I am the greatest hero of the land of Iran.

PART TWENTY-EIGHT

I shall give you nobility above all noblemen.
I shall raise you higher than you even desire,
And if you have a plan that could untangle
Your embroiled affairs, confide in me.
Since your position is so dire, do not seek to prolong it.
You know that I have forgiven you
And have opened the door of escape for you.
Otherwise you would have surely died like your father,
And neither your family nor your son
Would ever have a chance to set their sights on you.
Should you have a few friends keen on war,
Should you have a vast amount of treasure and gold,
Then, by all means, sound the timpani, resume battle,
For when one has wealth, one can always muster troops."

The envoy arrives and transmits his message.
Parmoodeh, who seeks to attain his goal,
Asks him to reply with the following:
"Abstain for as long as you are able to
From accessing the world's secret.
You are perhaps trusting fate, since the fatigues
You have endured have borne their fruit,
But do not allow yourself to be perverted by victory.
Though you are young, the world is ancient,
And no one knows the mysteries of its spinning sky,
Which never reveals to us its true, unmasked face.

"Sarcasm does not suit when it comes to a nobleman.
I as well have a host, elephants, and timpani.
But the powerful firmament tests us in our lies.
Guard yourself from becoming overly audacious.
My father was a vigilant world master.
You have witnessed his exploits on the day of battle.
The earth was the slave of his horse's hooves.
The sky spun at his will.
But he always reached the objects of his desires
And never suffered for having nourished
His mind with misleading ideas.
Value disappears when one makes use of spells,
And the enemy laughs from afar.

"You claim that the number of your troops

Is greater that the revolutions of Sun and Moon,
That your chargers and your elephants
Are akin to seeds of grass swept away
By the wind stirred by a mill wing.
All this will subsist until your day has passed,
For you will not always live in joy as light of the world.
Fear fate, for it sows seeds of vengeance.
It has the ability to convert antidote into poison.
Any man whose sole preoccupation is the spillage
Of blood and the terrorizing of his enemies
Will be slain with the same method he used to kill.

"If you destroy the land of Turks, retributions will ensue.
Nevertheless, I shall not engage in battle
With you without a vast army
Or else my friends would accuse me of folly.
I shall not present myself before you,
Though I do not fear that you will eventually kill me.
But you are a servant, and I am king.
Why would I debase myself before a subject?
There is no shame in asking for your king's
Protection out of necessity, at which point
The castle, my treasury, and my men will be yours,
And you may occupy this illustrious land.'"

The envoy returns to deliver the message
To Bahraam, who is filled with a sense of joy.

22 | Bahraam Choobineh Asks Hormozd for a Letter of Protection for Parmoodeh

A letter is composed addressed to King Hormozd
That could bear strategic fruit:
"The Tarkhan, Emperor of Chin, wishes to concede.
He is besieged in a fortress by the valiant Bahraam
And is in need of a letter sealed with the royal stamp
And holding the good news that he has been granted mercy,
A development that will be cause for celebration.
He requests our protection as he finds himself
In a predicament, having fallen from his high post.

May the King of Kings show a generous spirit to him
In view of his diminished and fading glory."

The letter's contents help raise King Hormozd's
Blessed crown all the way to the clouds.
He convenes the Iranians and seats them
At the foot of the imperial throne.
He asks someone to read the letter from Bahraam,
And they shower the reader with gems and jewels.

Hormozd Shah says, "Thanks be to Yazdan,
I shall pray three times a night for the emperor
To be my subject and the sublime sky my diadem.
The emperor raised his head to the wheel of sky
When he believed himself to be world master.
Now the army leader, this conqueror of provinces,
Has become the slave of a more powerful man.
It so happens that the chief of the Turks and Chin
Is in a situation in which he comes to pay homage to me.
Thanks be to the Creator of Sun and Moon,
Who has granted me the attainment of supremacy.
Let us distribute alms from our treasury to the needy.
And you as well address your prayers
And attempt to act righteously in all matters."

He summons the leader's envoy
And speaks to him at length with benevolence.
He asks for a belt decorated with stones worthy of a king,
A royal robe, and a charger with a golden bridle
With precious gems inset into every clasp.
Then he gives the messenger a crate full
Of dinars and many other valuables.

After having thus offered gifts to Bahraam,
Hormozd declares him his number one warrior.
Then he summons a scribe to write a letter on silk:
"The Emperor Parmoodeh is my friend,
And he is under my protection in all the lands.
I take, as guarantee of this seal and certificate,
Yazdan, Supreme Master, while we are lowly slaves."

Then he writes a reply to the ambitions Bahraam,
A letter as warm and beautiful as paradise:

"Drive Parmoodeh to our court in friendship.
Send me some of the booty you have seized,
And may the Creator look after you with affection!
Watch and see if we have enemies in any corner,
And if one of them hides in a shelter, seize him,
Put him under guard, and burn his house
With the aid of the happy and auspicious star
That will foretell a brilliant end.
If you require more troops, I shall add in numbers
And I shall increase your treasures.
Address me the demand in a new letter,
And I shall send as many troops as you may need.
Insert the names of the Iranians who are at your side
And whose conduct you have reason to appreciate.
They will receive rewards for their fatigues.
I shall entrust your army to guard the borders,
And I shall offer you the famed headdress of warriors."

23 | Bahraam Choobineh Receives the Letter of Protection for Parmoodeh

The illustrious hero's heart is renewed by the letter.
Full of admiration, he summons the Iranians.
He spreads the king's gifts before them,
And they praise and bless the glorious Hormozd.

Bahraam shares the contents of the letter with them,
And a cry of benediction rises in the hall
As if the earth is shaking.
He sends the king's lovely letter of protection
To Parmoodeh, whose soul lights up with joy.
The illustrious prince exits his castle
Uttering blessings on the king's name.
He hands over to Bahraam all his wealth
And prepares for his departure.

As Bahraam learns of his preparations
To travel to the renowned king,
He sends a supervisor to the castle to survey
And make a list of all the useful objects.

The proud prince descends from the castle
Seated upon a battle horse, as it suits
A man of war, and takes the road with his escort,
Without concern for the brave Bahraam.

Choobineh learns of the exit and feels wounded,
Although it is a king he is dealing with.
He dismisses everyone and calls for him
To rush over on foot in front of the army.

Bahraam, in a state of fury, says to Parmoodeh,
"Is this your custom in Chin and Tooran,
To set on the road insolently without notifying me?
This is an action that lacks sense and reason!"

Parmoodeh says to him, "Long ago, I held my head high
Before the assembly. I was independent.
I have fallen prey, at the mercy of the king.
I have fallen well below my prior status.
But today you did not display a good nature
By parading me in this lowly state before you.
O wicked man, I have in hand a letter of protection,
And I wish to present myself at the king's side
In the hopes that he will treat me as a brother
And that my ill fortune will be alleviated.
What do you want from me now that I have forsaken
My throne, my comfort, and my wealth?"

Bahraam, further enraged, his eyes full of blood,
Strikes Parmoodeh fiercely with his whip.
The prince's feet are immediately bound with iron chains,
And he is locked up in a narrow tent.

Khorraad Borzeen, witness to this, exclaims,
"This warrior's behavior is too irrational!"

He approaches the scribe and says, "The daring leader
Has as much wisdom as a fly has in its wing,
And for that reason does not respect anyone.
He must know that he loses himself without resource
And that his worst enemy is his wrath."

The two men march over to Bahraam,

Their tongues full of good advice, their faces dim.
They say to him, "You have abandoned
The fruits of your labors to the wind.
The head of a noble warrior must not be filled with fury."

Bahraam recognizes that he committed a vile act
And that he cast into the waters a dried brick.
He repents, removes Parmoodeh's bonds,
And strikes his own head, ashamed of his actions.
He sends for a charger with a golden bridle,
An Indian blade, and a golden sheath.
He goes to him to bring serenity to his troubled soul
And remains with him until he reclaims his weapons
And has climbed on an ardent horse.

Then the leader accompanies him on the road,
Recognizing that the emperor's face is not peaceful.
At the moment of taking leave of him, he says,
"You are angry with me in your soul.
But if it is so, do not tell the King of Iran,
For you would draw no honor in this affair."

Parmoodeh says to him, "My complaints are directed
At fate, and I have addressed them to Yazdan.
I am not one of those who likes to speak of others.
But if your king did not learn what happened,
He would not be worthy of being a ruler.
The revolving dome of sky is responsible for my fall,
And never will I disclose that a mere subject hurt me."

These words make Bahraam pale.
He writhes but bravely swallows his fury.
He replies, "An illustrious and powerful man
Once pronounced these memorable words:
        'Abstain from sowing seeds of evil, for if you do,
            Providence will make you taste its bitter fruit.'
In vain my heart leans toward you.
In vain I wrote a letter to the world king in your favor,
Keeping silent on all your shortcomings."

Parmoodeh says, "I swear by Yazdan
That I hold no hatred in my heart, now or ever.
Your kind deeds are more numerous than your crimes.

You were my guide on the path of righteousness.
But you must know that in times of battle,
One must exercise patience to reach a state of peace,
Although one may endure a serious defeat.
If you view war and concord as one,
It is evident that you can boast little sense.
When an army leader does not follow his ruler's path,
Misfortune results for having thought he is the wisest.
One must walk on the path of the Creator.
One must pluck from one's heart all darkness.
Now you must not speak of it anymore,
For past wicked deeds are worth as much as wind."

Bahraam listens and replies,
"I had hoped that it would remain secret.
But your complaints will not cause me harm,
And I shall not conceal my deeds behind a cover of silk.
Go to court and say what you must,
For my glory will never be diminished."

The emperor replies, "Know that a king
Who does not take good and bad actions into account
And would be silent on his subjects' crimes
Would be deemed foolish and mindless.
If a man, whether he is your protector or your equal,
Would see you from afar engaged in a wicked act,
He would consider you a good-for-nothing
And would call the King of Iran narrow-minded."

With these words, Bahraam pales.
Khorraad Borzeen observes him and fears
That the violent, bloodthirsty man, his pride wounded,
Would, on impulse, slay Parmoodeh.

He says to Bahraam, "O royal leader, calm your fury.
Let us return. The emperor has spoken well.
Listen to him, and do not give in to ill thoughts.
If you had not conversed in such a cold manner,
Neither he nor you would have suffered much."

Bahraam replies, "It seems that this clumsy man
Has only one wish: to join his father."

The emperor says to him, "Do not commit a crime.
Should I not attain old age because I have lost my father?
The heads of those the likes of you are filled with dust
And their hearts with the smoke of vanity.
They think only of evil, lack friends, and elevate
Themselves by means of cruel and tortuous paths.
You wish to instill fear in me for the King of Kings.
You wish to trouble my head
With the idea of what could happen.
But Hormozd is my equal among highborn men.
He does not appear to have wicked motives as you have.
Sensible and gentle, endowed with vast knowledge,
And highborn, he is acquainted with eminent men.
I implore you by the life and the head
Of the King of Iran to take the road and return.
Do not increase your wrongs with brusque replies.
Remain silent so that you need not hear a response."

Bahraam returns to his camp, head full of vengeance.
The experienced leader tells the noblemen
Of pure intentions: "Let Khorraad Borzeen,
The wise men, and the scribe write to the world king
On the events that occurred in private and in public."

Then he furiously addresses the grand wise master
And the sages: "O sensible men,
Travel to Aavaazeh castle in haste,
With the wind as your companion,
And assess the accumulated wealth
Contained within its walls."

The scribes leave at dawn, hearts full of terror.
They cover with ink many a sheaf
And yet are left with so much more to write
As three parts of night elapse.

In the castle, one cannot pass, so abundant
Are the untouched riches collected since ancient times.
They find, from the reigns of Arjaasp and Afraasiyaab,
Dinars and jewels, pearls and coral drawn from the sea,
Precious stones extracted from mines,
All this accessed only with the help of the skies.

This is the treasure found in the Castle of Aavaazeh,
Its name most renowned in the world.

Among the assets, they find Siaavoosh's belt,
Each button inlaid with precious jewels,
And his earrings, one of a kind in the world.
Kay Khosrow had given them to Lohraasp,
Who handed them down to Goshtaasp.
Arjaasp deposited them in the castle
At a time when no one remembers.

They create a record of every precious item,
One by one, found in the priceless treasury.
No one can estimate the proper value,
Neither nobleman nor astrologer.

Bahraam sends an eloquent scribe,
A good observer of serene heart
Who gathers the wealth in the fort and on the field.
They also find a pair of precious earrings
And a pair of boots embroidered with pearls
Weaved into the cloth with fine golden thread.
Two bolts of striped fabric are broached
In gold from the land of Yemen,
Each weighing seven mahns.[6]

The leader, in his perversity and presumption,
Cannot observe the rules of justice.
He sets aside two bolts of Yemeni fabric
And fails to mention the boots in his letter.
Then he commands Izad Goshasp to climb on a horse
And, with an escort of one thousand riders,
Return to the king's court with all the valuables.

One hundred caravans of camels depart
In joy and happiness in the direction of Iran,
The emperor at the lead, surrounded by his noblemen.

◇◇◇◇◇◇◇◇◇◇◇◇◇
6 Mahn: A form of weight measurement in the ancient Middle East equivalent to 3 kilograms or 6.6 pounds.

24 | The Emperor Parmoodeh Arrives at Hormozd's Court

The Chini ruler approaches the king's court
With his ancestor's treasures and his escort.
At the news, Shah Hormozd climbs on his horse,
A crown on his head, a mace in his hand.

He marches to the palace gate, where he remains
To see if Parmoodeh would dismount with his cortege.
He wishes to determine the level of respect
And then return to his palace to resume his duties,
As the ambitious and famed king is quite busy.

At that moment, Parmoodeh arrives
On horseback with Izad Goshasp,
Descends instantly and rushes to the King of Iran.
Hormozd Shah launches his bounding horse,
Not remaining a moment longer with Parmoodeh.

The emperor waits for the king to cross
The space between the gate and the palace.
Then he attempts to follow him,
But the chamberlain grabs his horse's reins.

Parmoodeh hurries to dismount and exhibits,
With a gesture of humility, his mind's flexibility.
He marches over to the throne, and the King of Kings
Receives him amiably, asks him the usual questions,
And seats him in front of him, regretting his suspicions.

They prepare a residence worthy of the emperor,
A sumptuous palace, supplied with all the necessary
Furnishings, with his escort settled close by.

The king charges one of his scribes with this matter,
And, upon hearing of Parmoodeh's gifts of valuables,
He sends them to the square so that the precious loads
Can be entrusted to the care of the chief camel driver.

For seven days, the emperor has a chance to rest.
On the eighth day, the king commands a banquet.

Parmoodeh, occupying a place of honor
Near the world master, asks for the camel loads
To be brought forth on men's backs.
Someone counts the number of carriers
And comes to a stop at ten thousand.

The next morning, at dawn, the king places
Wine on the tables and prepares to sit.
They bring in fifty thousand objects from the square,
A great burden for the backs of carriers.
Loads of valuables were seized from Aavaazeh,
And the mind of the king is resigned.

He asks for a package of clothing and earrings
To be placed before the court, along with inlaid belts.
It is as if all the gold and jewels of the world are there.

The king gives the goods to the envoy,
Who kisses the ground and departs.
The audience hall echoes with a cry:
"May the world master always be victorious!"

The king asks Izad Goshasp, with whom he shares
All his secrets, "What are your thoughts on Choobineh?
He valiantly puts a decided end to battles and wars."

The scribe Izad Goshasp replies, "O insightful King,
I have a hard time believing that Bahraam Choobineh's
Actions always follow the path of justice."

These words inspire suspicion in the king,
And his soul suddenly fills with worry.

25 | Hormozd Is Made Aware of Bahraam's Deceit

During this time arrives a vigorous dromedary
With a letter from the grand scribe, saying,
"May the world king live eternally!
May his crowned head remember his servant!
Know that there were two bolts of fabric from Yemen,
Boots embroidered with freshwater pearls,

And earrings dating back to the noble Siaavoosh,
Whose memory we continue to venerate.
The leader Bahraam took two parts of these,
But one must not be surprised and hold it against him,
As he endured immeasurable fatigues."

Hormozd, who seeks a good name, asks Parmoodeh
To recount in detail all that he knows on the matter.
The latter reports everything just as he witnessed.

The illustrious king grows infuriated and says,
"Choobineh has strayed and betrayed me.
He raises his head above the moon.
First he strikes the Emperor of Chin,
As one expects from a man of evil nature.
Then he could not resist earrings meant for royalty.
Has he elevated himself to the status of king?
All his labors have turned to wind.
All his good deeds have turned to evil ones."

He says this, asks Parmoodeh to sit in a place of honor,
And remain to drink wine until night
Is given the chance to unfurl its black mane.

Hormozd says to the emperor,
"You have deeply tired yourself on my account."
Then, while seated, he extends his hand,
Takes Parmoodeh's hand, confounding him.

The king says to him, "Take a new oath for me:
Place this affair on a completely different footing.
Swear by Yazdan, who is above the loftiest things,
Who brings light to Venus and Jupiter,
That, once you return to your land,
You will not turn away from me or from my noblemen."

Parmoodeh commits to a solemn oath, by the holy Yazdan,
By the bright day and the indigo night,
By the lives of the noblemen, by the crown and throne,
By the Sun and Moon, by Aazargoshasp, by seal
And diadem, to remain loyal to the king. In turn,
The king pledges to never afflict the emperor in any way.
They utter the words, rise, and retire to their chambers.

As the yellow sun appears beyond the mountain crests
And the heads of the rulers emerge from their torpor,
The illustrious king asks for gifts of gold and silver,
Horses, diadems, golden belts inlaid with gems,
Bracelets, torques, and earrings, Taazian steeds
With golden reins, and Indian swords with golden sheaths.
He sends the lot to Parmoodeh, Emperor of Chin.

He accompanies him on the road for two stations.
On the third day, the Chini ruler
Sets out for the long journey.
They bid farewell to each other
As the king swings the reins away.

When the army leader learns of the gifts of the king
And of the Emperor of Chin making his way back
After having been so well received at the court of Iran,
He goes to meet him with all his Iranian army friends.
He organizes provisions to be set up at every point
On Parmoodeh's passage, in cities and boroughs,
In stations, in the mountains and the plains.

Then he presents himself before him, asking
Forgiveness, his malevolent soul deeply ashamed.
But the Emperor of Chin turns his head away
From Bahraam and rejects his offerings,
Whether provisions, cases of gold, or slaves.

Bahraam escorts him on the road,
But the emperor avoids glancing his way.
Bahraam continues in this manner and follows him
For three stations without Parmoodeh addressing him.

On the fourth day,
He receives a message from the emperor:
"Return, for you have endured great fatigues."

Bahraam turns around and, in a fit of rage,
Heads toward Balkh where he remains for some time,
Regretful of his actions, nursing a mournful heart.

26 | Hormozd Sends Bahraam a Letter, a Spindle Box, and a Woman's Dress

On his side, the world owner is rather displeased
With Bahraam, and his anger is obscuring his mind,
First because of the leader's mistreatment of the emperor
And second because of his boldness in seizing
Valuables he had no right or permission to claim.

The king composes a letter to Bahraam,
"O malicious deev, you do not know who you are.
Do you think you are above the need for noblemen?
Do you not see that success comes from the Creator,
Yet you attempt to sit on the wheel of the sky?
Have you forgotten my efforts?
Have you forgotten that it is my army I gave to you,
My wealth that I expended for you?
You do not walk down the path of warrior heroes.
You attempt to raise your head to the firmament,
Turning away from my command and
Concluding the affairs contrary to my wishes.
Here is a present worthy of you,
Suitable and appropriate to your level of merit."

The king affixes his seal on the letter
And asks for a black box full of spindles,
Cotton, and many other degrading things.
Then he adds a blue silk tunic, red pants,
And a woman's yellow veil.

The king selects a messenger lacking substance
To transport the miserable present. He says to him,
"Take this to Bahraam, and tell him in my name:
'O man of little worth and little birth,
You bound the limbs of the Emperor of Chin?
You made it a game of debasing noblemen?
I shall make you plummet from your seat.
From now on, I do not count you among men.'"

The messenger departs with the present, as swift as wind,
While committing the words to memory.

27 | Bahraam Choobineh Dresses in the Woman's Attire

Bahraam receives the letter and the gift,
Maintains his calm upon receipt, and reflects in silence:
"This is the way the king rewards me, with an attack.
This poor action does not originate from his mind.
There is no doubt that he was influenced by my foes.
The world owner is the master of his slaves,
And he has the right to treat me with ignominy.
But I did not think that wicked men could reach him.
Since I have left the court with such ardor,
Accompanied by a weak host, everyone
Witnessed my deeds. Everyone witnessed
The worry, danger, and fatigues I have endured.
If the reward for all my troubles is humiliation,
If fortune only affords me indignities,
I shall complain to the Creator of the inconstant skies
Who withdrew from me the affection it once nurtured."

He invokes the Justice Master from whom originates virtue,
Then he dresses in the red and yellow attire,
Places before him the black spindle box
And all the items sent by the king, and, preoccupied,
He calls to his side the noble and illustrious army men.

As soon as the noblemen, old and young, arrive,
They are surprised to find the warrior
Dressed in such an unfamiliar and odd way.
Their hearts fill with concern, but Bahraam says,
"Here is a robe of honor sent to me by the king,
Who is world master while we stand as his slaves.
Our hearts and souls are full of affection for him.
You have witnessed my deeds, or if not, you have
Certainly heard the tales of my battles with javelin.
The king has grown weary of the Kianian throne.
Once the world was dark, but I brought light into it.
I wear this dress, a gift of our powerful king.
He enjoys world ownership, and we are his slaves,
Our hearts bound to him in devotion.
What do you think, O insightful ones?

What shall we tell the world king?"

They reply unanimously, "O illustrious
And most valuable warrior, if this is the sort of honor
The king reserves for you, then what status
Do his troops hold if not that of dogs at his court?
Reflect on what the old wise man once told Rei,
In his indignation at Ardeshir:
>   'I would be disgusted by the wise man
>   And the king's throne, since he has no qualms
>   About the harm he causes me.'
What do you expect from a disrespectful man?"

Bahraam replies, "Do not speak in this manner.
The king is a source of honor for the army.
We are all his slaves; he gives and we receive."

They reply, "From now on, we shall not bear arms.
We do not wish for Hormozd to maintain power
And for Bahraam to remain army warrior."

After speaking thus, the Iranians exit Bahraam's palace
And scatter across the plain. Bahraam gives them
All the advice he can, while restraining his tongue.

28 | Bahraam Has a Vision
of His Imminent Good Fortune

Two weeks pass.
Bahraam the leader exits his palace in the countryside
And arrives at a dense forest, a charming site
That invites men to rest and enjoy a cup of wine.
He spots a most beautiful deer in the grassland,
Which he pursues gently, without warming up his horse.

In the forest and at the place suitable for the hunt,
The deer crosses a narrow passage
And emerges into a plain full of gardens.

Bahraam rides; the deer prances.
The man and his charger are drenched in sweat.

He glances at the plain, notices a beautiful castle
Toward which he gallops, still chasing the deer.

He launches his horse to the steps of the castle,
Followed by Izad Goshasp, to whom he hands
The reins of his ardent charger, saying,
"May prudence always be your companion!"
Then the leader Bahraam enters on foot
Through the castle gate without a guide.

Izad Goshasp waits for some time,
Holding the leader's noble charger.
Yalan Sineh, who has followed them,
Arrives armed and mounted on a fiery horse.
The valiant Izad Goshasp says to him,
"Enter the castle, O fearless lion,
And look for our illustrious leader and master."

Yalan Sineh explores the garden,
Searching, his heart full of worry.
He finds a palace more beautiful than anything
He had ever seen or heard of in all of Iran.
In a part of the castle, he notices a vaulted room
Where his eye could not reach the heights.
There is a golden throne in this hall,
Inlaid with all sorts of pearls and jewels.
A sheet of Rumi brocade of pure gold,
Embroidered with fine stones, covers the seat
On which sits a crowned woman,
Slender as a cypress tree and beautiful as spring.
Her two black tresses frame her face
And enchant the hearts of warriors.
At the sight of her, Jupiter loses its luster
And wisdom drifts away.
She is like a column with a silver pattern.
At the sight of her, the dazzling sun
Cannot help but be seized by a fit of jealousy.

The army leader sits on a golden seat before her throne,
Surrounded by a great number of slaves,
Fair-faced beauties watched over by providence.

At the sight of Yalan Sineh, she says to a slave,

"My handsome friend, go tell this man of lion heart
That he has no right to be here,
And he may join his fellowmen.
His master Bahraam will soon advance ahead of him."

At the same time, she sends servants of the palace
To the side of Bahraam's escort with the order
To drive the horses of the valiant men to the stables
And to care for their saddles and covers.

The gardener opens the garden gate
On the order of the gorgeous hostess.
A priest, worshipper of Yazdan, enters the garden,
Murmuring prayers and holding the barsom.

Tables are placed outside, countless dishes brought.
Once the meal is complete, the horses are led
To the location of the banner,
And Bahraam says to the woman,
"May Jupiter be your crown's companion."

The woman replies, "May you be graced with victory!
May your heart remain patient!
May you always follow the counsel of prudence!
You are to be leader of Tooran and Iran,
King of lion-men, owner of Iran's crown and throne.
You are the support of the entire world.
Seize it all at the point of your dagger
From this dark dust to the bright stars above."

They further secretly speak, without witnesses.
When Bahraam exits her garden,
It is as if his eyes shed a shower of blood.
His humor altered, he speaks and responds differently.
It is as if his head reaches the Pleiades in the sky.

The male onager returns, the leader follows on horseback
And is guided all the way to the exit of the forest.
He rides from the hunting grounds to the city
And speaks to no one of his experience.

Khorraad Borzeen observes him and says,
"O powerful and true man, what is this marvel

104

That you encountered in the hunt and which
Surpasses anything I have ever seen or heard of?"

But the leader Bahraam fails to respond.
His mood is dim, and he travels on to his palace.
Besides Khorraad Borzeen, no one dares
Ask him what happened to him in the forest.

29 | Bahraam Choobineh Adopts the Demeanor of a King

The next day, when the mountaintop
Glows with a silvery sheen
And the brilliant yellow torch appears,
Bahraam asks for a carpet of Chini brocade
To be spread in a way that the earth resembles the sky.
He places golden seats everywhere in his palace
And covers them with cushions wrapped in golden cloth.

A small golden throne is adorned,
On which the leader sits.
He prepares a gathering worthy of the King of Kings
And places a headdress of power upon his head.

The great scribe observes his actions.
He notices Bahraam growing more bold and arrogant.
He approaches Khorraad Borzeen
And recounts to him what he observed and heard.

Khorraad Borzeen listens to the account
And understands that the events
Result from an ancient grief.
He says, "O noble scribe,
Do not take this matter lightly.
One must not speak of this, but immediately
Leave tonight in the direction of the king's court.
Our king, our master, acted foolishly
By sending this spindle box as a gift.
He did not think that it would provoke
The desire to rebel in this lion eager for battle.
Bahraam's heart is filled with the idea of a crown,

105

And he has boldly replaced his humble chair
With a resplendent ivory throne."

They debate on various courses of action
And agree on the need to leave for the court.
Once it is decided, they march out of Balkh at midnight.
The leader immediately suspects their plan,
For he is familiar with their brilliant minds.
He tells Yalan Sineh, "Run with one hundred
Cavaliers after these foolish men."

Yalan Sineh reaches the grand scribe
As furiously as a wolf, takes everything he has on him,
And brings him back burdened with chains.
He drags the innocent man to Bahraam
So that he may sentence him to death.

The leader says to him, "You have acted like a deev.
Why did you leave without permission?"

The grand scribe replies, "O warrior,
Khorraad Borzeen caused me fear when he said:
        'You must not stay here.
        Any delay in your departure
        Is only joy for those who speak ill of you.
        Since the valiant Bahraam, army leader,
        Sits at this court on the throne like a king,
        You and I must fear for our lives
        Unless we run away from here.'"

Bahraam says to him, "Such a thing could happen.
We must deliberate among ourselves
On what could benefit us and what could harm us."

He replaces everything for him with his own wealth.
Then he adds, "Go and reflect deeply on what
You have to do, and never attempt to run away again."

30 | Khorraad Borzeen Warns Hormozd of Bahraam's Deeds

On his side, Khorraad Borzeen wanders secretly
And in haste until he reaches the world king.
He recounts to him the developments
And reveals to him all his secrets.
In the end, he tells him the story of the forest
And the grassland, the arrival of the onager,
The parade, Bahraam's tranquility and slowness,
The palace and throne inlaid with fine jewels,
The slaves and the woman bearing a crown.
He goes through every point of what he witnessed.
The king is surprised, every word inscribed in his heart.

He remembers the discourse of the wise man
And exhales a great, deep sigh.
He remembers the words of the fortuneteller
Who predicted the leader
Would turn his back on the throne.
In haste, he summons the grand wise master.

He seats Khorraad Borzeen in the hall and says,
"Tell us all what you witnessed on the road."
Khorraad obeys, reporting all the facts, one by one.

The king asks the grand wise master,
"What could this be? We must gather these tales:
An onager serving as guide in a dense forest,
A castle rising in the middle of the desert,
A crown-bearing woman seated on a golden throne,
Servants worthy of a king surrounding her.
This story is like one of those dreams
We speak about in ancient legends."

The wise master says to the world king,
"This onager must have been a deev in disguise
Who turned Bahraam away from righteousness
And revealed the failings of his heart.
Take the castle as a place of sorcery and this woman
On the throne as its impious magician or witch.
She exalted Bahraam's pride.

When he left her, he was haughty, as if drunk.
Know that he will never obey you again.
He carries in his heart the wound of the spindle box,
And the path he was led onto by the deev magician
Has honored and celebrated him.

"You did not need to send an unworthy gift
To a man who was already so full of iniquity.
The Iranians have been shaken by it
And have ceased to place their hopes in the king.
Now seek a means to bring the army
From Balkh back to your royal court."

The king is ashamed of his actions,
Regretting the cotton and the embroidered clothes.
He asks Khorraad Borzeen what was said
On the subject of Bahraam and the woman.

Khorraad replies to Hormozd, "O King,
The army recounted that the renowned woman,
So beautiful and so dazzling on her throne,
Had to be Bahraam's star of good fortune."

These words fill the king with fear and dread
Over the calamities reserved for him by fate.

A few days later, an envoy dispatched by Bahraam
Arrives with a basket full of swords,
Their tips bent from overuse in battle.
He places the basket at the foot of the king,
Who examines the steel blades.
He has them shattered and returned
In the unfortunate basket to Bahraam,
Revealing with this gesture his secret thoughts
And intentions without having uttered a word.

Bahraam opens the lid of the basket to notice
The crushed tips of the long swords.
This man, whose judgment is already troubled,
Is filled with a sense of trepidation.
He summons the Iranians, seats them around the basket,
And says to them, "Look at the gift from the king,
And do not consider it of little value.

He wishes to say that the army is worthless.
The shattered tips of the swords are proof of this."

The warriors are appalled that the king
Would do such a thing, and they say,
"One day, he sends us a box of spindles
And women's embroidered clothing,
Another day, he breaks our swords,
Which is more cruel than injury and physical blows.
This king is not worthy of the throne,
Nor is he worthy of being remembered.
If Bahraam, son of Goshasp, passes his horse
Through the dust at the king's court,
Cursed be his brain, cursed be his skin,
Cursed be this man of little value, his father!"

The leader listens to their speech,
And, seeing that the army's heart is severed
From the world master king, he says,
"Be vigilant, and do not trouble yourselves,
For Khorraad Borzeen revealed to the king
What has been said in the open.
Seek a means to save your lives,
And act by concluding an agreement with me.
I must send some army men on the road
To observe our enemy's movements.
If I fail to do so, you can be sure that I will be lost
And the army will be exterminated."

He speaks in this manner, but his goal is otherwise.
Be watchful and you will be surprised.
He scatters the riders in all the provinces
So that they can bar the way to the Iranians
And prevent them from receiving letters from their king.
This way they will not arm themselves against him.

Some time passes, during which
No one receives a letter from the royal court.

31 | Bahraam Explains His Plan to Be King to Army Leaders

Then Bahraam convenes the noblemen
And shares many secrets with them.
Present are Hamdan Goshasp, the great scribe,
Yalan Sineh, an illustrious and audacious man,
The valiant Bahraam, of the race of Siaavoosh,
And the noble and intelligent Konda Goshasp.
They are all fierce lions and men of war
Who have lost their way.

Bahraam holds counsel with them and says:
"O famed and proud men, everyone needs your advice.
The king is displeased with you, though it is not your fault.
You well know how he has wandered off
The proper path and the way of tradition.
What shall we do? How do we resolve this affair?
Let us not weep over our fates as do the wounded.
When one hides his ailment from the physician,
One is reduced to shed tears of blood.
When one hides his secret from the sage,
One complicates an affair that is easily resolved.
My soul is afflicted, and you are my witnesses.
We left the land of Iran by order of the king to engage
In war, driving a small host against the enemy.
Our adversaries were more numerous
Than anyone has ever witnessed before.
Men such as Parmoodeh the Chini and King Saaveh
Initiated a war against Iran,
Deeming this land as insignificant as a ball of wax
And planning to attack Rum after their victory over us.

"Parmoodeh and King Saaveh experienced a sort of fate
The world has never witnessed before.
Despite all the weariness that they endured,
I did not allow them to hold on to an elephant or a valuable.
The king was able to establish a new treasury.
He has become wealthy as a result,
Yet he harbors anger toward his host.
How shall we heal this wound?

I have now revealed all of my heart's secrets.
I detach myself from this kingship, and from you,
If you know a way of salvation,
Hasten to speak on things that affect our joy and grief."

The illustrious leader voices his sentiment
Out of his heart's fear for his troops.
He has in his night chambers a fair-faced sister
Of brilliant mind, named Gordieh, who charms his heart.
She hears the conversation from behind the curtains.
She shudders, her heart leaping in a bout of fury.
She joins the assembly, her soul full of speech,
Her lips full of words on ancient wisdom.

Hearing her, her brother falls silent
And no longer answers questions for fear of misfortune.
The Iranian soldiers follow suit.

Gordieh comes forth to address the army leaders:
"O illustrious men, always in search
Of the righteous path, why do you keep silent?
How can you calm your hearts' ebullition?
What do you think of this affair,
And what game do you play on the bloody field,
For you are chiefs of Iran, valiant and wise.
You are noblemen of awakened minds."

Izad Goshasp, the rider, responds to her,
"O descendant of noble ancestors,
Were our tongues sharp blades, they would
Retreat before the vast sea of your reasoning.
Your every action comes from Yazdan
And bears the imprint of your courage,
Your wisdom, and your intelligence.
It is not necessary for us to engage in battle
And to follow the path of a leopard.
Do not ask me anything more, for my mind stops here.
But if you wish to fight, we shall support you,
We shall behave like riders faced with riders,
And if the warrior is satisfied with me,
I feel as if I shall always remain young."

Bahraam listens to the discussion

And understands that his sister's intention
Is to act as mediator between the two parties.
His eyes fall on Yalan Sineh, and he says to him,
"What secret observation have you?"

Yalan Sineh replies, "O valiant leader,
I can say that the one who walks in the divine path
Arrives at victory and glory through his wisdom.
Success is never reached through malfeasance.
When that is the case, blessings turn to malediction,
The wheel of the sky fills with wrath for the guilty.
The heavens granted you glory and good fortune,
An army, a treasury, a crown and throne.
Accept them; more will come your way.
Ungrateful hearts cannot fail but to dwell in anguish."

Bahraam Choobineh turns to Bahraam and asks,
"O wise friend, companion of reason,
Do share with me your thoughts.
Will the end of our search for throne and treasure
Be the attainment of dominion,
Or are we to wallow in grief and suffering?"

Bahraam smiles at the discussion,
He tosses his ring into the air, and says,
"A slave has the chance of ruling as king
For as long as this ring remains in the air.
The king is powerful, he does not evaluate the lows,
For one must not count a crown for little."

Then Bahraam turns to Izad Goshasp: "You are a lion
Who strikes with sword and launches his horse!
What thoughts have you on this affair?
Am I worthy of throne and supremacy?"

Izad Goshasp, the rider, replies,
"You are a remembrance of heroes: Your ancestors!
A wise man once said to Rei,
        'When a man endowed with wisdom
        And blessed footprints acquires kingship,
        His soul soars to the sky.'
It is better to desire the glory of a world master
Than to live a long and dreary life of servitude."

Bahraam addresses the grand scribe and says,
"O old wolf, open your lips to speak!"

The grand scribe keeps his lips sealed for some time,
Appears absorbed in thoughts, then he says to Bahraam,
"Anyone who searches for the object of his desires
Will realize it, as long as he is worthy of it,
For the hand of providence has the longest reach.
Know that if Yazdan, the just, accords something,
It is utterly useless to put up resistance."

Bahraam says to Hamdan Goshasp,
"You have endured good and bad fortune.
The words that you will utter in the presence of noblemen
Will drift in the wind without consequence to you.
Tell us what you think of this affair.
Tell us what are our chances, favorable and adverse."

The powerful Hamdan Goshasp replies,
"You are cherished by noblemen.
Why do you fear the prospective ills of the future?
Why do you ask questions about the crown of royalty?
Act and entrust Yazdan with the outcome.
Why extend a hand on the date when one fears its thorns?
Idle men can never rise to rulership.
Everything is for them either fear of death
Or fear of bodily harm."

The leader's sister suffers, saddened.
She does not open her lips to speak
From dusk to the middle of the night.

Bahraam says to her, "O my kind sister, what thoughts
Do you nurture on the outcome of the gathering?"

Gordieh refrains from answering.
She does not approve of the advice of the noblemen.
In the end, she says to the grand scribe,
"O evil man, you are as wicked as an old wolf.
Do you think that the crown and throne,
Army, power, and a victorious fortune
Have never been the envy of noblemen,
Men of upright character, since life

Is more gentle for a king than a servant?
One must shed tears on such wisdom.
Let us follow the customs that prevailed
During the time of ancient kings.
Let us listen to their ancient words."

The grand scribe replies, "If you do not agree
With me, then act as you desire,
Allow your heart to be your guide."

The sister repeats the same advice to Bahraam,
A stubborn and selfish man: "Neither your beliefs
Nor your intentions follow the path of sense and wisdom.
They are misleading you. Though the kingly throne
Has often been vacant, no subject has ever coveted it.
Most men valiantly protected the world to serve,
Their belts strapped tightly around their waist,
Their hearts attached to royal will and command,
Without casting a glance toward the Kianian seat.
Anyone outside the Kianian family
Need never give a thought to the throne,
For it is a status of power granted only by birthright.
Those who ruled in the past have been rightful heirs.

"Let me begin with Kaavoos Shah,
Who wished to infiltrate divine secrets,
Who wished to observe the celestial revolving dome,
Trample upon it, and count the stars in the sky.
He underwent a sad and shameful fall in Sari
As a result of his perversity and ill nature.
Goodarz and Rostam, the warrior, two mighty heroes,
Did not attempt to usurp the throne at that time.
Later, when Kaavoos went to Haamaavaran,
Where they bound and enchained his feet,
Again no one sought to seize the throne.
The heroes only nurtured a sense of warm solicitude
And genuine worry for their king's well-being.

"When the Iranians assured Rostam
That he was worthy of the Kianian throne,
That they would welcome him and acclaim him,
He shouted a cry of fury:

'You might as well tell me to bury myself in a grave.
How am I to have a golden throne
While the king remains captive and alive?
Cursed be power! Cursed be crown!'
He selected ten plus two thousand riders
From Iran able to conquer the world,
Mounted on stallions braced in iron shields,
To liberate Kaavoos, Giv, Goodarz, and Tous.

"Furthermore, when Pirooz was killed
And fortune abandoned the Iranians,
Khoshnavaz peacefully sat upon the throne.
Soofraay, from the family of Ghaaran,
Departed and restored the kingly seat.
At the news of his victory, the Iranian noblemen
Came to acclaim him as their world king.
But Soofraay said,
'Such a thing is not feasible.
Power and crown belong to the family of kings
And not to a mere subject. Though Ghobaad
Is still a child, he will grow and mature.
Let us not introduce a wolf into the lion's lair.
Do you really wish to offer kingship
To a man who was not born into royalty
And deliver his family to death and destruction?'
Once Ghobaad reached the age of maturity
And observed that Soofraay was worthy of the crown,
He had him, the support of the throne,
Executed at the instigation of a man of poor race.

"The army rebelled against Ghobaad
And placed Jaamaasp on the throne of justice.
Chains bound the valiant Ghobaad's feet, Kianian son,
And an ill-natured man handed him over to Zarmehr
In the hopes that he would avenge his father's death.
Zarmehr looked around, and, seeing no one
Worthy of the crown and throne of royalty,
He removed his bonds so that he could
Restore him to his affairs and return to him his life.

"None of the king's subjects sought the crown,
Although some were honored with the birthright.

115

Only one Turk, named Saaveh Shah,
Arrived to seize the seal and diadem.
But the glorious World Creator decided
That he must perish in Iran-Zamin.
In the glory of Yazdan and at your hands
The deed was accomplished.
Now you aspire to seize imperial rule,
But know that you will lose your life like Shah Saaveh.
Yalan Sineh will incite his horse to leap, saying,
  'I shall give Bahraam, son of Goshasp, kingship.
  I shall make him a memory in my name.'

"A wise king such as Anushiravan returned
To youth in his old age by looking at Hormozd.
Great noblemen from the provinces
Serve and support him as slaves and subjects.
Iran has three hundred thousand riders,
Illustrious warriors who are the king's slaves,
Who bow down at his every command and will.
The world king selected you as a valued nobleman,
For you have renowned ancestors who vanquished
The enemy at every time of need.
Now you are about to do harm as a reward
For the kindness you have received?
Know that the harm will only fall back on you.
Do not allow greed to dominate reason,
For wise men will never call you a pure man.
I am only a woman giving advice to men,
But I am not much younger than my brother.
Do not abandon to the wind
What your ancestors accomplished.
Heaven forbid you forget my advice!"

The leader bites his lips.
Everyone in the gathering is astonished
And understands that she speaks the truth
And only offers a way down the righteous path.

Yalan Sineh says, "O noble woman, guard yourself
From offering advice on the king's affairs.
Hormozd will die and disappear in little time,
And the warrior leader will enjoy the throne.

PART TWENTY-EIGHT

Since Hormozd has little merit, count on the fact
That your brother will be King of Iran.
If Hormozd wishes to enjoy the Kianian crown,
Why does he make gifts of spindles and cotton
To a leader of Bahraam's standing, a lion-man
Whose blade has the ability to shake up the world?
Were his sword to remain concealed in its sheath,
Few people would survive, neither Hormozd
Nor the land of Iran nor the land of Shaam.
Cursed be the king who sends cotton and spindles!
Let us not speak of Hormozd, son of a Turk.
May his lineage disappear from the world!

"If you count since the time of Kay Ghobaad,
The family of Kianians ruled with crown
And throne for one thousand years.
The era has come to an end.
Let us not utter the name of Kianian.
Let us not lend a thought to Khosrow Parviz.
The most intimate people at court hold a lower
Status than your brother's most humble servants.
If Bahraam tells his subjects to tie up Hormozd's feet
With heavy chains, they will instantly comply
And place your brother on the royal throne."

Gordieh replies, "The black deev
Will set a trap on your path.
Do not destroy us body and soul.
I see the pride and vanity that you kindle.
Our father was a mere border guard in Rey,
And you, by yearning for the throne,
By making Bahraam's heart simmer,
By inciting trouble in our tribe, you will toss
To the wind the fruits of our family's labors,
O miserable man of low race!
You will fuel the fire, insert chaos into our peaceful days,
And make yourself Bahraam's guide."

Having thus spoken, she withdraws to her chamber,
Weeping, her heart estranged from Bahraam.

Everyone agrees: "How well-spoken she is!

117

It is as if the holy woman's words come from a book.
She surpasses Jaamaasp in wisdom."

Gordieh's words deeply aggrieve Bahraam,
Whose dim soul is constantly fixed
On the throne of royalty in his dreams.
He reflects on the fact that "those who seek
World possession will only obtain it with difficulty."

He commands banquet spreads and wine,
Music, and singers, to whom he says,
"Give us today some heroic songs.
I wish for my guests to hear the ballad
Of the seven stages of Esfandiar's adventure
When he traveled to the impregnable castle
And the unfolding of the playful twists of fate."

The noblemen drink to the health of Bahraam and say,
"May Yazdan create many more leaders like you!
May the land of Rey always prosper
For bringing a mighty warrior into the world!"

They scatter in the dark night,
The heads of the drinkers blurred by the effect of wine.

32 | Bahraam Strikes Coins in the Name of Khosrow Parviz

As the sublime sun raises its spear point
And the dark night retreats in fear of light's splendor,
The audacious Bahraam summons the scribe,
And they write a letter to the emperor.
Worthy of Arjang, the letter is
Full of scent, color, and embellishments:
"Forgive my actions in a moment of contrariness.
My heart is filled with repentance and cold sighs.
From now on, out of respect for you,
I shall not cause any disturbance to your land.
If I am able to become world master,
I shall conduct myself like your younger brother.
Abandon all thoughts of vengeance.

Do not separate the lands of Iran and Chin.
Banish from your heart any memory of the past,
For Yazdan receives repentance from earthly servants.
I invoke benedictions on your undertakings,
On your character, your sword, your illustrious nation,
Your world-conquering hand, and your throne."

He closes the letter, and a highborn envoy departs,
As swift as wind, then arrives
At the side of the Emperor of Chin,
Covers him with praise, offers him homage,
And remits the warrior Bahraam's letter,
Dressing it up with an excess of flowery words.

The Emperor of Chin is thrilled with the missive
And offers Bahraam's envoy many gifts.
He writes without delay a reply,
Planting thereby a new tree in the garden of power.
He sends presents to Bahraam,
Who is quite satisfied with the response.

As the affair concludes to his liking,
Bahraam turns to a new one.
He opens the door to his amassed treasury,
Distributes dirhams, horses, and slaves to the troops,
Always with an eye on the throne of power.
He selects an army warrior to govern Khorasan,
And, in addition, entrusts him with troops.
He does the same for the cities
Of Nishapur, Balkh, Marv, and Herat.

Bahraam departs, full of strategies, from Balkh to Rey
On the joyous sixth day of the month of Dey.[7]
He thinks about all things, great and small,
And requests that new dirhams be printed at the mint
In the name of Khosrow Parviz.

One of the more intelligent merchants,
An eloquent speaker suitable for delicate matters,
Brings a crate of dirhams struck with the said stamp

◇◇◇◇◇◇◇◇◇◇◇◇◇
7 Dey: The tenth month of the year, corresponding to December.

119

And declares that they are to be transported to Ctesiphon
To be spent on the purchase of the most beautiful
Brocade from Rum embroidered in pure gold.
The new currency is to be taken to King Hormozd.

A messenger familiar with the affair departs.
He is prudent and courageous like the blessed Sooroosh.

33 | Bahraam Writes to Hormozd, and Khosrow Parviz Runs Away From His Father

Bahraam writes a letter to the proud King Hormozd
On various subjects, great and small,
Including Parmoodeh and the army of Saaveh Shah,
The battle waged by his troops,
And the present of a feminine costume
With the black spindle box sent by the king.

Then he adds, "You will never see me again,
Not even in your dreams.
Remove your fishing rod from the water.
Once Khosrow, your noble son, favorite of fortune,
Sits on the throne, I shall convert, at his command,
The mountainside into plains
And the plains into torrents of blood.
Although still young, he is worthy of the throne.
He is loyal and not a traitor like you.
I consider him the King of Kings,
And I shall stand as his slave and no one else's."

He holds on to the notion of time
Passing over the innocent youth
So that he may grow and mature in peace,
Fearing that his father, concerned over his power,
May secretly have him sentenced to death.
Bahraam worries about Parviz over everyone else.
Though young, Parviz would make a charming ruler.

Bahraam writes everything in a letter
And sends a messenger toward Ctesiphon, saying,
"When Hormozd sees the imprint on the dirhams,

120

He will squirm in pain, and when Khosrow Parviz
Is no longer his friend and support,
I shall prepare for him a terrible fate.
Once I get rid of the respect I hold for the king,
I shall pluck out the roots of the descendants of Sassan.
Yazdan did not create the world for them,
And the time has come for this race to be extinguished."

The messenger of auspicious path
Departs for Baghdad with notable men from Rey.
Upon receipt of the letter, Hormozd's face pales
To the color of the flower of the fenugreek.
Then he learns of the production of the coins,
Which adds a new sorrow to his ancient grief.
He trembles and conceives new suspicions about his son,
Which he communicates quickly to Ayeen Goshasp:
"Khosrow has become so valiant
That he wishes to be independent from me.
He has created new dirhams, and by doing so,
He could not have acted more disrespectfully."

Ayeen Goshasp replies, "May square
And horse never be deprived of your presence."
Parviz is your son, but for this act, he deserves prison."

Hormozd says, "I shall not waste time. I will make
This wretched son of mine disappear from the world."

The ambitious nobleman says to the glorious king,
"May your son never prosper once you are gone!"

They secretly call a man and sit him before the king.
At night, Hormozd says to him, "Obey me.
Liberate the face of the earth of Khosrow's presence."

The man replies, "I shall obey and free all affection
From him with incantations and spells.
We must have the king bring poison from his treasury,
And one night, when Parviz is drunk,
I shall mix poison into his wine.
This is a better course of action
Than if you were to dip your hand in blood."

121

Khosrow does not suspect the danger he is subject to
As he holds himself nobly in the palace.
He spends his time with maidens who charm his heart
And delectable wine, unaware of the secret, murderous plans.

His chamberlain receives the news of the machinations
And loses appetite and sleep over it.
He runs over to Khosrow and reveals everything to him.

Upon hearing that the world king contemplates his death,
Khosrow takes off in the middle of the night from Ctesiphon.
It is as if he has disappeared from the world.
He does not wish to surrender his precious head,
So he flees all the way to Aazar Abadegan.

The noblemen, border guards, and heads of provinces
Become aware of the fact that Khosrow,
Feeling threatened by the king,
Has left with a few illustrious riders.
They chase after him to question him.
They realize that the young man, loved by so many,
As strong as an elephant and as generous
As the flows of the River Nile, is in grave danger.

From Gorgan, Ostaay, divine worshipper;
From Oman, Khonjast, a drunken elephant;
From Shiraz, Saam, son of Esfandiar;
From Kerman, Pirooz, valiant cavalier,
Troops and their leaders hasten to Khosrow's side.

They acclaim him: "O son of the king,
You are worthy of throne, crown, and headdress.
So many sword-striking men will gather around you,
So many valiant leaders from Iran
And from the desert of spear-riders.
Do not fear misfortune.
Your glory will be the army's guide.
Live happy, joyous, and well-respected.
At times we shall charge our horses into the hunt,
At times we shall stand trembling before Aazargoshasp,
To glorify Yazdan and pray as fire worshippers.
If in Iran three hundred thousand riders were
To attack you, we would risk our lives to protect you.

We would celebrate the memory of the deceased."

Khosrow replies, "I am fearful of the king and his court.
But if the leaders wish to appear at Aazargoshasp
To pledge a solemn oath to guaranty my safety
And promise to remain loyal to me,
I shall remain trustingly in this kingdom
And no longer fear the possible harm of Ahriman."

The heroes listen to him, and, at Aazargoshasp,
Declare their oaths and their loyalty to him:
"We shall always be devoted to you!"

Finding himself thus secure before his noblemen,
He sends agents in every direction
To find out his father's views on his flight
And whether he is designing a new plot.

At the news of Khosrow's departure,
Hormozd sends someone to swiftly burden
Khosrow's wretched and bold maternal uncles,
Gostaham and Bandooy, with chains and prison.

Similarly, all of Khosrow's allies are dragged
Into captivity, despite the clamor arising from the action.

34 | Hormozd Sends Ayeen Goshasp to Battle Bahraam

The king says to Ayeen Goshasp,
"I know not how to resign myself.
Angst has lodged in me as my constant companion.
Khosrow has left. What shall we do about Bahraam,
The vile and arrogant slave?"

Ayeen Goshasp seeks to expedite his advice and says,
"O renowned King, Choobineh has often spoken of me.
He secretly seeks my death,
For I am the first to wound his pride.
Send me to him, feet bound. It will serve you perhaps."

The king replies, "I shall do no such thing.
It would be an act of Ahriman, evil creature.
I shall send out an army, take leadership of it,
And acquire glory in battle. Send him first
A skilled man to ascertain what is on his mind.
If he is in search of kingship, crown, and throne,
Fortune will turn its face away from him.
But if he is a loyal subject, he will realize
That the consequences will benefit him
As I shall offer him a part of the world to govern.
I shall place the diadem of heroes on his head.
There is no braver warrior than Bahraam in the world,
But he is my servant, even if he has the might of Rostam.
Let me know all his activities without delay,
And do not remain on the road for long."

Ayeen Goshasp executes the king's plan.
There is in the royal prison a man who comes
From the same city as Ayeen Goshasp.
This man seeks a way of salvation.
When he hears that the rider is about to leave for war,
He sends someone from his prison to say to him,
"O powerful path-seeker, I was born in the same city,
Yet here I find myself held in prison.
You know well my birth and my lineage.
If you wish to kindly ask the king,
If you wish to rescue me from captivity,
I shall accompany you to war,
Where I shall risk my life for you."

Ayeen Goshasp instantly sends someone
Running to the world king to say to him,
"There is a man from my city in prison.
He fears the harm he may subsist.
Should the world king grant me permission,
He will leave right away in my company."

The king replies, "I cannot imagine how
This wicked vagabond will fight in front of you.
He is a murderer, a good-for-nothing, and a thief.
There is no worse villain than him.
Still, you hope he will save you,

And I cannot refuse your request."

He frees the evil-natured, vile thief and assassin.
Ayeen Goshasp leads his army, as swift as wind,
All the way to the city of Hamedan,[8]
Where they stop to set up camp.
He asks who, in this vast town,
Knows the way of the stars and their auguries.

Astrologers tell him, "We shall send you
Someone who is very thankful
And who is versed in the study of astrology.
She is a famed, rich old woman who is the eye of stars.
There is no diviner more worthy than her.
Her speech does not have a word in excess.
Everything she predicts unfolds with precision."

Ayeen Goshasp sends a rider with one horse.
The woman arrives, and he questions her
On the king's affairs and on his army.
Then he adds, "Move your lips near my ear
To tell me if my soul will exit my body in bed
Or if I shall be struck by an enemy sword."

While he speaks secretly to the old woman,
Allowing no one to hear his voice,
The man who asked for mercy from the king
And whom he brought with him
Passes before the fortune teller,
Casts a glance on his master, and exits.

The old woman asks Ayeen Goshasp,
"Who is this man? We will have cause to shed
Tears on the wounds he will inflict upon you.
Your life will fall into his wicked hands.
Cursed be his marrow! Cursed be his skin!"

Ayeen Goshasp remembers the words of astrologers
Long ago, a prediction that he had forgotten:
"Your life will fall into the hands of a fellow citizen,

◇◇◇◇◇◇◇◇◇◇◇◇◇
8 Hamedan: A city and a province in western Iran.

125

A poor man of poor lineage.
He will come to your side after a long journey.
Though you helped him in his time of despair,
He will nevertheless rush to shed your blood."

He offers the old lady gifts and sends her on her way.
So upset is he that he can indulge in neither sleep nor rest.
He writes a letter to the king in which he says,
"I should not have liberated this man from jail.
He is of a more evil nature than the son of dragons.
His majesty warned his servant,
But I did not share the same clarity of mind.
Upon his arrival at court, immediately
Command the executor to cut off his head."

He affixes the seal to the letter, and once dry,
He summons his fellow citizen, praises him,
Offers him gifts, and honors him. He says to him,
"Swiftly and secretly take this letter to the world king.
Once you have his reply, hasten back to me.
There is no need to keep at the side of the king."

The young man takes the letter, but in his mind,
Worried about the voyage, he reflects,
"I am weary of prison, heavy chains, and hunger.
The Creator freed me from wretchedness,
From anguish, from worry and ill fortune.
Now I must return to Ctesiphon,
My mind and blood are simmering at the idea."

He remains on the road feeling troubled for some time,
Then he breaks the seal on the letter to the king.
He reads the message of the hero Ayeen Goshasp
And is confounded by the blow of fate.
He thinks, "Here is a man who asked Hormozd
For mercy on my life, telling him such an act is worthy
Of a king, and now he rushes to send me to my death?
Did this dreadful inspiration reach him through a dream?
He will see what it means to spill blood.
He will soon find himself resting from his ventures."

His soul full of such thoughts, he makes his way back,
Marching in tandem with the wind.

On the road, he notices that
No one is around his illustrious master.
Ayeen Goshasp sits in his tent without servant,
Without either his sword or his horse,
His heart full of worry on the king's affairs,
And on what fate reserves for him.

Upon seeing his fellow citizen entering his tent,
He understands that he has come to dip his hand in blood.
The murderer draws his sword
While his ambitious master attempts to soften him:
"O wanderer, did I not ask the king
To grant you a life you were about to lose?"

He replies, "You asked for it, but what did I do
That you later wished to destroy me?"
He strikes the powerful and illustrious man on the neck,
Ending the prospect of feast and battle for him.
He takes the bloody head out of the tent,
Away from observing eyes.

A man who seeks glory must not remain alone,
Especially if he is about to go to war.

He understands that the bloodshed renders him infamous,
And he quickly leaves to find Bahraam,
To whom he says, "Here is the head of your enemy
Who contemplated your death.
He advanced with an army against you
Without knowing your intentions."

Bahraam says, "Whose head is this?
Who in the world will shed tears for it?"

He replies, "It is the head of Ayeen Goshasp,
The rider, who rushed to fight you in war."

Bahraam says, "This pure man came from
The king's court to reconcile me with Hormozd.
You cut off his head during his sleep?
I shall pay you the retribution you deserve,
And people will weep bitterly over your death."

He asks for gallows to be set up at the door,
In plain sight of the people and the army,
And asks for the miserable one to be hung there alive,
Head down, to awaken the hearts of evil men.

When they learn that their leader has perished,
The court's cavaliers unite around Bahraam.
Another group takes the road to find Khosrow,
And a few of them return to the king.
They are like a herd deprived of their shepherd,
A herd that scatters on a windy, snowy day.

35 | Gostaham and Bandooy Blind Hormozd

Upon hearing of the fate of Ayeen Goshasp,
Hormozd, in his grief, refuses to give an audience.
No one finds him with cup in hand.
He loses sleep, appetite, and rest,
His eyes constantly shedding bitter tears.
Rumors spread about the king
And the fact that he bars access to court.

Warriors are surprised; each has a different opinion.
One of them says, "The belligerent Bahraam
Has designs to usurp the kingly throne."

Another says, "Khosrow Parviz is on his way
To Iran with his host as retribution for his treatment."

As the news from Ctesiphon
Spreads to far-reaching provinces,
Kingship loses its sheen and splendor.
The heads of servants are filled with sorrow and wrath,
And those who once blessed the king now curse him.
Only a few troops hold themselves at court,
And the world narrows for the king's heart.

Bandooy and Gostaham learn
That the imperial throne is subject to decline.
They free all the prisoners from their chains.
One of these prisoners is to assess the state of things

PART TWENTY-EIGHT

Amid the chaos, assess which of the noblemen
Have remained dutifully standing at the king's door.

When they learn the truth of the turn of events,
They rebel and break free. They smash prison doors
And shout cries that heat the plain to a simmer.
The troops remaining in town are embarrassed
And know not what actions to take.

Bandooy and Gostaham appear covered in mail,
Surrounded by their troops and war apparatus.
They reject humiliation and boldly march to the palace.
They meet the king's troops in the marketplace,
Riders who travel to Hormozd's court.

The valiant Gostaham says to his troops,
"Do not take this lightly. If you wish to act with us,
Strip yourselves of your attachment to the king,
Seize your weapons to avenge Iran's noblemen,
For Hormozd has executed many innocent men.
He turned his back on the virtuous prince,
His own son worthy of the throne.
May all those who have dignity and virtue
Walk the true path and refuse him the title of king.
Get to work to punish him as he deserves.
Render bitter to him the waters of Iran.
We shall place ourselves at the lead
And select a new king to sit upon the throne.
If you do not weaken in this venture,
We shall successfully seize Iran-Zamin for you.
As for us, a corner of the world will suffice,
Where we shall withdraw with our companions."

Everyone curses the kingly throne and says,
"May there never exist such a king
Who attempts to shed his son's blood!"

With these words, the troops surrender to insolence.
They set a blaze that consumes the palace gates.
They infiltrate the royal audience hall and arrive
At the side of Hormozd, who sits in pomp and majesty.
They pluck the crown off his head,
Fling him off his seat, and blind him with a flame.

The light in his eyes is obscured
As they extinguish his sight like a candle snuffed.

They abandon him alive in such a state
And proceed to plunder and pillage his treasury.

Such are the actions of the sublime wheel of sky.
Do not attach your heart to this fugitive dwelling.
At times it offers you a treasure,
At times it burdens you with fatigue.
Either way, you will not remain in this passing world,
Whether you are happy in it or not.
Whether it is one hundred years
Or one hundred thousand years,
Anything that can be counted must come to an end.
If you wish to attain happiness,
Abstain from speaking ill of others so that, in turn,
You are never exposed to the sound of ill words.

PART TWENTY-NINE

The Thirty-Eight-Year Reign
of Khosrow Parviz

1 | Khosrow Parviz Finds Out
How Hormozd Has Been Blinded

Gostaham and Bandooy hastily dispatch a rider
With a spare horse to relay news from Iran
Of the wounding of its monarch, King Hormozd.
The message is addressed to his son, Khosrow Parviz,
Who is stationed at the temple of Aazargoshasp.

The envoy arrives at the side of the young prince
On the first night of the new moon.
Pale like the flower of the fenugreek,
He recounts to Prince Khosrow all the troubles
And the current state of affairs in Baghdad.

Khosrow replies, "The one who strays from
The true path as a result of anger or lack of wisdom,
The one who dismisses the force of the wheel of sky,
Is sure to be plunged into a life devoid of happiness.
If you think that the misfortune you relate to me
Brings me the slightest intimation of pleasure,
I can tell you, you are in the wrong.
It feels like from now on my sleep
And my food will be tossed into the flames.
At the moment my father raised his hand to spill blood,
I realized I could not remain stationed in Iran.
But today I stand before him as his slave.
I shall obey every word he utters."

Khosrow Parviz marches off, as swift as fire,
His heart ulcerated, fearing that the rebellious
Bahraam Choobineh will reach court before him.
He charges ahead with a vast army
Drawn from Barda and Ardabil.
It trails the illustrious prince, corps after corps.
More troops from Armenia dash behind, as fast as wind.

Once word spreads in Baghdad that Khosrow Parviz
Is on his way to claim the throne of power,
The entire city is appeased by the news, allowing

The world seeker to ease into a sense of contentment.

The city's noblemen, all those who share in the power,
Trudge to his court to salute and greet him with tales.
An ivory throne is placed on the platform
On which rest the torque and the precious crown.
Khosrow enters the city in a state of grief
And presents himself full of sighs before his father.

What can one say about the speedy rotations
Of the relentless, restless vault of sky?
It offers one the royal crown
And casts another into the sea as fish food.
One has a bare head, feet, and shoulders,
And has neither rest, nor food, nor shelter to hide in;
The other is nourished with milk and honey
And dressed in brocade, furs, and silks.
In the end, both find themselves enveloped
In dust, their heads captured in the lakes of death.

If the sensible man had not been born,
If he had never seen days of struggle,
If he had never experienced this world,
His fate would have been more desirable,
More desirable indeed, no matter
Whether he is a humble man or a powerful one.

Now I shall consider the fate of Khosrow Parviz
And offer the reader new and interesting tales.

2 | Khosrow Parviz Climbs on the Throne and Asks Forgiveness

Once Khosrow Parviz is settled on the throne,
Worthy noblemen approach him
And scatter jewels on his new crown.

Khosrow says to the grand wise master,
"The throne and crown only fall
Into the hands of a man favored by fortune.
May I always act with righteousness,

For injustice leads one on the road to perdition.
My intentions toward others are pure,
And my head bars entry to wicked thoughts.
I have received the golden throne from the Creator
As well as this beautiful and new prized fortune.
Prepare your hearts to obey Yazdan,
And promise me to always abstain from three things:
Harming a pure and upright man;
Rebelling against the legitimate and rightful king;
And finally, extending a hand toward others' possessions.
The pain of this last one will reflect on the one
Who has sold his soul for something of no value.

"We must now renounce all this
And follow the path of righteousness.
Furthermore, wisdom must seek the things
That conform to the spirit of humanity.
I do not hold anything against anyone,
Not even against those who once intended
To greedily seize my throne and ring.
When one is blessed with a noble race and high birth,
One must speak only from the perspective of justice.
As for you, enjoy absolute security,
For I shall never surrender to the workings of Ahriman."

Everyone extols the throne and crown.
They depart happy to see him on the royal seat
From which he applies his good fortune.

At night's descent, Khosrow Parviz climbs down
His throne in joy with thoughts of his father Hormozd.

As the ebony veil of night dissipates
And one hears the rooster's call,
The world conqueror approaches his father,
His soul full of pain, his heart still wounded.

Khosrow Parviz moans at the sight of his father,
Then acclaims him. He stands before him for a long time,
Observing his pained face, and expels a cold sigh.
He kisses Hormozd's eyes, head, and feet
With a constricted heart and a tearful face.

He speaks to his father: "O misfortunate King,
Heir of Kesra Anushiravan, you know that if
I could have been your support, no one would have
Dared to even prick your finger with a needle.
Now reflect on what you wish from me.
Grief has fallen upon you; my heart swells with blood.
If you allow me, I shall stand here as your slave,
Steadfast at your side as your caring protector.
I do not desire to possess the crown,
Nor do I demand the command of a host.
I willingly offer my head to the king."

Hormozd replies, "O wise and sensible prince,
My days of misfortune will be ending as well as
The days of those responsible for my wretched state.
Their efforts and their greed will pass before me.
I ask three things of you and only three:
In the first place, at the dawn of every day,
You come to me to delight my ear with your voice;
Next, that you send me an illustrious cavalier,
One aware of our ancient battles,
A learned old man who has enjoyed the hunt,
Able to recite ancient tales of ancient kings,
One who brings me a book to ease my hardships;
My third wish is that your maternal uncles,
Servants of inferior rank to you,
Cease to see the world when you avenge
The grave injury they inflicted upon me."

Khosrow replies, "O King, may he perish,
He who does not weep over the state of your eyes!
May your enemies disappear from the world
If their crimes spring from their evil essence!
Reflect in your lucid mind on the fact
That Bahraam Choobineh is a bold hero.
He enjoys the support of a vast host
Of riders and sword-striking warriors.
If I raise a hand on Gostaham,
I shall no longer find shelter in the world;
His words and his actions have been foolish.
As for the aging, literate man who is able
To read beautiful stories to the king,

I shall always send you a new one.
May you find some relief in your suffering!
May your heart have the strength to endure your pain!
May patience align itself with your wisdom!
If providence allows me to proceed with justice
I shall seek revenge on Gostaham and Bandooy,
Abandon them to death and without a shroud
To the eager, hungering bites of vicious dogs.
May you dwell in peace and joy, O son of Anushiravan!
May you always be happy,
And may your soul remain forever young!"

After speaking in this manner,
He departs in tears, sharing his thoughts with no one.
The son is more affectionate than the royal father.
And Khosrow has spoken on the subject:
"A young man who is affable and soft-spoken
Is worth more than an old quarreling man
Weakened by the ravages of time and age.
In the end, whether he is valuable or worthless,
His head will, with great certainty, be buried in dust.
We must make every effort to acquire knowledge,
For no one can attest to the fact that a learned
Man and an ignorant man stand on equal footing.
Learning will undoubtedly benefit you in the future
And will send you to the peaceful paradise.
Just as you must nourish your body,
You must nourish your mind with knowledge.
Whatever you do, invoke the name of Yazdan,
Who is pure and victorious, and, above all,
Be sure to banish fear from your heart."

3 | Bahraam Choobineh Learns of Hormozd's Blindness and Takes Action Against Khosrow Parviz

Bahraam finds out about the fate of the king
Whose shining eyes have been consumed,
Two torches akin to two vibrant narcissi,
Snuffed and extinguished in the garden.
He learns that his son has climbed on the throne

And that the fortune of the father has fallen.

The valiant Bahraam is surprised.
His face pales as he deeply ponders the news:
"The time is ripe for me to engage in war
And seize the world with my power."

He gives the order for the beat of timpani
And the rise of the banner of supremacy.
He makes preparations for travel,
Commands his troops to climb on horseback,
Dresses in his armor, speaking at length
About the imminent battle with Khosrow.
The rebel and his army, a mountain in motion,
Advance toward Nahravan and the brave king.

Khosrow, concerned by the news of the march,
Sends emissaries to observe the action and says,
"We must bring this army's secret into light.
If the advice is to engage in war,
If the troops are united behind their leader,
It would make the situation drag on for too long.
We must observe and see if Bahraam
Is positioned within his army center or at the front.
We must assess his conduct at the time of an audience,
Find out if he gives into the hunt during his march."

The envoys depart from court unnoticed by the troops.
They observe and return unseen to Khosrow to report:
"The soldiers are in complete agreement with him,
Every one of them, young or old and experienced.
In an advance, he maintains his position in their midst.
At times he holds the right wing, at times the left wing,
And at times he marches besides the loads.
He is a visionary who can strategize for the future.
There is no nobler rider of his stature.
He consults his men and has no need for strangers.
When he gives an audience, he acts as a king,
And he hunts in the plain with cheetahs.
No ambitious man is more illustrious or more valiant.
He never strays from royal custom and has read

And completed the book of *Kalileh and Demneh*."[1]

Khosrow confides in his vizier:
"We must anticipate a drawn-out affair, for Bahraam,
When he launches his horse against an enemy,
Dragons in the sea are seized by tremors of fear.
Furthermore, he has learned royal ways
From my father, world master and King of Kings.
Thirdly, it appears that he has adopted as minister
The book of *Kalileh*, its contents superior to any scribe."

Then he says to Bandooy and Gostaham,
"We have become the companions of grief."

Illustrious wise men full of ardor,
Secretly hold a meeting with the King of Iran.
They include Gordooy, Shahpoor, Andian,
And Raadman, the leader of Armenia.

Khosrow says to his noblemen, "O valiant
And eminent warriors, those whose minds
Are full of light are protected by their wisdom
As one is protected by a shatterproof coat of mail.
Only the sword of death can administer blows
That can render helmets of steel as malleable as wax
And can thereby pierce holes through them.
I am your inferior in age and cannot assume
World governance because of my youth.
Tell me what remedy I must employ,
For none of us is exempt from the threat of wounds!"

The grand wise master replies, "May you live in joy!
May you be the light and the glory of righteous men!
Since the time of creation, wisdom has been divided
Into four parts: One part is attributed to kings
Who require majesty, birth, and insight;
A second part is linked to pure men;
A third part belongs to the servants of the king,
For they hold themselves close to him

---

1 *Kalileh and Demneh*: An ancient collection of animal stories originally written in Sanskrit but subsequently translated into Arabic and Persian (see Volume Four).

And in full sight of his vast sense and awareness;
Finally, a small part of wisdom remains
That sages attribute to farmers.
However, one finds a lack of insight in both
The ungrateful man and the faithless man
Who exhibits a deep contempt for Yazdan.
If the king wishes to listen to these words
Related by the sage old man, and if the king
Wishes to reflect on them, his mind will be edified."

The king says, "If I could write those words in gold,
I would give them the honor justly due them.
The words of wise men are akin to pearls,
But I have other worries weighing heavy on my heart.
When the two hosts stand to face each other,
When the tips of spears are two-sided like the month
Of Gemini, I shall emerge from the center formation
And fiercely advance toward the enemy host.
If I shout for Bahraam, impure and egoistic leader,
That is one thing, but if I show him a peaceful mien,
If I receive him with praise and acclaim,
If he accepts my propositions, it would be good,
For who else compares to him at court?
If he decides to engage in war regardless,
Well then, I shall be ready
For my troops to contend with his."

The noblemen and experienced warriors
Commend him as king and applaud his words:
"O King, may misfortune remain at bay!
May victory, glory, power, and the imperial crown
Remain forever yours!"

Khosrow replies, "So be it!
May we never be either vanquished or divided!"
He marches with his host out of Baghdad
And asks for the tent pavilions to be set up on the plain.

The two armies approach each other:
On one side, the leader's army;
On the other the king's.
Once the world's torch takes night into its noose,

Shaking its dark curls and spreading them all around,
The two sides send patrols to spy and protect the troops.

At the moment when night, trembling,
Lips parched, flees before the glory of day,
Drums resound on both sides,
And the sun above guides the battle.

The king commands Bandooy and Gostaham
To don their helmets of steel,
And they advance toward the River Nahravan.

A round warns Bahraam that a garrison looms,
Positioned within the space of two arrow lengths.
Immediately Bahraam sends troops,
Calls to his side skilled men,
And mounts his rearing, famed white horse
Of black mane and brazen hooves.
He is armed with an Indian sword
And strikes blows that echo like thunder.
He launches his horse like dazzling lightning.
To his left is the Ahriman-like Izad Goshasp,
Positioned next to Azar Goshasp, and Yalan Sineh,
Their three hearts keen and full of hatred.
These three fearless Turks,
Relatives of fhe Emperor of Chin,
Are resolved to serve Bahraam against Khosrow,
Having all three promised that if they see
The king apart from his host, they will rush him
To Bahraam's camp, dead or alive.

In this way, Khosrow is on one river bank
While the warrior Bahraam is on the other,
And in the middle runs the River Nahravan.
The troops look attentively on either side
To see if Bahraam prepares to approach the king.

4 | Khosrow Parviz Meets With Bahraam Choobineh

Khosrow and Bahraam prepare to meet in person
In order to assess how to proceed.
One's face is open, the other sports a grimace.

The world master is seated on his ivory horse,
A crown of gold and ruby on his head,
Dressed in a tunic of Chini brocade.
Gordooy precedes him as his guide.
Escorting him are Bandooy, Gostaham,
And Khorraad, son of Borzeen, with a golden helmet,
Covered in iron, gold and silver, and a belt
Where the gold disappears beneath a mass of rubies.

At the sight of the face of the King of Kings,
Bahraam pales with fury and says to his noblemen,
"This miserable son of a courtesan
Has risen from a base standing and
From a degree of stupidity to the level of man.
He has gained strength and acts with excessive pride.
Black down grows on his white face.
He thinks he is King Fereydoon with mace and crown.
He has proudly adopted imperial ways,
But his life will suddenly be extinguished.

"This king of dim soul drives his army
In the manner of Anushiravan.
Look at the troops from one end to another.
Observe and see if you see one illustrious man.
I do not find among them a rider eager for battle
Who would dare step forward to contend with me.
He will now witness the actions of valiant men.
He will witness the clash of horse and sword.
He will feel the dust of war and the shock of mace
And the raging shower of shots; he will hear the cries
Of warriors and the blows received and dispensed.
When I set my army into motion,
An elephant dares not hold a stance on the battlefield.
Mountains shatter at the sound of our voices.
The lion, full of heart, swiftly absconds.
I cast a spell on the sea with my sword.

I cover the plains with wide rivers of blood."

He speaks in this manner and launches his white horse,
Which looks as if it were a soaring royal eagle.
He selects a narrow battlefield,
And the army observes him in astonishment.
From there, he sprints toward Nahravan,
Approaching the blessed prince, attended by
A few Iranians armed for battle against Khosrow.

Khosrow turns to the men, "O illustrious ones,
Which of you is a relative of Bahraam Choobineh?"

Gordooy replies, "O King, look at the man
On the white charger, his tunic is white
And his sword's strap is black
As he sprints amid the troops."

At the sight of Bahraam, the world master
Fully understands his nature and says,
"Are you talking about the tall, dark rider?"

Gordooy says, "I most certainly am.
This man never entertains a caring or kind thought."

Khosrow says, "Should you question the warrior,
He will answer you rudely. He sports a boar's snout.
His eyes are half closed, and his heart is wrathful.
Look at his eyes and you will see
That he is an evil man and Yazdan's rival.
I do not see in him a hint of submission.
Proudful, he will never agree to obey anyone."

Then he turns to Bandooy and Gostaham and says,
"I shall shed light upon this affair.
When the donkey is unable to come to the load,
One is forced to take the load to the donkey.
Since Choobineh has been perverted by the deev,
How could he recognize the divine path?
A heart that is sick with ambition
Does not listen to the advice of wise men.
But once we engage in the fight,
Words will no longer be of service to us.

We must reflect carefully, from beginning to end.
Who knows who will emerge as victor in this battle
And who, on this side or the other,
Will bring glory and fame to his army?
We have before us a well-organized host,
With an ardent, warring commander in Choobineh.
He is as fierce and cruel as a deev
With troops standing by howling like wolves.

"If you agree with me, I do not think I shall
Dishonor myself with a few polite questions.
A willingness to negotiate is a more
Valuable strategy than exhibiting weakness.
If my encounter with him results in measured words,
His countless misdeeds will be forgotten.
I shall offer him a corner of the world
And shall not make demands of gratitude in return.
Then struggle and preparation for war
Will convert to acceptance and a peace accord,
A reconciliation that will be to our benefit.
Thus my sense of wisdom will forestall tragedies.
When a king conducts himself as a merchant,
The hearts of pure men rejoice."

Gostaham says, "O King, may you live eternally!
Your words flow as gracefully as dripping pearls.
You are the most knowing of men.
Do what you think is just and right.
You are the image of integrity, but Bahraam,
A slave, is lacking a sense of fairness.
Your head is full of insight and reason
While his head is full of wind."

Khosrow listens, then takes the road,
Advancing majestically, preceded by his escort.
He questions Bahraam from afar,
Wishing to convert an imminent threat into a feast:
"O renowned one, what are you doing
Standing fiercely on the battlefield?
You are the ornament of my court.
You are the foundation of the throne and crown,
The army's support in times of war,

A brilliant torch in times of celebration.
You are a hero full of ambition and drive,
A Yazdan worshipper.
May the Creator never fail you!
I have reflected on your fate.
I have weighed your position with kindness.
I shall offer you and your host my hospitality.
The sight of you will bring joy to my soul.
I shall name you leader of Iran.
I shall pray to Yazdan, the Creator, for you."

The valiant Bahraam listens and returns
The bridle to his white horse of musk-colored tail.
He salutes the king from high above his charger
And holds himself before him for a long time.

Then this man mounted on a white horse says,
"I am happy, content, and prosperous.
As for you, may you never achieve the heights of power,
For you do not know how to make use
Of kingship, neither justly nor unjustly.
When the King of Alaanans is made emperor,
Only miserable men are his partisans.
I have reflected on your fate.
I have just untied a noose destined to bind you.
I shall prepare, in haste, a high gallows,
Roll my noose around your two hands,
And suspend you to hang as you merit,
And hence propel you to taste the bitterness of fate."

Khosrow's cheek pales.
He understands that this man's heart
Will never renounce the throne and diadem.
He replies, "O ungrateful one,
What kind of a speech is this for a pious man?
When a guest arrives from afar to your banquet,
You overwhelm him with insults during the meal
And threaten him with the gallows?
Is this how you hope
To secure your fortune's foundation?
Such is not the custom of kings.
Such is not the behavior of noble cavaliers.

If you go back thirty centuries,
You will not find either a Taazi or a Persian
Who has behaved so wickedly.
A sensible man would be ashamed of it.
Guard yourself from indecent behavior.
When a guest addresses you with kind words,
Only a deev would answer in such a manner.
I fear that your wretched days are ahead
Because of your absurd comportment.
Your deliverance is in the hands of the king,
Who is eternal and master over all.
But you are a sinner, irreverent toward Yazdan.
You have exposed yourself to blame,
And your heart trembles.
When you call me King of Alaanans,
You poorly reflect on my descendance.
Am I not worthy of the title of King of Kings?
Does the diadem of power not suit me,
Whose grandfather was Kesra Anushiravan
And whose father is Hormozd?
Can you name anyone more worthy than me?"

Bahraam replies, "O cursed man,
You speak and act as if you are insane.
First you speak of a guest, but your lineage is new,
And yet you rely on ancient stories.
What do you know of the discourse of kings?
You are neither a sage nor a valiant rider.
You were King of Alaanans, now you are a subject.
You are the most inferior slave.
Your wicked acts bear no fruit in the world.
You are neither king nor worthy of kingship.
I have been acclaimed as king by the people,
And I shall not allow you to set foot on the ground.

"Furthermore, if I said that your star is weak,
That kingship and leadership do not suit you,
I have claimed so, O unworthy prince.
May you never sit upon the throne,
Because the Iranians are your enemies.
They will fight you and will uproot you.
They will tear you apart, body, skin, and veins.

They will surrender your flesh to lions and cheetahs."

Khosrow retorts, "O evil man,
When did you become so furious and so insolent?
Your vile words are humiliating to the human race,
But your nature was despicable from the start.
Reason has abandoned your mind.
Happy is the illustrious man nourished on wisdom.
Any deev who sees his end approaching
Will boast about himself in his speech.
Yet I do not wish for a warrior of your stature
To annihilate himself and lose himself.
Could you not free your heart from this hatred?
Could you not renounce this disruption
And ward off your anger?
Think of the Creator, Justice Giver,
And allow this thought to be your wisdom's guide.

"There stands a mountain before you.
Observe it, observe its height
Towering high above Mount Bisootoon.
To make a king of you would be akin
To asking a sterile thorn to bear fruit.
Your heart relentlessly dreams of power,
But yet Yazdan's will is to be determined.
I know not who has been your master
In all this evilness and who guided you
Down the path of Ahriman, but those who held
Such discourse with you only sought your death."

He says this, climbs down from his ivory horse,
Removes the precious crown from his head,
Turns toward the sun, filling his heart with hope
In Yazdan, and says, "O luminous Just Master,
You will provoke the tree of hope to bear fruit.
You know the nature of the slave before me.
One must shed tears for the crown.
If the race of Kianians were to fail in kingship,
If I were to be stripped of the royal belt,
I shall become a servant in the fire temple.
I shall take nourishment from milk and vegetables.
I shall own neither gold nor silver

And dress in coarse wool at the site of prayer.

"But if kingship is mine, I shall be your servant
And act according to justice and righteousness.
Bring victory to my army; do not surrender
My throne and crown to a slave.
If I obtain the object of my heart's desire,
I shall rush to the altar of Aazargoshasp to plan
An offering of this crown and horse, bracelets,
Chains, earrings, golden robe, and pearls.
I shall scatter one hundred pouches of dinars
On the temple's cupola of lapis lazuli.
Upon rising as world king, I shall send
One hundred thousand dirhams to the fire attendants.
Any prisoners seized from among Bahraam's supporters
Will be brought as servants to the blessed flame.
I shall delight the hearts of wise men and priests.
I shall rebuild any city devastated unjustly
That has become the lair of lions and onager.
I shall not allow it to be engulfed in thorns and weeds."

This oppressed man rises from the dust,
Stands up straight after having prayed,
And marches off to Bahraam Choobineh to say,
"O hellish man, slave of the odious deev,
Leader devoid of sense and reason,
Devoid of good manners and majesty,
A cruel, irascible, and violent deev has blinded you.
You have been infused with fury and a taste
For vengeance instead of sense and reason.
The deevs have acclaimed you as their king.
You take a thicket for a city and hell for a garden.
The torch of wisdom has been extinguished in your eyes
And removed the light from your soul and heart.
Only one deceitful sorcerer had the power
To bring you to the depth of such an abyss.

"Today you extend a hand toward a branch.
Its leaf is dipped in poison, and its fruit is bitter gourd.
Never did your relatives foster such an ambition.
The one who does so will not be blessed.
Yazdan did not grant you the right or a high post.

Do you not remember Gorgeen, son of Milaad?
O unjust, misfortunate man, do not
Lend a thought to what does not exist.
The crab does not have eagle wings,
And the eagle may not fly above the sun.
I swear by Yazdan, the pure, by throne and crown,
That if I find you isolated from your army,
I would only need to strike you with a cold blow
For you to expire even before you catch sight of me.
I have heard many harsh words on your account,
But my support is the One who grants victory.
And if I am not worthy of kingship,
Heaven forbid that I endure the life of a subject."

Bahraam replies, "O senseless man,
You are brisk and possessed by the deev.
Your father was an old, faith-loving world ruler
Who never blew coldly on anyone.
But you have not understood the value of such a man.
You shamefully deprived him of the throne.
And now you pretend to be world master after him,
You pretend to be a man of sense and reason?
You are an impure being, the enemy of Yazdan,
Whose benevolence will turn to adversity for you.
Even if Hormozd had not been a just king,
And even if the earth and the era
Roiled with complaints about him,
You are his son and unworthy of being King of Iran.
You have a right neither to life nor to the throne.
A casket will suffice, O miserable one,
Since I wish to avenge Hormozd
And since I appoint myself King of Iran.

"Now explain to me what righteous man
Will approve of the burning of the eyes of kings
Or the fact that you command others to burn them.
You will see that from here on, kingship will belong to me,
Along with everything from the sun high above to the sea
Below and the back of the fish, support of the earth."

Khosrow says, "Heaven forbid that a slave rejoices
At the expense of my father's suffering.

It was written, and events unfolded.
You wish to accumulate word upon word,
You attribute kingship to yourself,
And when death arrives, you will miss a shroud.
On your horse with lordly strappings,
You are a powerless ruler inept at achieving his goal.
You have neither home nor inheritance,
Neither land nor high birth.
Your rule is filled with nothing but wind.

"Despite a vast host, wealth, and a false title,
You will never shine on the royal throne.
Many ambitious men have come before you,
But none ever made claims to the empire.
None ever did, because as subjects,
They had no right to the throne and diadem.
You will always raise your head with anger,
Tears of shame never filling your eyes.
Fate will always accuse you of fury,
A sort of fury that will lead you to commit crimes.
Yazdan fashions a king with a sense of justice,
With high deeds and a high birth.
Kingship is bestowed upon the most worthy,
The most intelligent, and the most harmless.

"If my father appointed me King of Alaanans,
It is because he was worried about your traps.
But now the Creator has offered me
The empire, throne, royal crown, and power.
I have received them from the World Master
Who knows all that is revealed and unrevealed.
I have received them by order of King Hormozd,
Who inherited the crown from his father,
And by the grand wise master, by sages,
And worldly noblemen expert in courtly affairs.
I have received them according to the holy law
Brought from the sky by the sage Zartosht,
Who relayed the divine message to Lohraasp,
Who in turn accepted it and transmitted it to Goshtaasp.
All men are under my protection, whether they have
Caused me harm or donated their wealth to me,
Whether they are my friends or my enemies.

"I shall render wealthy any poor man
Coming my way from a demolished city.
I shall convert thickets into paradise,
Fill them with men, cattle, and harvest.
Until the day I depart from this unstable world,
I shall draw the worthy man out of oblivion,
Offer vast rewards, weigh him
On my heart's scale, and fortify his arm.

"Since Hormozd governed the world with justice,
And since the earth and the era
Enjoyed a time of happiness under his rule,
The son must inherit his father's throne,
As heir to the royal crown, belt, and fortune.
You are a man full of crime and treachery.
You were the first to attack Hormozd,
And misfortune followed at your command,
Stirred by your deceit, tricks, and machinations.
Yazdan willing, I shall obscure the light of the sun
For you in order to avenge the king.
Now who has a right to the crown?
If I am not most worthy of it, then tell me who is?"

Bahraam replies, "O valiant man,
The one who usurps the throne earns the right to it.
Did not the Ashkanian possess royal power
When the daughter of Babak gave birth to Ardeshir?
Did not Ardeshir gain supremacy when the throne
Fell into his hands after he killed Ardavan?
Five hundred years have passed since,
The heads and crowns of the Sassanians are weak.
The day has come when I am to seize the throne
And diadem, as my victory is assured.
When I see your face and your fortune,
Your army, your diadem, and your throne,
I extend a hand on the Sassanian power,
Like a tamed lion that grows ferocious.
I shall erase your names from the book.
I shall trample Sassan's throne beneath my feet,
For the power belongs to the Ashkanian,
If we are to hearken the words of men
Endowed with the knowledge of the truth."

Khosrow says, "O foolish man eager for battle,
If a king must be of Kianian lineage,
Where do you then belong?
The people of Rey, in the end, are hypocritical.
A small host emerged from Rey to unite
With Eskandar's troops and align with the Rumi cause.
Their goal was to seize the Kianian throne.
Mahiar, the impure, came from Rey,
And he destroyed Eskandar's family.
The Creator did not approve, and the people of Rey
Drew vast misfortune on the Iranians,
Who, from that time on, fought against each other.

"The World Master, always ready to protect,
Placed the diadem on Ardeshir's head.
Ardeshir was worthy of the Kianian crown
Because of his royal birth, though he lacked treasures.
The Creator only witnessed virtue from Ardeshir.
Are the names of the illustrious men forgotten?
Are my words nothing but wind?
Who is now worthy of power?
Who is master of this unstable world?
When you release and let go, your body feels liberated.
When you seek to gain or obtain something,
You live in a state of perpetual fear."

Bahraam replies, "I am a warring leader, for I shall,
Once and for all, pluck out the roots of the Kianian tree."

Khosrow retorts, "Have you heard the story
As related by ancient wise men?
        'The sword of power must never fall
        Into the hands of an ignorant man,
        A wandering man, or an infamous man.
        Should you desire to reclaim it,
        You will not succeed, since the holder
        Of the treasure is intoxicated by its pull.'
Follow the path of righteousness.
Answer my questions in truth."

"Furthermore, what did the soft-spoken man proclaim?
        'If you place a good-for-nothing at the pinnacle,

      You will be forced to endure pain and grief.'
Keep your distance from the ungrateful.
My inconsiderate, thoughtless father
Could not differentiate between
Appearances and your wicked soul.
Although he was surrounded by many men,
Great and small, he came to entrust
The Kianian sword to people of a base nature.
He offered you the command of illustrious warriors,
And you became the chief of the Kianian land.
You were valiant, ardent, and ambitious,
But your ill nature made you malicious.
The silver throne and the royal seal went to your head,
And you strayed off the true and righteous path.
Then your name, Choobineh, became Bahraam,
And your silver throne became a trap for you.
You wished to raise yourself above the moon.
You were a famed leader yet yearned to become king.
No man of sense would entertain such absurd thoughts.
There is no doubt that you united with a deev."

Bahraam retorts, "O wicked man,
You only know how to blame and insult others.
You count for nothing Yazdan's divine laws,
And you make claims to the throne,
Although you are rather unworthy of its glory.
You burn the eyes of the world king.
How could such a thing remain hidden?
All your friends are in truth your enemies.
In words they appear attached to you,
But in their hearts they are loyal to me.
The Emperor of Chin supports me in this venture,
As well as the armies that occupy the expanse
Between Iran and the far corners of Chin.
I am just and passionate, I brandish a sword,
And no adversary is able to contend with me.
I shall transplant the seat of power from Pars to Rey,
Decidedly ending the authority of the Kianian name.
I shall make justice flourish throughout the world

And raise the customs of Milaad.[2]
I am of the race of the illustrious Aarash.[3]
When I lead in war, I am an irresistible flame.
I am the grandson of world seeker Gorgeen.
I am the ardent flame of Barzeen.

"King Saaveh came to the land of Iran
To steal the throne, the seal, and diadem.
He wished to raze the fire temples to the ground,
To abolish the observance of the day
Of Nowruz and the feast of Saddeh.
He wished to turn the Iranians into slaves.
But I cinched my waist and picked up arms.
An arrow from my bow flew to slay Saaveh Shah,
Thereby defending and saving the land of Iran.
If you know not the number of insolent leaders,
Count four hundred times one thousands,
Plus twelve hundred war elephants.
It is as if all the paths on earth do not suffice.
This vast host was vanquished,
And I pursued it like a ferocious lion.
Know that a man who fails to accomplish high deeds
Cannot make claims to the throne of kings.
My helmet exudes the scent of the crown,
My sword will give me the ivory seat
While a mere fly that assails you
Has the force to propel you off your throne."

Khosrow replies, "O ill-fated man,
Why do you not remember Gorgeen in Rey?
He did not reflect on the throne.
He lacked power, glory, and good fortune.
No one in the world knew your name.
You were of a base condition and unknown
Until the noble Mehran Setaad arrived
And spoke of you to the reigning king.
This is how he extracted you from the dark dust.

◇◇◇◇◇◇◇◇◇◇◇◇◇◇

2 Milaad: Gorgeen of Milaad, from the lineage of Aarash Kamangir; ancestor of Bahraam Choobineh.
3 Aarash: Or Arash, is the famed archer from Persian legend in *The Avesta*. His arrow
travels for two days, and its landing determines the border between Iran and Tooran.

But you have forgotten all of that.
The king gave you treasure, weapons, troops,
And the banner of Rostam, shining bright as the moon.
Yazdan did not wish for the land of Iran
To be converted into a desert by the heroes from Chin.
Yazdan came to your aid in the battle,
And your helmet was raised to the highest clouds.

"When the Master of the revolving spheres
Resolved for the kingdom to prosper again,
You are the one who took on the honor.
May you never acquire either power or joy!
If this empire must escape the Kianian race,
Why do you seize your weapons?
Only someone like Eskandar can obscure
The fortune of the Kings of Kings.
But you, with your deev demeanor,
With your coloring in dark shades of dust,
May you only remain in the shallows.

"With your perversity and your maneuvers,
The day now grieves for the King of Iran.
You had dirhams engraved with my name
And, by doing so, wished to deprive me of life.
You are the very example of evil in the world.
You occupy the highest rank among the most aberrant.
You are responsible for the bloodshed on earth.
But you will not find the one you tracked down
By daylight fast asleep in the dark night.
O unfortunate, unjust man, do not spend
Your entire life in pursuit of wicked deeds.
Think of a reconciliation with Yazdan.
Make use of reason and righteousness,
For this world will end for you and for me
And time will count each of our breaths.

"Who would declare iniquity
More valuable than righteousness?
Why have you abandoned your heart to vice?
Should you concur with me, you would succeed.
You would own a part of this kingdom.
You would live happily in the world,

155

Free and safe from the attacks of your enemies.
When you leave this passing dwelling,
You will return to the Creator free of suffering.

"You must do neither more nor less
Than what Zartosht suggests in the *Zand*:
>   'If someone strays from the pure faith
>   And does not hold fear of the divine,
>   He must be given proper advice for one year,
>   And if he does not benefit from it,
>   He must be executed by order of the king,
>   His body, sullied by crime, flung on the road.
>   But if he has ill intentions toward the king,
>   He must be instantly killed.'
Furthermore, your blood will certainly be spilled.
Such is the conclusion received by your dismal fate.
Your life will from now on be miserable,
And after your death, your will be subjected to flames.

"If you continue to follow your path
And turn your head away from the king
And from divine justice, you will deeply repent
For your actions, your vile words and your deeds.
You are ailing, and my advice is your medicine.
I shall make every effort to cure you.
If your heart's sense of greed and envy dominates
And prevents you from listening to me, tell me,
So that I may summon another physician to you.
Regardless, your medicine must be good counsel,
And your cure must be wisdom,
As wisdom is the only thing able to pluck
From your heart the yearning for the throne.
Victory made you a man, but your greed
For the acquisition of wealth made you a dissident.
You have heard stories of Zahaak's impiety,
How he filled the world with terror for deevs,
And how, after he troubled many hearts,
The blessed Fereydoon handled him.

"Now your warriors are, in their hearts, my slaves.
They are mine in life and death.
You have given them a taste of glory,

Turned them away from justice.
But when I show them my treasury,
I shall fill their hearts with good will.
None of the troops will remain with you
Since you have neither name nor glory nor treasure.
When you overcame King Saaveh,
All the troops believed themselves invincible,
Satisfied and intoxicated by the loot they collected.
These fearless warriors must not perish by my hand.
I do not wish for them to battle until the land of Iran
Is depopulated and the throne of power is crushed.
Tell me who was king during the time of Aarash.
It will free me from your claims."

Bahraam says, "At that time, Manoochehr was king.
He was the master of the army, throne, and crown."

Khosrow replies, "O ill-natured man,
If you know that Manoochehr was world king,
How do you know that Aarash was his slave,
Curbing his head to royal will and command?
Then the vindictive Kay Khosrow rose to kingship
And had a servant like Rostam who could have seized
The power and majesty of the Kianian seat.
Yet he respected the rights of kings
And did not glance in the direction of the throne.
Why do you not recognize me as King of Iran?
It is because you are a deev Ahriman
With a dark complexion and a greedy constitution."

Bahraam says, "O ill-born man, the truth is
That your origins go back to a Sassanian family,
And Sassan was a shepherd, son of a shepherd.
Babak was not the first to entrust him with his herd.
For the sake of Aarash you blame me?
You only remember Kay Khosrow of all the kings?"

Khosrow says, "O wicked offender,
I do not flaunt pride merely for the fact
That I am a descendant of Sassan.
Every word out of your mouth is a lie,
And it is a dishonor to utter falsehoods.

You emerge out of a group of wrongdoers.
You are not from the race of Sassan."

Bahraam says, "The fact that Sassan was
A shepherd will never be forgotten."

Khosrow replies, "When Dara died,
He could not surrender the throne to Sassan.
Good fortune had vanished,
But how could his birth be overlooked?
Words do not render just what is unjust.
Is this the wisdom, intelligence, and dignity
With which you reclaim the royal throne?"

He smiles, turns away from Bahraam,
And heads back toward his camp.
The three audacious Turks, the emperor's subjects,
Avid for prey like wolves, had told Bahraam
That, to acquire fame and renown,
They would bring the king's body, dead or alive,
On the day of battle on the army front.
One of them, a rider of impure race,
Brave, angry, and unfamiliar with fear,
Springs into action, eager for battle,
A noose rolled sixty times hanging on his arm.

Approaching the royal ivory horse,
He aims for the noble crown of Khosrow,
Flings his noose, and, in its knot,
Snatches the head with the royal crown.

Gostaham slashes the noose with his sword,
And the head of the king is released, unharmed.
Bandooy quickly binds his bow, affixes to it
An arrow of poplar wood able to eclipse daylight.
He shoots at the Turk, who retreats to his troops.

Bahraam says to the Turk,
"May you be entombed in the dark earth!
Who told you to fight with the king?
Did you not see me standing before him?"
Then he returns to his camp,
His soul full of grief, his body consumed by flames.

5 | Gordieh Advises Her Brother, Bahraam

Upon hearing of her brother's return
From a meeting with the king,
Bahraam's sister removes her beautiful diadem.
A servant brings her veil, and she rushes to greet
Her brother, her heart pierced with pain, her mind dim.

Gordieh says to him, "O prince eager for battle,
How was your behavior in front of the king?
Tell me. If, because of his youth,
He gets carried away with acts of violence,
Do not allow yourself to reject a reconciliation."

The valiant Bahraam says to his sister,
"One must not include his name among Iranian kings.
He is neither an avid cavalier nor a brilliant man.
Ability is a more valuable asset than an illustrious birth,
And the greatest quality for a king is his valor."

The wise sister says, "O powerful man,
You are brusque and yearning for fame.
No matter what I tell you, you do not listen.
You only make a display of anger and petulance.
Reflect on the words of the eloquent man from Balkh:
        'It is a bitter thing to listen to the sincere words
        Of any man who reveals the truth of our shortcomings.'
You have a part of the world, you have land.
Do not strategize to convert it into a desert.

"A very wise man once recounted a story
In which a donkey who longed to bear
Buffalo horns lost his two ears in the middle of a herd.
Do not expose yourself to reproach in the world,
For no one in your family has ever borne a crown.
If this young man did not stand between you and kingship,
My mind would be neither wounded nor obscured.
But the father lives, the throne of royalty stands.
Yet you place yourself between the father and the son,
And for that my eyes are filled with blood tears.
You search only for anguish and imprecation.
You foolishly aspire for the perfume of a deadly flower.

People will say that Choobineh has lost his glory
And that the name of Bahraam
Has become synonymous to an insult.
Yazdan will bring divine wrath upon you,
And your soul will fall victim to the fires of hell.

"O brother, the world does not remain for anyone.
Only our good name will survive us.
Reflect on the fact that you never had a protector
In the world other than King Hormozd.
When the throne and the booty of King Saaveh
Fell into your hands, you raised your helmet high.
With the aid of Hormozd, you were able
To gain fame and glory in the world.
But now your sight is set on the imperial throne?
Understand that all good comes from Yazdan,
And do not be unjust with the wrathful king.
Do not be so proud of the battle you waged.
You admittedly acted with great valor;
Do not boast and submit to arrogance.
You have granted the deev access to your heart.
You have become a rebel in the eye of the Creator.

"When Hormozd had a fit of fury
Against the words of the wicked Ayeen Goshasp
And was struck by the calamity of blindness,
His son came from Barda to avenge him.
You should have remained calm in this affair.
It was not the time for a servant to incite war.
You should have gone to the young prince
And arranged the royal throne to his liking.
Then the youth would have followed your advice
And fate would have brought you only profit.
You would have been at peace and happy,
And destiny would have watched over you.

"Why then wish to seize the crown and throne?
You know there are princes young and old
From Ardeshir's family line,
Owners of vast treasure and innumerable hosts.
In view of this fact, what person in his rightful mind
Would agree to give you the title of king?

160

Only if you were a ruler with treasure and army
Would you be able to govern this land.
Only Saaveh Shah, commander of the vast
Chini host, ever dared attack Iran.
Yazdan, the pure, surrendered him to you,
Turning evil away from Iran and from the world.

"Since Yazdan created the world,
Since Yazdan drew from its bosom the sublime sky,
Never did anyone see a cavalier as bold as Saam,
Before whom a fierce lion would dare not appear.
But when fate willed for Nozar to commit awful acts,
When he trampled beneath his feet his father's advice,
All the noblemen wished to proclaim Saam king
And prepared for him the turquoise throne.
Saam vehemently refused, declaring,
        'Cursed be a leader whose sight is fixed on the throne!
        The dust at Manoochehr's feet is my home,
        And the foot of Nozar's throne is my crown.'

"O my dear brother, you are no more worthy than Saam,
Who, good-natured as he was, did not pursue the throne.
In turn, Zaal and Rostam, of elephant stature,
Did not attempt to usurp the royal seat.
I tell you this because one can obtain the throne
Only when one has a victorious fortune,
As well as a noble hand, an illustrious birth,
Intelligence, and a serene heart, full of justice.
I know not what will become of you,
For wisdom has vacated your mind."

Bahraam says to her, "As Yazdan is my witness,
You speak the truth, but this affair has gone too far.
My heart and my mind are full of greed.
I shall be king or else I shall give up my head,
A fate able to penetrate my warrior helmet of steel.
If I am defeated by the new king,
My host will seize his royal seat.
Attempt to place another on the throne,
For vengeance has corroded the hearts of my troops
When it comes to the subject of King Khosrow."

6 | Khosrow Holds Counsel With His Leaders and His Wise Men

On the other side, the world king returns,
And, having crossed the Bridge of Nahravan
Safe and sound, he convenes his army leaders
And seats them across his royal throne.

Khosrow says to them, "O illustrious and loyal ones,
O experienced chiefs tested in world affairs,
Here is the beginning of my exercise of power,
And I can only make more attempts.
I have not yet gained the right to receive gratitude,
No matter how well-intentioned I may be.
I have not yet provided you with happiness,
Rather I have burdened you with worry and weariness.
You have been the servants of my ancestors.
You have seen many troubles, endured much bitterness.

"I shall divulge to you a secret,
Which I shall keep from the army.
You as well do not reveal it to the Iranians,
For my fate will then be played,
That we are to attempt a night attack
To launch my warriors upon the enemy.
I have seen Bahraam and have spoken to him.
He is a rider able to handle his horse
And worthy of engaging in battle.
But I did not detect wisdom either in his head
Or in the heads of his famed army commanders.
He speaks only of his war against Saaveh Shah,
Continuously reviving the old epic story.
He takes me for a senseless child and believes
That he scares me with his mace and sword.
He does not suspect a night attack.
He does not deem me capable
Of stripping myself of timidity in war.

"If you wish to come to my aid, I shall not delay,
And we can spring into action at dusk.
Once night floods its dark face with gray amber
And floats its curly, musk-scented mane,

162

You will climb on horseback in battle armor
And brandish mace and dagger."
At this point, the troops promise to obey the king.

Khosrow enters his tent pavilion, dismisses
The visitors, and summons Gostaham, Bandooy,
And the valiant and skilled Gordooy.
He speaks to them of the nocturnal battle,
Expressing the hope that they will assist him.

Gostaham says to him, "O King,
How can you place your trust in fate?
You will wage a night attack with your troops
And perhaps lose the friendship in their hearts.
Your warriors are in accord,
United body and heart with the enemy.
On one side stand grandsons,
On the other their grandfathers.
How can we expect them
To use a ploy against each other?
On one side is a brother, on the other his father,
Both tightly bound to each other.
How could a father fall into battle with his own son?
Do not tempt your enemy with such a venture.
You must not speak of it to the army.
Just by the fact that you have brought it up,
The fight appears to be decidedly lost."

Gordooy says, "It is too late. Our entire past,
Our power and treasury, our valuables and army
Will soon be like wind blowing over the plain.
The heads of young men turn away from the path.
Do not remain tonight in this camp.
Do not wait for the loss of treasury and army.
I have no doubt that Bahraam's host is aware
Of our secret plans and preparations.
We must not surrender your royal head to the enemy."

Khosrow approves of the advice,
Recognizing and appreciating its importance.
Among the indomitable men, he selects a number
Who are devoted to him in good and bad fortune.

163

They are Khorraad, son of Borzeen; Gostaham, the lion;
Shahpoor; the valiant Andian; Bandooy;
Khorraad, the army's glory; and Nastooh,
Army destroyer whose fire consumes the enemy.
With them are those able to serve him
And to guard the treasury, the army, and his life.

Khosrow marches to a lush, green hill,
A proper place to set up a feast.
From its height, he can observe his army.
Members of his escort wait there,
Their hearts ready and keen on battle.

On the other side, the bold Bahraam mounts his horse,
And warriors, great and small, arrive.
The leader asks the chiefs,
"Have you received news of your families?
You all have in the other camp relatives
Loyal to us in words and faith.
Should they decide to come to me and obey me,
Should they engage their souls as guarantee to the treaty,
I shall enrich them with valuables from my treasury
And ennoble them with titles as I have you.
Troops from Barda and Ardabil remained
Loyal to Khosrow, but one or two corps
Of Armenians cowardly absconded.
We would have nothing to fear, for the people
Of Barda are to us equal to a fistful of dust."

The illustrious men listen to Bahraam
And assure him that he has attained his goal.
They select a literate army man,
Eloquent, erudite, and observant.

The hero, his soul full of secrets,
Goes to the illustrious and valiant Iranians,
Marching throughout the long night,
And repeats to them the words of the noblemen.

The Iranians reply to him, "As long as the hosts
Do not engage in battle, we shall not leave Khosrow.
We do not fear this state will last long.
Do not believe yourselves safe in your camp,

For Khosrow will launch a night attack."

The envoy returns to the hero's camp,
As swift as wind, to report the message.

Bahraam, learning how the army has prepared,
Asks for fires to be lit and torches to be placed.

7 | Bahraam Choobineh Launches a Night Attack

Bahraam, secure with the knowledge of his troops' loyalty,
Selects a valiant corps suited to conquer the world.
As the scribes enumerate them to him,
There are six thousand sword-bearing men.
Among the subjects of the emperor, there are three
Ferocious Turks who resemble devouring wolves.

He says to the warriors, "Once you hear
The sound of timpani at the hour of the cock crow,
You will shout a cry, you will attack the enemy,
And you will crown the leaders' heads with blood."

On the command of the hero, the company departs,
Preceded by the three renowned Turks.
It marches with ardor on the king's army,
Their hearts full of wrath set on vengeance.

The sound of mace, weapons, and arrows echoes.
The ground is made of steel, the clouds are of dust.
Each warrior cries, "Where is Khosrow?
Today victory and supremacy belong to us."

But Khosrow is on the hill, in a state of great distress,
His eyes full of blood, his face pale, gravely discouraged
And lost in thoughts about an event that confounds the world.
He remains in this state, terrorized by the blows,
Until dawn reveals itself over the mountaintops.

As the hem of night's cloak withdraws,
Khosrow observes the battlefield
Covered with corpses and wounded bodies.
He says to the illustrious gathering,

"Come to my aid; act against our enemies,
For the one who gives us victory is my protector,
And now the blows of swords concern me."

He runs toward the three Turks – what do I say,
Turks, they are more like fierce and vicious lions.
One of them launches his horse,
Arrives to confront Khosrow, draws out his sword,
And attempts to strike the king on the head.
But the valiant shah protects himself with his shield,
Strikes a quick blow below the Turk's armor,
And flings him to the ground, head first.
The troops turn away from the king.

Khosrow cries out, "O men rendered famous
By your battles, this is not the moment to hold back."
But they ignore him and deflect,
Shamefully abandoning their ruler.

The king turns to Bandooy and Gostaham:
"Now I have a bad opinion of this affair.
I do not have a son who has reached manhood.
I do not have a relative suited for the throne.
Should I be killed in battle,
There will remain no heir to the crown."

Bandooy says to him, "O noble man,
The world necessitates your majesty.
The army has left. Do not remain here,
For you will not find aid in this calamity."

Khosrow says to Gordooy, "Depart with Tokhaar.
Take with you the remaining one thousand cavaliers,
And take from camp all that you find in terms
Of tents, brocade, valuables, crowns, sacks of gold,
Slaves, and the precious ivory throne."

The noblemen gather the baggage and valuables,
Exerting themselves to carry the loads.
At that moment, on the horizon,
There appears a banner with the figure of a dragon.
It sends reflections of violet across the world.
Behind it runs the valiant Bahraam,

166

Who steals the light of the world in battle.

Bahraam and Khosrow come face to face,
Two warriors full of courage, two irritable lions.
They attack each other like war elephants.
They strike each other on the head.
Bahraam struggles fiercely,
But his weapons do not affect Khosrow's armor.
This battle continues in excess
Until the sun disappears from the vault of sky.

Tokhaar returns to the king's side
And tells him that he has driven
The treasure and the baggage to the bridge.

Khosrow says to Gostaham, "No one assists us in battle.
We are ten against a vast host led by a bold warrior.
The Creator has given me royal dignity,
But with no one to help us, we shall leave.
There are moments when flight is more valuable
Than battle, and when one is alone,
One must not seek ways to incur delay."

The inexperienced young man rides all the way
To the bridge of Nahravan, trailed by Bahraam,
Whose head is full of hate, his heart full of temerity.

Witness to this, Khosrow stops on the bridge,
Calls the worldly Gostaham, and says,
"Bring me my bow and my war interpreter."

The treasurer obeys and hands him bow and arrow,
As Gostaham is, in this affair, the king's vizier.

The valiant Khosrow takes the bow, fixes to it
An arrow, its spark erasing the light of day.
He sends a hail of shots, and at every strike,
He pins the helmet on the head of the enemy.

Bahraam, the lion, assails him,
Seated upon his dragon-like charger.
He holds only a noose in his hand,
And his horse is unprotected by armor.

Khosrow watches him with delight.
He attaches the cord to the two ends of the bow
And strikes an arrow into the horse's chest.
The creature instantly buckles and falls.

The leader, finding himself dismounted,
Seizes his shield and brings his hand
To his forehead in a gesture of despair.

Yalan Sineh rushes to him, as swift as dust,
But the Kianian prince, knowing that he is brave,
Immediately wounds his horse with his left hand,
Not considering him much of a warrior.
Yalan Sineh, on foot, absconds from the bridge.

All the Turks, young and old, run off as well,
And once Bahraam himself promptly withdraws,
Khosrow proceeds to destroy the bridge.
He then runs in distress to Ctesiphon,
Heart full of pain, eyes flooding with tears.
He asks for the city gates to be fortified
With iron bars, and he sits, besieged by worry.
He summons a notable man from every street
And places them as guards at every door.

8 | Khosrow Flees Toward Rum, and Hormozd Is Assassinated

From there, Khosrow travels to his father,
Eyes full of blood tears, heart deeply wounded.

Once in his presence, he pays homage to him
And remains standing before him for a long time.
Then he addresses him: "This valiant warrior
That you have selected, O King,
Came to me with royal pomp and a vast host.
I gave him all sorts of advice,
But it made little impression on him.
He only desired to engage in battle and fight.
May his name forever perish from the world!

"Against my will, we fell into a mighty battle,
And the stars brought down many soldiers.
My host abandoned me. It was as if my warriors
Could only see me when they passed before me.
They acclaimed Bahraam as their leader and king,
Unaware of the outcome of such a thing.
Bahraam followed me to the bridge of Nahravan
With an army that was like a mountain in motion.
When my affairs deteriorated, I fled to avoid
Being caught in the traps of destruction.
I have reflected on what could benefit or cause us harm.
I came to the conclusion that we could seek support
From the land of the Taazian, should the king allow."

Hormozd replies, "This plan is not a good one,
For you appear to have nothing to lean on.
To summon the Taazian would be a lost cause,
Since they have neither weaponry nor treasury.
They will refuse to come to your aid,
And you can do them neither good nor harm.
They will not respect you for your high birth
And will surrender you to the enemy for money.
May Yazdan be your support in this affair!
May fortune be your ally and smile on you!
If you decide to leave, run swiftly to the land of Rum.
Once you arrive, tell the Caesar my pleading words.
It is a land with religion and wealth,
Where weapons and troops are in good order.
Furthermore, the rulers are descendants of Fereydoon.
They are your relatives and will come to you
Should you fall into harm's way."

Khosrow kisses the ground at Hormozd's feet
And pronounces blessings on him.
Then he says to Bandooy, Gordooy, and Gostaham,
"Grief and fatigue have become our companions.
Prepare your affairs and prepare the loads for travel.
We shall not surrender the land of Iran to the enemy."

Gostaham exclaims, "O King,
May your eye never witness suffering!"

Khosrow says, "The revolving dome treats us
With aggression at times and at time with affection."

He hears the voice from the lookout shouting,
"O prince of blessed fortune and full of justice,
A dark dust is rising on the road.
One can see a shining banner in the midst of troops,
Followed by a banner the color of indigo
And sporting the image of a dragon, the very banner
Choobineh brandished on the bank of the Nahravan."

At the sound of this cry, Khosrow climbs on his horse,
As swift as smoke, and leaves the city,
Tailed by a banner the color of indigo.

He shakes his arms and his body, and, turning his head,
He notices Gostaham and Bandooy riding slowly.
He shouts at them in a bout of fury,
"O unworthy men, how could our opponents
Arrive as if they are among our men?
In any case, why do you not pick up the pace
Since Bahraam is now on our tail?"

Bandooy replies, "O King, do not worry about Bahraam.
He cannot see the dust we raise on the road,
Since his dark banner is still quite distant.
But here is what your friends are saying:
          'We have no reason to rush as you do,
          For Choobineh enters the king's palace.
          He will instantly give Hormozd the crown and throne
          And sit beside him as his vizier.
          He will cast into the sea a fishhook to attract bait.
          They will write a letter in the king's name
          To the Caesar to inform him that the vile slave
          Has fled the land of Iran and its border
          And must not remain in Rum in peace.
          Every time that he acted to his will,
          He incurred much damage and humiliation.
          If he arrives in your land, tie him up
          And fill his happy heart with pain.
          Return him to this court,
          And do not wait for him to gain power.

> The king's feet will be bound,
> And he will be returned to this court shedding tears.'"

Khosrow finds himself deeply troubled by these words.
Shadows frame his face as he asks,
"Is it possible for misfortune to bring us
An event of such magnitude?
There would be much to say,
And our position would be difficult.
Still we place our faith in the just Creator."

He launches his horse and adds,
"The good and bad fortune that the World Master
Inscribes on our foreheads will unfold,
And our worries have no power to change fate.
May our enemies never reach their goals!"

As soon as he draws nearer, the two scoundrels
Return to the palace, hearts full of hatred.
They enter the king's audience hall in anger,
Intent on committing a crime.
They cross the threshold and arrive at the throne.
They detach the cord from the bow
And wrap it around the neck of the venerable king,
To quickly strangle him.

In this way perish the crown
And the throne of the King of Kings.
It is as if Hormozd has never lived.
Such is the custom of this ever-changing world:
At times it provides honey, at times poison.
Since such is its nature, do not seek pleasures,
For its search will only attract pain upon you.

Once the rotation of Hormozd's days ends,
The throne and the blessed court are found empty.
The beating of timpani is heard,
The cheeks of the murderers are as pale as sandarac,
The leader's banner appears on the road in the army center.
Gostaham and Bandooy, two wretched criminals,
Flee the palace in haste, rushing to rejoin Khosrow.

When the prince sees their pale faces,

171

He understands why they had mysteriously vanished.
His cheeks drain of color,
Pale as the flower of the fenugreek,
But he does not show his despair to the bold men.
He says to them, "Let us part with the road,
For an army approaches. Take the long desert path,
And do not allow your bodies to bend to exertion."

9 | Bahraam Sends His Host After Khosrow, and Bandooy Seeks a Way to Rescue Khosrow

Once Bahraam enters the king's audience hall,
He surveys his vengeful army and selects
Six thousand men in chainmail and ready to strike,
And he sends them in pursuit of King Khosrow.
He entrusts this illustrious and valiant army
To Bahraam, son of Siaavoosh.

On his side, Khosrow enters the desert
To guard his life from enemy harm.
He runs in this manner until he arrives
At a fortified site, with walls so high
One cannot perceive the battlements.
It is a blessed site of prayer
Called the House of Yazdan, a place of rest
For penitents led by priests and clergymen.

Khosrow says to the divine servant,
"What food have you for me?"

The priest says to him, "O illustrious man,
We can offer you a dinner of unleavened bread
And watercress from the river, if it suits you.
May this meal be a simple snack for you!"

The king and his escort climb down from their steeds.
The ambitious world seeker and his two servants
Take the barsom in their hands to utter prayers.
Then they sit on the soft blue sand
And hastily indulge in the spread.

Then the king says to the clergyman,
"O old man of blessed footprint,
Have you not a cup of wine to offer us?"

He replies, "We harvest wine from dates.
We prepare it during the hot month of Tammuz.
We have some left, shining like rosewater
And as red as a ruby dazzling in the sun."

He brings a cup and a jug of wine
That eclipses the color of the sun.
The king drains three cups and eats the barley bread.
His mind heated by the red wine,
He reclines and falls instantly asleep on the sand,
With soreness in his soul and a wound in his heart,
His head resting on Bandooy's thigh.

Barely asleep, he is approached by one
Of the priestly leaders, who says to him,
"We notice a black dust rising on the road.
In its midst gallop numerous troops."

Khosrow says, "How unfortunate
That our enemies are so relentless!
Neither my men nor my horses can move.
Today marks the beginning of a deep state of despair."

Bandooy says, "We must find a solution.
The leader Bahraam is drawing near."

Khosrow asks, "O my dear friend,
How shall we escape our predicament?"

Bandooy replies, "O King, I shall find a way out.
But my life will be the ransom for his majesty's life.
Anyone who sows the seeds of fidelity
Is assured entry into paradise."

Khosrow says, "A learned man from Chin
Once said something on this subject.
When the walls of a city fall, the suburbs
And villages will not remain standing.
When a great city disappears,

173

The hospital will disappear with it.
If you think of a way of salvation,
Consolidate it swiftly, and Yazdan,
The almighty, will place you above need."

Bandooy replies, "Give me your golden crown,
Your earrings, your belt, and your ruby-colored
Chini tunic embroidered with golden threads.
You must not linger here as I dress in them.
Leave in haste with your escort.
Run like a boat hoisted onto the water by a sailor.

The young man obeys Bandooy and flees the site
As if he were the companion of the wind.
Gostaham runs with him, as swift as dust, head full
Of the desire for vengeance, heart full of grief.

As soon as Khosrow leaves his rescuer,
The skilled man turns to the monastery chief
And says to him, "You must withdraw
To the mountaintop and stay out of sight."

Bandooy runs to the sanctuary and bolts the iron door.
He dresses in the golden robe,
Places on his head the royal crown, and,
In a state of worry, he climbs onto the rooftop.
He notices troops surrounding the residence.
He waits for the warring army to near the walls.
Then he stands on the rooftop and reveals himself
To the troops with Khosrow's crown and torque,
The royal earrings and the royal belt.

They say to each other, "Up there stands the king
With his crown and his lavish, finely crafted attire."

Once Bandooy is persuaded that the army
Took him for the king, he descends,
Quickly changes into his own clothing,
And climbs back fearlessly up to the roof terrace.
He says, "O young warriors, who is your leader?
I have a message to relay to him from the world king."

The son of Siaavoosh says to him,

"I am the leader. My name is Bahraam."

Bandooy replies, "The king, world master,
Wishes for me to tell you the following:
    'I am suffering from the exertion of travel,
    My riders are all wounded and in pain,
    Exhausted from the long, arduous march.
    I have stopped at this house of penitents
    With five of my companions for a respite.
    As soon as the white light of dawn appears,
    I shall withdraw from my heart any affair
    Relating to this world, and I shall go with you
    On this long road to the renowned Bahraam.
    I shall not ask for a longer delay
    If the skies wish to come to my aid.
    All my ancestors, all the prior kings
    Observed the rules of majesty and faith.
    They never refused, in their long reigns,
    The needs of the most humble man.
    Now that fortune turns against me,
    I have revealed my heart's secret.
    Nothing is accomplished without the will
    Of Yazdan, the pure, nothing anywhere,
    From the brilliant sun to the dark earth.'"

The army leader listens and consents.
All those who hear Bandooy's discourse
Are moved deeply with a sense of pity.

The troops settle for the night, keeping guard
For fear that Khosrow may escape.
The next morning, Bandooy appears on the roof,
Goes to the wall near Bahraam, and says to him,
"Today the king is engaged in deep prayer
And will not bring his mind to his affairs.
Abstaining from sleep, he spent the night
In a stance of devotion before the World Master.
Now the sun rises in all its glory,
And Khosrow must not be affected by the heat.
He will rest today, and tomorrow at dawn,
He will show himself to your army."

Bahraam says to his noblemen, "This affair
Is perhaps unimportant or perhaps truly serious.
If we pressure Khosrow too much,
He may grow furious and wish to fight us.
He alone is worth an entire host.
He is ambitious, prudent, and valiant.
If he is killed on the battlefield,
Choobineh would sentence every one of us to death.
It is best to wait another day,
Although we are left with few provisions.
It is best to hope that he will surrender freely,
Without putting up a fight or a quarrel."

He remains in this way until night descends
With its army of stars united around it.
Then the troops spread on all sides
And light fires everywhere.

10 | Bahraam, Son of Siaavoosh, Takes Bandooy to Bahraam Choobineh

As the moon's face brightens like the sun,
The eloquent Bandooy climbs on the rooftop
And says to Bahraam, "O worldly man,
When the dust of your host rose on the plain,
Khosrow noticed you and left in haste toward Rum
With his escort, and today, if you flew like an eagle,
If you raised your head above the sun,
You would not see the king outside of Rum,
For he reached the land a long time ago.
Now, if you grant me life, I shall appear
Before the valiant leader and reveal to him
Matters great and small relating to the royal court.
Otherwise, I shall dress in war armor
And raise the dust of battle to the sun."

The heart of the young leader rapidly ages with grief.
He says to his companions, "What is the advantage to us
If I were to kill Bandooy at this very moment?
It is best to bring him well and alive to the chief

176

So that he may tell him what he knows about the king.
Perhaps he will grant his royal life mercy,
Or perhaps he will snatch his headdress from him."

He says to Bandooy, "O wicked man, full of ruse,
Plead your case before Bahraam Choobineh."
Bandooy, the lion, descends from the rooftop
And marches courageously with the noblemen.

Bahraam Choobineh learns of the army's approach
And how Khosrow has absconded to Rum.
Contemplating vengeance, he grows furious
Toward the son of Siaavoosh and says to him,
"O deceitful criminal, you did not follow my command.
Though you lack in skill, I made you army commander.
Your ill nature did not allow you to remain at ease."

Bahraam Choobineh asks Bandooy to come forward.
Ready to empty his fury on Bahraam, son of Siaavoosh,
He blurts out, "O evil man, you are worthy of blame.
You are only suited to instigate quarrels.
In your madness, you dared deceive my army?
You could not sit still because of your evil nature.
You united with the vile Khosrow, turning a child
Into a worldly, mature man, and now you come here
With a mind full of falsehoods with demands
Of returning the situation to its previous state?"

Bandooy says, "O illustrious one, seek righteousness
In me and do not act precipitously with my fate.
Know that the King of Kings is my relative,
That his grandeur and his nobility are everything to me.
I have devoted my life to him, as it is my duty.
Powerful as you are, do not surrender to iniquity."

Bahraam replies, "I do not wish to execute you
For this crime, but he will be the one to do so.
You will recognize that I am speaking the truth."

They burden Bandooy's feet with heavy chains,
And Bahraam hands him over to the son of Siaavoosh
To preserve him from danger.

Bahraam remains thus until the sun goes into hiding,
Then he reclines to sleep, his head full of worry.

11 | The Iranians Deliberate With Bahraam Choobineh on the Subject of Kingship

As the sun draws its dagger from its sheath
And its golden cloak appears to spread evenly,
Bahraam convenes the illustrious noblemen
And places his crowned chiefs on a carpet.
He sits happy on a golden chair,
Akin to a victorious king.

Then he says in a loud voice, "Give me, one and all,
Your answer to the thoughts that I nurture.
Listen to me; see how I bring peace everywhere.
Any honorable man knows that, no matter how long
You search, there is no king worse than Zahaak,
Who conspired to kill his father to seize the throne
And who took possession of Iran by this act.
Similarly, Khosrow, an unjust and vile man,
Killed his father and departed for the land of Rum.
We must find someone able to maintain the path
And the customs of the Kianian kings.
Whom do we know in the world,
An illustrious offspring of royal linage,
Worthy of the throne, diadem, belt, and royal fortune?
I swear by the Master of the sublime Sun
That I shall help you in this venture."

The noblemen listen to the speech of the powerful
And illustrious leader without contradicting him.
An old warrior and valiant nobleman
Named Hormozd Shahran rises to say,
"O glorious Bahraam, you have been
A benefactor to all of us throughout your life.
When Saaveh Shah invaded our borders with his army,
You were the only one stationed in Rey able to fight him
And free us from the threat of slavery and tyranny.
No one was in a state to contend with him.

You alone in the world armed yourself bravely
And spared the Iranians a grave calamity.

"In four instances, armies of one hundred thousand men,
Brave and suited for battle, withdrew at the sight
Of your shots of arrows of simple wood, and Iran
Was saved from anguish and from falling to ruins.
The fortune that always watched over you
Makes it evident that the throne of Iran belongs to you.
If an Iranian refuses to obey your command
Or if he stays away and does not recognize you,
We shall bring him according to your will,
No matter how valiant he may be
Or whether he has the fame of kings."

Having thus spoken, he returns to his seat.
The leader of Khorasan approaches Bahraam to say,
"I wonder what this ambitious and learned old man,
Who is in search of wisdom, bases his speech upon.
When he speaks of all the good in you,
The hearts of those gathered rejoice.
But there is a flowery speech that you,
Men of pure minds, may wish to listen to
And that Zartosht relates in the *Zand Avesta*:
        'Give advice and all the necessities for one year
        To anyone who strays from the almighty Creator.
        If, at the end of the year, he does not return to the faith,
        He must be executed by order of the king.
        When he becomes the enemy of the Justice Giver,
        His head must quickly be severed.'"

The leader of Khorasan returns to his seat.
Then Farrokhzaad stands up to address the assembly:
"O powerful and caring men,
Is it better to speak with truth or with smugness?
If justice is more valuable, cursed be the one
Who would disapprove iniquitous words.
If our speeches held nothing but complacencies,
Yazdan, the victorious, would not come to our aid."

Then he says to Bahraam, "May you be happy!
May your sight be nourishment for the world!

179

Sit upon the throne, for you are worthy of it.
You freed all the lands from the threat of danger.
Always live in joy, and may the hands
And hearts of evil men be kept at bay!"

The valiant man speaks, then sits back down.
Khosrow, the leader of the land of Khazars,
Rises like a lion and says,
"Now that young and old have spoken
With eloquence and everyone has listened,
It is up to you to carve a future path.
If in the end you decide, with a mindset of justice,
Send a camel, as speedy as wind, and do not delay,
So that the illustrious king need not undertake
This long voyage, his head full of concerns.
Ask forgiveness for the past, and do not allow
Your bold footsteps to walk the path of the throne.
As long as the king, world master, lives,
No leader can make claims to the royal seat.
If, in your heart, Khosrow inspires fear in you,
Leave Pars and Ctesiphon and settle quietly
In the land of Khorasan, where you will enjoy
The security and the power that you deserve.
Write letter upon letter to ask forgiveness,
And let us hope that Khosrow will come to you."

Khosrow Khazarvan barely reclaims his seat
When the noble Farrokhzaad rises again and advances.
He begins by speaking according to justice:
"O illustrious and high-born men, I have heard
The speeches of noblemen, chiefs of Iran's elite,
Abject words that touch on raising
A warrior to the noble status of king.
But no sensible man can approve of such discourse,
For it dishonors the way of humanity.
The chief of Khorasan spoke like an imperious man,
But I shall not say that it was in line with reason.
Farrokhzaad backed him up with audacious words
And muted the hearts of intelligent men.
The fourth one to speak was the leader of Khazaria,
Whose speech conformed with sense and reason.

"If we are to estimate from the time when Yazdan
Created the world and the rotation of fate began,
Zahaak, the Taazi, was the first unjust king
Of impure intentions who killed Jamsheed
And seized the world by way of an unjust crime.
Pure men were filled with grief over the fact
That a deev had risen to dominate the world.
The blessed King Fereydoon arrived to destroy Zahaak.

"The second one was Afraasiyaab, man of evil race,
Who came from Tooran to cross the River Jayhoon,
Who miserably severed King Nozar's head
With his sword and ruined everything.
The third one was Eskandar, who arrived from Rum
To Iran, devastated the nation, and caused the death of Dara.
He was ready to strike with his sword
And prevent the Iranians from enjoying their food and rest.
The fourth one was Khoshnavaz, of impure heart,
Who eradicated glory and contentment from the land.
When the Hephthalites unexpectedly killed King Pirooz,
Blessed world master and leader of rulers,
The throne of the King of Kings was brought down.
But no one has seen a more astonishing thing
Than what is happening now in the land of Iran,
Where a king such as Khosrow vacates his throne,
Flees the land and host to seek shelter with the enemy."

Having thus spoken, he sits down, weeping in pain.
Bahraam pales from hearing him out.
Sombaaz, an experienced man, rises
Armed with an Indian sword to speak,
"This noble warrior is powerful, just, and smart.
It is best for him to sit upon the throne until an offspring
Of Kianian lineage comes around equipped for battle.
He is valiant, he knows how to fight,
And is blessed with a propitious fortune."

The army commander seizes his sword, draws it,
And says, "If we find a woman of royal race
In one of the city homes,
I shall cut off her head with this sharp blade,
I shall make the breath of death pass over her life.

181

I shall not wait for a contender to the throne
To appear and to exhibit his courage among riders."

As the brave warriors Baabooy and Gord the Armenian
See the resolution of the impious and proud army leader,
They draw their swords, rise, and speak in a new tone:
"Bahraam is king, and we are his subjects!
Whatever we do will be to follow his command!"

Bahraam observes the bare swords
And responds with prudence and righteousness:
"If any of you rises from his seat or touches his sword,
I shall instantly cut off his hand unless he gains wisdom."

He takes leave of Iran's noblemen and enters the royal garden
As the assembly disperses, faces frowning, hearts broken.

12 | Bahraam Choobineh Ascends the Throne

As the pitch-colored drapery draws close
And the stars twinkle bright in the vault of sky,
The voices of the night guards are heard.
Bahraam asks for a reed and a piece of paper.
An intelligent and noble scribe arrives
And sets the inkwell and the reed before him.

Bahraam says, "We must compose a declaration
For the Iranians on a piece of silk to announce
That Bahraam Choobineh has risen as king,
That his fortune is victorious,
That he is worthy of the throne, and that
He is the ornament of the crown, seeking only
Righteousness in his actions, public or private."

The edict is written. They light candles
And pass the dark night in a state of unrest.

As the lapis lazuli veil of night dissipates
And the world is enrobed in the sun's warm golden tones,
A man of victorious fortune places a gilded platform
In Bahraam's hall, its surface swept as clean as ivory,

To support the golden throne.
Over it hangs the crown,
And once it is set, they open the audience hall.

Bahraam Choobineh takes a seat on the throne
And lowers the crown over his head.
His scribe displays a royal declaration,
Written on a valuable piece of silk,
And all the noblemen sign
And recognize Bahraam as world king.

Then Bahraam affixes his golden seal to the edict
And announces: "This kingship belongs to me,
As you and Yazdan, the pure, are my witnesses.
May kings of my race rule for thousands of years!
May my noble sons, one after the other,
Safeguard this crown and powerful throne.

"This declaration is executed on the day of Hoor[4]
In the month of Aazar[5] during the time
When the ferocious lion devours the onager's back.
Anyone who does not approve,
Whether he is a perverse person or an honest one,
Must leave the land of Iran after three days.
As soon as the world-illuminating sun appears,
He must return to the side of Khosrow,
For he will not find rest and peace in this land."

People acclaim him and shout,
"May the world never be deprived of your presence!"
But many among those gathered do not mean it
And do not pronounce the words in good faith.
In their hearts of hearts, they are loyal to Khosrow
And are deeply wounded by this intrusive kingship.

They depart from the land of Iran
And march to the border of Rum, where they scatter.

◇◇◇◇◇◇◇◇◇◇◇◇◇
4 Day of Hoor: The eleventh day of every month, the day of the Sun.
5 Month of Aazar: The ninth month of the solar year, equivalent to December.

13 | Bandooy Strategizes With Bahraam, Son of Siaavoosh, to Kill Bahraam Choobineh

Bandooy remains in Bahraam's prison,
Enchained like a cheetah, for seventy days.
His jailer is Bahraam, son of Siaavoosh,
Who is discontented about having to detain him.

Bandooy begins by abusing Choobineh,
For the chains do not appease his devious mind.
He says to his jailer, "Do not despair about Khosrow.
Either this dark night will turn into a bright day,
Or perhaps fortune will delay in reaching him.
His fate will be similar to the fate of Pirooz
When he came face to face with Khoshnavaz.
The World Creator favored him in the person of his son,
Ghobaad, whom he blessed with world possession.

"The crown will not belong to Bahraam for long.
What does this man of auspicious fortune think?
Cursed be the son of a farmer who
Madly indulges to destroy himself.
Count on your fingers two months from today,
And you will see an army march from Rum to Iran.
It will consume Bahraam's crown and throne,
And his diadem will be shattered on his head."

Bahraam, the son of Siaavoosh says,
"If Khosrow shows mercy on my life,
I shall use your advice as my soul's law.
I shall obey your commandment on every point.
I ask you to make an oath and swear by the moon,
By Aazargoshasp, by the throne and headdress
That, should Khosrow arrive in this land
Accompanied by the Caesar's Rumi army,
You will ask him to have mercy on my life
And you will neglect nothing in this affair.
In this way, my body will be safeguarded
From the king's wrath, and he will not be cautioned
Against me by aberrant words from Iranians."

Having spoken, he searches for the holy book

To seal Bandooy's word with a binding pledge.
Bandooy takes the *Zand Avesta* and says,
"May I suffer misfortune and pain
Given to me by the almighty Creator!
May I be deprived of security in this passing world
If I fail to see Khosrow as soon as he is on the road
And fail to entreat him to send you
The empire's ring and royal diadem."

Witness to the sincerity of Bandooy's pledge
And his commitment, Bahraam says to him,
"Now I shall reveal to you all my secrets.
I shall speak loudly and set a trap for Choobineh.
I shall bring vengeance down on him through ruse,
And if I can, I shall violently kill him
With my damasked sword during a feast.
There remains not a drop of water in the sea
Since we have assigned Bahraam the title of king."

Bandooy replies, "O worldly hero,
Know that I am a fine man, active and prudent.
Khosrow will soon come from Rum
And sit upon the throne, and you know
That he will refuse nothing to his servant.
I shall once again ask forgiveness for your past deeds,
And he will give you his crown should I demand it.
If you are as you say,
If your heart does not cling to detours and deceit,
Free my feet from these cuffs.
You will then recognize Khosrow.
You will manifest your secret,
And your kind words will reach his ears."

Bahraam listens, his face renewed with youth,
And he immediately removes the restraints.

As the musk-colored veil lightens
And the dawn of day grasps it in its fingers,
Bahraam says to Bandooy, "If my heart fails me not,
Today Choobineh is playing polo, and I have strategized
With five friends to bring destruction down on him."

He asks for a coat of mail, which he slips into

Under his tunic, and he gallops out of the palace.

The valiant Bahraam of Siaavoosh has a vicious wife
Who desires to see him lie beneath the ground.
She is secretly in love with Bahraam Choobineh,
Her soul full of hatred for her husband.
She sends someone to Bahraam to tell him,
"O my dear protector, be careful.
My husband has dressed in his coat of mail
And has fastened its clasps.
I do not know what actions he contemplates,
But you must stay away from him."

Choobineh, upon receipt of the wife's message
Suggesting that he abstain from the polo match
With her husband, softly strikes the back of those
Who arrive on the square and approach him
With their mallets, all the while speaking to them
Amicably and with a most gentle voice.

He continues in this manner until Bahraam,
Son of Siaavoosh, arrives and he undoubtedly
Feels the coat of mail on his chest.
He says to him, "You are more vile than a viper!
Who wears a coat of mail in the square beneath his fur?"
He draws out his sword of vengeance
And splits him in half from head to foot.

News spreads across the city that Bahraam
Of Siaavoosh has been struck and has perished.
The light of day disappears for Bandooy.
He dresses in armor, climbs on his horse,
Shakily straps his belt around his heroic waist,
And, to avoid being killed, he flees the city,
Accompanied by the allies of the deceased
And by those who trust him most.
At the first station, their company increases,
And they take the road to Ardabil in haste.

Leaving the square, Bahraam, in his fury,
Drags the hem of his robe through the blood.
He commands Mahrooy to watch over Bandooy,
But he is told: "O King, lend a thought to Bandooy,

For as soon as he learns of the fate of Bahraam,
He will undoubtedly run off, as swift as wind,
Repenting for having caused the death of his protector,
Who would make him realize his own state of danger."

Bahraam Choobineh replies,
"Woe to the brains and the bones of the one
Unable to distinguish between friend and enemy.
One sleeps on the point of an elephant's teeth,
Another counts on the blue waves of the River Nile.
Yet a third one braves the king,
While a fourth one snatches a lion by its front legs.
Have pity for these four men whose ends are near.
Another wishes to move a mountain
And asks the crowd to come to his aid.
He tires himself and is left with only wind in hand.
Better sift water out of a broken boat than to act hastily.
If you attempt to look directly at the sun,
You will be stunned and will turn away in anger.
When one takes for a guide a blind man,
One remains on the road at length.
When one seizes a dragon in his hand,
One is killed and the dragon runs free.
When one ingests poison as an experiment,
One gains only suffering and death.
I did not sentence Bandooy to death the first day.
And now, liberated, he has escaped me.
I must shed bitter tears over my own missteps
And wait to assess the will of the Creator."

On his side, Bandooy and his small company
Take to the road, as swift as a storm, with each one
Carrying as much load as he could seize.
They travel the road leading to Moossil, the Armenian,
Driving past a barren, waterless desert full of wild beasts.
In the end, Bandooy sees a cluster of tents.
He looks around and spots the Armenian
Surrounded by streams of water and heaps of provisions.

The world seeker Bandooy advances alone,
Runs toward the prairies, greets Moossil humbly,
And recounts to him his dramatic story.

Moossil says to him, "Do not leave this place.
You will receive news upon news of Khosrow,
His activities in the prosperous land of Rum,
And whether he is intent to make peace or war."

These words convince Bandooy to remain,
And he calls his companions from the desert.

14 | Khosrow Travels From the Desert to Rum

I shall now turn to Khosrow's adventures
After his escape from Ctesiphon.
While he makes his ardeous journey to Rum
With his most loyal men by way of the desert,
His warriors disperse, alone or in pairs,
To find their own places to stay

Once in the desert, Khosrow runs ahead,
Cheeks as pale as the flower of the fenugreek.
He finds neither water nor grass nor guide.
He runs wearily all the way to Baheleh,[6]
Leaving his charger's reins afloat.
All the noblemen of the city, anyone with
Some humanity, comes to meet and greet him.

Khosrow approaches them with troops.
But, having barely climbed down his horse,
A messenger accosts him, a carrier of a secret letter
From Bahraam Choobineh to the chief of Baheleh.

The letter says: "If armed troops enter your city,
Do not allow them to leave freely,
For my host is in pursuit of this company
And is expected at any moment.

The chief immediately rushes to Khosrow,
Whose attention is stirred by the contents
Of the letter and by the turn of events.

◇◇◇◇◇◇◇◇◇◇◇◇◇
6 Baheleh: Perhaps a reference to Deir al-Balah, an ancient city that would be located
in the Gaza Strip.

He fears to be trailed by this host, and his heart
Constricts at the thought of his men's weariness.

He quickly slips his Kianian body into a royal armor,
Exits the city, and continues his race westward,
Riding all the way to the edge of the Euphrates River.
He does not find a single blade of grass in the expanse.
By now, his men, young and old, are utterly famished.
They come across a forest with running water,
And Khosrow drives them to a lush, green site.

Watching his men, so exhausted and starving,
Khosrow binds his bow to capture game,
But nowhere is a living creature to be found.
There are only trees, grass, and freshwater springs.

At that moment appears a caravan of camels
Preceded by its young driver, who, at the sight
Of Khosrow's face, showers the king with praise.

Khosrow says to him, "What is your name?
Where are you going and to what end?"

The other replies, "I am Gheys, son of Haress.
I am a leader among free Arabs.
I come from Egypt with my caravan.
My tribe dwells on the banks of the Euphrates,
And I am on my way to the woods."

Khosrow asks, "What provisions have you?
Tell me, do you carry any carpets?
We are exhausted and suffer from hunger.
We have neither food nor baggage."

The Arab replies, "Wait here.
My fortune, my body, and my life belong to you!"

He begins a deep friendship with the king.
He brings a plump cow to be slaughtered.
A fire is ignited with dry wood,
On which the Arab grills the meat, and once done,
Khosrow's companions hungrily feast on it.

Worshippers of the true faith pray silently,
And the entire company sits to enjoy the banquet.
They eat a great amount of roasted meat without bread.
Then each of the noblemen prepares a place to sleep.
They rest for some time, then rise to pray fervently
To the just Yazdan, Creator of the weak and the strong.

Then the king says to his escort, "Those who have
Committed acts of kindness are those who are
Dearest to my heart and my most illustrious subjects.
But those who are guilty of crimes,
Who turned away from me and from the divine path,
Must place their hopes in me,
And you may relay the good news to them."

His companions bless him and say,
"O pure-hearted, faithful Khosrow,
May Yazdan always be your refuge!
May the Creator return to you the throne and crown!
You are blessed with a divine face, glory, justice, and love.
You spread wisdom everywhere with your fair ways."

These words delight Khosrow's heart
And he remembers that he must be on his way.
He asks for direction from the Arab who responds,
"You have ahead of you still more
Than seven farsangs of desert and mountain.
If you allow me, I shall bring water and meat
On the road for you, as long as you at a slow pace."

Khosrow replies, "All I can hope for
Is to have enough provisions and guidance."

The Arab sends a man on camelback to travel
At the lead of the convoy, and the guide
Runs ahead through desert and mountain,
Wearying himself and taking care of the men.

Another caravan appears in the distance,
Advancing toward Khosrow's escort on the road.
A rich merchant presents himself to the king,
Who asks him, "Where do you come from?
Where do you go in such haste?"

He replies, "I am a merchant
From Khorreh-yeh Ardeshir,
Blessed with literacy and the ability to write."

The king asks him,
"What name has your father given you?"

He replies, "Mehran Setaad."

The king asks him for provisions,
And his troop leader says, "O illustrious King,
We have an abundance of food, even if
The merchant would not show us a friendly face."

The merchant says, "I shall bring you all that I have."

Khosrow replies, "When one meets a host
During travels, it is always one more sign of comfort."

The merchant unfastens his loads of dirhams and dinars.
He brings provisions and sits on the ground,
Uttering blessings on the king.

Once the meal is complete, this man,
Respectful of his guest, reaches for a pitcher
To pour water over Khosrow's hands.
But Khorraad, son of Borzeen, observing him,
Rises, runs over to Khosrow, takes the warm water
From the hands of the merchant so that the prince
Does not think he is treated disrespectfully.

The merchant hastens to bring a wine
That shines as bright as rosewater, and once again
Khorraad grabs the cup and offers it to the king.
This service profits the servant whose status
Rises as he brings value to the king's honor.

Khosrow asks the road merchant what the troops can take.
The hospitable man indicates the goods.
Then the king asks him his name and his origin:
"Where is your home in Khorreh-yeh Ardeshir?"

He replies, "O King, may you live in justice.

I am a merchant from Kaarzi."[7]

He shows his signs in detail to Khosrow
And reveals to him all his secrets.
The king commands his scribe Roozbeh
To write the name of the young man and his district.
Then he says to the merchant, "You may go.
May wisdom be the warp and you the weft of the cloth!"

15 | Khosrow Enters the Land of Rum

As the royal company takes leave of the verdant place,
It marches in haste toward the border of Rum,
All the way to the great city the Caesar calls Karsan.[8]

At the sight of the troops from afar,
The Christians rush left and right
To gather their belongings inside the city walls.
Then they bolt and secure all the doors.

The world-illuminating king is disappointed
And remains on the outskirts for three days.
On the fourth day, he sends someone to say,
"I have with me only a minimum of troops.
I arrived in this city with no longing for war.
Brings us provisions, help us,
And guard yourselves from acting superior to us."

The townspeople scorn his words,
And the troops remain tired and hungry.
All at once, a dark cloud rushes to loom above,
Roaring like a lion in the midst of battle.
A fierce storm pours over the city with such force
That cries and supplications rise in the streets.

After half the dark night passes,
A part of the walls appears to have vanished.
Everyone is in a state of dismay and disarray,

◇◇◇◇◇◇◇◇◇◇◇◇◇
7 Kaarzi: A region of Pars near Shiraz.
8 Karsan: Perhaps a city in ancient Rum.

PART TWENTY-NINE

And the bishop implores divine forgiveness.

Provisions harvested in this lush green land
And clothing originating from Rum
Are collected in the streets and transported
By three bishops to Khosrow's camp.

They offer them humbly to the king and say,
"O King, it is apparent that we were at fault."

Khosrow, who is young and of noble soul,
Does not reproach their behavior.

There is a palace in the city full of slaves,
With a rooftop built by the Caesar that defies the skies.
Khosrow enters from the plain into the city,
Settles in the palace, and wanders through the streets,
Always greeted and cheered by the Rumis,
Who scatter precious stones at his feet.

Having thus found a fitting home,
He spends some time in rest
And writes a letter to the Caesar
On the subject of the wind, the rain,
And the roaring black cloud.

From there, he marches toward Manooy,[9]
A city worldly men refer to as celestial.
Its far-sighted, wise, noble, and powerful inhabitants
Come to greet Khosrow with presents and offerings.
They speak at length with the king
About the rain and the ancient city of Karsan,
Saying, "We are his majesty's slaves,
The subjects of his imperial words."

◇◇◇◇◇◇◇◇◇◇◇◇◇
9 Manooy: Perhaps an ancient city in Rum.

16 | A Hermit Predicts Khosrow's Future

Khosrow remains in the city for three days.
On the fourth day, as the world-illuminating sun
Pierces through the clouds with its cutting sword,
The prince takes the road toward Oorigh,[10] a great city,
That houses a piece of the cross and a hospice.

In an off-road site, there is a sanctuary,
And the king, at the sound of a hermit's voice,
Asks, "I hear someone speaking. Who is it?"

One of the residents answers: "An old man lives here.
He is so advanced in age that his skin has yellowed.
He is a skilled astrologer. Nothing is hidden from him.
Any event he predicts is sure to unfold.
One must never doubt his word."

The king approaches the hermit and says,
"May you never cease to serve the Creator!
If you wish to exit your old sanctuary,
May Yazdan, Giver of joy, sanctify you!"

At the sound of the voice, the hermit emerges,
Notices the king, and greets him humbly:
"You most certainly are King Khosrow,
Whose father's throne has brought him ill luck,
All because of a malevolent, vile, and proud subject."

The hermit elaborates on his discourse,
And the king's heart is renewed by his affection.
Stunned by his foresight, he summons divine grace on him.
From atop his horse, he extends a hand
And interrogates the Yazdan worshipper.

To test him, he says, "I am a man of little influence
In the army of Iran and bear a message to the Caesar.
Once I receive a reply, I shall return to my leader.
Tell me if my travels will bring me joy
And what will be my fate in the end."

◇◇◇◇◇◇◇◇◇◇◇◇◇
10 Oorigh: Perhaps an ancient city in Rum.

The hermit replies, "Do not speak in this manner.
You are the king and must not pretend to be a courier.
As soon as I caught sight of you, I said everything.
Do not attempt to put me to the test.
Your faith does not permit falsehoods,
Your path and dignity do not sanction deceit.
You have suffered and endured much pain,
And in the end, you fled before a wicked slave."

Khosrow is in awe of the hermit's insight
And, in his shame, asks forgiveness.

The hermit says, "There is no need for pardon.
Question me on the future.
Remain happy and proud of your voyage.
Become a fertile branch for the world.
Yazdan will fulfill your wishes
And give you glory and a powerful star of fortune.
You will obtain weapons and troops from the Caesar
And a daughter worthy of the throne and crown.
When you engage in battle with your slaves,
The World Master will come to your assistance.
In the end, the evil man will run away.
He will speak at length of his days of joy,
And, after the struggle, he will seize
And settle his residence in a far-away land.
But since he will prefer to run away than to submit
To kingly obeisance, you will demand his death."

Khosrow replies, "May it be as you say, O old man!"
What can you tell me about the time it will take
For the empire to be handed back to me?"

He replies, "After the span of ten plus two months,
You will recapture the crown.
Then ten plus five days will pass over your head,
And you will become the King of Kings,
The one to spread his light across the world."

Khosrow asks, "Who in my close circle will help me
The most in my pains and in my troubles?"

He replies, "The one who bears the name of Bastaam,

Your haughty and joyous maternal uncle,
Whom you deem your source of happiness
And whose age is equivalent to yours.
But beware of this pernicious Bastaam,
Who has also been named Gostaham.
He will bring you much pain, suffering, and harm."

Khosrow is troubled and says to Gostaham,
"The hermit has revealed to me your secret.
Your mother gave you the name of Bastaam,
But you pretend that you are Gostaham in battle."

Then he says to the hermit, "Here is my uncle.
He is my mother's true blood-related brother."

The hermit replies, "Gostaham will be
The cause of your pains and your struggles."

Khosrow says, "O my dear advisor,
What will happen thereafter?"

He replies, "There is no need for troubled thoughts.
After that, you will receive only blessings.
Never again will you suffer any harm, and,
If you have some difficult tasks to complete,
They will not be imposed by the Creator.
This rebellious spirit, Gostaham, will stir up your peace.
But in the end, all will unfold as you wish.
No matter how much this ill-intentioned man tries,
His fate will ultimately fall into your hands."

Gostaham says to Khosrow, "O King,
Do not afflict your heart on this subject.
I swear by Yazdan, the pure, Creator of the Moon,
Creator of a king of your stature in the world,
I swear by Aazargoshasp, by Sun and Moon,
By the life and head of the glorious king,
That as long as lives Gostaham, never
Will he stray from the path of righteousness;
Never will he betray you or knock at the door of perdition.
May his soul perish if he nurtures other designs!
Since the beginning of time and of creation,
No one can decipher the secrets of the world.

Why would you give credence to the words of a Christian?
Why would you listen to his unseemly discourse?
Assure yourself against the effects of his words.
Since I have taken an oath,
Do not seek a pretext to turn against me."

Khosrow says to him, "O fearful man,
Cease your useless, meaningless speech.
I have never experienced harm on your part.
You never displayed inclinations toward perversity.
Yet one must not be surprised if, by the effect
Of the sublime sky, you would at once turn wicked.
Once divine will is set on an action,
Wisdom and intelligence are unavailing."

Then the king says to the hermit,
"May your heart be happy and your fortune propitious!"
He exits the sanctuary and travels in the direction
Of the city of Oorigh, like a flash of lighting.

The noble and notable men of the region
Gather around him to acclaim him.

17 | Khosrow Parviz Sends a Letter to the Caesar

As the king enters Oorigh, a rider arrives,
Sent by the illustrious Caesar, to relay the message:
"Ask for anything you may want in this land.
Do not refuse to make your demands at court.
Although this kingdom belongs to me,
We estimate you to be my equal in every way.
Remain in peace and happiness in this city,
And free yourself from any thought of trouble.
All the Rumis from end to end are your subjects,
No matter how proud or powerful they may be.
I shall allow myself neither food nor rest
Before having organized your weapons and troops."

Khosrow is delighted. His soul freed from worry,
He summons Gostaham, Balooy, and the ambitious
Andian, and says to Khorraad, son of Borzeen,

197

And Shahpoor, the lion, "Saddle the horses at daybreak
And dress in gold-embroidered Chini tunics.
Remain unified and behave wisely.
Go to the Caesar, speak to him, and listen to him.
Make a show of caution and serenity.
Hear him out, and answer him graciously.
If the Caesar comes to the square and asks for his bow,
Or if he prepares for a game of polo,
Make every effort to avoid his courtiers' defeat.
May he learn that we bring from Iran
The art of riding and the courage and strength of lions."

The king commands Khorraad, son of Borzeen,
To ask for Chini silk and black musk and says,
"We must write to the Caesar a letter
Akin to the sun shining in paradise,
One of few words but infused with deep meaning
So that every man can inscribe it in his memory.
He has philosophers by his side,
Trained to speak on every subject.
Write in a way that they cannot find anything
Lacking sense in it or anything to be criticized.
Once the Caesar has read the letter, you will speak,
And no one will be able to resist your words."

Then he says to Balooy, "If the Caesar mentions me
To his court's assembly, if he mentions our alliance,
Our promises, our parentage, and our treaties,
Hand him a reply that is as sweet as honey.
You are my tongue and my interpreter in all things.
All of you make sure that you do not damage us.
Apply yourselves as best you can to the task.
Be the bearers of my promises,
And submit to memory his every word."

The worldly heroes of brilliant minds
Shower the blessed man with praise and exclaim:
"May no other ruler bear the royal crown!"
Then, as seekers of the true path,
They travel to the Caesar's court.

At the news of their approach,

The Caesar dispatches an escort ahead of them.
He asks for the palace to be decked with Rumi brocade
And decorated with statues crafted out of jewels and gold.
He sits on his illustrious ivory throne,
Places the dazzling crown on his head,
And asks for the entrance curtains to be drawn.

The envoys are quickly received through the portal,
With Gostaham at the lead, then the heroic Balooy,
Then Shahpoor, Khorraad, son of Borzeen,
And the valiant Andian, all donning crowns
And strapped with golden belts.

They dismount at the sight of the Caesar
And acknowledge him reverently.
They cover him with blessings and scatter
Gems and precious stones on his golden throne.

The Caesar questions them on the king, on Iran,
And the fatigues they endured during their travels.
Khorraad, son of Borzeen, steps forward with the letter.
On the order of the illustrious ruler,
Four golden seats are placed,
And three of the counselors sit
While Khorraad remains standing.

The Caesar says to him, "When one arrives
From the road, one must accept an offered seat."

Khorraad, son of Borzeen, replies, "My king has not
Raised me to be a man so powerful that I would sit
Before the Caesar while bearing a letter from his majesty.
By acting like a servant, I can gain your approval
And thereby be of use with the message I am to relay."

The Caesar says, "Reveal to me your secret.
What does your illustrious, intelligent prince desire?"

Khorraad, son of Borzeen, speaks as the Caesar listens.
First, he celebrates divine glory, then
Expresses his contempt for the world, saying,
"The One who is supreme above the sublime,
The One who is all-powerful and omniscient;

The One above time and space,
Creator of the sky and the stars and their seamless fit
And placement on the revolving sphere;
Giver of our soul, justice, wisdom, and love;
The One by whose order the skies revolve;
The One who draws from the earth all living things.
After the creation of dust on the earth,
Kiumars came into existence, then the other kings,
Down to Shah Fereydoon, favored above all.
In this way this family came into the world,
And the unrevealed was manifest.
All this unfolded until the advent of Kay Ghobaad,
Who placed on his head the crown of power.
Never did the royal family suffer misfortune,
For it always followed the path of Yazdan.

"But now, a vile and base being, a slave, intends
To usurp the Kianian throne, and I demand justice,
For he has no claims to the diadem, the throne,
The crown, or the belt of the King of Kings.
Anyone who is to sit upon a royal seat must possess
Wisdom, an illustrious birth, wealth, and good fortune.
May he learn to whom belong majesty and royal crown.
Act as my friend in this affair. Treat this man as you wish,
For you and I are known in the world as allies,
And now we find ourselves covered in shame,
As I have fled my land to walk across the earth."

The Caesar's cheeks pale like the flower of the fenugreek
And flood with tears as his tongue and soul lament.
This world master reads the king's letter,
And his pain doubles, his throne dims to his own eyes,
And he says to Khorraad, son of Borzeen,
"It is not a secret to any learned man that Khosrow
Is for me more than a blood relative and ally
And that I prefer him to my soul endowed with speech.
I possess weapons, treasures, and troops.
Let me know what you need, and even if you were to ask
For my eyes, I would gladly offer them without regret,
Though eyes are assets more precious than priceless treasures."

18 | The Caesar's Reply to Khosrow's Letter

The Caesar summons a worldly scribe
And seats him before the throne of power.
He commands him to compose a reply
Adorned like a pasture in paradise with countless
Embellishments, words of advice, and flowery writing
From the present era and going back to ancient times.

Once the scribe completes the letter,
The Caesar searches around for a horseman
Who is valiant, eloquent, observant, intelligent,
Learned, full of courage, and of serene heart.
He says to him, "Go to Khosrow and tell him:
        'O insightful King, seeker of the true path!
        I have treasure, warriors, and weapons.
        I have no need to upset anyone to acquire more.
        Even if I had no possessions, I would ask dirhams
        From all the noblemen residing in my provinces
        To assist you as you make your way back from Rum
        To your palace in Iran content, your wishes fulfilled.
        Banish sadness from your heart
        For as long as you visit my land.
        Such is the behavior of the dome of sky:
        At times it offers you shelter, at times your demise.
        At times it caresses you gently,
        At times it seizes you in the knot of a noose.
        Do not afflict yourself as I am about to bring you
        Troops, war apparatus, and vast wealth.'"

The messenger departs and repeats to Khosrow
The Caesar's words stored in his memory.

The Caesar dismisses all the visitors from his hall
And consults with his advisor, his heart full of worry:
"The supplicant seeks justice and shelter,
But what shall we do to help him succeed,
To relieve him of the shame and the beating
He has endured at the hands of his subject?"

The advisor replies to the Caesar, "We must seek
The advice of our philosophers of good counsel.

We shall allow them to deliberate on the matter."

The Caesar sends an envoy,
And four philosophers arrive,
Some young and some old, all of Rumi lineage.
They discuss at length the incidence and say,
"Since the death of Eskandar,
Our hearts have been at the mercy of the Iranians
Who have not ceased their pillage,
Their attacks, and the spillage of innocent blood.
Now Yazdan, the pure, has brought down
Misfortune upon them for their wicked actions.
But remain calm, since the prosperity
Of the Sassanians appears to be crippled.
If Khosrow regains hold of his imperial crown,
He will raise his head to the sphere of the moon
And will instantly demand tribute from Rum.
He will take advantage of his position to seize our lands.
Think about it wisely and consider
The words of the Iranians as nothing but wind."

These discussions force the Caesar to change his mind.
He sends a rider to the king with a letter
Indicating the proper path to follow,
According to the advice of the visionary sages.

Once the rider reaches Khosrow, he recounts
All that he heard from the mouth of his famed master.
He hands over the Caesar's letter and speaks at length.

Khosrow's heart constricts, and his concerns
Render his cheeks pale as he responds:
"If one must learn from ancient tales, one can deduce
That one's labors are as worthless as a fistful of wind.
Reflect on the fact that there does not exist
A single old man who remembers if my ancestors,
World masters and pure men elected by the Creator,
Engaged in wars justly or unjustly.
Ask your Rumi men who is guilty, the crow or the owl.
Anyone who came to Rum and reached fame and glory
Must not think that he no longer needs the Creator's help.
Our forefathers were powerful and famed world rulers

Who never tolerated any failings, such as pride,
Superiority, violence, or the lack of sense and reason.
But today these things have no value, for my head
Finds itself in close proximity of the dragon's jaws.
Take my greetings to the Caesar and tell him,
        'Princes must not, when faced with wisdom,
        Engage in discourse that has neither warp nor weft.
        In the end, both the good and the bad will pass.'

"From now on, I shall surrender to neither rest nor sleep
Before having drawn my robe's hem out of murky waters.
If I find the Rumis reluctant to assist me, I shall travel
To the Emperor of Chin, for all my words would have been
In vain, since the flows of your river are murky to its depths.
When my envoys return, I shall no longer be here."

He says to the Iranians, "Obey my command.
Do not despair for what is happening,
For Yazdan, the victorious, is our shelter,
And our duty rests on our valor."

He places himself above this affair in his heart
And sends Tokhaar with a letter, without lending
A thought to the consequences, good or bad.

Tokhaar takes leave of Khosrow
And travels to the court of the renowned Caesar,
Who reads the letter, his heart moved, and says
To his powerful vizier, "Reveal to me the mystery.
Summon the noblemen and army leaders,
And speak to them of what occurred.
Reflect on whether Khosrow will be happy in this war
Or whether he will yield when confronted by fate.
If you tell me that he will fail,
That he will never again have the chance
To partake in the celebrations of Nowruz,
We shall await his travels to the Emperor of Chin,
Where he will seek a remedy to his ailment.
But if he is meant to triumph, if he is to be
The master of his empire as was his father,
It is best for him to leave with an army so that
His heart does not retain a desire for vengeance."

The learned vizier hears him out and summons
Astrologers, who come with their antique tables
To discuss and deliberate through three parts of the night.
In the end, the chief astrologer relates his findings
To the Caesar, "O crown-bearer, I have studied
The ancient tables built by Plato[11] as relating to the stars.
Not much time will pass before the empire
Falls back into the hands of Khosrow
And Persian kingship profits from a new turn of fortune.
After thirty-eight years of his rule,
The dark dust will cover the body of the king."

The Caesar listens and says to his vizier,
"We have uncovered the secrets of fate.
Now how shall we proceed? How shall we reply?
What balm shall we apply to this festering wound?
If Khosrow travels to the border of Chin
And confers with the emperor, he will find relief."

The powerful vizier says,
"The stars have determined the outcome,
And nothing, neither value nor learning, can change it.
May the World Master protect you!
If Khosrow goes to the emperor's realm with demands
Of friendship, he will find safety and security.
If he procures himself an army elsewhere,
He will never cease to be your adversary.
Reflect on the fact that, at this moment,
You know the future better than Khosrow.
His demand makes you more powerful than him."

The Caesar says, "I feel obliged to send a host to the king.
The more I think about it, the more I am convinced that
It is best to risk my wealth to safeguard my well-being."

◇◇◇◇◇◇◇◇◇◇◇◇◇
11 Plato: Ancient Greek philosopher (fourth century BCE) and student of Socrates.
His contribution greatly influenced Western philosophy.

19 | The Caesar Writes Again to Khosrow Parviz

Immediately and quickly, he writes a letter
To Khosrow Parviz full of praise and blessings:
"My vizier, friend, and loyal advisor and I have
Openly discussed the good and the bad of the affair.
We have spoken on various courses of action
And have circled back to our initial plans.
Consultations and deliberations are now over,
And I have opened the doors to my ancient treasure.
Though I do not have enough troops in Constantinople
To watch over the land, we have arranged everything.
We have gathered forces from every part of the empire,
And, as they arrive, we shall dispatch them to you.

"Our hesitations, long discussions, and
The sting of the lion's bite derive from the fact
That our learned men reminded us of past deeds
During the time of Shahpoor, son of Ardeshir.
Back then, young hearts aged quickly
From pain and grief, from attacks,
Plunder, killings, and unfair acts of revenge.
Later, under the rules of Ghobaad and Hormozd,
Two monarchs who never lent a thought to justice,
The Iranians devastated thirty-nine of our great cities.
The plains turned into blood-filled lakes
As we witnessed the decline of our famed leaders.
Our women and children were taken captive.
You must not be surprised if the hearts of Rumi fighters
Beat with the burning desire to seek retribution.

"Yet our religion dictates that we never hold a grudge.
Heaven forbid our custom would lead us toward evil deeds.
We have recognized that righteousness is the highest value
And we must keep our distance from lies and deceit.
We have gathered here those who suffered the most,
Speaking at length of these affairs, and we have been
Able to, in artful ways, purify the hearts of men
And convert into theriac a corrosive and toxic poison.
I have convinced them never to bring up past deeds.
They will do as you wish and obey your commands.
They will offer their souls as guarantee for our alliance.

On your side, you must assure us you will not seek
To cause us any harm; you will declare that as long
As you remain king, you will never forget the pains
We endure for you, that you will never ask tribute from us,
And that you will never betray your gratitude to us.
Furthermore, you will relinquish the lands you have
Invaded in Rum and promise never to cross the border.

"Go beyond your present wish, make a deal with us,
And let us conclude the alliance for one purpose:
That in every occasion, when we are occupied with a matter,
Perhaps a foolish battle, we remain friends and brothers,
Even if one of us would be at times the weaker ruler.
When you no longer need the land of Rum,
Your ancient hatred may be reborn as well as
Thoughts of Toor and Salm and their wicked deeds.
But I now ask you for an enduring pact
Attested by a solemn seal
Whereby we forget the vengeance due Iraj
And all other struggles between our lands of long ago;
Whereby Iran and Rum unite to form one strong unit,
And no side will ever again attempt to separate the two.

"I have in my women's chambers a daughter
Worthy to be wedded to the greatest of great men.
Ask for her hand in accordance with our holy rites
And in harmony with our customs and ceremonies,
So that we may forget the wrong caused to Iraj.
Once you have a son of the Caesar's lineage,
And the world rests from its troubles and wars,
We may finally seek the true path through our faith.

"Now if you wish to perceive with the eye of wisdom,
You will be assured that I do not ask for anything
That is outside the framework of righteousness.
Our alliance is to be strengthened by our kinship.
Such is the desire of the order of Yazdan.
From Pirooz to Khoshnavaz, much time passed
During which our two peoples foolishly
Delivered their heads to the wind.
May there never exist a king disloyal to treaties!
The Messiah, our prophet, once said,

'Wisdom is smothered by a lack of justice.'
Khoshnavaz resorted to many means to save
Pirooz's head from falling beneath the shears of death.
Pirooz, when he acted harshly with Khoshnavaz,
Drew from the conflict only the anguish of fatality.
Once the head of the king strayed from justice,
His army and his royal throne perished.
You are still young and inexperienced.
If you wish to pluck the fruit of fortune,
Do not befriend a man who violates treaties,
For such a man is not deserving of the shroud.
Cursed be the throne and crown of a king
Who tears apart treaties and yearns for revenge.

"Read this letter from beginning to end.
Weigh my words and compose your reply.
Reflect in all sincerity and write beneath a lucky star.
I do not wish for a scribe to be informed of our secret.
Write yourself and bring to view your sagacity.
Once I receive your reply and recognize in it
The soul of a resolute man, I shall send weapons,
Troops, and dinars to ease your heart's affliction.
No matter what hatred you bear in your heart
To the most illustrious among your entourage,
Pluck from your soul the idea of vengeance.
Forgive their faults in the name of Yazdan,
For the day shines equally on friend and enemy.

"If you wish for your good fortune to treat you
As world master with army, crown, and throne,
Abstain to take the goods of others.
Direct your mind toward the path of righteousness.
Be benevolent toward your kin,
Act as the guardian of the poor and destitute.
If you are generous and seek to rescue others,
No one will extend a hand for your throne and crown.
Kings who watched over the world
And secured it against the enemy
Never suffered from their adversaries,
And the majesty given to them by the divine
Made them rise higher on the royal pedestal.
Princes ask for their daughters,

Either for themselves or for their virtuous sons.
Now I am asking you to become my son-in-law,
Giving you sage advice to seal our alliance."

Once the heading of the letter has dried,
A seal of musk is affixed on which the Caesar
Dips his ring, then gives the letter to the envoy
And dismisses him with many blessings.

The surprising news of an alliance reaches Khosrow,
Who gleefully addresses the Iranian assembly,
"Today the sun's revolutions have shifted in the skies.
An important letter from the Caesar has arrived,
And its contents are most favorable to us.
He seeks a path whereby we may erase
The enmity dividing our two lands."

The Iranians reply, "Once this deal is achieved,
None of the noblemen will dare yearn for the royal seat.
Many people will cease to live in poverty.
If this alliance comes to be during your reign,
Your name will be inscribed on all the crowns."

20 | Khosrow Parviz Writes a Letter to Seal His Alliance to the Caesar

Having received the Iranians' approval,
Khosrow dismisses strangers and visitors.
He requests his inkwell, reed, and Chini silk,
And calls a scribe to his side to write a letter
In the language of Pahlavi, with royal characters
And according to royal custom, to say:
"I, King Khosrow, swear by Yazdan, the pure,
By the turning skies and the peaceful earth,
That, for as long as I sit as king on the throne of Iran,
Possessor of treasury and army, I shall refrain
From asking tribute from the rulers of Rum
And refrain from sending a host to their land.
All the cities on the border, no matter how insignificant,
I shall return to the Caesar without exception.
I shall send all the deeds and the titles accordingly.

"Furthermore, I request in marriage,
Upon consent from the father, the Caesar's daughter,
Born of an unsullied mother of princely birth.
This request is rather close to my heart.
Dispatch a host and hand over your intelligent
And illustrious daughter to the Iranians who stand
Present at your court and under your protection:
They are heroes of the likes of Gostaham and Shahpoor,
Andian and Khorraad, son of Borzeen the Kianian.

"Through this alliance with you,
I shall be restored to the status shared
By the most glorious kings of long ago.
Kings of the likes of Kiumars and Jamsheed,
Who filled the world with fear and hope.
After them came men of blessed birth born from Iraj,
And the powerful crown-bearers of yore:
The famed Kay Ghobaad, Kay Kaavoos, and Kay Khosrow,
Who integrated lamb and wolf into the same family.
And so on and so forth down to King Lohraasp,
King Goshtaasp, and the blessed Esfandiar,
Whose offspring was the renowned Bahman.

"We come upon Ardeshir Babakan,
Who renewed the dimming star of the empire,
And upon Khosrow, son of Hormozd,
Who is one with the Caesar, body and soul.
Your ancient ancestor was the famous Salm.
I do not pronounce lies nor do I speak in vain,
For we have relinquished all thoughts of vengeance.
The Rumis and the Iranians are now united as one.
I gratefully receive from the Caesar his daughter,
Who is the diadem on the circle of fair maidens.
I accept her with her flaws and her assets
And invoke Yazdan, the pure, as guarantor
For everything contained in this letter,
Composed in my own legendary handwriting.

"I affixed the seal on the letter myself,
According to custom, form, and religion.
The souls and minds of future Caesars,
World masters, masters of throne and crown,

Will approve the covenant in this letter.
I shall never deviate from my commitment
And from anything written within, great or small.
Every word has been agreed to by both parties.
I shall forever hold my heart, my star,
And Yazdan, the pure, as my witnesses.
Make haste to send what you promised,
As my sojourn here has lasted far too long."

Having completed the letter, he hands it over
To Khorsheed, son of Khorraad, and the leader departs,
As wift as wind, riding a piebald horse.
He rushes to the Caesar and relays the message.

The Caesar unfastens the cords holding the letter
And reads the words of the powerful Khosrow.
He commands all the wise and eloquent men
To gather around him and consults with each of them:
"What remedy shall we apply at this moment?
This letter dispels all pretext of a refusal.
Iran and Rum have sealed a pact of friendship."

The learned noblemen rise and reply,
"We are your subjects and you are the Caesar,
World master, owner of throne and diadem.
Reflect carefully. It is for you to decide.
If you command us, we are yours, body and soul."

The Caesar approves the advice of the illustrious,
Sensible, and holy men and remains with them
Until the torch of the sun in the revolving dome
Loses its luster and begins to fade into dusk.

21 | The Rumis Prepare a Magical Figure to Test the Iranians

As the turning sun pales and a star
Appears in the sky's constellations,
The Caesar commands magicians to reflect.

He says, "Prepare a magnificent work of magic,

One that no one can differentiate from a human body,
The figure of a beautiful, moon-facced woman
Dressed in a long and modest robe
And seated on a bejeweled throne
With ladies-in-waiting on each side of her,
And slaves before and behind her.
She must remain speechless
And appear to be weeping.
Once in a while she will raise her hand
And wipe away a tear from her lash.
Anyone who sees her from afar
Will take her for a woman of dazzling, rosy cheeks,
Mournful for the Messiah, bitterly shedding tears
That flow from her eyes like a spring cloud."

Soon after, one of the Caesar's counselors
Appears before him to announce the completion
And the placement of the majestic, magical sculpture.
The Caesar marches over in haste to observe her.
He finds himself astounded by the skillful work
And presents dirhams and valuables to the sorcerers.

He summons Gostaham and says, "O illustrious hero,
I have a daughter as beautiful as spring.
She is now mature and at the age of marriage.
I have a relative ambitious for glory to whom
I offered her hand, in accordance with the Messiah's rites.
She had no knowledge of what the future holds for her.
One day, I sent her to the young suiter's palace.
Soon after, the soul of the latter soared to the sky.
Now my daughter sits in a state of mourning.
Her brilliant day has dimmed.
She rejects my advice, refuses to speak,
And the world that once appeared young to me
Has aged from the state of grief I am plunged into.
Would you not make the effort to visit her?
Have her listen to the advice of wise men.
You are young and of the race of warriors,
Perhaps she will open her mouth in your presence."

Gostaham says, "I shall obey in the hopes
That I shall awaken her heart's sensibility."

211

The illustrious man walks over to the sculpture
With an open heart and full of eloquence.
As he approaches her, she bends over on her throne.
The noble Gostaham sits humbly and addresses her.
He begins by giving her lengthy and wise advice:
"O offspring of the Caesar, a being endowed with sense
Does not complain about or protest her bitter fate.
The eagle in its flight cannot escape its death,
Neither can the lion in its thicket nor the fish in the sea."

The eloquent warrior's words are like wind
Since he stands before a body devoid of a soul
And a head devoid of a tongue,
A figure who incessantly sheds tears.

Gostaham remains thus, in a state of astonishment,
When the Caesar calls him to his side to ask him,
"What do you think of this daughter
Whose bereavement fills me with sorrow?"
Gostaham replies, "I have relayed to her much advice,
But my words have no effect on her."

The next morning, the Caesar says to Balooy,
Andian, and Shahpoor, "This man of high birth
Will assist you in allowing me to enjoy my daughter.
Go to my mourning child and speak to her of the king.
Perhaps you will receive a reply from her;
Perhaps you may alleviate the ardor
Of the fires of grief she crowds my head with.
Question my illustrious daughter.
She may listen and discern your status and your worth.
I believe that today she will answer you.
As soon as she speaks with her blessed voice,
I shall be free of the worry her state afflicts me with
As she continuously floods her breast with tears."

The three noble Persian leaders obey.
Each speaks of glory and battle, but none of them
Receives a response as the woman remains mute.

They exit the palace and return to the Caesar,
Having failed in their mission, and report:
"We have spoken to her, but the disconsolate

Creature is incapable of heeding our counsel."

The Caesar replies, "Misfortune has her
In a state of continuous, sorrowful mourning."
With no resource among the illustrious men,
The Caesar turns to Khorraad, son of Borzeen:
"O glorious and valiant man, elite of the race
Of Ardeshir, go and visit my daughter.
I hope that you can somehow hear her voice.
I am terribly afflicted by her state of apathy.
I know not what game fate plays with her,
And I find myself at a loss in this affair.
You may be able to unravel this adversity for me,
For you are a noble, prudent, and glorious man."

The Caesar sends him away from his palace
To the mournful woman with a trustworthy servant.
Once in front of the supposed Rumi princess,
Khorraad studies her face, head, and diadem.
He stands before her for a long time,
And the deceptive figure greets him.
He observes her at length from head to toe,
Observes the servants standing beside her,
Speaks to her, but she remains unresponsive.

The mind of the descendant of kings
Fills with suspicion as he reflects:
"If grief has rendered this woman insensible,
Why are her ladies-in-waiting not speaking to her?
If her eyes were to shed real tears,
It would be natural for her pain to diminish.
Her tears tumble down to her breast,
But she is unable to move left and right.
The tears she sheds always follow the same path,
And her hand always falls on the same thigh.
If this figure held a soul, her body would stir
And the movement would not be limited
Simply to her hand and foot.
Her tears would fall randomly, here and there.
I do not detect any life in her body.
I suspect it is merely a philosopher's trick."

He returns to the Caesar and says with a smile:
"This moon-faced woman has no soul.
She is a supernatural statue built by the Rumis,
And Balooy and Gostaham did not recognize it.
You wanted to mock the Iranians and bewitch our eyes.
When the king hears of this adventure,
He will laugh heartily and reveal his teeth."

22 | Khorraad Explains the Hindu Religion to the Caesar

The Caesar tells him, "May you live eternally!
You are worthy of being a royal vizier.
There is in my palace a marvelous room,
One beyond the most ingenious imagination.
When one sees it, one cannot understand
What sort of enchanting spell it contains,
Whether it is a work of magic or a divine creation."

Khorraad, son of Borzeen, visits the old building
To find a cavalier upon a horse suspended in the air.
He returns to the illustrious Caesar and says,
"O King of victorious fortune, it is a phenomenon,
A jewel, worthy of your throne.
No one has ever seen a more magnificent trick
Nor heard of such a thing from the most learned.
We must not hide this sight from the savants,
For there is nothing equal to it in the world."

The Caesar asks, "Who is able to raise in the air
A talisman that has neither soul nor fiber?"

Khorraad replies, "The rider is made of iron
And the vault of the room is made of a famous
Substance that learned men call magnet.
The Rumis placed it there above the metal horse.
Anyone who reads about this in Hindu books
Will find himself quite satisfied and enlightened."

The Caesar asks, "What point have the Hindus
Thus far reached in the path of science?

Where are they in terms of cult and religion?
Are they idol worshippers perhaps?"

Khorraad, son of Borzeen, says,
"The Indians regard the cow as both king and moon.
They give credence neither to Yazdan
Nor to the power of the rotating dome of sky.
They have neither pity nor affection for their bodies.
They consider themselves above the sun
And do not revere learned men like us.
Anyone who ignites a fire, jumps into it and burns,
Thinks that, by divine command, there is in space
A universal flame that their men of science call ether,
Of which they speak in beautiful and touching terms.
They say that when fire mixes with fire,
The sins we have committed evaporate.
That is why they ignite fires, and they believe that
They can be justified in being consumed by the flames."

The Caesar says, "This cannot be so.
The soul of the Messiah is my witness.
Do you not know what Jesus, son of Mariam,
Said when he revealed the secret? He said,
    'If someone steals your tunic,
    Do not heatedly argue with him over it.
    If he strikes you on the cheek in a way
    As to trouble your eyes from the force of the blow,
    Do not be wrathful; abstain from growing pale.
    Close your eyes on the gesture;
    Abstain from uttering a cold word.
    When food becomes scarce, be content with little.
    If you have no carpet beneath your feet, do not fret.
    By following these guidelines, you will not envisage
    Your misfortune as an adverse occurrence
    And will spend your days in peace.'

"Your desires are governing your mind,
And greed has led your heart astray.
Your palaces rise all the way to Saturn,
Camels carry loads of keys that open countless treasures.
Beyond your wealth, you have so many warring hosts,
Outfitted with countless Rumi armor and Rumi helmets.

You send your troops marching on every side
To commit wicked crimes without regard for justice.
You draw your swords out of a resting position,
Sullying all the springs and rivers with blood.
The Messiah did not wish for you to follow such a path.
He was a poor man devoid of fortune
Who gained his bread with his hands' labor.
He lived on only whey and milk,
Which he considered dietary luxuries.
When his enemies seized him and noticed
That he had neither protector nor means of defense,
They beat him up and hung him at the gallows
With the purpose of dishonoring his religion.
The place of worship for Christianity was his father,
And the place of worship for Judaism was his mother."

Pay attention to the response given by Khorraad:
"Jesus was created out of the cloth of human nature.
He spent his life in deep contemplation
And sought to distinguish between good and bad.
His mind was brilliant as he yearned
For wisdom, eloquence, learning, and reflection.
He became a prophet, gathered a following, and,
Through his subtle mind, acquired a name
At a very young age.
It was as if he were the son of the Creator,
As if he were smiling as he expired at the gallows.
But any intelligent man will laugh at such a thing.
If you have any sense, honor Yazdan,
Who has need for neither woman nor child,
And before whom all truth is manifest.
Why do you stray from the faith of Kiumars
And the path of the cult of Tahmures?
They declared that the World Master is One,
And you must entirely submit to the One.
The worldly peasant bard, Yazdan worshipper,
May not consume a single drop until he holds
The Barsom in his hand while murmuring prayers.

"Even if, by an excess of thirst,
He were imagining water in his dreams,
He takes refuge in Yazdan on the day of battle

And need not ask for fresh water during the fight.
His Kiblah[12] is above all things, above water, earth, and air.
Our kings do not tamper with their faith;
They lend an ear to divine command.
They are attached to neither dinars nor jewels.
They seek glory and distinction only in justice,
In the gift of lofty palaces and in the joy
They infuse into the hearts of wretched men.
Finally, our kings call a man of sense the one who,
On the day of battle, covers the face of the sun
With dust and protects the land from the enemy.
Cursed be the one unworthy of praise who seeks
In religion something other than righteousness."

The Caesar approves of words that are beneficial to him.
He says to Khorraad, "The one who created the world
Created you to be the most illustrious of noblemen.
One must listen to your holy discourse,
For you possess the key to the door of mysteries.
The one with a subject such as you
Can raise his head above the diadem of the moon."

He asks for dirhams and dinars from his treasury,
A glorious diadem, and gives it all to Khorraad,
Covering him with praise and blessings:
"May the land of Iran prosper with you!"

23 | The Caesar Sends His Daughter to Khosrow Parviz With an Army

Once the Caesar is aware of his army's arrival,
The world growing hazy with the dust raised.
He selects one hundred thousand Rumi men
Who have distinguished themselves with their skills.
He asks for weapons, dirhams, and battle steeds,
And in this way passes the delay he had called for.

He has a daughter named Mariam, intelligent,

◇◇◇◇◇◇◇◇◇◇◇◇
12 Kiblah: Or Qiblah, is the direction of the Sacred Mosque in Mecca, which always determines the direction of prayer.

217

Of good counsel, solemn, and strong-minded.
He engages her to Khosrow in accordance with the rites
Of his religion and invokes divine blessings upon her.

The valiant Gostaham receives her to hand her
Over to Khosrow in line with royal ceremony.
Then the Caesar asks for loads of dowry
So heavy that they burden the strongest horses.
There are objects of gold and gems worthy of kings;
Rubies, gold-embroidered robes, carpets,
And Rumi brocade stitched with pure gold and silver;
Dazzling bracelets, torques, earrings,
And three opulent and very precious crowns.

He prepares four golden litters with covers
Embellished with royal jewels and forty carriages
Of ebony gleaming like a rooster's eye with fine gems.
Then come three hundred moon-faced members
Of the queen's following, dazzling with color and scent;
Five hundred intelligent, awakened slaves,
Mounted on stallions with gold and silver strappings;
Next are forty charming, fairy-faced, Rumi eunuchs;
Finally, four learned, famed and shrewd Rumi philosophers.

The Caesar indicates to them what they must say,
Then speaks secretly with Mariam on the subjects
Of peace, generosity, worth, desires to be manifested,
Ability, duty, food, and propriety.

The Rumis calculate and record the wealth,
Which amounts to more than
Three hundred times thousands of thousands.
The Caesar offers bolts of fabric, horses,
And gold to the royal envoys at court,
Bearers of gem-encrusted diadems.
He offers them an abundance of riches
Worthy of their standings and ranks.

Then he commands a scribe to write a letter
To convey all the necessary information
To the King of Iran: "The king's subjects
Can raise their heads to the moon.
There does not exist in the world,

Among men great and small,
A more capable person than Gostaham.
There does not exist a more valiant man than Shahpoor,
Nor one more able to serve as intermediary in affairs.
Moreover, Balooy is able to keep a secret
And will never betray the Persians, not for anything.
For as long as we are on the earth,
One will never see a man like Khorraad, son of Borzeen.
Yazdan created him so that he may reveal the mysteries.
He is unsullied and shines like the brilliant sun.
All his actions and words come from the Creator."

Having committed all this to the letter,
He summons his guide, who appears with an astrologer
Able to determine an auspicious day to start the voyage.

The Caesar sets off on Bahraam day,[13]
Under a favorable star and bright omens.
He marches for the duration of three days.
On the fourth day, he takes position at the lead
Of the cortege, asks for Mariam to approach him,
And speaks to her for a long time.
He enjoins her to maintain her belt around her waist
Until she reaches the land of Iran
So that she may appear covered before the king,
As unveiled would be a most inappropriate state.

Having spoken, he takes leave of her tenderly
And says, "May the skies protect you in your travels!"

The valiant Niyaatoos, the Caesar's brother,
Is to command the army on its journey.
The Caesar says to him, "Khosrow is now your kin.
I give you this mission because he resembles you
In character. I entrust you with my daughter,
My treasures, and this well-equipped army."

Niyaatoos takes charge of it all,
And the world master circles back, weeping,
As the procession begins its journey to Oorigh,

◇◇◇◇◇◇◇◇◇◇◇◇
13 Bahraam day: The twentieth day of every month in the solar calendar.

With Niyaatoos at the lead,
Armed with mace and blade.

At the news of their approach,
Khosrow exits the city with troops
And takes his position on the road.
The dust stolen from the leaders lifts in the distance.
The banners of ironclad cavaliers emerge
As the army advances swiftly,
Drowning in helmets and corselets.

The king's heart smiles like a spring rose
At the sight of the advancing illustrious troops.
His shining, noble soul lifts.
His charger leaps under the weight of his heel.
He notices Niyaatoos, takes him in his arms
With effusive expressions of gratitude.
He asks him the customary questions
And showers the Caesar with praise
For having exerted such effort and,
Beyond the tremendous effort and the army,
For having emptied his treasury for him.

Then he approaches the litter
To catch a glimpse of Mariam's face beneath the veil.
He questions her and kisses her hand.
The aspect of this beautiful moon pleases him.
He accompanies her to the women's chambers
And prepares a secret apartment for her.
He speaks to her and remains with her for three days.

The fourth day, as the world-illuminating sun
Raises its shining orb, a magnificent tent is prepared,
And Niyaatoos is summoned to Khosrow's side
With Sarguis, the warring Koot, and a few army leaders.
The king asks them, "Who are your chiefs and warriors?
Anyone who wages battle with mace and blade
Is more than willing to risk his precious life.
Whether he is faced with a lion or a leopard,
He never flees before the prospect of a fight."

Niyaatoos indicates seventy men,
Each able to drive an attack on battle day.

He assures that he has, beneath his banner,
A cavalry of one thousand elite, sword-striking riders.

When Khosrow sees the selected host,
The illustrious riders avid for battle,
He addresses prayers of grace to Yazdan,
Creator of sky, time, and space, to Niyaatoos
And his army, to the renowned Caesar and his land.

Khosrow says to the noblemen,
"If the Creator wishes to aid me in this venture,
I shall show my power, render the earth prosperous
And shining with precious gems like the glistening ocean.
Rejoice for having come here! Speak freely!
We shall have no other worry than those of our friends.
The sky is my greatest support,
And my bond to noblemen is my garden."

24 | Khosrow Drives the Army to Aazar Abadegan[14]

On the seventh day, the sun-faced king
Commands his army like the revolving skies.
The sound of timpani rises over the gates,
Dust colors the earth in shades of ebony.
He forms an army composed of Iranians
And sets out in the direction of Aazar Abadegan.

For two weeks, troops advance under the king's
Command and arrive successively at camp.
The king sets up his enclosure on the plain of Dook.[15]
His host includes many adherents to the land of Rum.
He hands over the lead to Niyaatoos and says,
"You are the appointed master of this herd."

From there, he and his ardent riders
Return the bridle to their keen chargers
And travel to Chichast,[16] charging

◇◇◇◇◇◇◇◇◇◇◇◇◇
14 Aazar Abadegan: Same as Azerbaijan.
15 Dook: Somewhere on the way to Aazar Abadegan.
16 Chichast: Same as Lake Urmia in northwestern Iran in Azerbaijan.

Restlessly and keenly devouring the road.

Bandooy, Khosrow's maternal uncle,
Lives in a camp and under the protection
Of Moossil, the Armenian, an independent prince.
As soon as they hear that the king has resumed his march,
They rush from the desert to greet him on the road.

The two men break away from their escort,
And Khosrow, at the sight of them, says to Gostaham,
"Who are these two valiant men rushing on the field?
Go to them, find out their identity, and find out
Why they are racing toward us in this manner."

Gostaham replies, "O King, I believe that the rider
On the black and white horse is my brother,
The intrepid Bandooy,
But his companion belongs to another host."

Khosrow says to Gostaham, the lion,
"How could this be, O valiant rider?
Do you truly believe Bandooy is still alive?
If it were so, he would most definitely be in prison.
However, I believed he was dead,
Hanging at the gallows in some square."

Gostaham replies, "O King, look carefully.
You will distinguish the features of your uncle.
Should he near us and not be Bandooy, you have
Every right to end the life of the talkative Gostaham."

At that moment, the two men reach the king
And dismount in a shaded place.
They approach Khosrow and greet him reverently.

Khosrow questions Bandooy and exclaims,
"I was sure to find you buried beneath the ground!"

Bandooy recounts what happened to him,
The way Bahraam, son of Siaavoosh,
Ttreated him with humanity, instigating his escape,
The ruse he employed dressed in royal robes
With the clever intentions of fooling Choobineh.

After his elaborate account, Khosrow weeps briefly,
Then asks, "Who is this man with you?"

Bandooy replies, "O sun-faced King, why do
You not address amiable questions to Moossil?
Since you left Iran and traveled to Rum,
He never had a chance to sleep in a cultivated land.
The tent and the desert have been his dwellings,
His palace is made of felt and canvas.
But there are many troops around him,
An abundance of weapons, and a silver treasure.
He stationed himself on this road until you arrived,
For his greatest wish was to set his sight on the shah."

World master Khosrow asks Moossil,
"We shall not allow your efforts
On our behalf to go unnoticed.
I shall work to make your days
Be filled with joy and to have your name
Shine among the greatest noblemen."

Moossil replies, "O King, give me for once a day of joy.
Allow me to approach your majesty, kiss your stirrup,
And pay homage to your grace and your glory!"

Khosrow says, "As a reward for your fatigues,
I shall, from now on, add substantially to your wealth.
I shall grant you the object of your desires
And shall elevate your name above the proudest men."

He removes one foot from the stirrup,
To allow the intelligent man of restless heart
To kiss the royal foot and stirrup
In a state of shock and in fear of the king's splendor.

Khosrow, seeing the devoted Moossil undone,
Commands him to climb back on his horse.
He himself launches his charger to exit the barren
Desert and to gallop to the temple of Aazargoshasp.

He enters the sanctuary in silent prayer, heartbroken.
A priest comes with the Zand Avesta
To greet the world king, Yazdan worshipper.

Khosrow unfastens his golden belt to release it
And throws a few precious stones into the holy flame.
Then he utters his prayers, pleading louder than the priest:
"O pure, just Creator, cast to the dust my foes' heads.
You know that each of my breaths is devoted to justice
And my thoughts are directed only toward the good.
Do not approve the unjust deeds of an unjust man."

He says this, picks up his belt, and straps himself.
He turns toward the plain of Dook and departs
In a state of despair, searching for the way.
Upon his return to camp, the world is plunged
Into the blackness of a dark and long night.
He sends prudent emissaries to observe the affairs.

Once the army of Nimrooz learns
That the world-illuminating king is on his way,
They attach timpani to the backs of elephants,
And the world ripples like the flows of the River Nile.

The report of Khosrow's return renews his people,
Who rush to him to affirm their support.

25 | Bahraam Choobineh Learns of Khosrow's Return

At the news that the majesty of the King of Kings
Radiates with a new sheen, Bahraam casts his eyes
On an illustrious, learned, and honored army leader
Named Dara Panah, who has been loyal to him.

He summons a renowned scribe, speaks to him at length,
And commands him to compose forceful letters
To a number of powerful and audacious leaders:
To Gostaham and Bandooy; the valiant Gordooy,
Who surpasses others in glory and courage;
To Shahpoor; the rider Andian;
And other illustrious and heroic warriors.

He begins the letters: "I always quietly praise
The World Creator for allowing you to awaken
From your slumber and for guarding you

From rushing down the path of wicked deeds.
Since the Sassanian race appeared,
It has caused, in its search for world domination,
Nothing but perversity and iniquity
At the center and the confines of the earth.
Ardeshir, son of Babak, initiated the hostility.
The era has been obscured by his sword.
Noblemen's heads have been plunged
Into a state of insecurity and trouble.

"I shall speak first of Ardavan[17] and illustrious men
Of shining minds whose names have disappeared
And whose loss is still mourned by the royal throne.
You have indeed heard of the fate Soofraay endured
As a result of Pirooz's dreadful designs.
He had freed Ghobaad's feet from chains
And avenged him of the Hephthalite princes.
The wicked Ghobaad regained his power,
Rejected virtue from his heart, surrendered to vice,
And sentenced to death Soofraay, his loyal friend,
Thereby wounding the hearts of noblemen.
But a man who cannot act honorably with his kin,
Who prefers greed over his own children,
Cannot behave respectfully with strangers.
No one will search for ivory in a throne of ebony.

"Do not place any hope on the Sassanians.
Do not seek rubies in the red willow tree.
When you receive this letter on the day of Ormazd,
May fortune be propitious to you!
You have a brilliant position at my side,
Where the shirt's front and its sleeves
Are sewn out of the same cloth,
Where you will enjoy rest and sleep day and night.
When you all come to unite with me,
My troubled soul will regain its serenity.
I shall fear neither the Rumis nor the Caesar.
I shall trample beneath my feet their heads and thrones."

The king's seal is affixed, and the cunning envoy

◇◇◇◇◇◇◇◇◇◇◇◇◇◇
17 Ardavan: Ashkanian king whose reign ended with the rise of the Sassanians.

Departs, disguised as a merchant.
He speeds to Khosrow's courtly hall,
Taking a caravan loaded with all sorts of wealth,
For he is carrying many presents with the letters.

The old man sees the king's power
And a host so vast it is as if the earth is too small for it.
He reflects, "I have engaged in a hopeless venture.
Who will ask the valiant Bahraam for protection
When faced by the majesty and glory of the king?
I am a humble Persian man with no enemy
While I lug thirty loaded camels in my caravan.
Why would I allow myself to be killed
Just because the king has climbed out of the abyss?
I shall hand over these letters to the king.
I shall offer him gifts such as one has never seen."

He presents himself at court, his mind full of thoughts,
Bearing the vengeful letters and the gifts.
He hands out the dirhams, the presents, the letters,
And recounts everything to the world ruler.

Khosrow reads the letters, seats the envoy
On a golden seat, and says to him, "O wise man,
I do not make much of the leader Bahraam.
You have now attained the object you proposed.
Try not to seek fame by speaking of this affair."

He summons a scribe to reply to the letters,
Asking him to write a long message that says,
"O valiant and illustrious warrior, we have
Read your letters with the envoy seated before us.
We stand by Khosrow in words but not in actions.
Our hearts are loyal to you as you resemble spring.
When you drive your army to this land,
We shall draw our swords and kill the Rumis.
At the sight of your host, at the sight of your courage
And your high post, Khosrow's heart will tremble
In fear on battle day, and he will take off like a fox."

The king affixes a seal to the letter.
He summons the envoy whom he coddles and says,
"O intelligent man, you will draw

The rewards for your efforts in this venture."

He gives Dara Panah gems, gold, and high-priced rubies,
And says to him, "Take these to Choobineh,
And repeat to him all that you have heard.
When my proud fortune shines in all its splendor,
I shall raise you above all need in the world."

Dara Panah leaves the king's court, takes the road,
As swift as wind, and hands Choobineh the letter,
Addressing him with the sweetest, gentlest words.

26 | Bahraam Choobineh Marches Against Khosrow Parviz

As the ambitious Bahraam reads the letter,
He chases reason away and calls on his ardor,
Determined to make preparations for departure,
A resolve that astonishes the Iranians.

The older men go to him to dissuade him
From engaging in such a dark and risky plan.
They say, "Do not leave, for if you do,
Your young and brilliant fortune is sure to fade.
If Khosrow enters Iran-Zamin,
He will find only the mace and sword of vengeance.
But if you conspire against the royal throne,
Fate will mislead you in the most cruel ways."

Their words have no effect on Bahraam,
Who commands his troops to charge the loads,
To climb on their steeds, and to sound the timpani.
He leads his valiant host of Iranians out of the city,
Marching in haste at the lead toward Aazar Abadegan.

There the two armies come face to face
In a way as to bar passage to the smallest ants and flies.

Avid for retaliation, the warrior says,
"I wish to scrutinize the army, to assess the nature
Of its Rumi riders, their numbers, and their skills."

227

The heroes climb on horseback with Yalan Sineh
And the powerful Izad Goshasp, and they march
To survey the Rumi host, avid for battle.
They return, dismount, and report to Bahraam,
"The enemy is comprised of innumerable troops,
Many more than what we had estimated!"

On the other side, the king's Rumi riders
Rush to the audience hall dressed in armor
And exclaim, "O King,
We are eager to fight against the Iranians!"
There is nothing Khosrow Parviz desires more
Than to grant the Rumis their wish.

As the sun raises its head over the dark mountain,
A great clatter rises from both camps.
It is as if the earth is the turning sky,
For if the sun is eclipsed by the gleam of swords.
The troops form into left and right wings,
And the ground becomes a mountain of steel.

The neighing of horses and the clatter of troops
Are so loud that the plain takes refuge in the mountain.
Witness to this state of things,
The warring Bahraam draws his shining sword
And makes the rounds of his host,
Inspecting the right and left wings.
His lion heart is split in two, though he has no fear.
He says to the Iranians, "Take your positions
At the center front, for today, we shall lead the attack."

Bahraam surveys the battlefield and tells
Yalan Sineh, "Place yourself at the vanguard.
Today it is my turn to fight.
Today I shall surrender or flee."

Khosrow notices that the world is obscured by troops,
The face of the sun is black like the lion's jaw,
And it feels as if a shower of swords falls from above.
Niyaatoos, Gostaham, and Bandooy escort the king
Away from the field to the top of Mount Dook,
Eyes fixed on the warriors bellow.
From his vantage point, the king can better

Observe the army wings and the proceedings.

The sound of timpani rises on both sides.
The warriors, eager for battle, advance.
It is as if the earth, a mountain of steel,
Is engaged in a raging war with the sky, its enemy.

At the sight of the state of things, at the sight
Of earth and sky weaved into a firm warp and weft,
The king addresses Yazdan in Pahlavi:
"O You who are the highest being that exists,
You are unique and just. You have insight
Into the outcome of the battle;
You know whose fortune will weaken today,
Whose spear tip will be converted
To thorns and blades of grass."

Khosrow's heart and soul fill with concern.
The world appears like a dark forest before his eyes.
Koot, mountain-like in his armor of steel,
Emerges from the army center, climbs to the heights,
And says to Khosrow, "O illustrious King,
Search with your eyes for the deev-like slave
Against whom you fought in Iran,
Who vanquished you and before whom you fled.
Search the army left and right, find his position,
So that I may teach him a lesson or two,
So that I may show him the power of the heart
And the force of a most able contender."

These words revive an ancient grief in Khosrow,
Reminding him that he fled before a subject
And cast aside his weapons of war.
He does not answer him, his heart mourning
And his mouth expelling deep sighs.
In the end, the king says to Koot,
"Go to the rider on a white and black horse.
When he sees you, he will advance to fight,
But you must remain staunch and never bolt."

Koot returns to the field as swiftly
As if he were the companion of the wind,
Boiling with ardor and brandishing his spear,

Charging like a drunken elephant.
Koot asks to be led to Bahraam the leader.

Yalan Sineh warns Bahraam: "Beware,
O valiant cavalier, here comes a deev,
His noose wrapped around the saddle knob
And his spear gripped firmly in his hand!"

Bahraam draws his sword from its sheath,
As swift as wind, and shouts his name.
At the sight of the exploit, Khosrow rises,
Fixes his eyes on Koot and Bahraam,
Tearful, his heart boiling with fury.

The advancing Rumi, brandishing his spear,
Comes into view of Bahraam whose body stiffens.
He sustains the shock of Koot's spear
Without having incurred an injury.
He protects his face with his battle shield,
Strikes Koot's head and neck with his sword,
And splits his dark body down the chest.

The crash of the blow reaches Khosrow,
Who bursts into laughter at the act of Bahraam.
But Niyaatoos closes his eyes, furious, and says,
"O illustrious ruler, it is not right to laugh in war.
You only know how to make use of ruse,
And I see that your heart has fallen asleep
When it comes to avenging your fathers.
There is no man equal to Koot in strength
In the prosperous lands of Iran and Rum.
He is equivalent to one thousand men.
Though you laugh at the death of this warrior,
You must know that your fortune dies with him."

Khosrow says, "I do not laugh at his death
Or at the fact that his body was split in half.
Anyone who engages in mockery will, in turn,
Receive a fatal blow from the spinning skies.
He told me that I fled before a slave, that I did not
Have enough heart to measure myself against him.
But it is not a subject of shame to take flight before
A capable subject, one able to administer such blows."

On his side, Bahraam exclaims, "O illustrious
And high-born men, Yalan Sineh, Raam,
And Izad Goshasp, we must fasten the corpse
To his horse and return him to his camp
So that the king may witness his maimed body."

The warriors quickly tie up Koot's corpse
Onto the saddle, and the horse takes off.
Khosrow's heart is deeply afflicted at the sight of Koot.
The king asks for the body to be untied
And the wounds filled with musk,
Then dried up and sewn in a fine linen cloth
To be finally dressed in his coat of mail and belt.
Then he sends the body to the Caesar with a message:
"This is the way the sword of this deev-like slave
Strikes on the day of battle. You can surely see
That there is no shame in the fact that I took flight."

All the Rumis are heartbroken, and those
Who did not battle feel wounded at the soul.
The Rumi patricians shed copious tears,
Their faces drenched and their hearts ulcered.
One hundred thousand illustrious, valiant,
Catholic riders, advance to activate an offensive,
Assailing in a way as to make the mountains
Split from the cries of the mass of Rumi fighters.
The clash of arms, the voices of the leaders,
The blows of sword and heavy mace resound.
It is as if the sea is on the boil and the spinning
Firmament shouts terrifying cries of blood.
There are so many bodies in the midst of troops
That they obstruct passage to the fighters.

The Rumi corpses form an army with fallen leaders.
Khosrow's heart is stabbed by the points of grief.
He asks for soldiers' wounds to be dressed
And the bodies to be stacked into a mound
That they name Bahraamcheed.[18]

Khosrow loses his hope in the Rumis. He reflects,

◇◇◇◇◇◇◇◇◇◇◇◇◇
18 Bahraamcheed: The killings of Bahraam.

"If these warriors appear twice on the battlefield
In this way, there will no longer be a Rumi host.
Their swords of steel have turned into wax."

Then he says to Sarguis, "Tomorrow, take time to rest.
Guard yourself from trudging with your troops to battle.
I shall march forth with my countrymen avid for vengeance."

Then he says to the Iranians, "Tomorrow
You shall, without delay, engage in a fierce war."

They all respond, "We shall fight so fiercely,
Mountain and plain will flood with torrents of blood."

27 | Khosrow's Warriors Fight With Bahraam Choobineh

As the sun's white banner rises over the sea
And the stars despair from the depths of darkness,
Elephants march in tandem with the beating of drums.
The sound of clarion, trumpet, and timpani
Placed on the backs of elephants is such that it feels
As if plain and boulders shake, and the sun's face
Appears as black as a raven's plumage.

Once the Iranians form their lines of battle,
Wielding spears and Indian swords,
The earth seems wrapped in an armor of steel,
And stars borrow their luster from spear points.

Khosrow aligns the center corps.
The troops, full of heart and obeisance,
Flawlessly shift and fall into line.
The leader of the right wing is the ambitious Gordooy.
At the left wing is an illustrious Armenian shielded
In armor and wielding a sword worthy of Ahriman.
The army champions are Sepansaar, Shahpoor,
And Andian, who secure their belts, eager for battle.
Gostaham positions himself next to the king
To serve as a shield against the enemy.

PART TWENTY-NINE

Bahraam fails to see the Rumis among the troops.
He pauses, utterly silent, then commands
The timpani to be strapped to elephants.
The face of the world stirs like the flows of the Nile.
He climbs on a white elephant,
And his battle companions despair of his fortune.

Launching his beast toward the right wing
Bahraam says to Shahpoor, "O miserable traitor,
Did you not promise in your letter that you would
Come to me but not on a bloody battlefield?
This is not a behavior worthy of an Iranian!
You freely abandon your body to annihilation."

Shahpoor says, "O deev face,
Have you lost your head to slavery?
What is this letter you mention to our noblemen?"

The powerful Khosrow interjects, and says to Shahpoor,
"This letter conformed to this man's intentions.
As a result, you will be recompensed by me
And by the members of my royal court.
When the time arrives, I shall explain to you
And refute any suspicion that may be tied to you."

Bahraam understands Khosrow's strategy.
He is troubled by this affair and ashamed.
In a state of irritation and mounted on his elephant,
His mind intent on battle, the usurper swiftly
Charges alone toward Khosrow's army center.

At the sight of him, the king says to Andian,
"O valiant and fierce lion,
Bring down a shower of shots on his elephant,
Convert your bows into moist spring clouds."

All the Iranians, favored by fortune, bind their bows,
And the elephant trunk is so riddled with shots
That its beastly body turns the color of the River Nile.

Bahraam instantly demands a hand horse
And a helmet that would befit a king,
But a shower of shots rains down once again

233

On the proud warrior's charger.
This man, avid for battle, dismounts,
Picks up the sides of his coat of mail, tucks them
Into his belt, protects his head with his shield,
And draws his sharp, piercing sword
To bring death into the ranks of the combatants.
Many run away at the sight of Bahraam,
Dropping their Chaadji bows and arrows.

The leader swiftly climbs on a fresh charger.
He rides it into the Iranian army core,
Targeting the king's position at the lead.
He causes the troops in the center division to scatter,
And the banner of the world master disappears.

From there, Bahraam prepares to assail the right wing,
The location of the supplies behind the Iranian line.
Khosrow rushes forth like a wolf chasing a lamb.
Gordooy commands this wing, a valiant, ambitious
Man who, recognizing his brother, raises his bow,
And the two craving men, fall on each other.
It is as if they mix one with the other.

Some time passes with them wrestling body to body.
Bahraam says to Gordooy, "O fatherless man,
How could you bind your bow against your brother?"

Bandooy replies, "O forest wolf, have you not heard
The great story, that anyone who has a friendly brother
Is happy, but better have neither vein nor skin
Than to have a brother who is your enemy?
You are a man eager for blood. You are evil,
As vile as Ahriman, and your heart negates the Creator.
A man should never rush to attack a brother
If he has the slightest respect for his name and honor!"

A furious Bahraam turns away from Gordooy
Who rushes to Khosrow, his heart
Full of horror, his warrior face black.

The king blesses him affectionately and says,
"May the spinning sky reward you!"
Then Khosrow marches to the center front,

And, seeing that his brave men are stirring,
He sends someone to Shahpoor to tell him,
"Support Moossil, fight, and depend on each other.
Perhaps you will be able to ride the wave of good fortune."

Then the king says to Gostaham,
"If a single Rumi were to engage in fight
And if Bahraam were to be killed
Or wounded in the scuffle,
All the Rumi warriors would raise their heads
To the vault of sky and would boast beyond measure.
But I wish not for them to raise their heads
And assume airs before us in the fight.
I have witnessed their high deeds.
They are like a herd on a tempestuous day.
It is best that I assail Choobineh once and for all
With a small company, wishing in this affair
Aid from none other than Yazdan,
My protector and shelter."

Gostaham replies, "O King, do not conspire
Against your sweet life, but if you are resolved,
Select warriors and avoid death on the field of vengeance."

Khosrow says, "You speak fairly.
Let us select a number of friends in the army."

Gostaham indicates ten plus four illustrious men
Among the most audacious Iranian riders.
First he writes his own name at the top of the list,
Then he adds Shahpoor and Andian;
Bandooy; Gordooy, the support of kings;
Aazargoshasp; Shirezil; Zangooy,
Who braves lions and elephants;
Tokhaareh, a man confident in the face of combat,
Who fiercely detests Yalan Sineh;
Farrokhzaad and the proud Khosrow;
Oshtaa, son of Pirooz, in the face of whom
The enemy melts like an object on fire;
The blessed Khorsheed; and Ormazd,
To whom adversaries are as weak as withered grass;
With Gostaham marching at the lead,

A noteworthy combatant in the war against Bahraam.

Having completed the selection of two times seven men,
Gostaham instructs them to move out of the ranks
And gather around Khosrow, who declares,
"O illustrious ones, draw your support from Yazdan.
May your hearts smile in merriment!
All things unfold at Yazdan's command.
Such is the way of the ancient dome of sky
From the beginning of time.
It is best to be killed in battle than to suffer
The elevation of a slave to a master.
You must protect me fiercely in this fight.
We must not delay when it is time to launch."

They pay homage to him in unison,
Acclaim him as world king, and swear
That they would never abandon him on this day.

The army master is appeased by their words.
He is happy that his subjects respond to him.
He hands over the army command to Bahraam[19]
And departs with his fourteen valiant companions.

At this moment, the voices of sentinels announce
To Choobineh the arrival of a sword-wielding division.
The ambitious man of awaked heart climbs on his horse,
A noose hooked on his saddle knob.
When he sees from above his charger
The handful of men, he selects a few brave warriors
And says to Yalan Sineh, "This man of ill race
Has proved his worth in battle, and I now know
That he is the only one who would dare advance.
He comes for retribution with a few men, but perhaps
He is flinging himself into the jaws of the whale.
He has no more than twenty warriors with him,
None of which I am able to recognize.
If he comes to me, I shall destroy the world.
If I prove less than him, I am not my father's son."

◇◇◇◇◇◇◇◇◇◇◇◇
19 Bahraam: Warrior in Khosrow's army, not to be confused with Bahraam Choobineh or Bahraam, descendant of Siaavoosh.

Then he says to Azar Goshasp and Yalan Sineh,
"Men must not hide their courage.
If we retreat before them, we shall be dishonored.
It is not necessary for us to be more than four,
For fortune is more favorable to me than to Khosrow."

There is a man whose name is Janfoorooz,
Who prefers the dark night to the light of day.
Bahraam entrusts him with the army
And departs with three lively companions.

Khosrow catches sight of him approaching
And says to his company, "Here comes a host.
Uphold your courage, for the moment
Has arrived when my life may be in danger.
My mace and I will take on the infamous Choobineh.
You may battle with his rebels.
You are fourteen friends against their three.
Heaven forbid for us to find ourselves crushed."

Niyaatoos and all the Rumis dress in armor,
Fasten their belts, and hasten toward
The battlefield by way of the mountain.
From its vantage point, they can observe the two hosts.

Each one says, "Why should a noble king risk his life,
Dismiss his warriors on the plain,
To foolishly fight alone for the crown?"
They all raise their hands to the sky,
Thinking that Khosrow's fate is surely dim.

When the warring Bahraam Choobineh, Yalan Sineh,
And Azar Goshasp launch their horses,
Khosrow's companions cut their ties to their king.
They are the herd, and Bahraam is the wolf,
All worried at the sight of the unrestrained deev.
With only Gostaham, Bandooy, and Gordooy remaining,
The crown-bearing hero invokes Yazdan.

With no other option in sight,
The world master swings his horse around
With Azar Goshasp lunging to chase after him.

The king says to Gostaham,
"Fate enchains me to a constricted spot.
What purpose did this foolish massacre serve
Since now they have witnessed me in flight,
Turning my back on them once again?"

Gostaham says, "The riders ran off.
How could you fight all alone?"

Khosrow glances behind him and notices
That Bahraam is galloping ahead of the others.
In an attempt to escape his enemies,
He cuts his horse's caparisons,
Hoping to lighten the load for him.
The three valiant, vengeful riders fall behind
But doggedly continue their pursuit.
Before him is a narrow slit in the mountain,
It's end blocked by a boulder,
And the world master remains far from his army.

The noble young man dismounts
And swiftly climbs on the boulder.
He stands there, on foot, the road blocked to him,
His royal heart in a state of great distress.
He could neither stop there nor find a path of escape.
Behind him rushes the terrible Bahraam, declaring,
"O deceitful one, the abyss opens to your greatness.
How did you hand over your fate to me?
How did you burden your shoulders with it?"

The position of the king is dire.
He has a sword at his back and a boulder in front.
He addresses Yazdan and says,
"O Creator, you are above the rotations of fate.
In this place of deep agony, you are my Savior,
And I shall neither pray to Saturn nor to Mercury."

As soon as his cry rises over the mountain,
The blessed Sooroosh appears on a white horse,
Dressed in a green robe. The sight reassures Khosrow.
Approaching him, Sooroosh takes his hand,
(One must not be surprised by this divine act),
Picks him up under the enemy's nose,

And takes him effortlessly away to then release him.

Khosrow, at times speaking, at times weeping,
Asks the archangel for his identity. The other replies,
"My name is Sooroosh, and you are now safe.
You may cease to lament since you are to be
World king, and you must behave with a pure heart."

After speaking, Sooroosh instantly disappears.
Never has anyone seen a more astonishing thing.

A stunned Bahraam invokes the name of the Creator
And shakily says, "Heaven forbid that my courage wanes
When my enemies are human, but now that I have
To fight with fairies, one must weep over my fate."

From there, Bahraam departs, heart full of pain,
Repenting for all his ventures and designs.

Niyaatoos, standing on the mountaintop,
Also implores divine grace,
And Mariam tears her cheeks with her nails
In her concern for her husband, the world master.

The army takes position on mountain, plain, and road.
The hearts of the Rumis are burning with ache.
When Niyaatoos no longer sees Khosrow,
He places Mariam on a golden litter and says to her,
"Remain here. I fear that our king has perished."

At that moment, Khosrow appears
On the other side of the mountain,
Far from the crowd, filling the army ranks with joy.
Mariam's heart is swiftly liberated from sorrow.

Khosrow reaches Mariam's side and recounts
To her the marvelous thing that happened:
"O moon, from the lineage of the Caesar,
The Creator, Justice Giver, vindicated my being.
I did not run away out of cowardice or fear,
For only the evil man is a coward in a fight.
In the slit where I was abandoned without an ally,
I invoked the Creator in my distress,

239

The One who keeps all the affairs of the world veiled.
There, Yazdan's servant received a divine revelation.
Never did the blessed Fereydoon, Toor, Salm,
Or Afraasiyaab see in dream a presage of victory
And royal power such as the one I witnessed today.
O illustrious one, reignite your will to resume battle
And initiate the war in the name of Khosrow."

28 | The Third Battle of Khosrow Parviz With Bahraam Choobineh

The army sets in motion, leaves the mountain,
And the world obscures with the stirring dust.

On his side, a pained Bahraam regrets his actions.
With no option left, he launches his troops.
The day is deprived of its light as he says,
"The one who drives his host must make use
Of wisdom, courage, and skill.
Those who have witnessed the blows of my javelin,
Those who have observed the nature of the warrior,
Selected me above the race of kings.
I shall bring down, once and for all,
The glory of Anushiravan!"

He advances recklessly at the head of his host
Toward the king, binds his bow, and throws
An arrow of simple wood aiming at the king's belt.
The shot rests without penetrating,
Suspended at the silk-covered strap of the belt.

One of the king's servants sees the blow,
Rushes over, and removes the arrow from the brocade.
At that moment, the king lunges toward the evil
Bahraam Choobineh and strikes him with his spear.
The spear does not penetrate the meshed rings of his belt,
But the point breaks in two, terrifying the leader's heart.

The king, at the sight of his broken spear, is furious
And strikes his enemy's helmet with his sword.
The shattered blade is fixed in the headpiece of steel.

All those who witness the sight,
All those who hear the sound of it, bless the king
And rush on his trail to break the vast host.
The royal troops are renewed by the king's feat.
With the moon and the sun growing obscure,
Bahraam turns his back on the king.
He knows that this challenge has placed him
Short of the ability to turn things around.

In view of the king's heroic deeds,
The Rumis and the Iranians launch their steeds.
They draw their swords of vengeance
And, like a massive mountain, assail enemy troops
Who fall in defeat and in a state of disarray.

Bandooy approaches the king and says,
"O King whose crown surpasses the sphere of moon,
Here come innumerable troops, like ants and locusts,
To cover the plain, the sand, and the barren land.
It is not worthy of you to spill further blood.
It is not worthy of a king to persevere against his subjects.
Better to allow them to ask for mercy
Than to wound or kill them on the battlefield."

Khosrow replies, "I have nothing against
People who renounce acts of iniquity.
They all fall under my protection.
They are the pearls lodged in my royal crown."

As it is, night advances over the dark mountain,
And the two armies withdraw to their respective camps.
With the constant sound of watch guards
And bells, few people are able to fall asleep.

The ruthless Bandooy emerges from camp,
Advancing between the two hosts.
He has singled out a courageous, eloquent
Herald gifted with a beautiful voice.
He commands him to climb on horseback,
Ride to the middle of camp, near the enemy,
And make the following proclamation:
"O criminals, slaves, seekers of fortune,
The world king has sworn by Yazdan

241

That he will forgive all your sins,
Whether public or private,
Even those belonging to the one who,
In times of war, has committed the most crimes
And has made an infamous name for himself."

All ears prick up at the sound of the night voice,
And the noble warriors in Choobineh's faction
Prepare to decamp and to disperse.

As the world-illuminating sun raises its head
Above the mountain and day dresses the earth
In a sumptuous, silken, golden cloak,
The plain is strewn with abandoned tents
While Bahraam ignores the night's occurrence.
No one is left in his camp except his most intimate friends.

Once apprised of the developments,
He crosses the line of tents and says to his allies,
"It is best to take flight than to wait around and be killed."

He asks his camel leader for three thousand
Strong camels able to endure strain and fatigue.
They are loaded with as much wealth as possible
In terms of clothing, carpets, golden and silver crockery,
Ivory thrones, bracelets, golden torques, and crowns.
Bahraam climbs on his horse to initiate his retreat.

29 | Bahraam Choobineh Takes Flight and Seeks Aid From the Emperor of Chin

As the dazzling sun decks its throne,
A patrol guard exits the king's camp
And fails to find anyone in Bahraam's enclosure.
The tents are still intact but vacant.

The king is infuriated by the sentry's report
Of the escape of his aggressive opponent.
He selects three thousand chain-mail-clad warriors
Mounted on barded steeds.
He commands Nastooh to straddle his horse.

The hero arms himself for the race,
Charging away, heart full of worry,
For he is not Bahraam's equal on the day of battle.

Bahraam, at the head of his troops, is not sure
Whether they are loyal to him or loyal to the land.
He runs off by way of roundabout paths,
His heart full of terror,
His load full of gold and silver.

Yalan Sineh and Azar Goshasp ride beside him
And drive the division on the same paths,
Recounting stories relating to ancient kings.
From afar, they spot a squalid village,
Unfitting to receive a noble lord.
Bahraam urges his horse forward, full of repentance,
His heart chagrined, his mouth parched.

Choobineh enters the house of an old woman.
They take care to speak softly to her
And gently ask her for bread and water.

The old woman listens to them,
Unfolds before them an old, tattered sheepskin spread,
And sets upon it a loaf of barley bread.

Yalan Sineh hands the barsom to Bahraam,
But to their chagrin, they forget to utter prayers.
Having eaten the bread, they ask for wine
And then quietly murmur prayers.

The old woman looks on and says to them,
"If you desire wine, I do have some,
And I also have an old squash
Of which I cut off the top when it was fresh.
I turned it into a cup and placed it as a lid
On the vase that contains the wine."

Bahraam says, "As long as there is wine to drink,
Who needs a more lavish cup?"

The old woman fetches the wine and the cup,
And Bahraam rejoices. He shares the drink

With his host, placing a full cup in her hand
So that she may enjoy as well, and says to her,
"O esteemed mother, what news have you of the world?"

She replies, "I have heard so many things,
My brain has grown weary.
Many people from town have come to our village
And have spoken at length of the war with Choobineh.
They say that his troops have united with the king's army
And that the leader has fled without an escort."

Bahraam says, "O holy woman, do tell me,
Were Bahraam's plans out of his mind's wisdom
Or did they belong to the world of fantasy?"

The woman says, "O illustrious man,
How did the deev trouble your sight?
Do you not know that since Bahraam,
Son of Goshasp, launched his horse against
The son of Hormozd, sensible men laugh at him?
He is no longer included in the company of noblemen?"

Bahraam reflects, "If such is the case
And I went after my dreams, I am now
Drinking wine out of a vessel made of squash
And eating barley bread on an old scrap of sheepskin."

Night falls, and he reclines in this dark place,
His tunic as a cover and his shoulder leaning on his armor.
But sleep does not wash over him, so unsettled is he.
Here is a man intent on winning his goals
Who is met with nothing but disappointment.

As the sun reveals its secretive face in the dome of sky,
The leader summons his troops, and they march off.
On the road is a beautiful field of reeds
With numerous men scattered about, cutting the stems.
They spot Bahraam in the distance with his escort
And exclaim, "O warrior, may your life be eternal!
Why have you traveled to this field of reeds?
There stand here before you many men who have
Washed their hands with blood in the throes of battle."

Bahraam replies, "There can only be
Warriors from the king's regiment here.
I have learned that the king, once we decided
To leave our camp and prepare for the long road,
Charged Nastooh to follow us in haste
With three thousand riders with specific directions
To attack us en masse.
But this warrior has neither warp nor weft.
If I see him, I shall quickly put an end to his life."

He commands the horses' straps to be stretched
And roams the length of his line of troops.
His riders tighten their belts, seize their Indian blades,
Set the field of reeds on fire, and destroy the army.
The entire plot is consumed, some men are slain
While others are ravaged by the flames.

At the sight of Nastooh, the bold Bahraam
Returns the bridle to his keen charger,
Removes Nastooh from his horse with his noose,
And proceeds to tie up his powerless hands.

Nastooh asks Bahraam for mercy:
"O illustrious ruler, why would you spill my blood?
Have pity on my overthrown fortune and forgive.
Do not kill me, so that I may assist you
And be your most humble servant."

Bahraam says, "My urgent desire is to encounter
Other foes on the battlefield the likes of you.
I shall not cut off your head.
It would be a source of shame for me
To have overcome a cavalier such as you.
Now that I release you from my grasp,
Run and tell Khosrow what you have witnessed."

Nastooh, at these words, kisses the ground,
Blesses him numerous times, and departs.
Bahraam leaves the field of reeds
And marches to Rey with his valiant companions.
He remains there to rest, then sets off
In the direction of the palace of the Emperor of Chin.

30 | Khosrow Parviz's Letter to the Caesar Announcing His Victory

On his side, Khosrow plunders the camp
That was occupied by Bahraam and his host.
He distributes Bahraam's pouches of gold and crowns.
Then he takes a racehorse and prepares for his prayers.

He finds a thicket full of weeds, dismounts, and enters.
He rolls around in the dust, addressing the Creator:
"O Master of Justice, pure and perfect,
You banished the enemy from this land.
You helped me beyond my greatest hopes.
I am your worshipper, your unworthy servant.
I walk to the beat of the World Master."

From there he strides to his own tent enclosure
Where his advisory is and summons a scribe.
They compose a letter on a sheaf of silk.
The king dictates to the Caesar the contents
Relating to the unfolding of the battle.

He begins in praise of Yazdan, Justice Giver,
Giver of power, fortune, and virtue:
"I have only beheld good deeds from the Creator.
We reached to Bahraam Choobineh with my host,
Rushing forth eager to execute vengeance.
He came at me in fight leaving me no way of escape.
If it had not been for the aid of Yazdan the pure,
I would have died at that moment.
The one with the breath of fire lost his strength
And his superiority, lost his army and his support.
At the crack of dawn, Bahraam absconded.
Alone, he left with just a handful of troops.
We set ablaze the land and the battleground.
At the command of Yazdan, the victorious,
I shall cut off his path once and for all."

They affix the king's seal to the letter,
And the emissary rides off with it.
He travels to the Caesar's palace and enters.

After reading the letter, the Caesar,
An enlightened man, steps down from his throne.
He speaks to his divinity: "O eternal Guide,
You always show us the right path!
You are the reason why your servant, Khosrow,
Has achieved great acclaim and victory.
You have raised his status far above anyone."

He gives an abundance of dinars, food, and fare
To the poor, then writes a reply as beautiful
As a tree in the garden of paradise.
At the start of the letter, he brings to mind
The World Owner, Creator of victory, glory, and justice;
Creator of Sun and Moon;
Creator of majesty and strength;
Giver of power and good fortune.
Remember to be grateful for as long as you live.
Only act with justice and righteousness in mind,
Whether in public or in private.
I have a crown, a memory of ancient Caesars,
Which I kept to be used at some future time;
One royal torque and two earrings;
One thousand one hundred golden costumes;
One hundred camel loads of golden dinars
And just as many of pearls and rubies;
A green war outfit sewn with golden threads,
Boasting a dazzling stone sewn at each end;
One bejeweled cross; one throne full of royal gems."

Four Rumi philosophers depart with the gifts.
At the news of their approach, Khosrow sends
A procession of one thousand to meet them.
The philosophers present themselves before Khosrow
With their letter, their gifts, and their offerings.

Surprised at the wealth and the abundance of the gifts,
Khosrow reads the letter, then turns to his vizier,
"The attire is for Christians. It is not appropriate for us.
Wearing such a thing with a cross would give
The impression that we have converted to their faith.
But if I fail to dress in it, it will sadden the Caesar.
Wounded, he will nurture undesirable thoughts of us.

Still, if do wear it, our noblemen will say,
    'Look at our king, who wears a robe and a cross,
    All for the sake of self-aggrandizement.'"

The vizier replies to Khosrow,
"An outfit cannot dictate your faith.
You are loyal to the Zoroastrian prophet,
And, furthermore, you are a relative of the Caesar."

The king dresses in the attire
And sets the bejeweled crown on his head.
He welcomes the noblemen to his court,
The Rumis, the Iranians, and all levels of people.
Those who have wisdom say,
"The robe was a gift from the Caesar."

Others claim, "The world ruler
Has secretly converted to Christianity."

31 | Mariam Diffuses the Anger Between Niyaatoos and Bandooy

The next day, Khosrow sits at court
And places the Kianian crown on his head.
They set up a spread in the garden
And summon the Rumi warriors.

Niyaatoos arrives with the army
And the four philosophers to sit around the spread.

Khosrow climbs down from the throne
With his bejeweled Rumi attire.
He happily takes his place among the guests.
Bandooy is in a state of anger, though he holds
The barsom and murmurs his prayers.

Niyaatoos, at the sight of him, tosses his bread aside
And rises to exclaim: "How could you utter
Zoroastrian prayers with the cross nearby!
It is as if the Caesar is insulting the Messiah."

Bandooy strikes the face of one of the Rumis
With the back of his hand.

Khosrow is saddened by the developments.
His cheeks are as pale as the flower of the fenugreek.
He turns to Gostaham and says,
"This senseless warrior should not
Be drinking wine with animosity.
What he did to Niyaatoos will only turn against him."

Niyaatoos abandons the court and the palace,
Half drunk, and returns to his army.
He dons his Rumi chain mail
And walks off to disturb the royal gathering.

The Rumi riders, in a state of hostility,
Make an appearance at Khosrow's palace.
One of them was sent by Niyaatoos to say to Khosrow,
"Bandooy the wicked slapped one of our worshippers.
Either you send him to me or I shall instill chaos.
You will suffer more from me than you have
Endured at the hand of Bahraam Choobineh,
Who yearns to be the usurper of your royal throne."

Khosrow retorts, "No one hides his religion toward Yazdan.
Kiumars, Jamsheed, all the way to Kay Ghobaad,
No one ever mentioned the name of the Messiah.
Heaven forbid that I abandon the faith of my fathers,
Who were noblemen and world masters, holy parents;
Heaven forbid that I adopt the religion of the Messiah
And would pray at the table and convert to Christianity.
You have been misled, for I have seen
Many skilled Rumis on the day of battle.
No one ever incites war for no reason."

Mariam says, "I shall end this quarrel in your court.
Bring the high-born Bandooy to me
So that the Rumis may catch a glimpse of him.
I shall bring him back to you safe and sound.
No one ever seeks a senseless struggle."

The king sends Bandooy, ten cavaliers, and Mariam,
A wife so prudent her lips only utter sensible words,

To Niyaatoos to convey the message:
"Go to your father's brother and say,
    'O evil man, you voraciously seek battle
    Have you not seen how the Caesar assisted
    The king in maintaining his power and glory,
    How he concluded a peace accord with him,
    Formed an alliance, gave him wealth and men?
    Now you are about to break the terms of the treaty
    And deprive me of the respect due me
    As the daughter of the Caesar?
    Haven't you heard from the Caesar that Khosrow
    Would not abandon his religion upon his return to Iran?
    Do you not know that a wise poet bard
    Never strays from his ancient faith?
    Why do you speak with such brutality?
    Hold Bandooy's head close to your chest,
    And do not address him with unpleasant words.
    If he speaks outrageously, defending his faith,
    Do not ask for reason from a senseless man.
    Do not destroy the work of the Caesar
    Or the effort he has exerted.'"

At the same time, Khosrow confides in Mariam:
"I do not count Bandooy for much.
My heart weeps for my father's blood.
I am in a state of endless mourning.
My soul is full of the desire to avenge him,
And my tongue is charged with curses."

Mariam listens to him, departs as swift as wind,
And reports his speech to Niyaatoos, who blushes,
Accepts and approves the advice and the words.
When he sees Bandooy, he rises brusquely,
Asks for a magnificent horse from his treasurer,
Questions Bandooy on the customary subjects,
Smiles at him, and makes him an offering.
Then the two present themselves before the king.

Khosrow, at the sight of Niyaatoos, says,
"The heart of a malicious man does not seek virtue.
Bandooy only yearned for struggle and fight.
Guard yourself from dimming the earth for us.

Do not allow your impetuous nature to force
The Caesar to lose his hard work to the wind.
Stay with us for some time.
Let us engage in feast and revelry."

Niyaatoos replies, "O world master King,
Do not ask for sense from a drunken Rumi.
Continue in the faith of your fathers.
A sensible man does not change his religion."

They speak for a long time,
Then Niyaatoos returns to his camp.

32 | Khosrow Parviz Forgives Niyaatoos, Who Returns to the Caesar With the Rumis

The king says to Khorraad, son of Borzeen,
"Prepare to review the Rumi army
And estimate the number of troops, young and old.
Distribute two parts of our treasure to the Rumis.
Our generosity may ease their suffering."

He prepares robes of honor for deserving warriors
Who executed their duty on the day of battle.
They call for their horses from the royal stables.
He offers Niyaatoos so many precious stones,
Horses, and golden-belted slaves that he elevates
His head higher than the most noble of noblemen.

Then all the cities that Ghobaad, Hormoz, and
The highborn Kesra once seized from the Rumis
Are returned in accordance with a written edict.
By this action, he sprinkles honey on a bitter cup.

The Rumis take leave of the flourishing border
To return to their prosperous land of Rum.
Khosrow accompanies them for two stations,
Then he bids farewell to Niyaatoos
And makes his way back.

The following week, he takes the road

With ten intelligent and illustrious riders.
He marches to a camp in Aazargoshasp
And dismounts at the sight of the sanctuary.
He advances on foot, tearful, cheeks as yellow as the sun.
He crosses the threshold, arrives at the fire,
His face inundated with tears.
For one week, he recites the Zand Avesta,
Humbly and despondently circling the flame.

On the eighth day, he leaves the fire temple
Close to the time of the Feast of Saddeh.
He donates to the temple his part of the spoils of war:
Gold and silver crockery, fine stones, dinars, and gems.
He accomplishes everything
He had announced to his noblemen.
He distributes to the poor a wealth of dirhams,
Leaving no one wanting for anything.

From there he travels to the city of Andiv,[20]
Where he spends some time in rest and joy.
It is a city on the limits of the salty desert,
Its soil of little value to anyone.

A beautiful hall is prepared in Anushiravan's palace.
A throne is decked in gold.
Khosrow arrives and assumes his grandfather's seat
As victorious world master and Yazdan worshipper.

He summons a scribe and his ingenious vizier.
They write qualifications for the Iranians,
According to the ways of famed kings,
Favorites of fortune. The worldly Bandooy,
Noble and wise, directs the affair.

Khosrow assigns Khorasan to Gostaham, commanding
Him to establish new customs and spread justice.
Borzmehr is to be his vizier in all his ventures,
A worldly scribe with a handsome, inviting face.

The king, seeing the sky spinning to his favor,

◇◇◇◇◇◇◇◇◇◇◇◇◇◇
20 Andiv: An ancient city. Unclear of its exact location.

Places the governance of Daaraab-Guerd
And Estakhr in the hands of Raam Barzeen,
Appends a golden seal to the diploma,
And commands him to take slaves
And robes of honor to Shahpoor.

According to Kianian custom, Khosrow orders
Another diploma and seal to be taken to Andian,
Entrusting him with the land of Kerman,
Since he counts among the most renowned chiefs.

He offers another region to Gordooy
And places a golden seal on the letter.
At the same time, he gives Balooy the land of Chaadj,
Sending him a diploma and an ivory throne.

He gathers and counts the keys to his treasury
And gives the lot to the son of Tokhaareh.
After these actions, he addresses the noblemen,
Commands them to obey Khorraad, son of Borzeen,
Whose wishes are to be executed in the world
And whose name appears on all the writings.
All the army members who remained loyal
To the illustrious king during the time of war
Receive from him royal robes of honor,
And each is offered a district to rule over.

An eloquent herald, a great and prudent man
With a beautiful voice, proclaims everywhere:
"O subjects of the world ruler, may you
Only celebrate the king with acts of justice.
Guard yourselves from exercising vengeance,
Spilling blood, and being the instigators of crimes.
If a subject complains about having to suffer
From the wicked deeds of an oppressor,
The evildoer will end up on the gallows in this life
And in the throes of fire in the other world.
You are all the masters of your treasures,
Of everything you have acquired by your hard labor.
Consume, enjoy, or give away what you have.
Those who have nothing may make a request.
I have a treasury in every city,

Either amassed by my ancestors or by myself.
I commanded the treasurer to provide
Clothing and food to those in need.
If someone lacks a meal in the morning, he will
Obtain three mahns of corn from my treasurer,
Under the condition that he invokes divine blessings
On the king and he works to cultivate the land."

Since he converts the world into a paradise
With his sense of justice,
We must always acclaim the king.
Let us praise him for making the world flourish.
Such a king is far better than one who,
Though gifted with vast knowledge,
Surrenders to impure actions.

33 | Ferdowsi's Lament on the Death of His Son

I have passed my sixty-fifth year.
It would be futile to extend a hand to gain wealth.
If I did not apply the advice I offer others to myself,
I could only fix my sights on my son's death.

He left in his time of youth, though it was my turn to go.
The grief I must endure makes my body devoid of soul.
I hasten in the hopes of joining him soon, and,
If I reunite with him, I shall reproach him lovingly:
"It was for me to depart. Why did you go against
My wishes and steal from me my days of peace?
You were my support in times of misfortune.
Why did you drift away from your aging companion?
Have you met new and youthful friends
Along the way that you would choose
To leave me behind so hastily?"

At the age of thirty-seven, this young man
Did not find the world to his taste and departed.
He had a way of being quite harsh with me.
He grew angry, decided to turn his back on me.
He left me with my grief and affliction.
He left me to drown my eyes in tears of blood.

Presently he travels toward the light,
Where he will save a place for his father.
He has left for some time now,
And none of his traveling companions came back.
He must be waiting for me,
Ready to scold me for taking so long to join him.
I have passed the age of sixty-five.
He was only thirty-seven.
He failed to ask the old man his permission.
He hurried away while I linger on here,
Hoping to witness the completion of my work.

May the Creator bring splendor to your soul!
May wisdom be your mind's armor!
I implore the holy World Master,
Giver of our daily bread and our nurturing parent,
To forgive all my sins
And shine a bright light into my dimming moon.

PART THIRTY

The Thirty-Eight-Year Reign
of Khosrow Parviz (continued)

1 | The Story of Bahraam Choobineh and the Emperor of Chin

Now recount the ancient tales,
Recount the events that unfold
When Bahraam Choobineh reaches
The land of Turks and meets with
The Emperor of Chin and his aging leaders.

Ten thousand heroes of awakened hearts,
Elite cavaliers, march forth to meet him on the road.
At the head is the son and brother of the emperor,
Each accompanied by a wise man and advisor.

Nearing the throne, Bahraam dismounts,
Greets and blesses the prince.
The emperor rises at the sight of him, kisses him,
Takes him in his arms, and strokes his cheek.
He questions him on the hardships of his journey,
His grief, and the fight against the king and his host.
Then he addresses questions to two vengeful heroes,
Izad Goshasp and Yalan Sineh.

Bahraam sits on the silver throne,
Takes the emperor's hand into his,
And says, "O glorious prince,
Chief of the army of Turks and Chin,
You know that no one feels safe
In the presence of the wicked Khosrow Parviz.
Should he find you resting from your fatigues,
He will take the opportunity to cause you harm.
Should you live your life in peace, he will
Trouble you and double your heartaches.
If you receive me, if you can be my support
In good and bad fortune, I shall be your friend.
I shall act as your lieutenant in every circumstance.
But if your intention differs from mine,
I shall leave to find another haven,
Perhaps I shall make my way to the land of India."

The emperor replies, "O illustrious one,
May you never abandon us and our land!
I shall treat you as my ally. What do I say, ally?
I shall consider you as dear to my heart as my son.
My land and my people, subjects great and small,
Will assist both you and me in this venture.
I shall place you above the leaders of Turks.
I shall make you independent from my noblemen."

Bahraam asks for a solemn oath.
Until then, these are mere words, and he asks
The emperor to engage his soul in a covenant.

The emperor says, "By the mighty Creator,
My Guide and yours, I swear to remain
Your most sincere friend for as long as I live.
I swear to share your fate in good and bad fortune."

Then they prepare two palaces for the guests.
The emperor sends all sorts of fabrics, servants,
Clothing, provisions, necessary carpets,
Gold and silver crockery, dinars, brocade,
And jewels worthy of a king. With the gifts,
The gleam returns to Bahraam's dim soul.

Never does the Emperor of Chin
Engage in a game of polo, an assembly,
Or a hunt without the presence of Bahraam.
They live in this way for some time,
As close friends, with the emperor
Blessing Bahraam and praising him.

One of the great leaders, a friend of the emperor,
His assistant in times of battle, a man of high birth
By the name of Maghaatooreh, to whom the emperor
Owes his glory and triumphs, arrives every morning
At the ruler's side to kiss his hand and pay homage to him.
At every visit, he takes a part of the princely treasure,
In excess of one thousand dinars.

Bahraam observes the transaction for some time
In astonishment, and one day he says to the emperor,
"O powerful man, respected among princes,

Every morning, at the hour of the audience,
This Turk receives one thousand dinars from you.
Is this a gift to him or is it the army's monthly salary?"

The emperor replies, "It is my custom,
And my religion dictates to never refuse a raise
To a man who distinguishes himself by his courage
And by his tenacity in moments of danger and of war.
This man, now more powerful than I am,
Is ambitious and hardworking,
So I use the gold as a charm on him.
If I were to neglect him, my host would boil in rage,
My troops would obscure my brilliant day."

The resourceful Bahraam says, "O chief of the land,
Have you designated Maghaatooreh as your ruler?
When the world master is valiant and aware,
He must not surrender power to an inferior.
Would you like me to get rid of him,
Or would that be a source of humiliation for you?"

The emperor says, "You have my permission
To undertake any venture your heart desires.
If you free me from his presence and his grip,
You would put an end to all the disputes."

Bahraam says to him, "Tomorrow at dawn,
When Maghaatooreh comes to demand his dinars,
Do not smile at him, do not look at him,
Do not even offer him a reply,
Or if you must, speak to him with resentment."

The night passes, and at the dawn of the next day,
Maghaatooreh arrives and demands his golden coins.
The emperor, world master, does not glance his way
Or even lend an ear to the demanding, belligerent Turk.

Infuriated, Maghaatooreh says to the ruler,
"O renowned man, why do you treat me with scorn?
Perhaps the Persian nobleman,
Who arrived in our land with thirty of his companions,
Works at turning you away from justice
And wishes to ruin your army."

Bahraam says, "O hostile leader, why speak so bitterly?
If the emperor follows my advice and my path,
His mind will never forget my counsel.
I shall not allow you to strip him of his treasury.
If we agree that you are worth three hundred riders
And that in battle you contend with a lion as prey,
Still it does not justify the fact that every morning
You demand from the king loads of golden coins.

Maghaatooreh's head fills with hatred and outrage.
He extends a hand in an outburst,
Draws from his quiver an arrow of poplar wood,
And says to Bahraam,
"This is my sign and my interpreter in battle.
If you present yourself tomorrow at court,
You better beware of my arrow's point."

At these words, Bahraam grows more eager to fight.
He advances wielding an arrow of poplar wood
With a tip of steel. He hands it to Maghaatooreh:
"Here is a souvenir of me; see if it will serve you."

Maghaatooreh stomps out of the emperor's court
To return in haste to his tent pavilion.

2 | Bahraam Choobineh Kills Maghaatooreh

As night gently gathers its dark cloak
From across the earth to fold it away
And dawn blossoms on the mountaintop,
Maghaatooreh dresses in his battle chain mail,
And exits, his Tooranian blade firm in his hand.

At the news, Bahraam calls for his charger
And his armor worthy of a king,
And they select a field so dry and barren
A leopard would never leap into it.

The emperor mounts his horse
And rushes over with his Turkish servants to see
Which of the two leaping lions would be victor.

Maghaatooreh arrives on the battlefield,
Raising the dust to the clouds and shouting to Bahraam,
"What have you to say now about your courage?
Are you the one who will engage in this fight
Or the Turk of lion heart, the emperor's servant?"

Bahraam replies, "You come forward,
Since your words instigated this hostility."

Maghaatooreh invokes the World Master.
He hooks the rope to the two ends of his bow,
Cheerfully takes the arrow, and releases his finger.
The arrow strikes the rider's belt,
But the gleaming steel fails to bore through the mail.

Bahraam stays away for some time
To allow Maghaatooreh to grow weary of battle.
Maghaatooreh, assuming Bahraam dead,
Shouts and is about to leave the battlefield.

But Bahraam shouts back at him, "O eager fighter,
You have not successfully killed me yet.
What are you doing retreating to your tent?
You have spoken; remain and listen to the reply.
If you are still alive upon hearing it, you may go."

He picks up an arrow able to pierce a breastplate
And next to which iron is as malleable as wax.
He flings it toward the valiant rider's waist.
The leader's mind instantly abnegates
Any lingering craving he may have for war.

When Maghaatooreh had climbed on his horse to fight,
He tied his two feet firmly to the stirrups.
Now his head bows low, his eyes are filled with tears.
His saddle of poplar wood functions as his bed.
Yet, as wounded as he is, he remains on the seat.
As struck as he is, he ushers his war horse forward.

Bahraam says to the Emperor of Chin, "O prince,
This ambitious man is asking for a gravedigger."

The emperor replies, "Look closer, you will find him

Lying down on his horse's back, quite alive."

Bahraam says, "O noble-minded prince,
His frame is about to tumble down into the dust.
May your enemies' bodies always recline,
Just as this one is on his Tooranian horse."

The emperor sends a valiant rider
To the lion-like, illustrious man,
And he notices that he is as fierce as a beast.
He sees that, still tied up to the horse,
Maghaatooreh has died wretchedly
And may now reach a time when he may
Rest from the vicissitudes of life and fate.

The emperor secretly smiles, in awe of Bahraam,
So unique in the world. He sits in his palace, pensive.
In his joy, his headdress rises to touch Saturn.
He asks for silver, weapons, horses, slaves, a crown
And an imperial throne, dinars, jewels worthy of a king,
And all sorts of weaponry and gear for battle.

A messenger takes the lot from the emperor's palace
And hands it over to the valiant Bahraam's treasurer.

3 | Kappi the Lion Kills the Emperor's Daughter

Some time passes in this way,
During which peace reigns supreme.

At this time, there lives in the mountains of Chin
A number of incredible wild beasts.
Among them is a creature larger than a horse,
With two black horsehair curls akin to ropes,
A yellow body, black ears, and black jaws.
He prefers to reside in the warmest corners,
And only appears visible to people at the noon hour.

His two front talons are like lion claws,
And his roar pierces the densest clouds.
He is referred to as the lion Kappi.

The fear he instills in the people is so tremendous,
For they are stunned at the destruction he causes.
He is able to inhale boulders with his breath,
Swallow men, whether on foot or on horseback,
Obscuring the day for the bravest warriors
And wreaking havoc all around.

The emperor has a daughter as beautiful as the moon,
If the moon were to have two black curls, red lips,
A nose like a silver reed, a smiling coral mouth,
And two dreamy black eyes of narcissi.
Her father and her mother tremble in fear for her,
Even dreading the graze of the sun rays on her head.

One day she marches to the plain,
Wishing to wander through the prairies,
While the world emperor is on the other side,
Engaged in the hunt, and, in the castle,
Her mother is in consultation with a trusting wise man.

The young daughter advances into the fields
With her companions, with wine and cupbearer.
The lion Kappi spies on them from the mountaintop.
He descends, draws in the princess with one inhale,
And proceeds to quickly devour her.
The beautiful maiden disappears from the world,
As her life instantly comes to an abrupt halt.

At the news, the emperor's cheeks turn black,
And the mother plucks her hair out.
They mourn her for many years,
Consumed by the ardent fire of grief.
They spend every moment of their days
Strategizing ways to destroy the dragon
And free Chin from his calamitous presence.

After Bahraam's battle with Maghaatooreh
And the death of the latter,
The emperor's wife wishes to see him.
She highly praises him and his high deeds.

One day she sees him striding on horseback
With one hundred illustrious Iranians, preceded

By men on foot and accompanied by a guide.

The empress asks for the identity of the man
Who appears so powerful and majestic.
Her attendant tells her, "He is an illustrious ruler."

A second servant says to the first,
"You are ignorant if you do not know his name.
He is Bahraam Choobineh, the warrior,
Who ruled as king in Iran for some time,
His crown rising above the sphere of the moon.
Noblemen call him Bahraam the valiant,
For he surpasses all the kings in courage.
Since he arrived from Iran to Chin,
The earth shakes beneath his charger.
Our master, the emperor, called him prince
And placed on his head a royal crown."

The Chini queen says, "Since he is so glorious,
We could live happily beneath the shade of his wings.
I shall go to him straight away and ask him for a favor,
Should the emperor agree with me.
I hope that he will aspire to avenge us from the dragon.
I hope that he will listen to my grief and maledictions."

The servant says, "If you recount this to the prince,
You will never hear from the lion Kappi again
Except for the fact that he is dead and the wolves
Have dragged his limbs into the forest to devour."

The empress rejoices, somewhat relieved
And hopeful after her daughter's devastating loss.
She rides her horse to the emperor
And tells him what she saw and heard.

The emperor says, "It would be humiliating for us
To speak of how Kappi the lion seized our daughter
In a land with a leader of my stature.
It would be a dishonor to my name and my race.
Bahraam does not know that this ferocious dragon
Can tear apart a mountain of steel with its breath.
No matter how illustrious a princess may be,
Life is nevertheless dear to a king."

The empress replies, "I long to execute retribution
And avenge the life of my precious daughter,
Who was the shining light of my eyes.
Whether there is shame or glory,
I yearn for my wish to be granted."

Many days pass. The woman hides her vengeful plans.
The emperor asks for a feast to spread his splendor.
He sends for the valiant Bahraam
And, upon his arrival, seats him on a silver throne.

At the sounds of the feast, the emperor's wife
Hurries out of her chambers and approaches Bahraam.
She showers him with praise and says,
"May our lands prosper by your power!
O nobleman, I have a favor to ask of you.
May you be kind enough to grant it."

Bahraam says, "I am at your command.
My will and my duty dictate my obeisance."

The queen tells him, "Not far from here
Is a meadow worthy of a site for feast.
Chini youths hold festivities there every spring.
At an arrow's length from the woods,
You will see a mountain as dark as tar in which
Dwells a dragon that brings us tremendous grief.
We have named him the lion Kappi,
And I know no other name for the beast.
The Emperor and I had a daughter
To whom the sun paid homage.
She left the palace sauntered to this place
While the emperor hunted nearby with his host.
The fierce dragon emerged from the mountain
And seized our daughter, light of our eyes,
In its rapacious, ravenous, savage jaws.

"Every spring, Kappi goes on the hunt,
Barring youths and warriors their chance to live.
They have all died in the grips of the wicked creature
Who has vastly destroyed this once-flourishing land.
Valiant riders and steadfast men have led expeditions
To this mountain, but at the sight of Kappi's claws,

His chest, his black ears, his head and limbs,
At the sound of his earth-shattering roar,
Their hearts instantly quivered in retreat.
Next to him, what are lions, tigers, and whales?
With such knowledge of the stakes,
No one dares contend with the beast."

Bahraam replies, "I shall go tomorrow at sunrise
And look around to survey this site of feast.
I swear by the power of Yazdan, Giver of my force,
By the Creator of Moon and Sun, that
I shall free the meadow from the dragon's presence
If only someone can show me the way at dawn.

4 | Bahraam Choobineh Kills Kappi the Lion

As the disk of moon appears in the sky and dark night
Shakes its black ringlets, members of the assembly,
Well inebriated, retreat to their respective dwellings.

Upon the withdrawal of night's indigo manes
And the appearance of the golden sun in all its splendor,
The valiant Bahraam dresses in his special coat of mail
And entrusts his illustrious body to Yazdan.
He picks up his noose, his bow, three arrows
Of triple wood, and a two-pointed hunter's spear.

At the foot of the lofty mountain,
He commands his escort to leave him and turn back.
He nears Kappi, whose massive form dims the mountain.
He arms himself in the midst of the boulders,
Launches his horse with his noose rolled up
On the saddle hook, rubs his bow to stretch it,
And raises it, invoking the help
Of Yazdan, Giver of joy and happiness.

The lion Kappi is in the basin of a spring,
Rolling in the water for some time. Then he emerges,
His skin moist and impenetrable by arrows and shots.

He notices the valiant cavalier advancing

Toward him, as aggressive as a male lion.
He sharpens his teeth and battle claws,
And his head ignites with warring ardor.
He thunders a vicious growl and grabs a boulder
With his claws, which sets off a spray of sparks.
The formidable dragon takes a stance of attack,
Ready to engulf the warrior hero.

The valiant Bahraam rubs his bow once again.
The gleam of his arrows has the power to eclipse sunlight.
The bold man flings an arrow that fills Kappi's heart
With disgust and dissolves any lingering desire to fight.

Bahraam shoots another arrow to his head,
Provoking blood to gush out like a waterfall.
Witness to the strength of the attacking beast,
Bahraam sends a third shot into its paw.
Then he detaches his noose, climbs the mountain,
Pierces the wild beast at its waist, and, with his spear,
Colors the naked boulder red with blood.
Then with his sword, he strikes the dragon's body
And cuts it in half. He separates the head
From the corpse and flings it away like a vile thing.
Then he descends the mountain, marches gaily
To the emperor, and recounts his adventure.

The emperor and his wife stride to the forest
And climb to the mountain heights.
The leader of Chin embraces Bahraam,
And from then on gives him the title of king.
When the empress arrives, she kisses Bahraam's hand.
The valiant members of the emperor's family
Approach, along with the leaders of Chin,
And shout triumphantly as if the earth is about to split.
They shower Bahraam with praise
And toss gold and gems over him.

At his palace, the Emperor of Chin selects a friendly
Messenger to give Bahraam one hundred crates
Full of silver, bolts of fabric,
And many other gifts including slaves, .
He says to the envoy, "Go to the hero and say,

'In the women's chamber, I have a daughter
Who is the diadem over the heads of princesses.
If you ask for her hand in marriage,
I shall offer you my army and my land.'"

Bahraam replies, "That is all very well.
The world owner rules over his slaves."

The emperor summons a scribe who writes
An investiture on silk whereby Bahraam
Is to receive the royal daughter
As well as the command of the nation.

An offering is prepared according to Chini custom,
Bringing in many diadems and belts,
And the emperor says to Bahraam,
"Distribute all of this among the Iranian warriors
And leaders who are rightly deserving."

Bahraam abandons himself to feast, to giving,
And to the hunt, without further thought
Or worry over the rotations of fate.

The renowned noblemen of Chin express
Deference to the hero, and the Chini people say,
"We are your slaves, living only to serve you."

5 | Khosrow Parviz Learns of Bahraam's Feats and Writes a Letter to the Emperor

Bahraam continues to enjoy life and to give generously.
Everyone pays homage to him, and this state remains so
Until news reaches Iran and the king of brave men:
"Bahraam has acquired, without much effort,
A kingdom and a treasure greater
And more valuable than yours."

Bahraam's deeds send tremors through Khosrow's heart.
Chagrined, he holds counsel with his noblemen,
Speaks at length and suggests all sorts of strategies.
In the dark night, he summons a scribe

Who hones the end of a reed as sharp as an arrow's tip.
He composes a letter to the Emperor of Chin
As if he is writing with a sword instead of a reed.

He begins in praise of the Creator,
"The all-powerful, omniscient, nurturing
Parent of all things and all beings,
Who places above us Moon, Sun, and Saturn,
Who seats the king upon the royal throne,
Who brings down criminals and infuses
Divine wisdom in those who possess it.
If you declare that Yazdan is One, free of mate
And equal, you will surely evade ignorance,
Iniquity, perversity, weakness, and perdition.
Anyone in search of virtue will find happiness.
Cursed be the one who reaches to commit a breach.
If you walk down the Creator's path,
You must turn away from ingratitude.

"The king once had an ungrateful subject
Who rudely and disdainfully failed
To recognize his superior and the divine Master.
His name is Bahraam Choobineh,
May he never attain the object of his desires!
He was a poor child, a nameless soul,
Whom my father drew out of obscurity.
When the world king made him his army chief,
His answer came from his wicked essence.
What he accomplished in the world
Is well known to nobleman and commoner.
No man of distinction, no man of elevated
Intelligence would tolerate him by his side.

"He came to you, and you received him.
You extended a hand to him
As if he is holder of a noble status.
No man endowed with righteousness
Will understand your gesture.
As for me, I deeply frown upon it in disapproval.
Have you forgotten his actions and the way
He mistreated you, slashing you with his noose?
You must not turn your glory sterile

269

And sell your sense of peace to Bahraam.
When they hand you this letter,
Allow your penetrating mind to reflect.
Should you send the slave back to me,
Feet enchained, you would have chosen wisely.
Otherwise, I shall send an army from Iran and
Render black the shining day to Tooranians."

The Emperor of Chin receives the letter, reads it,
And says to the envoy, "Tomorrow morning,
When you appear at court, ask for a reply."

The envoy departs with an anguished heart
Unable to either sleep or rest during the night.
He is still until the torch of sun shines above,
Then goes to the emperor's court.

The emperor calls a scribe equipped with a reed,
Musk, and Chini silk, and dictates a reply
Beginning in this way: "As a slave, I give thanks
To the Creator, in the manner of rulers and kings.
I have read your letter and sat the envoy before me.
The way you address me is not the way of kings
But rather the manner in which one addresses a slave.
It does not suit a descendant of your ancient line
To fail to distinguish between great and small
And assign a rightful ruler the place of a subject.

"The entire lands of Chin and Tooran are mine.
The Hephthalites obey my command.
I have never transgressed from the terms of a treaty.
Do not then address me in such a way.
I have taken Bahraam's hand into mine.
But if I fail to keep my word to him,
Men will not consider me of pure race.
I do not fear Yazdan, the holy, and,
No matter how much your power prospers,
A better thing would be to expand your intelligence."

He affixes his seal on the letter and says to the envoy,
"You must consider wind your companion."

The envoy returns to the side of the king,

Crossing the land in less than a month.
Khosrow Parviz reads the reply, writhes
In his seat and begins to fear the rotations of fate.
He convenes the Iranians and repeats to them
The words of the emperor from beginning to end.
He shows them the letter, which, once read,
Sends the noblemen into a state of deep reflection.

Finally the Iranians answer him:
"O King, you are the glory of the throne
And Kianian crown. Hold counsel with an old man.
Such an affair cannot be dealt with in a letter.
Do not dim the flame of your ancient majesty.
Select in Iran an intelligent, eloquent, brave,
And literate old man to send to the emperor
So that he may speak to him and learn of his intentions.
He will reveal to him Bahraam's true wicked nature,
How he abused his post of leader
Only to reach a higher state of power,
And how he wished to reduce his master to captivity.
Let the envoy remain for one month or one year,
As long as needed for him to succeed in his mission.
If Bahraam is the emperor's son-in-law,
It will not be easy to speak against him.
The mystery must be penetrated by gentle means."

6 | The Emperor of Chin Prepares an Army

The bold Bahraam learns that a letter
From Iran has reached the Emperor of Chin.
He runs to him and says, "O glorious prince,
I hear that the cursed one writes letter upon letter.
Let us muster a valiant host so that
The land of Iran can fall into your possession.
I shall seize Iran and Rum with my sword
And declare you king of these territories.
Sentries will shout your name in the conquered lands.
I shall execute Khosrow, man of evil race.
May his head and his footprint be damned!
If I consent to strap my belt as your subject,
It is to pluck out the roots of the Sassanian race."

271

The emperor grows pensive.
Worry proliferates in his heart, like trees in a forest.
He convenes the most eminent, eloquent,
And wise old men, each endowed with a superior memory.
He relays Bahraam's words and divulges the secrets.

The sages, who are not only allies but just
As many relatives as are strangers, respond to him,
"It is a wicked and difficult affair to declare
That the measure of the Sassanian race has been filled.
However, if Bahraam commands the army
And shows the way to intelligent men,
He will gain friends in Iran,
Since his ally is the Emperor of Chin.
The venture will conclude with the aid of good fortune.
We must lend an ear to Bahraam's discourse."

Bahraam's heart is transformed by these words.
He smiles and makes a new resolution.
All the heroes are of the advice that they must
Select two young men able to take command,
Two unfaltering and inexorable warriors.

The emperor calls two Chini commanders to his side.
One is Chinooy, a nobleman,
The other is Zangooy, a stubborn warrior.
He seats them in the office, offers them a salary,
And advises them: "Be vigilant on battle day.
Keep an eye on Bahraam, whether in joy or in fury.
Seize the banks of the Jayhoon,
And make the dust rise to the dome of sky."

He entrusts them with a valiant army
Composed of illustrious and bold lions.
The sound of timpani rises at Bahraam's palace gates.
The dust renders the sun's face as black as ebony.
Bahraam turns westward, toward Iran
On the morning of the day of Sepandarmaz.[21]

---

21 Sepandarmaz: The fifth day of any month on the solar calendar.

7 | Khosrow Sends Khorraad, Son of Borzeen, to the Emperor

The great king learns that the wolf has left the woods
And the brave Bahraam brings an army so mighty
It steals splendor from the skies.

Khosrow Parviz says to Khorraad Borzeen,
"Take the direction of the emperor's palace.
Go to the despicable man and talk to him,
For you are the wisest, most eloquent man in Iran."

He opens the door to his treasury and offers him
Jewels, swords, and golden belts in such abundance
That the stunned Khorraad invokes the name of the Creator.

He travels to Chin with the gifts
And crosses the Jayhoon River,
Attempting to follow the roads less traveled.
At the emperor's court, he takes precautions
And selects a messenger to announce his arrival.

The emperor prepares the audience hall
And commands him to be introduced.
Khorraad approaches, greets him, and says,
"Your slave awaits your permission to speak."

The emperor replies, "A gentle voice
Restores an old man's heart to youth.
Tell me what you are here to say, for words
Constitute the core while omission forms the rind."

The discussion reminds Khorraad, son of Borzeen,
Of ancient words. He begins with gratitude:
"To the supreme Creator of the vault of sky,
Of Earth and Time; Giver of power and powerlessness.
The revolving dome, devoid of any support,
Burst into life suddenly at divine command.
One cannot ask why or how.
Glory be to the One who creates all things,
Sky and Sun, night and day, rest and sleep.
Power is with the divine, and we are slaves

273

Praising divine perfection and divine creation,
Which gives to one crown and splendor,
And to another misery and enslavement.
The World Creator holds no favors for a king
And has no hostility for an inferior subject.
One and all, great or small, we are all born
Out of dust and to the dust we shall return.

"Beginning with Jamsheed, the sublime,
And with Tahmures, the glorious world master,
And continuing with Kay Ghobaad and others
Of whom we have conserved the memory:
Kay Khosrow, the illustrious Rostam, and Esfandiar
All retained from the world nothing more than a casket.
They sucked on poison instead of theriac.
Now the King of Iran is your relative,
His happiness and grief are dependent
On either your growth and victory or your decline.
In the time of the glorious kings,
The Emperor of Chin was Khosrow's ancestor
On his mother's side, keeping our alliance tight,
But now things have changed.
May the Giver of Victory shower you with blessings!
May the heads of kings form the ground beneath your feet!"

The emperor replies, "O nobleman, seller of wisdom,
If there is in Iran another man like you,
He is in a state to celebrate the skies as one should."

Khorraad is assigned a place of honor next to the ruler,
By whose order he produces the king's gifts,
Which are then handed over to the treasurer.

The emperor says to him,
"May you never be deprived of wealth.
If you wish to accept something from me, tell me,
So that I may in turn receive what you bring to me.
In any case, you shine brighter than any present
As the diadem over the heads of learned men."

A sunny residence is prepared for Khorraad,
Decorated with all sorts of wall coverings.
He is welcomed at the emperor's table,

At the hunt, in feast, and during times of drinking.
He awaits a moment when the emperor is inactive,
Rushes to speak to him and says,
"Bahraam is a man of evil race,
Far worse than the wicked Ahriman.
He is ready to betray the wisest at any price.
King Hormozd brought him out of nothingness
And raised his status above the sun with his favors.
No one in the world even knew his name,
And everything worked to his favor.
If he shows some loyalty to you, he will
Eventually turn his back on you and betray you.

"He acted in the same manner with Khosrow,
But he reveres neither king nor Creator.
Once he became powerful with the aid of his majesty,
He rejected his loyalty and his duty toward him.
He coveted the dignity of the King of Kings,
Saying that the land of Iran belonged to him.
Although his actions may have benefited you,
In the end, he will break his bonds with you,
Just as he has ruthlessly shattered his ties to Iran.
He is devoted neither to the king nor to Yazdan.
If you send him back to Iran's court,
You will elevate the head of the Iranian king.
At that time, Chin and Iran will be yours,
And you may establish your residence
Anywhere you please."

The emperor is troubled by this discourse.
His eyes dim at the sight of Khorraad.
He replies, "Do not speak in such a way,
For my esteem surely would elude you.
I am not a wicked man.
I do not breach the pacts I commit to.
The violator of treaties gains only dust as a shroud."

Khorraad Borzeen says to the emperor,
"You originate from royal lineage.
Do you remember these words?
        'The King of Iran is a better ally than Choobineh,
        For he was born into your family long ago.'"

275

The emperor replies, "Let me divulge to you a secret:
What would you say if the Rumi Caesar had broken
His covenant with Khosrow?
What would you say if I were to follow such an example
And deceive him by retrieving my promise?
Just like Khosrow, I have thousands of servants
And slaves; my essence is glorious; my lineage is pure.
Your king cannot be compared to the Rumi ruler
Who gave him arms and army, treasure and land
So that he may return to Iran and reclaim his throne.
Just like the battles of Bahraam the warrior
Are written in detail in books. He is my son-in-law,
How could I ever come to breach our agreement?"

A concerned Khorraad searches for a solution.
He reflects, "Since he has planted the seed of hope
That the land of Iran is within his reach,
The emperor will not remember.
Further speaking on my part would be useless."

In a state of despair, he turns toward the empress,
Searching for someone to enlighten her mind.
Bahraam encounters an attendant in the palace
Who is in close contact with her.
He visits the misbeliever and addresses him
Words about Khosrow to charm his heart.
He says to him one day, "Help me find a way
To become the scribe of the emperor's wife."

The attendant replies, "You will not attain your goal
With her, for Bahraam Choobineh is her son-in-law
And draws his power from her.
You are literate. Search for another means,
And reveal your secret to no one,
Not even to the wind."

Khorraad understands neither the beginning
Nor the end of this man's discourse.

There lives an old Turk named Gholoon
Who is considered with little regard.
He dresses only in a coat of sheepskin
And lives on curdled milk and millet.

Since the fatal day when Maghaatooreh,
His relative, perished at the hands of Bahraam,
Gholoon's heart has simmered with grief, day and night,
And with a burning desire for vengeance.
He unravels his tongue to curse Bahraam at length.

One day, Khorraad hears him and summons him.
He invites him into his noble residence,
Gives him dirhams and dinars, clothing,
And plenty of food, and at the table, he seats him
In the company of the most illustrious noblemen.

Khorraad, a man eager to learn, is of a patient nature,
Prudent, ingenious, and expert in affairs.
Day and night, he appears discrete toward the emperor,
While on the other side,
He questions the palace attendant on the wife.

One day, the old Gholoon says to the mighty Khorraad,
"If you, so eminent and so learned as you are,
Knew something about medicine,
And if your famous name was far-reaching,
You would thereby be the diadem
On the head of the empress, especially
Since she has a daughter who is gravely ill."

Khorraad replies, "I am indeed in possession of science.
If you wish to speak of it, I shall take charge."

The palace attendant runs to the empress
And tells her that a new medicine man has arrived.

She replies, "May your life always be happy!
Bring him to me right away,
Without taking time to scratch your head."

He returns and says to Khorraad, son of Borzeen,
"You must keep your secret. Go to her,
Conceal your identity, and pretend to be a physician."

Khorraad presents himself before the wife.
He sees that the patient has an ailing liver.
He asks for water, pomegranate juice, and an herb

277

That grows on river banks named white chicory,
Hoping they will help bring down her fever.
By Yazdan's will, after seven days, the daughter
Is as healthy as the world-illuminating moon.

The empress brings a treasure, a pouch of gold
And silver coins, and five robes of golden thread.
She says to him, "Please accept this humble present,
And ask me for anything else you may wish."

He replies, "You may keep all these.
I shall tell you in due time what I require."

8 | Khorraad, son of Borzeen, Sends Gholoon to Bahraam Choobineh

Bahraam travels toward Marv and assembles
An army as beautiful as a pheasant's plumage.

Someone approaches the emperor and says,
"Guard all the Turks and Chinis from crossing into Iran.
If Khosrow receives news, his conduct may change."

The Emperor of Chin makes a proclamation:
"If anyone crosses without an order
Stamped with my seal into the land of Iran,
I shall split him in two from the waist.
I swear by Yazdan he will not have the opportunity
To buy his freedom with his wealth."

For three months, Khorraad, son of Borzeen,
Secretly observes all the developments.
In his anguish, he calls Gholoon, seats him
In his magnificent home, and says to him,
"You know that no one is exempt
From a heart that does not bear secret grief.
You have often asked people in Chin
For barley bread, millet, and sheepskin.
Now you find yourself eating cheese and lamb
And dressed in sumptuous clothing.
There was the state you were in long ago,

And this is the present state you find yourself in.
So many curses and blessings you have received.
Your life surpassed ordinary measure.
You have exceeded one hundred years.
You have seen many days and nights,
Many a mountain and many a plain.

"I have for you a frightful job
That may lead you either to the throne
Or to lie beneath the somber earth.
I shall obtain from the emperor the imprint of his seal.
You must leave with it, and ride
As if you wish to roll up the ground beneath you.
You will go to Bahraam and remain in Marv.
You will dress in a coat of black sheepskin
And take with you a knife.
You will wait for the day of Bahraam[22]
To present yourself at the door of the hero.
He holds this day as a day of misfortune
Because of the bad omens he received in the past.
He will, for that reason, bar entry to his home.
His head will be covered with a turban of Chini brocade.

"Tell him that you bear a message
From the emperor's daughter
Addressed to the blessed prince.
During this time, hold the knife in your sleeve
Until you are offered an entrance.
Once in Bahraam Choobineh's presence, you will say,
      'The eminent princess, daughter of the Emperor of Chin
      Wished me to communicate her secret
      In your ear and away from strangers.'

"He will say, 'Tell me this secret. Be quick!'
At that moment, you will approach Bahraam,
You will strike him with the hidden knife,
Tear apart his navel, then lunge to find an exit.
Anyone who hears his screams will rush
Either to the stables or to the treasury.
Your action will not attract any attention

◇◇◇◇◇◇◇◇◇◇◇◇◇◇
22 Day of Bahraam: The twentieth day of the month.

279

Or put you at harm's way.

"Even if they were to kill you, you are weary of life.
You have endured many trials and tribulations.
This is your way of executing vengeance
And to achieve your ultimate goal.
But most probably, no one will cause you harm.
If you escape death, you will have paid the price
And renewed life for yourself.
The victorious king will reward you
With a city to rule and a part of the world."

Gholoon says to the learned Khorraad,
"I have no need for further instructions,
But I shall require a knowledgeable guide.
Although I have passed one hundred years,
I still yearn, in my distress, to acquire something.
May my body and soul be your ransom and our pact,
For you provided me with nourishment
As I languished in a state of poverty."

Khorraad rushes out of his house
And appears at the empress's side to say,
"The time has arrived for me to ask a favor,
Which I will explain, O good-natured woman.
I wish to liberate my family held captive
On the other side of the river.
If you could procure me with the imprint
Of the emperor's seal, you will save my life."

The emperor's wife says,
"My lord is asleep and in a state of inebriation.
Perhaps I could take the imprint in clay."

She asks Khorraad to bring her the clay
And goes straight to the drunken ruler's bedside.
She takes the imprint of the ring
And returns to hand it to the learned hero.
He thanks her and leaves
To give the seal to the old man.

9 | The Death of Bahraam Choobineh at the Hands of Gholoon

Gholoon takes the seal and departs,
Running secretly like a pheasant to Marv.
He stays there until the day of Bahraam,
A day of misfortune for Choobineh,
Who is in his room with a single servant,
Surrounded by pomegranates, apples, and quince.

Gholoon arrives at the door alone
And says to the guardian, "O fame-seeker,
I have been sent by his wife, the emperor's daughter.
I am neither a warrior nor an Iranian.
The holy woman confided in me a secret
That I am to relay to the leader.
Her door is closed due to his absence,
And she is ailing and expecting.
Can you please tell him so that I may give
Her message to the crowned and glorious king?"

The venerable guardian rushes to Bahraam's door:
"An emissary has arrived of somber mien,
Dressed in sheepskin claiming to be the carrier
Of a message from the emperor's daughter."

Bahraam replies, "Tell him to come to my door."

Gholoon advances to the threshold, looks in,
And, at the sight of the old, exhausted, wretched man,
Bahraam says, "If you have a letter for me, hand it over."

Gholoon replies, "Sire, I only have one message
Of which I may discharge myself only to you."

Bahraam says, "Enter quickly and murmur it
In my ear without causing any trouble."

Gholoon moves forward, the knife in his sleeve,
The moment of the crime close at hand.
He advances as pretending to be
About to murmur in Bahraam's ear,

Then he swiftly strikes him with the dagger.
A cry of pain echoes in the chamber.

Immediately, men rush to the leader's side.
Bahraam says to them, "Quick, seize him!
Ask him who instructed him to commit the crime."
Everyone in the palace arrives to pull the old man
By the head and the feet. Furious at him,
They strike him with their hands and fists.

He tolerates the blows without parting his lips
From midday to midnight.
In the end, his feet and hands are shattered.
They throw him into the palace courtyard,
And the menservant return to Bahraam,
Heartbroken and full of anguish.
Blood flows from the body of the wounded man,
His lips exhaling deep sighs,
His cheeks the color of lapis lazuli.

Bahraam's sister arrives, tears out her hair,
Places the head of the injured on her chest and laments:
"Alas, O valiant rider, before whom the lion flees!
Who dared knock down this support of the world?
Who is the instigator of this evil strategy?
Alas, O mighty cavalier, world conqueror,
You once were a fearless lion vanquisher!
What kind of a person would dare
Strike your elephantine body?
Someone who is neither a Yazdan worshipper
Nor a servant of the king.
Alas, this powerful, lofty mountain,
Who would dare pluck it out of the bottomless sea?
Who would dare overturn this verdant cypress tree,
Lower the royal crown to the ground,
Fill with dust the deepest sea,
And raze to level this walking mountain?

"We are strangers, alone, devoid of friend or protector.
We are despised in someone else's land.
I had warned you, O leader of the people,
Not to pluck the roots of the tree of loyalty.

If just one daughter was left from Sassan's race,
She was meant to place a diadem on her head.
The entire land would be her slave,
And her brilliant crown would rise to the sky.
All the cities of Iran would obey her mandate.
Never would hearts abandon this family.
Now the leader who did not heed my advice
Or my good words repents for his actions
And will travel to the Creator with a guilty soul.
Misfortune struck this powerful home.
We have become sheep, our enemy is a wolf."

Hearing these words and seeing the heart
And the wisdom of this woman with scratched cheeks,
Pulled hair, her heart and eyes full of blood,
Her face full of dust, Bahraam opens his lips sadly,
And, with great effort and difficulty, whispers,
"O my dear sister, you were born to be holy!
Never have I received better advice from anyone.
Yet my measure has reached its capacity.
I did not follow your counsel.
It was as if in all things I was guided by the deev.
There was never a king greater than Jamsheed,
Who filled the world with fear and hope,
Yet the deevs led him astray and caused his downfall.
Later the prudent Kay Kaavoos, world master
Of blessed star and auspicious footprints,
Allowed himself to deviate from the proper path.
You have heard the hardships he drew onto himself.
He wished to fly to observe the spinning skies
And the way they conduct the journeys of Sun and Moon.
Instead he fell from the air only to be plunged
Shamefully into the water on the border of the city of Sari.

"I have also been led astray by the deev
Who forced me away from the path of virtue.
He told me that kingship was mine
From the house of the Ram to the sign of the Fish.
I repent for all the harm I have caused.
If the Creator wishes to forgive me,
It would be through divine grace.
All this was written in my destiny.

Why should I grieve over my past actions?
The water has now risen over my head,
And sorrow and joy are nothing but a gust of wind.
It was written and so it unfolded,
For one cannot add or strike out from the writing.
Your words are for me rare and precious pearls,
But the time to behave justly or unjustly has passed.
Therefore, do not remind me of what you have said.
Turn your eyes toward Yazdan.
Lean on the side where fortune shines.
The Creator is your only support in times of trouble.
Do not discuss your pains and joys with anyone.
I only obtained from the world the part due me,
And now fate demands that I depart from here."

He turns to Yalan Sineh: "I entrust you
With throne, rulership, and the army's command.
Take care of my sister, this excellent woman.
You will not have need in the world
For any other advice than hers.
Never drift apart from each other,
And may there never be disunity between you.
Try not to linger in this hostile land.
I came into the world to conquer,
Only to find myself ultimately disgusted by it.

"Go together to Khosrow, speak and listen to him.
Tell him that Bahraam holds no hostility toward him.
If he forgives you, hold him as your sun and moon.
I have heard that Khorraad has come
As a messenger to the land of Chin.
Take greetings from me to Gordooy and relate to him
The fact that my demise is at Khorraad's instigation.
Raise a coffin for me in the land of Iran,
And destroy the palace of Bahraam in Rey.
The Emperor of Chin has been a friend to me.
Not a single day passed without him
Expressing his affection to me.
He certainly is not the one to reward me for my efforts
By sending this evil deev to attack me.
But it is probable that, when he learns of this,
He will not understand how it could have happened.

This can only be a blow from the Iranians,
And the deev must have been the mastermind."

He summons a scribe and writes a necessary letter
To the Emperor of Chin in which he reveals:
"Bahraam has passed away. He died sadly
And miserably, having failed to achieve his goal.
Bring happiness into the lives of those he leaves behind,
Safeguard them from misery and evil.
He never caused you any hardship and always
Sought to follow the path of righteousness with you."

Then Bahraam gives his sister much advice,
Holding her beloved head to his chest.
He places his mouth on her earlobe.
His eyes fill with blood tears as he expires.

Everyone mourns him bitterly.
They survive him with wounded hearts.
His sister shouts cries of anguish.
She repeats his words all day, heartbroken with grief.
She prepares for him a narrow, silver coffin,
Decks his heroic body with brocade
And envelops him in fine linen beneath his tunic.
She pours camphor over his body
Until his head is immersed in it.

Such is the condition of this passing dwelling.
Do not tire yourself, since you know
With certainty that you will not stay here for long.
Great and small, we are born from dust,
And to the dust we surrender our body
At the moment of our death.
Do not give into fear and worry.
Drink wine day and night.
Hold your hearts full of joy
And your lips parted in smile.

10 | The Emperor Learns of Bahraam's Death and Destroys Gholoon's House and Family

Upon receipt of the letter and the circumstances
Surrounding his ally's death, the Emperor of Chin
Understands that Bahraam's glory is about to fade.
The messenger speaks, and he listens to the account.
The update fills his soul with sorrow.
His eyes flood with tears, his lips turn blue.
Stunned by Bahraam's fate, he calls to his side
His old advisors and speaks of the fate of Bahraam.
Everyone present weeps with grief.
The entire land of Chin sheds bitter tears.
Terror consumes the land as if by flames.

The emperor searches Bahraam's past deeds
To find out who is responsible for the crime.
He quickly understands that Khorraad is guilty
Of venturing into ruse and injustice.
He sends on every side keen race camels
Without any success in capturing the Iranian.
He ceaselessly repeats, "How could a dog
Who spreads such dishonor on my head escape?"

Gholoon has in Tooran two sons
As well as relatives and friends of every sort.
Once the emperor learns that he is guilty,
He burns down his house and the enclosure.
He throws his two sons into the flames
And plunders all their belongings.

He continues to send race camels to every corner
In search of Khorraad Borzeen, but with no luck.

Then it is the turn of his wife, whom he drags
By the hair out of the women's chambers.
He seizes all her wealth and brings it to his palace.
He never speaks of the misery that he reduces her to.
He dresses all his Chini servants in blue
And for a long time mourns Bahraam,
Feeling shame for his fate and remembering him fondly.

11 | Khosrow Learns of Bahraam Choobineh's Death

When Khorraad, son of Borzeen, reaches Khosrow,
He recounts to him all the developments.
The heart of Khosrow Parviz rejoices
As he feels freed from the evil enemy.
He gives dirhams, alms, clothing, and goods to the poor.
A letter is written in Pahlavi to every ruler and
Every independent prince to announce Yazdan's deeds
And how the king's enemy was eliminated.

Khosrow writes a royal letter to the Caesar
According to customs and rites.
For one week they hold assemblies
And call for wine and music in every neighborhood.
The king sends an offering to the fire temple
And presents gifts to his wise noblemen.

Khosrow Parviz says to Khorraad, son of Borzeen:
"With your actions, you deserve for me
To hand over the throne and crown to you."

He fills Khorraad's mouth with precious stones
And gives him one hundred thousand dinars
That the treasurer spills at Khorraad's feet
In a way as to hinder his movements.

He says to Khorraad, "Anyone who strays
From the path of the king will see his days dim,
Even if he were the most valiant on the battlefield,
Like Bahraam, who ended up slain by an old Turk."

All the wise men pay homage to Khosrow:
"May your subjects never see the world
Deprived of your throne and crown!
May Bahraam's fate strike anyone who,
Despite your grace and clemency, attempts
To bar your face from shining on the world!"

12 | The Emperor Sends His Brother to Gordieh, Bahraam's Sister

The land of Chin is transformed into
A spread of mud as a result of the bloodshed.

One day, the Emperor of Chin declares,
"Anyone who dwells in idleness and languor
Can produce only work that is incomplete or incorrect.
Thanks to the noble Bahraam, my life was
One of ease, and I was able to attain my goals.
Why did I not take care of his relatives?
People will point the blame at me.
No one will ever again agree to seal a pact with me.
I did not pay attention to his small child or his kin.
He was my son-in-law, united to me.
Ever since he wed my daughter, he abandoned
His heart to affection and his soul to wisdom."

The emperor summons his brother
And speaks to him at length:
"Travel as swift as a bird from here to Marv
To observe the members of Bahraam's family.
Tell them that, in the name of Yazdan,
We had no idea of the plots against Bahraam.
As for me, I am weary, and my grief is everlasting.
I washed the surface of my land with the blood
Of vengeance, leading some to curse me
And others to highly praise me.
With my heart's pain and sorrow, I wish
To bring down the sky and merge it with the earth.
Any act I undertake as retribution is not even
One to one hundredth of Bahraam's heroic feats.
No one can overrule Yazdan's command.
Any wise man is well aware of this fact.
It was so for as long as Bahraam lived,
But it was turned upside down by the deev's spell.
I wish to uphold my agreements and my pacts."

He sends a separate letter to Gordieh,
"O pure-hearted woman, your actions are driven
By righteousness and humanity.

Positioned far from scarcity and lack,
The source of your essence is abundance.
I have reflected at length on your account.
It is as if wisdom has taken a seat next to your heart
And is engaged in secret communications with it.
I do not see a better candidate for you than myself.
Come and bring honor to my women's chambers.
I shall worship you as if you were of my own flesh
And shall never breach my covenant with you.
Thereafter, your command will rule over the city,
And my heart will be yours for any desire you may have.
Gather your belongings, consult with advisors,
Then make a decision based on deep-seated wisdom
And an open mind, for wisdom is the king of language.
Relate to me your ultimate decision."

The emperor's brother takes flight toward Marv
Like a bird searching for a far-away cypress tree.
The world seeker carries the letter to Bahraam's relatives
And relays the emperor's message to them,
As they are deeply aggrieved by the death
Of the hero and eager to execute retributions.

The envoy says to them, "O skillful and wise warriors,
This is not a death to be taken lightly.
I hope that the Just Creator is Bahraam's companion."

Then he hands over the letter to the sister
And reports the words of the Emperor of Chin,
The desire for him to unite in marriage,
With reflections on ancient deeds and new actions.
He speaks of "the chastity of a woman and how
She is able to grieve with you as well as guide you."

The pure-hearted woman hears him out
But refrains from furnishing him an answer.
She reads the emperor's letter,
Joins her insight to her knowledge,
And proceeds to compose a reply:
"I have read the letter through the eye of wisdom.
The emperor's plans are no different from other rulers.
May the emperor always bring light into our eyes

289

For his wishes to seek revenge on the death of Bahraam.
May the world never be deprived of his rule!
May the land prosper with his kingly crown!
May grief and sorrow never seep into his heart,
For everyone is dependent on his reign!

"We shall read the letter from beginning to end.
Any illustrious man endowed with wisdom
Will contemplate the words and wishes within.
My entire family is in a state of deep mourning,
And now is not the time to speak of this matter.
Once our bereavement has ended,
We shall obey the emperor's command.
I do not wish to travel to Iran.
It is best for a chaste woman to marry.
If I quickly travel to his court,
What will his majesty think to me?
Am I to revel in joy when I am in mourning?
Such an action goes against my nature
As a warrior and as a pure woman.
Wise men will accuse me of being shameless.
The emperor himself will view me in this way.
I have heard all that I needed to hear,
And will listen to anything else that is said.
After four months of grief, I shall send an ambassador,
Carrier of a letter in which I shall include my terms."

She turns to the envoy, offers him many gifts, and adds,
"Go in joy to the emperor and relate to him what I said."
The aging man happily departs from Marv
And travels back to the land of Chin.

13 | Gordieh Holds Counsel With Her Noblemen and Flees From Marv

After this, the wise young woman
Sits peacefully with her advisors and says,
"I am faced with a new matter that bears
The necessity to be reflected upon,
For I wish not to keep this sentiment in my heart.

The Chini world ruler has asked for my hand
And has spoken on various subjects.
He is not an insignificant monarch,
For he is a king, a valiant, skillful rider,
And the commander of Tooran's army.
The bold Bahraam took great care of me
For two times ten years after my father's death.
If, in the past, anyone wished to marry me,
His hostility was such that his brain
Would simmer to a boil.
No one dared look my way
For as long as my brother was alive.
Now the emperor is a proud ruler.
He has holdings, power, sovereignty.
He wishes to unite the Turks to the Iranians.
The only thing he now holds on to is grief and pain.
Look and see how Siaavoosh, as bright as the sun,
Brought splendor and light to Afraasiyaab
Yet ultimately lost his head in kinship.
He was a youth like no other.

"In the same way, Bahraam, the son of a hero,
Converted to dust the lands of Iran and Tooran.
Let us take this exchange with the Turks to Iran-Zamin.
Having endured difficult reflections for a solution,
I have decided to write a letter to Gordooy
So that the king may be aware of our situation
And know our concerns and our worries.
Yazdan willing, he will accept and understand
My predicament and reflect on my condition."

The advisors say to her, "Whether you are queen
In Iran or in Chin, you will nonetheless be a support.
As a guide to warriors, not even
A mountain of steel can make you budge.
You are more enlightened than the wisest men,
More vigilant than the most knowledgeable.
We are your inferiors, ready to apply your command."

Subsequently, Gordieh reads the number of troops,
Surveys them, and distributes dinars to them.
She selects one thousand one hundred sixty warriors,

Each one equivalent to more than ten riders.
She gives them dirhams, returns to her home,
And addresses her host:
"Anyone who has witnessed the bridle of a horse
Will never change his seat for another, no matter
How many ups and downs life challenges him with.
He will not fear contenders, even if a cloud of shots
Were to rain down on his head.
He will never turn away his horse's reins,
Even when faced with a mortal enemy.

"We must travel to Iran and to the king of the brave.
We are strangers in Tooran; we have no support
And lack allies among the powerful men of Chin.
We must run away from here at nightfall
And before the enemy wakes up.
Do not fear our flight, even if the Chini army
Rushes after us with their heavy maces.
Place your lives into your own hands,
Even if we must fiercely engage in fight and battle.
But if you are not in agreement with me,
Then it is best for you to remain here."

They repeat their pledge: "We are your inferiors
And shall never stray from your command."
Determined, they rise and ready themselves
For battle with the warriors of Chin.

Yalan Sineh and Yzad Goshasp saddle their steeds
And say, "We would rather die than
Allow the Chinis to gain victory over us."

They ride to the caravan on the plain
To select three thousand camels, on which
They load up the provisions and the baggage.

As night descends, Gordieh mounts her stallion
Like a brave leader, brandishing her mace.
They dress the horses and warriors in armor,
Don their war helmets, and wield their swords.

The army moves, as swift as wind,
Traveling through the day and the night.

14 | The Emperor Learns of Gordieh's Flight

Many transgressors leave Gordieh's army
And seek protection from the emperor.
The emperor's brother says, "O valiant prince
Eager for battle, a company marches to Iran,
And many defectors are accosting us, asking for mercy.
People will laugh heartily at you and your army,
And such a thing would bring our court eternal shame."

Anger pales the cheek of the ruler of Chin.
He says, "Observe the roads they have taken.
Hurry to lead an army. They know not our strategy
Unless we have an informant in our midst.
Go and join them, and do not show your wrath.
Greet them well, with kind words. Praise them.
Praise their valor. Elevate their humanity.
These tactics will help reduce
Our enemy to powerlessness.
If one of them attacks you,
Act as a man and do not hesitate.
Fill the cemetery in Marv with corpses so that
The earth becomes like a pheasant's plumage.

The leader departs with six thousand elite Turk riders.
He reaches the Iranians on the fourth day.
The lion woman is unmoved, confronted with a vast host.
She runs out of the troops toward the caravan leader,
As swift as wind, and places the baggage at the rear.
Then she inspects the battlefield,
Dresses in her brother's armor, and climbs on her charger.

The two hosts form their lines of battle.
The troops place their lives in the palm of their hands.
Tevorg, whom the emperor calls the old wolf,
Presents himself at the front of the Iranians and says,
"Is the holy woman not present in this gathering?"

The bold Tevorg does not recognize Gordieh,
Since she is dressed in heavy mail,
Armed like a man of war.
He strikes his horse with his heel,

Advances toward her, and says to her,
"Where am I to find the king's sister in this host?
I have much to talk to her about,
New subjects as well as ancient ones."

Gordieh says to him, "Here I am.
I launch my horse like a shredding lion."

Tevorg is astonished to hear Gordieh speak
From atop her formidable charger.
He says, "The Emperor of Chin singled you out,
In his entire kingdom, so that you may be
A souvenir of the lion Bahraam, a superior rider.
He promised that, if you wish to listen to him,
He will reward you with kindness.

"The emperor said to me,
        'Hurry to her and tell her:
                "If you do not approve of what they tell you,
                Consider my words as if they were unspoken.
                I would reject the idea as well myself.
                You do not wish to leave our land.
                Guard yourself from doing so,
                Even If you dismiss my offer of marriage.
                Prepare your affairs, and if the emperor's advice
                Does not suit you, seal a treaty with him."'

"Anyone who believes the emperor is capable
Of acting in the way you most fear
Surpasses what is allowed to be expressed with words.
The emperor confirmed that if you do not comply,
We are to bind you and take you captive.
Anyone who provokes your movements
Is surely acting beyond the necessary measure."

Gordieh replies, "Let us distance ourselves
From the battlefield and from the vanguard.
I shall reply to all your points
And provide you with excellent arguments."

Tevorg withdraws from the army front
And follows the proud and illustrious woman.

Once the diligent Gordieh finds herself alone with him,
She shows him her face beneath the black helmet
And says to him, "You have seen Bahraam.
You have admired his horsemanship and warring skills.
Beyond brother, he was to me both mother and father.
Now he is deceased, and I shall
Put you to the test and fight with you.
If you find me worthy of a husband, tell me.
I shall perhaps accept you as my mate."

She launches her horse with Izad Goshasp on her trail.
The Chini leader attacks her on his side,
And the two battle lions fight without respite.

The sister of the illustrious hero
Rushes after Tevorg with her spear.
She strikes him mid-waist and
Penetrates his coat of mail and his belt.
He falls from atop his horse, and
The sand beneath him shifts in a pond of blood.

Yalan Sineh, at the head of the elite army,
Charges with his horse on the battlefield.
He breaks the army of Chin, flings men to the ground,
Kills some and wounds many others.
The Iranians pursue the Chini warriors for two farsangs,
Allowing only a few of them to remain on horseback.
The plain, from end to end, is a river of blood,
Strewn with corpses, some with heads, some without.

After her victory, Gordieh departs for Iran
To meet with the king of brave men.
On the fourth day, she arrives in Amoy.
Never have you seen a woman leader of her might.
She remains in Amoy for some time,
Her heart obsessing over much concern.

She writes to her brother Gordooy a letter
Full of grief, and she recounts to him her affairs:
"Right before his imminent death, the valiant Bahraam,
His mind full of brotherly concern, addressed me
Words of wisdom destined for you and me.
May his soul never be exposed to reproach!

Then he commanded me to repeat to the king
All the advice he had shared with me.
A great army composed of illustrious and bold men
Pursued us, but I treated them so poorly during battle
That they will never again see either fight or feast.
I have with me many noble leaders
Who must be preserved from any form of calamity.
I remain in Amoy, hoping that my lucky star
Will bring back a reply from you."

15 | Khosrow Kills Bandooy to Avenge the Death of Hormozd

With the valiant Bahraam eliminated,
The king sits on the throne feeling safe and secure.
He does not see anyone among his noblemen
Able to rebel against him and overcome him.

One day he says to his loyal vizier,
"Until when must I conceal my thoughts?
Will my father's murderer continue to pass before me
And remain at my side here as a relative?
Since my shining soul is so full
Of the memory of my father's bloodshed,
How can I perform my kingly duties?
What are the consequences that could result?"

A table is placed before him. They drink wine,
And on that same day, he imprisons Bandooy.
Then he says to his advisor,
"Let us immediately cut off his hands and feet.
Without hands, he will no longer seize weapons
To destroy and execute descendants of Kianian lineage."

With hands and feet severed, Bandooy dies instantly,
Abandoning his criminal soul to the Creator.

16 | Gostaham Rebels Against Khosrow and Weds Gordieh

Khosrow dispatches someone to Khorasan
With profuse recommendations, saying,
"Do not open your mouth to speak to anyone.
Travel from here to the border guard
And say to Gostaham,
      'Do not delay for a moment.
      Come here as soon as you have read our letter.'"

The envoy obeys, arrives at Gostaham's court,
Where he lives peacefully, and communicates to him
The order of Parviz, a young king eager for bloodshed.

At the command, Gostaham summons his dispersed
Troops and takes the road all the way to the land
Of noblemen, passing the cities of Sari and Amol
And stopping in the region of Gorgan.
He learns there that the King of Iran has become fierce.
That he killed his brother one night in a drunken bout.

Gostaham bites his hand
And dismounts from his yellow horse.
He tears out his warrior attire
And tosses dust over his head.
He bellows, understanding that the world master king
Seeks to kill him to avenge the death of his father.

He returns from this place in a state of rage.
It is as if he is the companion of the wind.
He gathers loyal troops
And marches them to the Forest of Nahravan.
There he positions them at the foot of Mount Amol.
He races every which way to assail and exercise vengeance.
He turns every idle man he encounters into a servant.
He destroys every warrior of the king crossing his path.

On the other side, Gordooy, in the king's presence,
Recounts to him the feats of his sister and her army
Against the leaders of the emperor's borders
And how she triumphed over the land of Marv.

Gostaham learns that the valiant Bahraam perished,
That Gordieh gathered a powerful army
And left the side of the fierce emperor,
That a host chased her to contend with her,
And that she dealt fiercely with famed Chini warriors.

He commands his troops to climb on horseback,
To march out of the forest and to greet Gordieh.
At the news, Gordieh departs from Amoy
With her illustrious leaders to meet him.

At the sight of the troops on the road,
Gostaham launches his horse ahead of his army,
And, full of grief, he approaches Gordieh.
He speaks to her at length of the pain he endures
From the death of Bahraam, then he recounts
His sorrow over the miserable execution of Bandooy.
Blood tears flow from his lashes,
And he wipes them with his robes' sleeves.

At the sight of Yalan Sineh and Izad Goshasp,
He dismounts, weeping, and says,
"The king executed Bandooy, and my own life is in danger.
It is as if Khosrow Parviz has no relation to Bandooy's sister,
As if Bandooy did not spill blood for him,
As if the king had not declared that he valued
Bandooy's head more than his own, and that his life
Would serve as ransom for the dust at Bandooy's feet.
The king, in a state of drunkenness,
Ordered his hands and feet to be cut off,
As one would expect from a man of his nature.

"With what sort of hope are you going to him?
You are better off waiting for the willow tree
To bear fruit during the summer months.
He will use you as an ax to strike your companions.
He will make the meat cheap at the butcher shop in town.
At the sight of you, Yalan Sineh, he will grow furious
And surrender to a renewed sense of vengeance,
For you have been Bahraam's army chief,
And he was the one to give you power in the world.
Anyone who knows him better must avoid him.

Even better would be to cut his throat with a sharp blade.
If you chose to remain at my side,
We shall hold counsel on all things, great and small."

Those who hear this discourse accept his advice,
Wishing to emerge from the path of misfortune.
Then he addresses urging words to Gordieh,
Reminding her of Bahraam's high deeds.
Gordieh is touched, sensing the truth in his words.

They ride to Gostaham,
And his dim hopes regain their luster.
Time passes, partly in joy, partly in sorrow.

One day, Gostaham says to Yalan Sineh,
"What does this brilliant woman think of a husband?
What sort of man do you think she seeks?"

Yalan Sineh replies, "Wait for me to speak to her
And prepare her heart for the need of speech."

Yalan Sineh says to Gordieh,
"O woman, I have always found you of sound counsel.
You have distanced yourself from the emperor,
Wisely rejecting his offer of marriage,
For you preferred the company of Persians.
What do you think of the valiant Gostaham,
The king's uncle, a powerful leader and army chief?"

She replies, "An Iranian husband would
Never have the ability to destroy my lineage."

Yalan Sineh marries her to Gostaham,
Who is a valiant hero of royal race.
He takes care of her like a fresh apple.
In his grandeur, he does not believe any fall possible.
All the armies who come from the side of the king
Witness their old fortunes change, and Gostaham,
Seeing one of them fall, would give shelter to others.

17 | Gordieh Kills Gostaham
at the Insistence of Khosrow and Gordooy

After some time, the king feels uneasy about Gostaham.
One day he says to Gordooy,
"Gostaham has joined Gordieh in marriage.
Masses of men are driving to him,
And I think that she has enticed them.
One of my spies has returned from Amol
And has revealed all the secret machinations."

He continues to speak until nighttime,
When the heroes' eyes can no longer see clearly.
While the servants bring candles and wine
And prepare the hall, the king expedites
The visitors and sits on the throne with his advisor.

Gordooy and Khosrow discuss all sorts of things,
Great and small, and the king says, "I have sent
Numerous troops to Amol to battle vengefully,
But they have all either been taken captive
Or returned defeated and full of laments.
Now I only have one resource, although a weak one
When it relates to throne and crown.

"When Bahraam Choobineh deserted the royal way,
Gordieh remained on the straight and loyal path.
Today this fact offers me a way of salvation.
But do not speak of this matter to anyone at court.
We must address a letter to Gordieh,
Similar to a river of wine in the garden of paradise.
We must say to her,
> 'You have shown me affection for a long while
> And have served me in all things and at all times.
> Never did my tongue betray my heart's secret.
> But the moment of confession has arrived,
> For Gordooy is as dear to me as my own body.
> Reflect on a way to make Gostaham disappear.
> He is an evil, malicious, and execrable man.
> Find a way to crush him, and you will conquer,
> Through this act, both my heart and my home.
> Once you have accomplished the deed,

Your army and any friend you have in the world
Will find protection at my side
And will never be oppressed by me at any time.
I shall offer provinces to anyone you desire,
And they will be placed at the head of the land.
You will enter my golden women's chambers,
And you will put an end to all the vengeance.
I swear to be true to my words, and, should I ever
Turn away from my engagements with you,
May my allies abandon me once and for all!'"

Gordooy replies, "May you live forever in happiness!
May you shine like Venus under the house of Virgo!
You know that, next to your valued head,
I deem as insignificant my life, my children,
My cultivated lands, as well as my allies,
No matter how precious these possessions are to me.
I shall send someone with this message to Gordieh.
I shall fill with joy her dim soul.
I request a letter with the king's seal,
Written by his hand, a letter as bright as the moon.
I shall send my wife to my sister
And shall keep at bay ill-intentioned men.
This message must come from a woman alone,
Especially one of good counsel.
The more I reflect upon this, the more I believe
That we must entrust your message to my sister.
You will see, the matter will unfold
And conclude speedily and to your liking.
We must plan to do neither less nor more."

Khosrow rejoices at the proposal.
His heart lightens from the burden of worry.
He asks his treasurer for paper, ink of black musk
Dissolved in water, and writes a letter
As embellished as a garden full of vibrant flowers,
Like the cheeks of a friend, a letter full of promise,
Engagements, pledges, prayers, and sound advice.
Once the writing has dried, they apply black musk
To the seal and press the ring
Inscribed with the name of Khosrow Parviz.

Gordooy, on his side, writes a letter
Full of instruction and kind words.
He begins with the deeds of "Bahraam, who infused
Shame into his family's name and into his land.
May Yazdan forgive him, and may he not have
To repent for the quarrels he instigated.
The man whose soul does not possess wisdom
Does not think before taking on his actions.
But those of us who will one day die in his example,
Let us surrender to the justice of the World Master.
When my wife arrives at your side,
She will enlighten your troubled mind.
Do not turn away from her words,
For if you neglect them, our fortune will fade."

He places the king's letter within his message,
Seals the two in a silken envelope,
And hands it to his resourceful wife.
She listens to the imperious words
And travels as swift as wind to the Forest of Naarvan.

The female messenger greets her female counterpart.
Gordieh is as delighted as spring to welcome her visitor,
Her face shining with all its charm, scent, and beauty.
The two women speak at length of Bahraam
And shed copious tears over his demise.
Then Gordooy's wife secretly delivers to Gordieh
Her husband's letter enclosing the king's words
And explains to her what she was told.

When her eyes fall on the royal letter,
It is as if Gordieh sees the moon on the earth.
She smiles and says, "This affair is easy
For a person who has five friends."

She reads the king's message to five men,
Hiding it from the assembly of noblemen.
Then she addresses them,
Swiftly concludes the convention with them,
And takes each of their hands.

Gordieh welcomes the five men into her residence
And arranges accommodations near her bedroom.

As the deepest part of night
Exterminates any remnant of light,
She quickly places her hand over her husband's mouth.
The five men come to her aid,
Rushing to the side of the illustrious leader.
She struggles for some time with the drunken man.
In the end, she stops his cries, and, in this way,
The leader dies in total obscurity, abandoning the nights
And the brilliant days to his ambitious wife.

Cries and clamor rise in the city.
In every street a fire burns and a storm erupts.
The audacious woman dresses in Rumi armor.
She summons the Iranians during the night
And speaks at length of the man she killed.
Then she shows them the king's letter
And exalts their courage and their pride.
All the noblemen acclaim Khosrow
And spread jewels over the letter.

18 | Gordieh's Letter to Khosrow Accepting His Offer

The fearless woman asks for an inkwell and a reed.
She sits with her advisors to write a letter to the king
On the subject of her friends and her enemies.
She begins by celebrating the praises of those
Who wash their hearts of the ancient hatred.
Then she adds, "The deed requested by the king
Has been achieved according to his heart's desire.
The menacing army has dispersed as a result
Of his majesty's good fortune.
I remain here for now, awaiting his command,
Waiting to see what sort of earrings
He will choose to place on his servant's ears."

The woman's letter arrives at court
To King Khosrow's great delight.
He asks for a pure, soft-spoken messenger
Endowed with a powerful star and a serene mind.
A letter is composed so beautiful, it is as if
Arjang the Chini himself has painted it.

In it the king covers the noble woman with praise
And invites her to court as the diadem of the moon.

The messenger rushes as swift as dust to Gordieh
And relays to her Khosrow's words.
The king's letter makes the lioness
Shine as radiant as a spring rose.
She gathers her army at her door, pays the salary,
Then, at dusk, she packs her bags and departs.

Soon after, she approaches the royal city
To find that an escort has advanced to meet her,
And once at the gates, she's ushered in.
At the sight of her standing before his throne,
The master of crown is full of attentions for her.

She brings her entire treasury and her leaders.
One after the other, she offers the king valuables,
Handing the royal treasurer gold coins and gems
Worthy of a king and in such abundance
That estimating the count would be utterly useless.
There are bolts of golden brocade, crowns, belts,
A golden throne, and a golden shield.

The king observes the noble cypress tree
Blessed with a moon face, a pheasant's stride,
Cheeks that resemble day in their luster,
And curls that resemble night in color and sheen.
It is as if her mouth unfurls a cascade of pearls.
The king leads her to the women's chamber
And assigns her a rank above all the others.

Then he asks after her brother, after the well-being
Of Gordooy, his vizier, his affairs' keeper.
He asks for her hand in marriage,
According to religious rites, obtains her consent,
And considers her as valuable as his own soul.
He offers Gordieh's friends robes of honor,
Dirhams, dinars, and all sorts of wealth.

19 | Gordieh Proves Her Worth to Khosrow

Two weeks pass, then the king says to Gordieh,
"I conjure you by the Sun and the Moon,
By the throne and the diadem, to recount to me
The struggle you encountered with the emperor's troops
In which you dressed yourself boldly in armor."

She replies, "O King, may you always dwell in joy!
May your sight serve as nourishment for our souls!
Request a horse, a saddle, a bow, and a battle noose;
A spear, a helmet, chain mail, and a quiver
Complete with arrows of poplar wood."

The king commands a servant to set up a place
In the garden, by the blooming rose bed.
Open-hearted slaves, Turk and Rumi servants,
The beautiful women of Khosrow's palace
All arrive, numbering one thousand two hundred,
Filling the garden so that no path can be carved through it.

At the head advances Shirin, akin to the sun.
She is tall and as white as a silver column.

Gordieh rises from her seat, advances on foot
Toward the king, belt strapped, spear in hand.
She asks a slave for a coat of mail and a Rumi helmet.
She tightens her belt and grabs her spear.
She turns to the world king and says,
"May evil always remain distant from you!
May I have your permission to proceed?"

The king commands the skillful woman
To bestride her black horse.
Gordieh buries the end of her spear into the ground
And swiftly jumps onto the saddle.
She selects a closed field in the garden
And exhibits astonishing acts of prowess,
Launching left and right, flying about,
And shouting cries that pierce the darkest clouds.

She says to the king, "This is how I was,

Like a ferocious wolf when I fought Tevorg."

Shirin says, "O King, you offer weapons to our enemy,
For she will never forget that you killed her brother.
I fear that she will seek to destroy you.
You sit on your golden throne with a simple robe,
Free of armor, giving her full access to you."

Laughing, the king assures Shirin:
"Expect only acts of amity from this woman."

During this discussion, Gordieh continues
To execute warrior-like twirls on the arena.

Khosrow exclaims with praise: "Bravo!"

She says, "Please Yazdan that there was
Before me on this battlefield an enemy of the king!
I would instantly remove him from the saddle
In full view of his majesty as I removed Tevorg."

The king, astounded by her tall stature,
Her arms, and her shoulders, says to Gordieh,
"You are fearless in the face of the rotations of fate.
Let us test you before the cup of wine
And see if you are weak or firm on your feet."
He offers her a full royal goblet,
And the warrior woman accepts it.
She stands proudly before the assembly
As everyone watches her every move.
She drains her cup to the health of the king in one swig.

The ruler is quite stunned and says,
"O moon-faced fighter, I have in the world
Four army leaders, guardians of my life.
Each one of them is at the head
Of ten and two thousand bold Iranian riders.
Similarly, in my golden women's chambers
And in my gem-encrusted palace, there are twelve
Thousand servants, all wearing torques and earrings.
I wish to make you the overseer, for you have always
Worked for yours and have taken good care of them.
I do not wish for anyone else, young or old,

To tell me anything about them but you."

Gordieh feels happy and safe
Against the malfeasance of the enemy.
She sweeps the ground with her face
In celebration of the king's majesty.

20 | Khosrow Appoints a Cruel Governor to Rey

A long time passes during which
The king's star turns in his favor.

One night he drinks wine with his wise men,
Noblemen skilled in world affairs.
On the table spread is a cup
On which the name of Bahraam is engraved.
The king commands the cup to be cast aside.
Everyone empties his heart
And curses Bahraam and the maker of the cup.

Khosrow says, "The land of Rey is being trampled
Beneath the feet of war elephants.
The city has been converted to a desert,
And its inhabitants have been expelled."

The noble vizier says to the king,
"O Kianian heir, reflect on the fact that Rey
Is a great city that must not be destroyed.
Reflect on the fact that Yazdan would not approve
Nor would any of the earth's just men."

The king replies, "Then I must find a man
Of ill nature and low birth to govern Rey,
An ignorant man endowed with coarse speech."

The vizier says, "If the king could indicate
The signs by which one recognizes such a scoundrel,
I shall search for him and bring him to court,
For I cannot find him without instruction."

Khosrow says, "I am in need of a talker
Born beneath a baneful star, with red hair,

A vile body, a crooked nose, a yellow face.
One who is malevolent, small, wicked, ignoble,
With a bitter heart, lacking distinction, his head
Full of hatred, his tongue full of lies, cross-eyed,
His teeth wide and with the stride of a slouching wolf."

The wise men are astonished to hear
Khosrow's detailed description of such a being.
They search here, there, and everywhere,
In cities and towns, among men, great and small.

One day, someone appears at the king's throne
To say, "On my way, I have met such a man.
If the king permits, I shall bring him to his majesty
To assess whether he is right to govern Rey."

The king agrees.
The sight of the odd being sends a roar of laughter
Among the troops and the townspeople.

Khosrow asks him, "O wicked, foolish man,
What evil actions do you remember?"

Here is his reply:
"I have no way of stopping my vicious acts
And I have no intelligence whatsoever in me.
I say one thing but do the exact opposite.
If someone interrogates me,
I make him bleed, body and soul.
Falsehoods are my capital, and that is all.
I am incapable of any righteous thought or action.
If I make a promise to someone, I never hold it.
Any noble sentiment I may have I toss into the dust."

Khosrow says, "May your vile star keep you this way!"

The investiture of his title of Governor of Rey
Is written in the offices, and this lucky man
Gains power by way of villainy.

The king gathers troops and hands him leadership.
He departs from court with a reputation of indignity.
Once in Rey, the impure man banishes

From his heart and eyes any shame before Yazdan.
He commands all the rooftop gutters to be removed,
A feat for which he fully rejoices.
Then he sentences all the cats to death,
Thus distressing all the homeowners.
He travels with a guide in every direction,
Preceded by a herald who proclaims:
"If I come across a home with a gutter or a cat,
I shall set fire to the property and make the stones
Tumble down on the heads of its inhabitants."

Everywhere he goes, he spies and pries and,
Upon finding a single dirham,
He persecutes the owner.
People flee their homes for fear of this man.
People despair of the land, once so prosperous.
During rainfall, there are neither gutters nor guardians.
In this way, the miserable and vile man,
Who was sent to Rey from Khosrow's court,
Completely devastates the lush region.

The sun beats down on men's heads.
The city is replete with wounds and laments
To which no one in the world pays attention.

21 | Khosrow Appoints Gordieh as Governor of Rey After She Displays Her Skills

Life continues in this way until the month of Farvardin,
A time when the ground is carpeted with rose petals,
When clouds rain down their tears as morning dew
To add a gentle luster to tulips in mountains and plains.
Paths and fields are striped like the backside of a panther,
And the earth appears as lush and colorful as Rumi brocade.
Noblemen enter the gardens to play games;
Sheep and deer scatter to graze on the plain.

At the sight of the open garden doors
And the bathing doves gathered at the fountain,
Khosrow asks for the sound of clarions
And for platters of fragrant herbs.

They sit among the greenery to drink wine
And engage in happy discourse.
Someone approaches Gordooy from Rey
And relates to him a story from his city.

Disturbed, Gordooy reflects to find a solution
And addresses his sister, Gordieh:
"We cannot keep this information from the king.
Attempt to find a way to appease him."

Gordieh appears with a little cat.
She mounts a horse of golden bridle,
With a saddle ornate with jewels and gems.
Earrings drop from the cat's ears,
And its claws are painted the color of a tulip.
Its eyes dreamy and drunk, as if it has consumed wine,
Are as black as tar, its face as fresh as spring.
A golden cover floats over the horse's back.
In this way, Gordieh throws the cat
Across the garden as if it is a child.

The King of Iran laughs heartily,
A sort of laughter that is infectious.
Khosrow says to Gordieh, "O good-natured wife,
Tell me what you desire most from me."

The shrewd woman greets him humbly,
Bowing down reverently, "O illustrious King,
Offer me the land of Rey, be reasonable,
And free its people's hearts from grief.
Summon from Rey the evil being,
And give him his true name of miscreant.
He has chased away all the cats from their homes
And has plucked out all the gutters."

Khosrow smiles at the words of the woman
And replies, "O courageous army-destroyer,
I give to you the city and its district."

Gordieh recalls the miserable being
Who resembles Ahriman from Rey, and
Her fortune continues to grow beneath the shade
Of the royal tree that bears the crown.

22 | Khosrow Distributes Governments and Sends Armies to Iran's Borders

As the king's hand spreads across the empire
And the entire world submits to his rule,
Crown bearers become devoted to him,
And all his subjects grow more wealthy.

He selects in Iran forty-eight thousand men,
Skilled riders, valiant and able to fight.
He opens the doors to ancient treasures
Gathered by Pirooz and the blessed Ghobaad.
He divides the world into four regions
And nominates the governors of all the cities.

He sends to the border of Rum twelve thousand
Illustrious riders, prudent and ready to strike,
To guard the lush and happy lands against an invasion,
To allow every person to value the border
And appreciate the wealth of his possessions.

He sends twelve thousand glorious riders
From the rose garden to Zabolestan, all eager
To fight on the battlefield, and says to them,
"Bring gently back to the path those who stray
From the truth and do not keep their tongues.
Should they transgress again, bind them, imprison them.
Send spies to every corner
To ensure that nothing remains hidden.
Make the rounds day and night.
Never sleep in your tents without a watchguard."

Then he summons twelve thousand more valiant riders,
Powerful and full of warring ardor.
He gives them much advice and sends them
In the direction of the land of the Alaanans.
He entrusts them to protect the door to the empire's west
So that enemies are barred from crossing over.
He says to the illustrious men: "Be vigilant
And remain under the Creator's protection."

Then he selects twelve thousand more suitable riders,

311

Sends them to Khorasan, and gives them much advice:
"No one may cross into our land anywhere from
The border of the Hephthalites to the border of Chin,
Except for men whose souls are devoted to me,
And only if I am able to grant them permission.
I possess in every land a valuable treasure,
A resource that must not be out of reach.
Ask anything that suits you and satisfies you.
Be prudent, and you will be exempt from grief."

He opens his treasury's door, demands a great
Quantity of dirhams, coins minted by Hormozd.
Shedding tears, he distributes them to the poor
And supplies them with additional gifts and clothing.

Then he cuts off the heads of all of Bandooy's friends,
As well as anyone who approached Gostaham
And assisted in his father's murder.
In this way, having exhausted his vengeance,
He walks down a new path of learning.
He fixes and divides into four parts
The hours of night and day,
Assigning one to his wise man who reports back
The good deeds and reveals what occurs in public
And in secret in the army and around the world.

As soon as he sees something that is not quite right,
Whether in the army or among his subjects,
He instantly acts with a sense of justice,
Examines the problem, and finds a solution.

Another part of the day is dedicated solely to joy.
Seated peacefully among noblemen,
They listen to musicians without lending
A thought to hardships, as is the way of princes.

A third part is devoted to prayer and praise of Yazdan.
A fourth part to the observation of the skies
And to questions regarding nature,
The motion of the stars, and their numbers.
Astronomers stand before the king
As his guide in learning and understanding.
Nevertheless, a good part of the long night

PART THIRTY

Is devoted to drinking and enjoying
The company of beauties from Taraaz.

Khosrow proceeds to divide each month
Into four parts so that he may further
Instill joy and contentment into life.
One part is for games in the square
With mallet and ball, and target shooting
As the court's noblemen stand to mark the score.
A part of the time is consecrated
To mountain and plain and to the hunt,
An activity through which life is renewed.
Every time he returns from an expedition,
Whether by daylight or late at night,
All the men of power would raise
Rich pavilions of feast in the city.
A second part of the time is given to the games
Of chess and backgammon, and to war tales.
In the third part, he seats before him in turn
Anyone who is learned or literate
And able to recite an elaborate piece
Or sing ancient ballads to him.

In the fourth part, envoys are summoned,
And Khosrow would write replies to their letters
And hand them to the highborn men
Who would return from his court
With robes of honor and satisfied.
On the same day, he would write the deeds
To various lands and would give them to noblemen.

At the start of the new year,
During the month of Farvardin,
When the gardens dazzle with the sun's light,
He secretly establishes a treasure,
Well-guarded from his subjects.

23 | Shirooy, Son of Khosrow, Is Born Under Inauspicious Circumstances

With the passing of five years over his reign,
Khosrow finds himself with no equal in the world.
Upon the sixth year, Mariam, the Caesar's daughter,
Gives birth to a son who resembles the moon.

At this time, it is not the custom
For people to pray in a child's ear,
One meant to be raised with tenderness.
But his father assigns him two names:
A secret name, which he whispers in his ear: Ghobaad,
And a public name, which he proclaims loudly:
Shirooy of blessed birth.

The child is born during the third part of the night.
The king summons astrologers to his side.
He asks them to delve into the stars, reveal
Their observations , the results of their calculations,
And what sort of fortune the prince is to expect
As apparent in the cosmological tablets.

The chief astrologer says,
"We cannot escape the rotations of the sky.
The earth will be deeply troubled by this child.
The army will not easily give him its blessing.
He will drift away from the path of Yazdan.
What more could we reveal to you?"

The king, afflicted by this unfavorable report,
Says to the learned man, "Watch your words carefully
And take care not to disclose any of this to the noblemen."
The astrologer keeps quiet on the ill-fated horoscope
And locks it under royal key and seal.

The king remains deep in thought over this affair.
He closes his audience hall for one week,
Abstains from hunting and drinking wine,
And does not see anyone during this time.

The noblemen visit the grand wise master

And question him, wishing to know
What has happened to the illustrious Khosrow
To make him refuse access to his subjects.

The wise man relays their message to the king,
Who replies, "I am worried about my fate.
The words of the astrologers cause me
To protest against the spinning skies."
He commands his treasurer to bring
The silk envelope containing a written sheaf.

The treasurer obeys.
The wise man reads its contents.
His heart constricts, and he remains silent.
In the end, he says, "The Creator is everything,
Far above universal knowledge.
If the firmament, which follows its law
By turning an unfavorable face to the curious,
Yazdan, with divine mercy, can change this woe.
Nothing is resolved with complaint and fear.
No one can predict future events.
Do not pay attention to their words.
May you always have reason to rejoice!
May the Creator be your support and protector!
May the stars be your adoring friends!
We have no choice but to accept any seed sown
By the rotating skies, whether good or bad.
At times we are handed justice and compassion,
And at times war, suffering, and strife.
Everything, whether to our benefit or to our detriment,
Is distributed by providence.
We must lean on wisdom, for wisdom eradicates fear."

The king smiles at the wise man's words
And shifts his attention to another matter.
He summons his favorite scribe
And converses with him for a long time.

24 | Khosrow Writes to the Caesar, Who Replies by Asking for the Messiah's Cross

The king composes a letter to the Caesar
In which he says, "Place upon your head
A diadem worthy of kingship, for Mariam
Has given birth to a son resembling the moon,
A child of such beauty you have never seen,
A child who is worthy of acquiring knowledge,
Of obtaining fortune's grace, and of winning,
By his merit, the throne and the means to be generous.
May you live in joy, as happy as I am,
For happiness and pride are your rights!"

The letter arrives at the Caesar's court.
He examines it and sees Parviz's handwriting.
He calls for the blare of trumpets at the palace gates,
And the land fills with noise and clatter.
Festival pavilions are erected on and off the roads
To honor Shirooy, son of the victorious king.

The sound of music is heard throughout the land,
From one Rumi border to another.
Many crosses are carried in procession to court.
The scent of roses and incense fills the air.

For seven days, people celebrate with music
And wine the birth of Shirooy, the Kianian.
On the eighth day, the Caesar summons
A caravan of camel drivers to the palace door
And charges one hundred camels with dirhams,
Fifty more camels with gifts of dinars;
Two hundred with loads of Rumi brocade,
So dazzling with gold that it is
As if the cloth did not have a network of silk;
Forty gold tables with legs of coral worthy of a king;
And finally, sculptures of wild animals
In gold and silver with fine stones inlaid for the eyes.

He sends to Mariam a great quantity of jewels,
A golden peacock, silken garments, Rumi furs,
And a vase of beryl inlaid with pearls.

Then he sends tribute from his land,
Amounting to four loads of thousands
And thousands of Rumi dinars.
Forty Rumi men of insightful minds are led by Khanegi,
A valiant leader, who has no equal in knowledge.
In this way they depart with the camel driver
And ten camel troops loaded with dinars.

At the news that an envoy sent by the Caesar
Is appearing on the road, the victorious king
Summons Farrokh, who is devoted to him
And holds the rank of a border guard,
Commander of Nimrooz.
He tells this noble and valiant man,
Ornament of the army, to climb on his horse.
He takes with him royal cavaliers with golden helmets.

At the sight of the riders in the distance,
Khanegi advances to greet them as it suits
A stranger, and in this way, the Rumis arrive
At the side of the king and his glorious court.

When their eyes fall on the king's face
And on his magnificent throne, they bring
Their foreheads to the ground in homage.

Khanegi rubs his face in the dust for some time,
Then he says, "O just master, may Yazdan bless you
With victory, and may you always rule in happiness!"

The noblemen help him rise and assign him
A seat near the royal throne. Khanegi says to Khosrow,
"You have no equal in wisdom and insight.
You dazzle brighter than the sun in the vault of sky,
More ingenious than the most eloquent mind.
May the world never be deprived of your diadem and rule!
May fate shower you with an abundance of power!
May the day never come when your will is ignored,
You, whose name is inscribed on the face of the sun!
May your empire never be without its host!
I relay to the illustrious world king greetings
From the Caesar, who pays homage to his majesty.
May any man displeased and disgruntled

In the shadow of the king be deprived of light!
We arrive with presents and tribute from Rum.
We arrive to your glorious nation,
Escorted by scholarly philosophers
To safeguard you from disappointment.
May it please the king to accept the tribute
And the presents from the Caesar,
Along with lavish expressions of praise."

The king smiles at the man full of merit,
Whom he places on a seat near him.
He dispatches all the presents to the treasury,
Addressing the envoy and insisting:
"You did not have to take such pains!"

Then he turns to Khorraad, son of Borzeen:
"Read the Caesar's letter before the assembly."

The scribe, an eloquent, observant man, obeys:
"This letter is addressed to the great king,
The renowned Parviz, son of Hormozd,
Prudent master of the happy land of Iran,
Servant of Yazdan, the Creator, who bestowed
Upon him intelligence and the royal seat;
He who is the ornament of the crown and throne;
From the part of the Caesar, the young prince's
Mother's father, a ruler who bears a lion's name.
May his fame and his power endure forever!
May he be glorious, victorious, and bear fruit!
May all his days resemble the day of Nowruz!
May his influence extend from Iran to Tooran!
May he never find himself a rival in the empire!
May his heart always dwell in happiness
And his mind in peace! May his intelligence
Always be mature and his power young!
The noble prince of the race of Kiumars,
Descendant of Hooshang and Tahmures,
And so on from father to father and son to son,
Down the line, from generation to generation,
May this family's lineage never be severed!
May Yazdan, the holy, the realm's noblemen,
And the followers of the faith all bless you!

"There is no bolder rider than you,
Nor is there a more joyous spring than you,
Nor a Chini painting more dazzling than you.
You are full of humanity and righteousness.
May you never experience scarcity!
Yazdan allowed you to be born
Into the purest race that exists in Iran, Tooran,
And India; among the Turks and the Rumis
As well as all the lands where sorcerers dwell.
Never did a holy mother give birth to a son like you.
When Fereydoon offered Iraj the land of Iran,
He removed from Rum and Chin the glory of kingship.
He blessed his youngest from the very first day,
Purging darkness and perversity out of his heart.
It is as if Yazdan has endowed you with all the wealth,
A star of good fortune, power, courage,
And the art of alchemy.

"Employers of high merit, noblemen
Who lavish their wealth on others,
Men of this race never experienced hardship.
They imposed on their enemies tribute
And royalty fees, and those who wished
To harm them bore the burden like buffaloes.

"In the time of Kesra Anushiravan,
May his manes always be youthful,
For never has there been nor will there ever exist
A prince of such highborn race,
Who crossed the deep waters of the Jayhoon River
And climbed over the great wall
Built by a shrewd Kianian.
In his time, they freed the Forest of Naarvan
From the oppression of the Turks
And returned peace to the people.
The great land was liberated from the enemy.
May the benediction of men fall on Kesra's soul!
The Taazian, the Hindus, and the Iranians
Cinched their waists and composed an army.
From the Sea of Chin to the land of Khazar,
From Armenia to the western borders,
From the lands of the Hephthalites and the Turks,

319

From Samarkand and Chaadj,
All the noblemen, despite their authority,
Their honor, and their crowns,
Became your subjects and honored their servitude.
Your kings were of the race of Fereydoon,
And the others have no right to claim otherwise.

"The alliance I contracted with you
And by which I have wisely
Increased my power, delights me
As much as water delights
A parched man or a scorched plant.
May the prudent world master dwell in happiness!
May he give me a response today,
For I have a demand to make of the king,
A demand for something that has no value to him.
You have in your treasury the cross of the Messiah.
If you look, you will recognize that I speak the truth.
It has been in your possession for many years.
Would it please the king to return it to us?
By granting us this favor, the world king
Would benefit all of us, great and small.
The entire world would praise him and wish
That time and earth would never face his absence.
I shall receive the cross from King Khosrow
As an act of kindness, and I shall pray for him
During the day and during three portions of night.

"May he accept my presents along with the tribute
And the royalty fees that I send to court.
I shall welcome the cross as a blessing.
May his eye never perceive the face of a criminal!
Our feasts and our rites will then be complete.
Our faith will shine throughout the world.
We shall fast piously the first day of the week.
We shall worship Yazdan everywhere.
The afflicted will brush their faces against the cross.
We shall burn an abundance of incense,
And it will be a happy moment for our hearts,
As it will erase the ancient hatred that took root
During the time of Fereydoon and entered
The depths of souls in the era of Salm and Toor.

"The land will be freed from incursions
And vengeance of all sorts that have erupted.
Rumi women and children have been kidnapped,
Wounding our hearts in all sorts of ways.
The world has been pacified by our alliance.
These foolish acts have been calmed.
May the grace of the Creator shine on you and your land!
May you be showered with endless blessings!"

The world master, having listened carefully,
Is pleased and feels a royal fortune blossom in him.
He showers Khanegi with praise and says,
"Do not consider yourself a stranger in our land."

An apartment is prepared for the nobleman,
Consisting of two beautiful rooms
With all the necessary furnishings and items.
He visits his dwelling, then presents himself at court.
He never leaves the side of the worshipping prince,
Neither during meals nor during times of revelry,
Neither during the hunt nor during rest.

In this way, the Rumis pass one month
At court, spending it joyously and amicably.

25 | Khosrow Parviz Replies to the Caesar's Letter

At the end of the month, Khosrow writes a reply
To the Caesar, expressing kind and sensible words:
"May noblemen pay homage to the pure-hearted one
Who accepts from Yazdan the true, the good,
And the bad; who blesses the Master of the Sun,
Keeper of the sky as we perceive it.
First, I have to say that I understand the praise
You address me in your letter
As well as your show of friendship.
I delight in your manner of speech,
Worthy of a perceptive sage.
I have received your magnificent presents.
I did not wish for you to expend so much on my behalf.
You are able to do so, since Yazdan, the holy,

321

World Master, raised your realm to be above
The star of Arcturus,[23] thrusting your empire
To a higher status than those of India or Saghlaab,
Higher than those of the lands of Chin or Khazaria.
What courage, what knowledge, what virtue and faith!
The Creator has truly blessed you.

"When I was in need of you, you came to me
As a friend and freed me from my concerns
With all the resources of your wisdom.
Our alliance filled me with delight
As did you and your virtuous daughter.
I find nothing greater than her, than your land,
And this pure friendship we sealed with you.
Other rulers had turned away from me,
Abandoning me with disdain in my time of need.
You alone took the place of a father.
You were even more than a father to me.
Continue to treat me in this way, now that you,
My father, see me as a free king,
With a heart full of affection for you.

"I understand everything you tell me
On the subject of my son Shirooy,
A child of pure body, who will be my support
And my strength, and I thank you.
For this reason, I call you a man of pure faith.
My scribe has read the kind and touching words
You emitted on the subject of your religion,
On your custom of fasting and your devotions.

"I am not ashamed of my ancient faith.
There is nothing in the world better
Than the faith of Hooshang, which fully consists
Of justice, generosity, decency, and charity,
As well as the observation of the stars' motions.
I am convinced about the existence of Yazdan.
I apply myself sincerely to the execution of justice.
We recognize in the Creator neither companion nor ally,
But a being who will never hide and never disappear.

◇◇◇◇◇◇◇◇◇◇◇◇◇
23 Arcturus: The fourth brightest star in the night sky.

PART THIRTY

Our thoughts cannot embrace our Guide
When it comes to recognizing divine existence.

"As for the Messiah's cross of which
You speak in accordance to ancient traditions,
Consider the dictates of wisdom:
Any religion that is founded on a trivial
Piece of wood goes against sense and reason.
Those afflicted by such notions
Bear the responsibility for attaching
Their own prophet to the cross.
Who says that he was the son of Yazdan?
Who says that he smiled on this elevated perch?
If he truly were the divine offspring,
He would have returned to his father.
For that reason, you need not distress yourself
Over a piece of useless, rotting wood.
If the Caesar utters foolish words,
Any old man would laugh at him.
The cross of Jesus is not worthy enough
To be placed in the royal treasury of kings.
If I were to send from Iran a piece of wood to Rum,
I would be the laughingstock of my people.
Wise men would think that I have converted
And become a Christian priest for Mariam's sake.

"Ask me for anything else you may wish,
No matter what it is, the path is open to you.
I admire your presents for which you have labored.
I have bestowed your hard-earned valuables
To my son, Shirooy, to quickly start his own treasury.
I am full of worry for the lands of Rum and Iran
And spend countless nights with my thoughts.
I fear that, upon reaching the age of maturity,
Shirooy renews the ancient hostilities
First provoked by the fierce Salm and then
Continued by Eskandar, an old and vengeful wolf.
I fear for new and old hatreds to be reintroduced.

"As to what you have heard of your daughter,
Know that she has renewed your diadem.
She practices the religion of the Messiah

323

And rarely listens to what I tell her on the subject.
She is happy with the restful life she leads
And proud of the new offspring on the royal tree.
May the World Master always be your protector!
May your star of fortune never leave your side!"

The king's seal is affixed to the letter,
It is handed to Khorraad, son of Borzeen.
Then they open the treasury of valuables
Accumulated arduously by the king
Over a lengthy period of time.

First he takes one hundred and sixty pouches
Of coins that the Persians call Pandavsi[24]
And fills them with precious stones.
Each bag is carefully sealed, each inscribed for the value
Of one hundred thousand dirhams in the king's books.

Then he takes two thousand one hundred and forty
Thousand spindles of Chini brocade,
Embroidered with golden thread and precious stones;
Five hundred pearls from the beautiful far east,
Each in the shape of a droplet of water;
One hundred and sixty rubies akin to pomegranate
Seeds and vastly admired by experts.
Finally, he sends from Iran to the illustrious Caesar
Three hundred camel loads of sumptuous fabrics
From Chin, India, Egypt, Barbarestan, and Shushtar,[25]
All items selected among the finest of the region,
Luxuries the world has never seen.

He dresses Khanegi in a robe of honor,
More beautiful than what one offers parents or strangers.
He gives him horses, a cup, a throne, attire, bridles,
And sumptuous textiles to be loaded on camels,
Ten of which bear a heavy load of dinars.

Then he gives the lot to the Rumi philosophers,
Who depart from the land quite content.

◇◇◇◇◇◇◇◇◇◇◇◇◇
24 Pandavsi: A Pahlavi currency, each coin equivalent to five dinars.
25 Shushtar: An ancient fortress city in the province of Khuzestan, Iran.

PART THIRTY

All the noblemen sing the praises of the world king.

I shall now renew an ancient story and turn
To recount the adventure of Khosrow and Shirin.

PART THIRTY–ONE

The Thirty-Eight-Year Reign
of Khosrow Parviz (continued)

The Adventure of Khosrow and Shirin

1 | The Beginning of the Story

The ancient book detailing the words
And the actions of good men has grown old.
I take it upon myself to reintroduce it to the world,
To renew the memory of prominent and proud men.
It will be composed of six times ten thousand couplets
And consist of beautiful lyrics able to cast aside grief.

One may come across a book in the Persian language
One hundred times thirty couplets in length.
If we were to look and count the weaker verses,
They would most likely number less than five hundred.

Yet the generous king, a bright light among world kings,
Does not pay attention to my tales and stories.
His graces on me were stolen by my poor fortune
And by slanderers envious of my work.

Once the army commander takes the trouble to read
My stories, once he reflects upon them in his clear mind,
I shall receive a just reward from the royal treasury.
May the harmful reach of his enemies never touch him!
The army commander will share my work with the king,
Perhaps allowing the seeds I have sown to bear fruit.
May the diadem and the throne remain eternally,
And may the king's fortune shine brighter than the sun!

Here are the words of an aging and learned poet bard:
"Knowledge always comes to the assistance of men.
One has no choice but to accept grief and joy.
The taste of bitter, unsavory flavors is unavoidable.
No matter how wealthy or well born a youth may be,
He can never acquire merit without exerting effort."

When Parviz was a young, fearless man, whose father still lived
And whose son exercised the life of a warrior,

He had a friend named Shirin,
Who was as dear to him as his shining sight.
She was the only one in the world who pleased him
Among the most beautiful, noble ladies.

Once he became world king, he separated from her
For some time, wandering through the world restlessly,
Absorbed by the war that pinned him against Bahraam.
Through these months, Shirin wept day and night,
Feeling Khosrow's rejection of her love and affection.

2 | Khosrow Sees Shirin Again
and Invites Her Into His Women's Chambers

One day, King Parviz prepares for the hunt,
An activity most enjoyed by noble rulers.

Three hundred hand horses of golden bridle
Are gathered for the glorious king.
One thousand one hundred and sixty servants
Depart on foot, armed with javelins;
One thousand forty swordsmen
Wearing brocade over their coats of mail.
Behind them march seven hundred falconers
With hawks, hunting whips, and royal falcons.
They are trailed by three hundred riders
Leading the cheetahs, and, farther back,
Seventy chained lions and leopards
Raised for the hunt, muzzled wiht golden chains,
And tightly attached with Chini brocade.
Finally, seven hundred dogs braced in golden chains
Able to seize gazelles racing on the plain.

Following the procession are two thousand musicians,
Masters of hunting tunes.
They bear golden diadems and ride on mules.
There are eight hundred camels charged with seats;
Tents, great and small; fabrics for the enclosure
Of the royal encampment; and all the necessary
Equipment for the upkeep and feeding of the animals.

Farther back are two hundred slaves
To fire up the casseroles and burn aloe and ambergris.
Two hundred young servants carry before the king
Roses, narcissus, and saffron,
So that the scents emanate into the air
And drift back toward his majesty.
These men of fragrance are preceded
By one hundred carriers of wineskins
Filled with water with which they sprinkle the road.
It appears as if they spray rosewater on amber
To keep the path fresh for the procession.
It is so that the wind does not lift the dust
To adversely affect the ruler of glorious birth.

Three hundred young princes accompany Khosrow
On horseback, dressed in yellow, red, and purple.
The King of Kings is preceded by the Kaaviani banner
And wears a crown, earrings, bracelets, a royal robe,
A torque, and a golden belt inlaid with fine jewels.

At the news of the approaching cortege,
With the world leader at the head,
Shirin dresses in a yellow tunic, perfumed in musk,
Brightens her cheeks the color of a pomegranate flower,
Slips into a red robe of Rumi brocade woven
In pure gold and with patterns of precious stones.
She places on her head a royal crown inlaid
With jewels worthy of the wife of a warrior hero.

She climbs from her hall to the terrace,
But despite her youth, her humor is not joyous.
She awaits the king's arrival,
Tears flowing down her cheeks.
At the sight of Parviz's face, she rises,
Shows herself standing, speaks to him in a gentle voice,
And reminds him of their past encounter.
She sprays her cheeks with tears
Flowing out of her dreamy, narcissus eyes,
For hers are ailing eyes,
Though the roses of her cheeks blossom.

In this blend of tears and beauty,

She addresses him in the language of Pahlavi:
"O King, O lion, O fortunate Kianian blessed
With a warrior body, O hero, vanquisher of lions,
What happened to your love?
What happened to your tears of blood
Magically healed at the sight of your treasured Shirin?
Where are your nights converted to days when our hearts
And eyes wept while our lips shaped into smiles?
Where are the oaths and protests,
The promises and the sworn faith?"

She speaks shedding blood tears on her grieving face.
At the sound of her voice, Khosrow weeps
With her, and his face pales as yellow as the sun.
He sends his hand horse of golden bridle
And forty renowned Rumi slaves and orders them:
"You will bring her to the golden chambers.
You will lead her to the gem-studded room."

From there he goes to the hunting plain.
He spends some time with music and wine
And with his companions of revelry.
Having delighted in mountain and plain,
He returns to the city happily and eagerly.
Pavilions are set up on the road and in the city
To celebrate his return from the hunt.
The sound of clarion and song is such
That it shatters the thread and weft of the air.

This man of royal stature and powerful limbs
Enters the city and his lofty palace.
Shirin approaches the king,
Kisses his feet, his hands, and his head.

The world king says to the grand wise master,
"Guard yourself from having a poor opinion of me.
Wed me to this fair-faced woman
And relay this happy message to the realm."

He marries her according to ancient rites,
Just as prescribed by the era's customs and laws.

3 | The Noblemen Advise the King on the Subject of Shirin

The news spreads among the noblemen and
Warriors that Shirin is in Khosrow's palace
And that the ancient affair has been rekindled.

The townspeople are terribly afflicted,
Full of suspicions, sorrow, and curses.
For three days, no one appears at court.

On the fourth day, as the world-illuminating star
Rises to shine, the king summons his noblemen,
Seats them in their assigned positions,
And says to them, "I am chagrined that I have not
Had the pleasure of your company for so many days.
I fear that I have caused you pain,
And I am worried about your intentions."

No one replies to him. Those who are resentful
Cast their glances at the grand wise master,
Who notices, rises, and says to Khosrow,
"O righteous man, you became king in youth.
You have endured joy and misfortune from fate.
You have heard of the good deeds and evil deeds
Of noble and powerful men in the world.
Now the race of kings has been sullied,
And majesty will be erased from your essence.
Know that a pure son cannot be born
From a pure father and a corrupt mother.
A son will never raise a hand to precipitate
His father's death unless the mother spoils the race.

"Just like Zahaak approved of his father's death
And provoked Jamsheed to plunge into his end;
Just like Eskandar spilled Dara's blood,
Thus igniting the flames of hatred among us.
Dara considered his brother as a father,
And Filghoos considered him as a son.
The father was pure, but the mother was of ill nature
And could not bear a pure son.
No one seeks righteousness in a perverse man,

For the perverse will stray from the righteous path.
Our hearts are afflicted by the actions of the deev,
An atrocious being who is the companion of the king.
Is there no other woman in all of Iran
Who may equally please the king?
If Shirin was not in the women's chambers,
The king would be welcomed everywhere.
Never did your sensible ancestors
Have to speak of such an adventure."

The wise man continues on this subject,
But the King of Kings fails to offer a reply.
The wise man says, "Tomorrow at dawn,
We shall return to court, hoping for a reply,
For we have spoken at length today."

The next day, the noblemen rise at daybreak
And prepare to attend court. One of them says,
"The wise man does not speak effectively."
Another says, "His words appear reasonable."
A third one says, "Today the king must offer a reply.
He must say things that will bring us good luck."

All the wise men march and solemnly enter court.
After they take their seats, they see
A man arrive and pass before them holding
A burnished basin filled with warm blood.
At the king's side, he gently sets it down.
Everyone turns their sights away from the basin
As the court fills with murmur and buzz.

Khosrow looks around at the present assembly
As they exhibit signs of fear.
He asks the Iranians, "Whose blood is this?
Why have you placed it in front of me?"

The wise man says, "It is impure blood.
Anyone who sees it is disgusted by it."

After these words, the basin is removed
And passed from hand to hand.
They toss aside the blood and rinse the cup
To clean it with water and sand.

The vessel purified and rendered shiny again,
It is filled with wine, mixed with musk and rosewater.

Khosrow says to his wise man,
"This is, nevertheless, the same cup,
Or has it changed in nature?"

The wise man replies, "May you live eternally!
The pure has taken the place of the sullied.
With one word, you have changed hell into paradise,
And the object of beauty is under your command."

Khosrow says, "Shirin was to the city
What this disgusting and poisonous vessel was to us.
She has transformed, in my women's chambers,
Into a pure cup of wine.
In this way, my scent touches her
And drenches her in fragrance.
Because of me, she had acquired a bad name,
And hence illustrious men did not approve of her,
Though she never asked for material riches."

The noblemen pay homage to the king:
"May the earth never be deprived of your crown!
The one who spreads his generosity will, in turn,
Gain more benefits and kindness in abundance.
Mighty is the one who will thrive and flourish.
You are king, noble wise man, and powerful warrior.
You are a reflection of divine glory on earth."

4 | Shirin Kills Mariam, and Khosrow Imprisons Shirooy

Later, the king's power augments even more,
And what was once the moon
Becomes as bright as the sun.
He passes his days at the side of the Caesar's daughter,
The reigning queen in the harem.

The favors granted to Mariam deeply afflict Shirin,
Whose cheeks pale with jealousy.

In the end she poisons her opponent, quickly
Plunging the Caesar's beautiful daughter to her death.
No one is aware of her crime,
For Shirin guards her secret closely.

One year after Mariam's death,
The king offers Shirin the golden seat in the harem.

When Shirooy reaches the age of two times eight,
He is taller than a thirty-year-old man.
His father summons masters to teach him well.
At the order of the king, a wise man
Watches intently over him day and night.

One day, the wise man exits
The court in search of Shirooy.
He finds him as usual occupied with games.
He sees that the young man sits with a book
Entitled the *Kalileh and Demneh*.[26]
In his left hand the youth holds a wolf's claw,
Cut off and dried up, while in his right hand
He brandishes a buffalo horn and head
And strikes the two objects together.

The master grows concerned,
Deeming the game worthless
And considering the objects ill-fated.
He is disturbed by the child's evil character
And disastrous fortune, especially after having
Seen the horoscope drawn from his birth
And having questioned the vizier on the subject.

He goes to the grand wise master,
Explains the situation, and says,
"This prince only thinks of fun and games."

The grand wise master rushes to the king,
Who reflects in awe on the affair, his cheeks pale.
He is filled with concern on the fate menacing the world.
The words of the astrologer fill his soul with alarm

◇◇◇◇◇◇◇◇◇◇◇◇◇
26 *Kalileh and Demneh*: An ancient collection of animal stories originally written in
Sanskrit but subsequently translated into Arabic and Persian.

And bring fear into his heart.
He says, "We shall see in which way
The Creator will look upon this affair."

By the time Khosrow's reign
Reaches its twenty-third year,
Shirooy's limbs are well formed,
And the noble king is disquieted
To see the child growing bold and defiant.
Khosrow's soul more and more troubled,
He proceeds to lock up Shirooy
In his own palace with his milk brother,
Who has fallen into disgrace due to his sibling's mischief.
Similarly, he detains all those with ties to his son
Who seek the council of the prince.

At count, they find three thousand supporters,
Some of high birth as well as a number of commoners.

The king's attendant opens communications
Between the residences that enclose them,
Provides the palaces with carpets and clothing,
Provisions and all the means to distribute gifts.
He summons servants and slaves, wine and musicians.
The prisoners are give an abundance of dinars,
And they spend their time in joy and feast,
Under the guard of forty men.

Now I wish to insert here another story,
One recounted to me by a man of pure heart.

5 | Khosrow Builds the Throne of Taakhdis

We shall narrate now, according to sincere and truthful men,
The elaborate story of the throne named Taakhdis
That Khosrow Parviz raised in the hippodrome.

It is a story that began in the era of Zahaak,
A most impious and impure man.
When Fereydoon, the hero, arrived and overthrew
The Taazian ruler, there was a man living

337

On Mount Damavand whom the king singled out.
His name was Jahn, son of Barzeen.
He was prosperous in all the lands.
He was commissioned to build
A throne encrusted all around
With fine gems for the illustrious king.

King Fereydoon was most pleased with his work
When his magnificent throne was completed.
He gave Jahn thirty thousand dirhams, a golden seat,
And earrings, and he asked for a certificate
To assign him governance of Sari and Amol.
Jahn made these lands flourish like paradise.

When King Fereydoon, world master,
Handed over Iran to Iraj, his youngest, noble son,
He added to the gift of a kingdom three more gifts:
One was the throne, another was the bull-headed mace,
Still famous in the world, and the third was the jewel
Named Haft Cheshmeh[27] by the just ruler.
Iraj died and left behind these three assets,
Which Manoochehr in turn was able to enjoy.

Since then, every person
Blessed with the crown of kingship
Added something of value to the throne,
And when the blessed Kay Khosrow
Inherited it, its height increased.
The throne reached Lohraasp and, after him,
Goshtaasp, who exclaimed at the sight of it,
"One must not hide the work of powerful kings."

The noble Goshtaasp said to Jaamaasp, his advisor,
"What are you able to add to this work of art?
Examine it from every side to see how you could
Complete it, so that it may honor me after my death."

Jaamaasp surveyed the throne.
He discovered a key to the door of knowledge
And a representation of the sublime firmament

◇◇◇◇◇◇◇◇◇◇◇◇◇
27 Haft Cheshmeh: Seven Sources.

Where one could calculate nature,
The arrival of various phenomena, and their duration.
By order of the king, a depiction was made on it
Of all the constellations from Saturn to the Moon.

In this way the throne fell into the hands of Eskandar,
And each successive king added certain elements
And ornaments of gold and silver, ivory, and ebony.
But in the end, Eskandar ruined it in his ignorance,
Completing his work of destruction in one fell swoop.

Noblemen secretly kept fragments of the throne,
Trading them from hand to hand
All the way up to the reign of Ardeshir,
After which time the name of the throne was forgotten.

Meanwhile, the king did not find a hint of the throne
And applied himself with passion to build another
According to certain requirements,
But the end product was not to his satisfaction.
He died, and the throne went to his successors.
The affair was left alone until
The noble Parviz Shah acceded to kingship.

Once he assumed his place on the royal seat,
Parviz Shah summoned the land's noblemen,
And they spoke at length of the throne.

He said to them, "O illustrious lords,
I have a longing desire to renew the famed throne
In order to leave behind a memory of my reign.
I wish to examine the writings the famed Jaamaasp
Executed at the time of the rule of Shah Goshtaasp."

The wise man fetched the fragments of said writing
And Khosrow received them,
Joyously taking on the task of assembling them.
They showed him the throne of King Ardeshir.
He called on the most ingenious men of Iran,
And they constructed, during the king's reign,
A magnificent royal throne.

Carpenters arrived from Rum and Chin,

From Mokran, Baghdad, and the land of Iran.
They were one hundred thousand and twenty masters
Whose only ambition was to restore the throne.
Each master worked with thirty craftsmen
From Persia, Rum, and Baghdad.

The king commanded them to work incessantly
And to collaborate with each other
In order to complete the work in two years.

Once they built the lofty throne,
The powerful king's fortune radiated its light.
It measured one hundred and seventy arrash in height
And one hundred and twenty arrash in width,
Being less wide than tall.
The throne was so lofty that it collided with the sky.

Every morning of the thirty-day month,
A different carpet was spread before it.
The throne comprised twelve parts.
The glory of the day borrowed its sheen from it.
One hundred and forty thousand ornaments
Adorned its surface
With intricate patterns of turquoise and gold.
All the pegs and clamps were made of pure silver,
Each one weighing sixty-six mithqal.

The throne was placed in such a way that
When the sun's torch shone in the house of the Ram,
Its back was like the plain and its face like a garden.
When the sun was most ardent in the house of the Lion,
The back of the throne still faced it.
In the summer months, during the season of fruits
And feasts, the throne faced the garden
So that the scent of the fruit drifted toward it.
In the winter, during the time of wind and snow,
No one suffered from cold, for the entire top area
Was surrounded by a curtain of beaver skin
And sable furs worthy of a king.

The wardrobe valets warmed in a fire
One thousand gold and silver balls,
Each one weighing five hundred mithqal

And each turning the color of coral in the heat.
Half of the balls were always in the flames, and
The other half were offered to the highborn noblemen.

The twelve signs of the Zodiac and the seven
Planets were represented on the throne,
The moon dazzling among the constellations.
The astronomers saw in them wandering stars.
They saw how part of the night unfolded
And how the sky journeyed over the earth.
A portion of the constellations were made of gold,
And some were inlaid with precious gems.
No one, no matter how learned he may have been,
Was able to estimate their numbers.
The most insignificant stone incorporated into it
Was worth at least seventy dinars,
And many were valued at over seven hundred,
The average of the most pricy and the least valuable.
Then there was an endless string of priceless rubies,
Able to render luminous the dark face of night
And each appearing as Venus dazzling in the sky.

Three seats were on the steps of the royal throne,
Embellished from top to bottom with jewels.
From one to the other, there were four
Golden steps inlaid with precious stones.
The lower seat was called *mishsar*, or ram's head.
The seat one level higher was *laajevard*, or lapis lazuli,
As the wind and the dust never could reach it.
The third was entirely made of turquoise
And charmed the hearts of onlookers.

Poet bards and landowners sat on the *mishsar*.
The throne representing the blue vault of sky
Was intended for the riders intrepid in battle.
The turquoise throne was the seat of the vizier
And the treasurer who dealt with the affairs of governing.
To be worthy of such a seat, one required
Intelligence and unyielding devotion to the sitting ruler.
Once one arrived at the position of royal advisor,
How could one not have a seat at the side of Parviz?

A golden sheet covered it, fifty-seven arrash long.
On the fabric of the fringe, fine stones
Were introduced, held in place by golden threads.
In it, one could discern the image of the sky:
Mars, Saturn, Jupiter, and the Sun;
Venus, Mercury, and the spinning Moon,
Predictors of the king's fortune.
Next was a representation of the earth's seven realms
And the Persian and Rumi wise poet bards.
Next came portraits of the forty-seven noble kings,
Figured with their heads, golden crowns, and thrones.
Never had the world seen a more lush fabric.
It was spun in Chin by a man with no equal in skill
Who devoted seven years of his life to the labor.

At the start of the new year, on the first day
Of the month of Farvardin, the Chini man appeared
Before the king with this tapestry worthy of a Kianian.
The noblemen opened the way for him to pass,
And he spread his rich fabric on the day of Nowruz.

The powerful king was beside himself with joy.
Everyone gathered around the textile.
Wine and musicians were called for.
A musician named Sarkesh exalted the artist's praises
In song and congratulated the King of Kings.
The noblemen scattered jewels on Khosrow
To acclaim his power's glory and majesty.

6 | The Story of Sarkesh and Baarbad the Musician

Sarkesh continues to pluck the strings of his lute
And sing a song in praise of the king's splendor
As Khosrow's supremacy continues to spread.
His reign reaches its twenty-eighth year.
Everyone at court prospers.

There lives another talented musician named Baarbad.
People tell him, "The world king prefers
The company of musicians to noblemen.
If we place you across from Sarkesh,

You will rise above him with your voice."

Baarbad grows ambitious, although
He is in no way in need of fame and fortune.
He leaves his land and goes to the royal court
To observe and assess the king's musicians.

Sarkesh hears him sing, and his soul grows troubled.
He addresses the chief chamberlain,
Offers him dirhams and dinars, and says,
"There is at the palace door a musician
Who has the advantage of youth and talent.
He must not find access to Khosrow Parviz,
Or else he will be deemed a novelty while I shall
Be viewed as an increasingly more tiresome habit."

The guardian of the king's door listens to him
And bars entrance to the newcomer.
Baarbad continues to address him to no avail.
The chamberlain continues to reject him,
And no one intervenes in his favor.

Baarbad despairs of ever accessing the court.
With his lute, he goes to the king's garden
Where there is a guardian named Mardooy.
It is the royal garden for a period of two weeks
As king and court celebrate Nowruz.

Baarbad approaches Mardooy and befriends him.
Hopeful and happy, he says to the gardener,
"It is as if you are the soul and I am the body.
I must ask for a favor you can easily grant me.
When the world king enters the garden,
Allow me to be present so that I can secretly observe him.
Since this is the site where he spends his days of joy,
I could, while keeping hidden, gaze into his face."

Mardooy replies, "I shall grant you this favor,
And, for the affection I have for you,
I shall silence my doubts and my scruples."

When the king readies to step into the garden,
The heart of the gardener becomes a shining lamp.

He calls Baarbad and informs him that the king
Is about to enter his garden of delights.

Baarbad dresses in green clothing, takes his lute,
And prepares epic songs of battle and glory.
He goes to the location of the king,
Since every spring he selects a new site.

There is a verdant cypress tree with dense foliage
And thick branches akin to the brawl on the battlefield.
Baarbad climbs up, and, the lute leaning against his chest,
He hides until Khosrow arrives on the pleasant lawn
Where the gardener prepares a seat for him.

A fairy-faced cupbearer approaches the king
To offer him a wine so red
It renders the cup's crystal invisible.

Once the sun begins to pale, languishing
Until hues of lapis lazuli usher in night,
The musician atop the cypress tree begins to play
His instrument and sing a song about kingly exploits.
It is a ballad so beautiful it leaves the king
Of awakened fortune in a state of bewilderment.
Baarbad sings with a gentle voice
The air called *Daad Aafareedeh*, or "Just Creator."

Members of the assembly cast admiring glances
At each other, with inquisitive expressions.

Sarkesh is mad about the unexpected touch of lute.
He knows well to whom it belongs, yet he keeps silent.
He knows that none other than Baarbad
Has the skills to strike the chords
And chant so heroic a ballad.

The king commands the noblemen
To search the four corners of the garden.
They go in quest of the mystery singer
For a long time, then return empty-handed
And sit at the side of Khosrow.

The cunning Sarkesh speaks to say,

"It would not be astonishing that,
By the king's good luck, the roses
And the cypress tree would be musicians.
May his royal head and diadem be eternal!"

The cupbearer brings a new cup of wine,
And, just as the king takes it from his hand,
The musician suddenly begins a different melody,
Called *Paykaarkard*, or "The Battle of the Brave,"
A title assigned to the song based on the lyrics.

The musician sings, and the king listens,
All the while sipping his wine.
Then he asks for the singer to be brought to him.
They search once again for a long time.
They bring torches to finely comb every corner,
But nowhere do they find anything but cypress
And willow trees, and pheasants sprinting beneath.

The King of Kings asks for another cup of wine,
Raises his head in anticipation of the voice.
The sound of the instrument
As well as the chords of a new melody fill the air.
This one is called *Sabz dar Sabz*,
Meaning "Green on Green,"
And is used for incantations and magic.

At the sound of the song, Parviz rises suddenly,
Asks for a cup of wine to be enjoyed over a bed of roses
And as bright in color as the enchanting garden.
This cup contains a wine weighing one mahn.
With one swallow, he drains the cup and cries,
"If he were an angel, he would be of musk and amber.
If he were a deev, he would not have the ability
To sing or to pluck at the strings.
Search the garden and the rose bushes, left and right,
To see where hides this musician.
I shall fill his mouth and the folds of his tunic with gems
And place him at the head of my musicians."

When Baarbad hears the gentle and friendly words,
He climbs down the branch and heartily rubs his face
In the dust before the glorious Khosrow.

The king says to him, "Who are you? Speak!"

Baarbad replies, "O King, I am your slave.
I subsist only on the sound of your name."
With confidence, he recounts the incidents
Leading to this moment and reveals the identity
Of those who treated him with friendship.

The king, at the sight of him, is as happy
As a rose garden at the height of spring.
He says to Sarkesh, "O incompetent man,
You are the bitter quince and Baarbad is the sugar.
Why did you hold him away from me?
Why did you not allow him to sing for us sooner?
Never again will you perform before my assembly!"

Khosrow continues to drink happily
To the sound of Baarbad's voice
And to repeatedly empty his cup of wine
Until sleep washes over him.
Later he fills the singer's mouth with freshwater pearls,
Thereby appointing Baarbad as the king of musicians,
A most important figure among influential courtiers.

The story of Baarbad comes to an end.
May you never lean toward evil deeds!
Life passes over all people, great and small.
Why does a sensible man bemoan this fact?
Many greater and less significant people have preceded me,
And I would like to never wake up from sleep,
For an old man cannot be happy beyond the age of sixty-six.
Once this glorious poem is complete,
My name will echo throughout the land
And grace me with immortality.
I shall live on for having scattered the seeds of wisdom.
Anyone with sense and reason, with soul and faith
Will celebrate me long after my death.

Now I shall begin a new tale about the city of Mada'in
And the story of the building of Khosrow's palace.

7 | Khosrow Builds a Palace in Mada'in

A Persian man of serene heart,
Over whom four times thirty years passed,
Once recounted to me Khosrow's desire
To build a palace and how he sent messengers
To Rum, India, Chin, and all the wealthy lands.

After a search, three thousand artisans arrive,
All celebrated artists in their respective lands,
One hundred of the most skilled in the art of brick
And mortar, who originate from Ahvaz, Iran, and Rum.

Among them, they select the thirty most valiant,
And of these thirty, two are from Rum and one from Iran.
Of the three, the king chooses one noble Rumi,
The likes of which are few in the world.
He is a surveyor able to speak the Persian language.
The worldly man presents himself to Khosrow
And explains to him the plans
And the apparatus of construction.

The king says to him,
"Accept this commission from me.
Pay attention and absorb everything I tell you.
I want a palace in which my sons and my family
Can live for two hundred years
Without the chance that it may fall to ruins
From the ravages of sun, rain, and thunder."

The surveyor takes charge of planning the king's palace,
Affirming, "I have the skills to accomplish this task."
He digs the foundation up to ten king arrashes,
Each of which is equivalent to five ordinary arrash.
The foundation is reinforced with mortar and stone.
He performs his job like a man wishing to excel.

Once the walls are raised, the Rumi man appears
Before the king and says, "If his majesty knows
An expert of mature age and learned in many subjects,
He may send him to me with some wise men of his choice."

The king offers him such a man with a few others,
And they successfully certify that the walls are solid.
The Rumi brings silk, with which they braid a fine rope
To assess the height from top to bottom.
Then he measures the length of the rope
Before the assembly and takes it
To the royal treasury to be placed under the seal.

Later, he appears before the king and explains,
"The palace wall rises to the moon, but it must dry
For forty days so that it has a chance to settle.
During this time I shall require more workers.
When the time arrives to finish the palace,
Its roof will reach Saturn,
But you must not show impatience
And rush me or burden me with work."

Khosrow says, "O wicked man,
Why are you demanding so much more time?
You may not interrupt your work.
Have you no need for dirhams and dinars?"
He asks for the Rumi to be paid thirty thousand
Dirhams to appease him and convince him.

But the architect knows that
If he were to rush to complete the project,
Men aware of the nature of the work
And those building a dome would blame him.
Should one day the structure collapse,
He would lose his bread and his honor.
As soon as night thickens, he disappears,
And no one knows of his whereabouts.

The king is furious to hear of the Rumi's flight:
"How could a man lacking know-how
Be so presumptuous?"

Then he commands someone to examine the work
And imprison all the Rumis.
He summons architects,
Asks for mortar, bricks, and large stones,
But all those who are witness to the walls
Run away and disappear from the king's land.

He finds himself forced to abandon everything.

He turns his ear and his heart toward Ahvaz,
Where there dwell many construction workers.
He does not wish to allow a work of this magnitude
To remain incomplete and without its dome.

For three years, the king searches
For a suitable master architect, without success.
There is no one distinguished enough,
And they cannot stop talking about the artist who left,
Until one day, after four years, he reappears.

A wise and illustrious man relays the news to the king
While the Rumi rushes to present himself at court.

The king says to him, "O criminal, what is your excuse?
Why did you execute such a wrongful act,
Thereby barring yourself access to paradise?"

The Rumi says, "If it pleases the king
To have me accompanied by a trustworthy man,
I shall show the expert how I can be forgiven."

The king sends one of his trusted friends to the master.
With the rope, the learned Rumi measures
The height of the wall before the observer,
Showing him how the construction
Settled by seven king arrash.

They take the rope to court,
And the king's friend reports what he witnessed.

The Rumi then says, "O King, if I had raised the dome,
There would have remained neither wall nor dome,
Neither building nor the likes of me able to stand
Safely and respectably at the king's court."

The king understands that he speaks the truth.
No one can resist validity.
He releases all those he had incarcerated,
Whether they were guilty or innocent.
He gives the Rumi architect a pouch of dinars

And offers the prisoners valuable gifts.

The work continues for a long time,
With the king eager to see the final product.
After seven years, the palace is completed
In a way that earns approval from men of good faith.

Khosrow showers the Rumi with honors and praise
And offers him land, dinars, and dirhams.
Everyone wishes to visit the palace.
The king moves in on Nowruz, the first day of the year.

No one had ever seen or heard of such a dome.
There is a ring of melted gold to which
Is attached a circle with a chain of crimson gold.
Every link on the chain is inlaid with jewels.
When the King of Kings sits on the ivory throne,
The crown is hung on the chain.
During Nowruz, the king places
His blessed wise man closest to him.
Below are the leaders and army intendants.
Farther down are the merchants and the professionals.
Farther down are the poor people
Who gain their earnings from their hands' labor;
And farther down are men who have lost limbs,
Crippled ones who have been deposited at the palace gate.

A voice rises from the hall, moving the hearts
To proclaim, "O subjects of the world king,
Guard yourselves from nurturing
A sorrowful or a malicious heart.
Anyone who casts an eye on this lofty palace
Will find that his troubles disappear.
But one must look further than the Kianian throne.
One must respect one's inferiors and take care
Of the wounded one encounters on the road."

No one remains in the king's prison,
Whether guilty or innocent.
The king dresses the prisoners from head to toe,
Gives them dinars and all sorts of presents.
All the poor in the city unable to celebrate Nowruz
Are invited to the palace gate,

Where they are showered with royal dirhams.
All the criminals fear Khosrow,
And all those asleep are awakened by him.

Another herald enters the audience hall
At the time of departure and says,
"O worthy, skillful leaders, observe those below you,
For one must weep over the fate of the wretched.
Above all reflect on what you have to do
So that you preserve your safety and your strength.
Reflect on every affair and project, and take action.
Do not break the hearts of men of poor minds.
Listen to the words of wise men.
Anyone who holds to the true faith
May sleep before the throne without fear.
But anyone who extends a hand
Toward the possessions of another
Will not escape our wrath."

8 | On the Power of Khosrow Parviz

Now I shall speak a few words
On the subject of Khosrow's supremacy
And thereby renew the ancient days.
His power is so vast that no one, neither great
Nor small, ever remembers anything like it.

Anyone who has read the history of kings
Must shake his robe's hem in disgust for the world.
I shall say one word on which sensible men will agree:
This world, which contains more poison
Than its antidote, must not render you insolent.
It is merely a place of passage.
It is not a permanent dwelling.
Follow your path; disclaim feelings of greed or hatred.
You are an old man; the young are taking over.
One arrives; another departs.
Each person prances into this station
Only to gaze into it momentarily.
When the drumming of departure beats,
The heads of lion and elephant

Equally plummet into the dust.

Pay attention to my stories of Parviz,
And learn from its lessons.
They will astonish you, for no matter
How much you interrogate learned men,
You will never hear anything
That will surpass the dignity, the power, the grandeur,
The glory, majesty, and the army of the king.

During bright days and dark nights, he receives tributes
From India, Rum, Chin, and all the cultivated nations.
Every court sends him slaves and servants,
Pearls, rubies, and all sorts of jewels.

He has countless dinars and endless treasures.
Never has there lived a ruler of his stature.
Falcons and gyrfalcons, high-flying eagles,
Lions and leopards, whales in the seas,
Every being obeys him,
And his soul shines as bright as the sun.

The first treasure he forms with the tributes
From Chin, Bulgaria, Rum, and Russia
Is named *Aroos*, or "bride."
The second is the treasure of *Baadaavar*, or "windblown,"
Which they attempt to estimate without success.
The third treasure is *Dibah Khosravi*, or "royal silk."
The fourth is the celebrated treasure of Afraasiyaab.
No one, neither on land nor on the sea,
Has ever owned an equal amount of wealth.

The fifth is the treasure of *Sookhteh*, meaning "burnt,"
One that dazzles the world with its gleam.
Another is a wealth of freshwater pearls,
A heap as tall as the length of an arrow.
Taazian noblemen and skilled wise men
Have assigned it the name of Khazraa, meaning "green."
The seventh is the rich treasury of *Shaadvard*, or "giver of joy,"
Often featured in the ballads of singers and musicians.
Another treasure is called *Baad*, meaning "wind,"
Unique and never seen by men, great and small.

As for musicians, Khosrow can boast the talents
Of Sarkesh and Baarbad, never lacking sweet music.
In the golden women's chambers live
Twelve thousand young women as fresh as spring.
There are one thousand two hundred war elephants,
So numerous they allow little space on earth.
Forty-six thousand war stallions dwell in the royal stables.
An astonishing twelve thousand red-skinned camels
Stand at the ready, with ten and two thousand pack camels,
And six hundred and sixty-six more to carry the litters.

Never has the world witnessed such magnificence.
Never have the most experienced old men
Heard of such splendor and majesty!

There are thousands and thousands of warrior
Riders from Tooran, Chin, and Rum;
A number of black horses who never tire in war.
Shirin reigns in the night chambers,
Illuminating the rose garden.

Such a person as King Khosrow
Was killed at the hands of one of his assistants
And is now dead and gone.
Such a person as King Khosrow is dead and gone.
Why should you lament over the state of the world?
Why should you worry so much about your affairs
If you wish to boast the justice in your judgment?

The good and the bad in the world come and go,
And time counts our every breath.
Whether you are blessed with a throne, a crown,
And a treasure, or whether weariness is your lot,
You will, in the end, own nothing more
Than a cover of dust and a pillow of brick.
Attempt to sow only seeds of righteousness.

Every time we open the book
And read the story of Khosrow Parviz,
We are plunged into a state of astonishment.
Let us learn from its lessons; let us not forget them.

9 | Khosrow Becomes Unjust, and the Army Rebels

The world master is not satisfied with what he has:
His illustrious throne, his grandeur, his power,
And his brilliant diadem of the King of Kings.
He incites the ruin of Iran and Tooran.
This prince, once so fair and benevolent,
Turns unjust, favoring the evil acts of his servants.

Farrokhzaad, son of Azar Mahan, arrives,
Fierce of demeanor and seriously displeased
With the behavior of the king.

Khosrow imposes incredible labors,
With the goal of furthering his wealth.
He extorts riches from everyone, confuses everyone,
And blessings he earlier received now turn into curses.
Having always had the nature of a sheep,
The king adopts the character of a wicked wolf.

The people are miserable, having neither bread nor water.
They emigrate from Iran and relocate in enemy lands.
Anyone who suffers from the king's arrogance
Shouts his sighs and loudly curses kingship.

There is a worthless man named Goraaz,
Who blindly obeys the king,
Procures him rest, and always flatters him.
He keenly and carefully watches the border of Rum.
He is a man with the behavior of a deev,
Unjust and vile, and when the king, once so fair,
Turns to injustice, Goraaz is the first to betray him.

Then there is the famed Farrokhzaad,
A favorite of Khosrow,
Who is in charge of providing access to court.
When the king's life approaches its end,
Farrokhzaad's heart becomes corrupt.
He bonds intimately with Goraaz
And plots a conspiracy that stretches from land to land.

The leader Goraaz writes a letter to the Caesar

And incites in him an evil thought by writing:
"Rise and, with my assistance, seize the land of Iran."

The Caesar reads the letter and prepares for war,
Swiftly driving a host from Rum to the border of Iran.

10 | The Caesar Returns to Rum According to Khosrow's Plan

Upon hearing the news,
The king makes light of the matter.
He understands that Goraaz is responsible
For having advised the warring Caesar.
Khosrow summons the wicked man,
Who refuses to obey and show his face.
He fears the king, his court, and the noblemen.

The King of Kings sits with his leaders to deliberate.
They search for a long time for a way out.
Struck by a brilliant idea, Khosrow writes to Goraaz:
"I approve of your deed and have praised you
At court for having surpassed all in artifice
And having brought the Caesar's head
To the edge of a vertiginous precipice.
Upon receipt of this letter, reflect in your subtle mind.
Remain in place until I set out,
Then take the road to meet me.
The Caesar will lose, for he will find himself
Surrounded on both sides by our troops,
And we shall capture him and countless
Rumi prisoners and lead them to Iran."

The king selects a shrewd man from court,
Eloquent and learned, and says to him,
"Secretly take this letter as if you were a spy.
March in a way that you cannot be discerned
By any Rumi warrior who may interrogate you,
Seize you, and take you to the Caesar's army leader,
Who will ask you where you come from.
You will tell him that you are a poor man
Who seeks to earn a living,

355

That you have made the long and arduous journey
As carrier of a letter to Goraaz.
You will attach this letter to your right arm,
And if the Rumi takes it from you, it will be good."

The messenger leaves Khosrow's side,
The letter fastened to his arm,
And continues on the road.
Nearing the Rumi court, a patrician sees him
And takes him to the Caesar, powdered in dust,
Cheeks pale, lips a deep blue.

The Caesar says to him, "Where is Khosrow?
You must reveal to me only the truth."

The poor subject stands dumbfounded
In front of him, seized by a swell of panic.
He replies with a distressed mind.

The Caesar snaps, "Search this ill-intentioned man!
He has ill thoughts and utters ill words."

They investigate, and an intelligent man
Detaches the letter from his arm.
They appoint a learned leader able to read
The missive in the language of Pahlavi.

The cheek of the prince turns
As black as pitch with the message.
He says to his army, "Here is an ambush
Planned by Goraaz, who wishes to destroy us.
The King of Kings sets a trap for us
With three hundred thousand men,
Countless war elephants, and a vast treasure.
May his heart and his dreams dwell in obscurity!"

The Caesar withdraws with his army,
And the desire for conquest abandons his heart.

At the news that the Caesar is on his way back to Rum,
Goraaz's heart fills with pain and his cheeks pale.
He selects a cavalier among the bravest as messenger
And writes a letter full of complaint and wrath:

"Why is the Caesar disgruntled with me?
Tell me why you have left the land of Iran,
Thereby making me a man of few resources.
The king knows that I am the author of this venture.
His wounded heart will fill with rancor toward me."

The Caesar sees the letter and reads it.
He selects a nobleman from his army
And sends him to Goraaz to say,
"Has the Creator given you a level of prosperity
That leads you to destroy my crown and throne?
For you consume my entire army with a fierce blaze.
O man of ill race, your letter caused me
To cast to the wind my wealth and treasure!
You sought to surrender me to Khosrow.
May you never attain power and happiness!
Understand that the Iranians,
As long as they count a prince of Kianian lineage,
Will never ask a stranger,
Not even one from the Caesars' ancestry,
Not even the most intelligent man on earth."

Goraaz searches for a long time to justify himself
And to regain the Caesar's graces.
But despite all his efforts,
He could not release himself from the trap he fell into.

Khosrow selects a noble, eloquent, learned envoy
And writes a letter to Goraaz: "O worthless,
Evil man, you act in the way of Ahriman.
I have repeatedly summoned you to my audience hall,
But you refuse to follow the rules and the path.
Now this army that you have with you, with troops
You believe support you throughout the year,
Is in fact devoted heart and soul to the Caesar.
Send my way the soldiers who have been shaken
And who meditate thoughts of a rebellion."

Goraaz, deev-like leader, grows concerned.
He selects twelve thousand illustrious riders
And says to them, "Remain united.
Do not give credence to anyone's words.

Stay still for some time on our side of the water.
Do not hasten your footsteps.
As long as you are united and agree with each other,
You will have the strength to tear out
The very foundation of a boulder."

The army marches to Khorreh Ardeshir,
Young and old, as one, undivided.
At the river's edge, they await the order of the king.

At the news, Khosrow commands Farrokhzad
To travel in haste to the side of the royal army,
Bearer of the following message:
"Long ago, you regarded me with good dispositions.
Why have you left the road open
In a way that allows the Rumi Caesar
To cross over with his host?
Any one of you who has transgressed
From my directions has fallen off Yazdan's path."

The warriors' faces dim with terror.
No one dares reveal the secret.
They feel pained and burdened by worry.

The king's messenger who conspires with Goraaz
Hides this secret even to the wind and the earth.
He furtively visits the leaders
And brightens their dark souls by saying,
"O powerful men, do not nurture fear.
The king is not aware of any transgression from you.
Remain united in heart, intention, and word.
Do not reveal who among you is the king's enemy.
Say that if there has been an enemy,
You all stand beneath the same cloak,
And you all support each other bravely."

The warriors understand the secret.
They rise and reply accordingly.

Farrokhzad returns to the king, as swift as dust,
And reports to him the words of the warriors.
The king commands him to tell them:
"Which one of you wishes to burden others with pain?

Has the Caesar of dim fortune corrupted you with
The promise of treasures, weapons, crowns, and thrones?
That man has failed in his duty toward me
And is deemed a rebel to my crown and my throne.
Send to my court the one who has failed
Or else the gallows and the dungeon await
The entire army for having veered off the path."

Farrokhzaad departs and repeats the king's words,
And the young warriors' cheeks crease in grief.
No one dares open his mouth.
They remain silent and aggrieved for a long time.

Suddenly, Farrokhzaad gives free run to his tongue
And speaks wicked words: "Here is a young
And valiant army in which I do not see a weak man.
Why do you then hold such fear for the king?
He has distanced his troops from his palace,
Scattering them across the world.
There does not remain at his court a nobleman
Able to shed light on his star and his moon.
Scorn the words I deliver to you on behalf of the king.
Do not fear the misfortune I menace you with.
Reply to the reproaches addressed to me
Or to the king who holds his head high."

With this speech, they understand
That the king's fortune has passed.
They rise and voice their indignation.
Farrokhzad departs and reports to the king
That the entire army is united in sentiment,
Adding, "I fear for my life
Were the king to send me back to them."

Khosrow understands that this man of perfidious
Words is able to mix truth and falsehoods.
But he does not reply, for fear of Farrokhzad's brother.
He keeps to himself what he knows as truth.

Goraaz has turned away from the king and government.
He commands ten thousand sword-striking men.
He observes the intentions of Farrokhzad
While turning his troops away from Khosrow.

11 | The Iranian Noblemen Free Shirooy

Farrokhzaad understands that Khosrow
Would soon hear of the army's betrayal.
Once he exits the palace, he does not
Dare present himself before the throne.
He stands by the door and makes every effort
To entreat those who seek an audience,
Convincing everyone, warrior by warrior,
To turn their back on the king.

He is able to persuade most Iranians of the need
To replace Khosrow with another ruler,
Since he has digressed from the ways
Of dignity, royal custom, and good fortune.

An old man full of experience in the affairs
Approaches Farrokhzaad and says to him,
"Khosrow attributes to you the army's defection.
We cannot go farther until you bring forward
A new ruler, or else this prosperous land of Iran
Will be converted into a barren desert.
We must assess which one of Khosrow's sons is
Most humble and meets with the least opposition.
We must place him boldly on the throne
And shower his crown with golden coins.
We must proceed with caution
If we wish to taste sweetness after a bitter morsel.
Since Shirooy, his eldest son, is intelligent
And finds himself in prison, he must be the one."

Everyone shares the same mindset.
Not much time passes before Tokhaar
And his host raise the dust, firm in their resolve.

Farrokhzaad meets with Tokhaar,
Accompanied by innumerable troops.
They dismount together and speak
At length in public and in private.

Farrokhzaad exposes the ailments caused by Khosrow
And adds, "The army wishes to reestablish

Royalty through its value and its wisdom."

Tokhaar replies, "As for me, I have no talent.
But when I fight against the heroes,
World champions cannot contend with me.
The king, in his youth, was dear to noblemen
And warriors. When one sees
The days of such an illustrious man obscure,
One cannot wish the crown and throne for another.
Khosrow lost his power the moment he became
Unjust and approved of his subjects' wrongdoings."

With these words, Farrokhzaad selects Tokhaar
Among all the Iranians to execute his plan.
He says to him, "Let us go to the prison.
Let us approach the wretched men held within,
And, without hesitation, let us release Shirooy,
The young, brave, and ambitious prince.
There is a prison supervisor who deserves
To be robbed of his brain and skin.
He and six thousand riders guard the captives."

Tokhaar replies to Farrokhzaad,
"We have treated the affair of the supervisor lightly.
If fortune were to return to Parviz,
He would not allow a single Iranian warrior to live.
No one would escape chains and would end up
Either on the gallows or in dungeons."
As he says this, he launches his horse forward,
Taking his army into battle as swift as Aazargoshasp.

The supervisor boldly advances toward Tokhaar.
But his illustrious troops are thrown into disarray,
And he himself is killed in the chaotic brawl.
The king's army scatters.
The day dims for Khosrow, and his power is lost.

Thus Tokhaar finds a way into the narrow prison.
He calls Shirooy in a loud voice,
And the prince responds,
Understanding the reason for Tokhaar's visit.

At the sight of the leader's radiant face,

His heart and soul exhale his anguish,
And he says through tears,
"Where is Khosrow?
Have you come to liberate me?"

Tokhaar says to the king's son,
"If you consider yourself a man,
Do not scratch at the lion's palace.
If you do not agree with us in this affair,
Guard yourself from mixing your hand in it.
We can pass on one prince out of sixteen,
Since we have fifteen more of your brothers,
Each of whom is worthy of royal status.
If not by you, the throne of power
Will happily be occupied by one of them."

Shirooy, weeping and in a state of confusion,
Emerges from his confined dwelling.

12 | Khosrow Learns of the Army's Deeds

During this time, Farrokhzaad stands alone
At the palace door barring entry to anyone
Who may reveal information on recent incidents.

As the sun begins to pale beneath its veil
And the noblemen prepare for sleep,
Farrokhzaad commands the night guards,
All the ones with a certain amount of authority,
To assemble at the palace gate,
A place of joy and rest for the king.

He says to them, "Tonight, we must adopt
A cry different from previous nights.
The guardians must shout out
Ghobaad's name in recognition."

They agree, "We shall do so
And thereby chase away Parviz's name."

As night renews its pitch-black veil,

The guardians raise their voices over city and marketplace
To proclaim: "May Ghobaad,
Descendant of great kings, live in happiness!
May his name be acclaimed in all the lands!"

The world king is asleep in the deep of night
With a troubled Shirin sitting at his bedside.
She grows concerned when she hears the cries.
Her heart, once so happy, is stirred into a state of grief.
She says to Khosrow, "O King, what will ensue?
We must discuss what is happening."

The king awakens at the sound of her voice,
And, irritated, he says to her, "O moon face,
What are you trying to tell me at a time of sleep?"

She replies, "Open your ears,
And listen to the cries of the night guards."

At the sound of them, Khosrow's cheeks
Grow as pale as the flower of the fenugreek.
He says, "Three parts of the night have unfolded.
Summon the astrologers, and ask for their advice.
When this evildoer was born from his mother,
I secretly gave him the name of Ghobaad,
While out loud and in public I called him Shirooy.
I painstakingly kept his secret name hidden.
We must leave in the dark night for Chin or Maachin,
Or perhaps for the land of Mokran.
We shall outpace our enemy by means of a ruse,
And I shall ask for an army from the Emperor of Chin."

With the dimming of his star of fortune,
His affairs on earth take a course for the worse.
He does not execute his plan swiftly
Under the cover of night,
Taking a serious affair much too lightly.

He says to Shirin, "Our time has arrived.
Our enemies have gained more power and overrule
Any effective ruse or strategy we may have.
May you live forever!
In your wisdom, devise a way of salvation.

Heaven forbid that our foes reach their goals.
When daylight arrives, they will undoubtedly
Be advised to descend on our palace."

The king asks for a coat of mail from the royal treasury,
Two Indian sabers, a Rumi helmet, a quiver,
Arrows, and a golden shield.
He summons a valiant slave avid for battle,
Then exits into the garden when night is still deep.
It is at the precise hour when the black crow awakens.

He selects a place in the vast garden,
Beneath a mass of trees,
To set a plan on which he could sit.
He suspends from a tree branch his golden shield
At an isolated spot, away from the passage of men.
He sits amid the narcissus and the saffron blooms,
His heavy sword in one hand, his mace in the other.

As the sun launches its rays from above,
Khosrow's bitter, relentless, deev-nurtured enemies
Enter the magnificent palace and search its every corner,
But the king is nowhere to be found.
They abandon his treasures to pillage,
And no one lends a single thought to the labors
And pains Khosrow endured to amass them.

They return, eyes full of tears
And surprised by the unfolding of fate.
What can one ask of the spinning dome of sky
That never rests from its motion?
It gives one a royal crown
While abandoning the other to the fish in the sea.
It leaves one naked from head to toe,
Without rest, food, or a hiding place,
While nourishing another with milk and honey
And dressing him in brocade, furs, and silks.
In the end, both end up in a dark spot,
Deep in a lowland beneath the ground.
If a sensible man had not been born,
He would not have to endure grief, shame, and pain.
It is more valuable to not see the world at all,

Whether you are a subject of the king or the king himself.

Now I shall take great pains to furnish
The singers with a new tune or story
On the demise of King Khosrow Parviz.

13 | Khosrow Parviz Is Taken Prisoner by His Son Shirooy

Khosrow remains in this field
Beneath the shade of a majestic tree.
Half of the long day passes,
And the king's hunger intensifies.

In the garden there is a laboring servant
Who has never cast his eyes on the royal face.
Khosrow, who shines like the sun, addresses him:
"Do cut a part of my fine-looking belt."
The piece sports four golden buttons,
Costly because of the inlaid gems.

Khosrow adds to the gardener,
"These buttons will serve me well today.
Take them to the bazaar
And buy some bread and a piece of meat.
Do avoid the major paths traveled.
These gems are worth thirty thousand dirhams
For any man who is in need."

The gardener runs to the baker with them
To purchase some bread. The baker says,
"I know not the value of this object
And am not able to gain a return on it."

The two take the belt strap to the jeweler and say,
"Make use of your skills and give us a price."

The expert jeweler sees the gems and says,
"Who would dare buy such a valuable piece?
There are similar chain links in the king's treasury.
Every year, new ones are added to it.

Where did you steal these from?
Did you seize them from a slave asleep?"

The three men go to Farrokhzaad and Shirooy
To return to him the precious object.
As soon as the leader sees the fine stones,
He rushes to the side of the new king.

Shirooy says to the gardener, "If you do not
Give us an indication of the whereabouts
Of the owner of this belt scrap,
I shall have your head cut off,
As well as all the members of your lineage!"

The gardener replies, "O King, there is in the garden
A man dressed in mail and holding a bow.
He has the stature of a tall cypress tree,
A face as fresh as spring
And in every way sports a royal mien.
He makes the garden dazzle with his presence,
As he shines in his armor as bright as the sun.
A golden shield hangs from a tree branch.
A slave bearing a belt stands before him.
He removed from his body this piece with gems,
Handed it to me with the command:
        'Run to the market and bring me back
        Some bread and seasoning.'
        I left him instantly, rushing as fast as wind."

Shirooy is certain that the description
Of so regal and unique a demeanor
Matches his father, Khosrow.
He sends from the palace three hundred
Speedy riders to the edge of the river.

Khosrow, at the sight of the approaching company,
Pales and draws his sword of battle.
When their eyes fall on the King of Kings,
The troops retreat and return weeping to Farrokhzaad,
To whom they give an accounting:
"We are mere subjects, and he is the king.
Misfortune is a new thing to him.
No one will dare send his way even a cold breath,

Either in the garden or in battle."

Farrokhzaad approaches the king's garden,
Taking from his palace a vast escort.
He advances alone to address him a few words.
Khosrow listens to him attentively as he says,
"If the king grants me an audience,
If he wishes to give me amnesty for my deeds,
I shall tell him the truth, otherwise I shall go home."

Khosrow replies, "Speak as you say you will speak.
Though you may not be a sympathizer,
Neither are you an enemy."

The eloquent man says to the king,
"Cast a more insightful look at this affair.
You are not in a state of killing one thousand warriors.
The people of Iran have grown hostile toward you;
They are united body and soul to contend with you.
Come and see what the skies hold in store for you.
Perhaps fate's clemency will erase the hatred."

The king's heart fails upon hearing the words
Of Farrokhzaad because of an old memory.
Long ago, astrologers had pronounced words
That had made a profound impression on him.
They foretold that he would meet his death
At a place between two mountains
And at the hand of a slave, away from the crowd.
One of the mountains would be made of gold
And the other of silver, and he would be
Seated between the two, his heart vastly broken.
The sky above him would be golden, the earth
Of solid iron, and his fortune full of rancor.

Now Khosrow reflects, "This coat of mail
Is my seat upon the earth, the shield is my sky,
The two mountains are the two treasures
Placed in the garden, the delight of my soul.
Without a doubt my days have reached their end.
Where has gone my world-illuminating star?
Where is my power and my sense of security,
Me, whose name was once inscribed upon crowns?"

Out loud, Khosrow says, "Yes, it is true.
I fear evil men. I fear their curses on me."

They drive an elephant to him,
Filling his dim soul with grief.
The king climbs on it, and the army
Guides the elephant out of the garden.

Khosrow says in Pahlavi from atop his beast:
"O my treasury, although you proved your enmity,
Do not befriend my adversaries, for today
I am in the hands of Ahriman.
You did not come to my rescue in my distress.
Hide and do not show yourself to anyone."

Ghobaad commands the vizier:
"Do not address him a word of reproach.
Drive him to Ctesiphon and place him
In the house of my favorite advisor.
He will remain there for some days,
And no one must hurt him in any way.
Let him be under the guard of Golinoosh,
A sure man who commands one thousand riders."

Khosrow Parviz reigned for thirty-eight years,
When the spinning sky passes in this way over him.
It is the day of Dey, during the month of Aazar,
A time when people light fires, roast poultry, and drink wine.
On that day, Khosrow loses royal glory and his crown.
Once he boasted to be the famed King of Kings.
He is now lowered to the status of subject or slave.

Ghobaad ascends, places the crown over his head,
And sits happily on the throne.
The army of Iran pays him faith and homage,
And the king distributes the troops' yearly salary.
But his life subsists for only seven months.
Call him king if you want, or call him nothing.

Such is the custom of this oppressing world.
One must not expect it to keep its promises.
Anyone familiar with its ways
Knows that it always holds a grudge.

Attempt to perform good deeds
And entertain good thoughts.
When you attain the object of your desires,
Beware, for the goal may have a hold on you.
As much as you can, give up wicked thoughts
And listen to the words of the wise man.

As long as your words and deeds are virtuous,
Your soul will maintain its purity in the world.

PART THIRTY-TWO

The Seven-Month Reign of Ghobaad, Known as Shirooy

1 | Shirooy Ascends the Throne

As Shirooy happily takes his seat on the throne,
He places the Kianian crown of justice on his head.

Iranian leaders arrive to pay homage to him
As is due famed rulers. They loudly declare,
"O noble, rightful King, just as Yazdan bestowed
The crown and peacefully transferred
The ivory throne to you, may you, in turn,
Similarly deliver kingship to your son."

Shirooy replies, "May you be victorious and joyous!
We shall never give in to evil acts, so glorious
Is justice when united with a benevolent nature.
We shall assure that the world lives in security.
We shall destroy the efforts of Ahriman
With the aid of rules passed down by our ancestors.
Our work will make our religion dazzle and shine.
I shall send a message to my father
To make him know the state of our affairs.
His name will retain a layer of disrepute
Because of his unreasonable conduct as ruler.
He will ask of Yazdan forgiveness for his sins.
He will comport himself according to the rules
And walk down the proper path.
If he consents to follow my advice,
He who so afflicted my heart,
Then I shall apply myself to world affairs.
I shall attempt to act with justice in public or in private.
I shall bring happiness to good people
And never break the hearts of the poor.
Now I need two noble and eloquent men
With knowledge of what happened long ago."

He turns to the assembly and adds,
"Who is willing to serve me?
Point out the purest, most prudent leaders of Iran?"

The heroes glance in the direction of two learned men,
And Shirooy understands the selection
If they are willing to take on the responsibility.
They are Oshtaa and the aging Khorraad,
Son of Borzeen, two learned, eloquent, observant men.

The king says to them, "O intelligent ones,
You have experienced and accomplished much.
Do not deem the affairs of the world harshly,
For noblemen acquire wealth through hard work.
You must go to my father, the king.
Perhaps you can effect a change in his thinking.
Discuss with him various subjects, old and new."

The two wise men rise unwillingly
And prepare to depart, their lashes full of tears.
Khorraad, son of Borzeen, and Oshtaa, son of Goshasp,
Climb on horseback according to the king's command:
"Take the road to Ctesiphon with goodwill,
And take the message to my exalted father."

He addresses Khorraad: "Be vigilant,
Since you were the king's vizier.
Remember the message from beginning to end.
Tell Khosrow,
            'It is not our fault that your reign abruptly ended.
            The Iranians alone could not overthrow you.
            You were struck by Yazdan's vengeful wrath
            When you turned against the true faith.
            First, a wellborn son would never shed
            His father's blood, as impure as he may be.
            He would never be sanctioned by storytellers.
            Furthermore, the world is filled with your wealth,
            And your exactions spread to all the lands.
            You filled with grief the hearts of good men,
            And in this, no one can approve of your actions.
            So many valiant, illustrious riders lived in Iran
            Without the chance to enjoy home and children.
            Some traveled to Chin and others to Rum,
            Many scattered throughout the lands.

            'Furthermore, you ignored the Caesar

Who did so much for you,
Who gave you an army, a daughter,
An abundance of gold, and countless precious valuables.
You ignored his request to return to Rum
The Messiah's cross so that the land may flourish again.
What is the point of this cross in your treasury
Next to the Caesar's pleasure if granted this favor?
Yet you refused him out of foolishness,
Straying from the path of humanity.
Another seized you, the eyes of reason troubled,
And you failed to interfere when
The goods of the unfortunate were extorted.
They cursed you,
And their curses caused your downfall.

'In addition, you killed my two kind uncles,
Whose reflection dazzled your throne.
You had two times eight children
Whose days and nights passed in prison.
No one at your court was able to sleep
With a sense of security for fear of you.
People distanced themselves secretly.
Know that your defeat is brought on by the Creator.
Take the time to reflect on your wicked actions.
I am not the instrument of your downfall
But merely the threshold over which things cross.
I swear by Yazdan that I am innocent,
That I never sought to usurp the royal throne.
Ask forgiveness for what you have done.
Ask forgiveness from Iran's noblemen.
Turn toward Yazdan for your misdeeds,
Your Guide in virtue, and I hope
That the divine hand will draw you out
Of the troubles you precipitated upon yourself.'"

Having delivered the message, the two men depart,
Their souls wounded and tormented.
They travel to the land of Ctesiphon,
Eyes full of tears, hearts swelling with blood.

From the city, they march to the king's palace
Of Maroosepend, where they find Golinoosh,

Before whom the earth appears on the boil.
His host is equipped, dressed in armor and helmets,
Mounted on strapped Taazian stallions.
Golinoosh holds a mace of steel,
His tempestuous heart on fire.

When Khorraad Borzeen and Oshtaa Goshasp
Dismount, Golinoosh instantly rises, delighted
To see them and honoring them as illustrious men.

The eloquent Khorraad is the first to bravely
Speak to Golinoosh, "The blessed Shirooy
Peacefully placed upon his head the Kianian crown.
It has been announced in Iran, Tooran, and Rum
That he occupies the throne of the King of Kings.
Why have you dressed in armor and helmet,
Brandishing your mace and bow?
Who is your enemy?"

Golinoosh replies, "O worldly man,
May all things unfold according to your will!
You free my body from the burden
Of this heavy tunic of steel.
I shall praise you for your affection
And scatter jewels over you.
You will always utter kind words.
May the sun be your protector!
Tell me what brings you here, and ask for a reply."

Khorraad says, "The blessed Ghobaad gave me
A few messages to relay to Khosrow.
If you would kindly ask him for an audience,
I shall tell him what the world master
And the people have charged me to say."

Golinoosh replies, "O noble man,
Who could repeat their words better than you?
But Ghobaad, King of Iran, lavished me with advice
And recommended that neither by day nor by night
I allow anyone to speak to Khosrow
Unless I can give attentio to what is said,
Whether in Persian or in Pahlavi."

Oshtaa says, "O fortunate man,
My message is not meant to be secret.
It is a biting one such that
This blade will have to bear fruit
And the proudest heads will have to be flung
Into the folds of their respective tunics.
Ask Khosrow for an audience right away
So that I may acquit myself of the king's message."

Golinoosh listens to him, rises, fastens his armor,
Enters the king's hall, arms crossed as suits a servant,
And says to Khosrow, "O King, may you live forever!
May your heart never find its way to affliction!
Oshtaa and Khorraad, son of Borzeen,
Bring a message from the royal court."

Khosrow smiles and says loudly,
"Your words are not reasonable.
If my son is king, then what does that make me?
Why am I held in this constricted cell,
And why do you ask me for an audience with people
Who will tell me either falsehoods or truths?"

Golinoosh returns to the heroes,
Reports to them the royal response and says,
"Enter now, arms crossed at your chest.
Speak to him and listen to his reply."

The two wise men, bearers of sincere words,
Cover their mouths with a piece of Chini fabric.
At the sight of the king, they bow low
And remain in this way for a long time.

The world master slouches on a lofty throne,
Ornate with ram and wolf heads.
The seat is embroidered with gold interweaved with gems.
Beneath his feet is a stool of yellow brocade.
His back rests on pillows the color of lapis lazuli.
His mien somber, he holds in his hand a large quince.

He notices the two powerful men who excel in wisdom.
He sits up and invokes in his soul the Creator's support.
He sets the beautiful quince on a cushion

377

And prepares to question the two slaves.
But the quince slides off, spinning and rolling down
The slope of brocade, bouncing off the royal throne.

Oshtaa runs to catch it, rubs the dust off,
And places it on his forehead.
The world master turns away from Oshtaa
To avoid the color and the scent of the quince.
Then the two men place the quince on the throne
And remain standing before the king.

Khosrow is worried about this affair
With the quince tumbling down,
As he senses it to be a bad omen.
He turns his eyes toward the sky: "O true Judge,
Who can ever raise to heights the one you overthrow?
Who can reinstitute the thing that you have shattered?
When a shining good fortune abandons a family,
Grief is soon to replace the days of joy."

He says to Oshtaa, "What message do you bring
From the vile, malicious, and suspicious young man?
Without wisdom, men cannot attain contentment.
Good fortune will abandon my family,
And no one from my lineage will ever be happy.
The crown and throne will fall into unworthy hands,
And the royal tree will plummet to its demise.
The common man will reach heights of power
While the souls of noblemen
Will fill with grief and sorrow.
Power will not remain in the hands of my son
Or any of my parents and allies.
Their friends will become their enemies.
They will attack our family with words and deeds.
The quince revealed the secret:
The throne of the King of Kings will cease to bear fruit.
Now repeat to me all that was said.
The message of this prince is as meaningless
To me as water flowing through the river."

The two men open their eloquent lips
And repeat to him his son's words.

The king listens to them and sighs deeply.
Then he says to the illustrious Oshtaa,
"Listen to my reply, and report it to the new king:
> 'Do not blame anyone before
> Having yourself washed your hands of blame.
> The message they relay to me is not yours.
> May the one who inspired you fall ill!
> Never utter foolish words that fill your enemy
> With a sense of joy and satisfaction.
> He will understand that your brain has not
> Intelligence enough to nurture a wise thought.
> When you place your trust on sterile words,
> You distort your heart and your mind.
> A man who calls you a villain and then salutes you
> As world king is not worthy to sit at your side
> Or to be charged with state affairs, great or small.
> Never again send messages of this sort,
> For your enemies would revel in joy.
> Yazdan has decided on my fate.
> My wishes now relate only to the other world.
> But you will never acquire glory
> With false accusations directed at me.'"

2 | Khosrow's Response to Shirooy

Khosrow continues:
"Listen to my reply, and do share with the others.
As my truthful words are my witness,
I shall indeed be remembered posthumously.
Once I unveil the multitude of hardships I have endured,
It will be clear how they produced my wealth.

"First, you speak of Hormozd, his wrath,
And the unfortunate incidents of days of yore.
My father lashed out at us on account of slander.
His anger and unfounded suspicions
Drove us into a state of chaos.
He could not be convinced of my innocence
And wished to kill me by feeding me poison.
Once aware of his murderous intentions,
The antidote to my demise was to take flight,

379

Searching the way by night through roundabout paths.
We fled to avoid being caught
In the snares of misfortune's swells.

"Once I was informed that something
Happened to him, I rushed from Barda.
Bahraam, the criminal, mustered an army
And faced us, head on, on the battlefield.
The day of the fight I fled once again
To avoid falling captive into his hands.
Then I returned and bravely reengaged in war.
The entire world observed our struggle
With Bahraam as it broke out at a fort.
The fight was not determined by a single blow.
I conquered him with my strength
As our star of misfortune withered.
The world was witness, and, at the command
Of Yazdan the benevolent, Giver of good and bad,
Iran and other nations swiftly surrendered
And were reinstated as lands under our dominion.

"All of Bahraam Choobineh's desires fell short.
With the war over, I felt I had avenged,
Before anything, my father's death.
Bandooy and Gostaham, my mother's brothers,
Did not have their equals anywhere.
They risked their lives to save mine.
They were attached to me as my closest relatives.
But between us was my father's blood
And a precipice of grief within my heart.
For that reason, I did not hesitate to take vengeance.
I ordered Bandooy's feet and hands to be cut off
Because he deprived my royal father of the light of day.
Gostaham disappeared from the world,
Retreating into a dark, unknown corner.
I had him killed unexpectedly, and good fortune
Decidedly abandoned the bloodthirsty murderers.

"Later you spoke of your own affairs,
Your narrow prison, and what happened to you.
My goal was to prevent my son from mischief
And actions that would bring misfortune to him.

380

You were not bound up in a dungeon.
You did not endure indignities.
There was no threat upon your head.
I did not treat you with harshness,
And instead I expended my wealth for you,
Always conforming to the ways of ancient kings.
You were never deprived of participating in the hunt
Or enjoying the company of musicians in a feast.
You lacked for nothing, neither gold nor jewels,
Neither cheetahs nor falcons.
You merrily lived in a palace that took the name of prison
But where life unfolded in a constant state of revelry.

"As for the words of astrologers on your subject,
They inspired fear in me for presaging
The developments of great calamities.
I confined you to avoid falling victim to you.
I did not forget or let go of the horoscope.
I put the document under seal, entrusting it to Shirin.
Once my kingship reached its thirty-sixth year,
Once you were enjoying your happy days,
You did not lend a thought to the predictions.
You received a letter from India, which was handed to me
And came from the highest-ranking rajah.
It came along with jewels, fabrics of golden silk,
An Indian sword, a white elephant, uncut stones,
And many valuables one may desire in the world.

"I called a scribe of Indian origin, discreet and eloquent,
Able to read and translate the letter written on silk.
His face flooded with tears at the contents:
        'May you live happily forever!
        May you merit, with your golden crown,
        To be an ornament for the dignity of kings.
        You will rise to rule as world master
        During the month of Aazar on the day of Dey,
        At the time when your father will have
        Reigned for thirty-eight years.
        This is the way the stars will spin.
        The time of joy will then shine, and you will
        Place upon your head the royal crown.'

"These words were verified for me that day,
But the heart must not reject affection.
I knew well that fortune, a high position,
And the splendor of your throne
Would bring me nothing but grief and pain
And that my shining days would dim.
Yet, through generosity, affection, the spirit of family
And faith, I did not concede to anger.
Having read it, I handed the letter to Shirin
And surrendered to all sorts of reflections.
Shirin secretly keeps the letter with your horoscope,
And no one knows anything about it.
But if you wish to lay your eyes on it, you may do so.
It is possible that you will not accuse me of a crime.
I think that once you see it, you will repent
And seek to find a resolution to the conflict.

"Next, you speak of prison and bondage,
As if anyone has suffered at my hand.
Such is the law of the world for as long as time
And the law of noblemen, kings, and princes.
If you do not know about it, ask your vizier,
And he will ease your mind on this point.
It is not right to allow an enemy of Yazdan to live.
My prisons detained only obvious deevs
Against whom good men raised concerns.
My custom was neither to shed blood
Nor to insist on extreme conditions.
I imprisoned evil men in my dungeons
To bar them from committing offenses
That would impede my people's sense of safety.
Many had warned me that they were enemies.
But since my mind was pure, I did not listen.

"Now I learn that you have released these men,
Who are more vicious than dragons.
It is as if you have sinned against Yazdan,
As if your words and your actions are pitiful.
Now that you are world master, act cautiously.
If you lack knowledge of an affair,
Consult a man who is familiar with it.
Do not forgive those who offend you,

Even if you can extract wealth from the situation.
What better punishment for any man
Whose crimes you witness than iron bonds?

"Furthermore, when it relates
To the wealth of which you speak,
You did not prove your acumen,
And you concealed your good sense.
I never asked for anything more than tributes
And fees from anyone with the ability to pay.
I accepted the throne and crown from Yazdan
And, as a result, endured much hardship.
The Supreme Judge willed my fate to change.
All unfolding developments are by divine command.
My actions have always been guided by my faith.
One can never escape the wheel of destiny.
When the Just Giver questions me,
I shall confess both the manifest and the hidden.
The One interrogating you is more learned
Than you and exceeds you in supremacy.

"The guilty people around you
Are neither your friends nor your relatives.
Be sure that they will soon
Spread rumors behind your back.
They are merely the slaves of gold and silver.
You will be at a loss to find among them a loyal man.
They fill their hearts with corruption,
A sort of filter for their crimes.
Without a foundation of wisdom,
Your words will never profit anyone.
Falsehoods cannot bring glory to kingship.

"Nevertheless, this letter written in Pahlavi
Will be a memory of me in the face of my enemies.
It will come as a sort of comfort to wise men
And all those who, after my death,
Will read these words and appreciate my plans.
I brought armies from Barda and Chin,
Placed leaders and commanders everywhere.
I invaded my enemies' lands,
And no one dared raise their heads.

"Once my adversaries fled and scattered here and there,
Our treasuries were overflowing.
People from all the lands worked for me.
Seamen drew from the sea so many pearls
That they labored constantly and grew quite weary.
The plains, the seas, and the mountains belonged to me.
When my treasure of dirhams ran over,
I filled pouches with new dinars, rubies,
Fine jewels worthy of a king, fabrics, and war gear.

"After twenty-six years of rule,
My treasures burst with precious valuables
And I minted a new dirham with joy and glory.
Upon count, we had one hundred loads of dinars,
Each holding one hundred thousand coins.
We had plenty of Pandavsi, each pouch of gold
Holding ten plus two thousand royal dinars.
So many tributes and dues came from India,
So many from Rum and the land of sorcerers!
So many presents and fees poured in from every land,
From every nobleman and every prince!
So many offerings customary to the festivals
Of Nowruz and Mehregan!
So many horses and fair-faced slaves!
So much armor and helmets,
So many maces and swords
Were distributed freely to everyone!
Such an abundance of musk and camphor, beaver skin,
White and black ermine fur, and marten fur!
My subjects would charge camels
With these valuables and rush to my court.
No one dared evade our wish and our command.

"I worked hard and long to fill my treasury.
I have deliberated at length about a name.
In the end, I called one part *Baadaavar*,
While another became the treasure of *Khazraa*.
Furthermore, I own the treasure of *Aroos*,
Which I founded for days of misfortune.
In this way, from the twenty-sixth year of my reign
Until the thirty-eighth year, the sky turned to my will.
All the noblemen enjoyed a sense of security

While my enemies trembled in fear.

"Now I am told that you are world master.
I witness our land going adrift
From the obedience pledged to you.
Joy will be eradicated,
And people will have to keep quiet.
You will burden the earth with calamity upon calamity.
Everything will become pain and hardship,
With no benefits anywhere to anyone.
Evildoers will surround you and guide you
In the dark nights to cast your throne to the wind
In a way that you will never again find happiness.
If you had at your side a sensible man
Who could bring light to your dim soul,
There would be no harm in being generous,
For your treasures would reach the poor and the needy.

"O my dear son, whose life is short
Snd whose mind is weak, your soul will soon
Be stripped of joy and instead be riddled by worry.
Know that these amassed treasures are your support
And that your fate is entirely in your own hands.
Wealth is your means to exercise kingship.
A world without wealth is a lost world.
A poor king becomes unjust when he finds himself
Empty-handed and without dirhams.
The situation leaves him without the means to act.
If he lacks the power to give,
He becomes an object of derision to noblemen
Who renounce the notion of him as a rightful ruler.
If his treasury is seized by his enemies,
If all the idols fall into the hands of brahmans,
Believers will turn their backs on Yazdan
And dishonor your name and your memory.
If you have no wealth,
You will not be able to unify troops,
And your subjects will not call you king.
A dog asking for bread is tame,
But once you fully satisfy its hunger,
It will become your enemy for life.

"Furthermore, you bring up the troops
I positioned on the roads to provinces.
You point the blame out of ignorance,
For you have not a clue what leads to gain and loss.
Here is what I offer you as a reply:
My wealth was acquired through great pains.
I snatched many cities from strangers.
I overcame myriad adversaries.
I divided my cavaliers on the borders
To distinguish the worthy from the unskilled
And to secure my position on the throne of delights.

"By recalling your hosts from every corner,
You allow your rivals to notice the open roads.
Iran is like a spring garden blooming with roses,
A garden vibrant with the most fragrant narcissi,
Apples, pomegranates, and quince.
As soon as the orchard is abandoned,
People will uproot the basil
And break off the branches
Of the quince and the pomegranate trees.
The army and the weapons are the walls,
And the spears on the battlements are the thorns.
If you foolishly bring down the garden wall,
What difference will there be between the garden
And the barren desert, or between the garden
And the sea, or the mountain?

"Take great care not to destroy the wall
And thereby shatter the Iranians' hearts and backs,
For then pillage and incursions will ensue,
The cries of cavaliers and the execution of vengeance.
Do not endanger the women and children of Iran,
Or else after one year of reign,
Wise men will consider you unwise.

"I hear that you have enlisted incapable,
Undeserving men with the execution of important tasks.
Know that Kesra Anushiravan, son of Ghobaad,
Wrote the following in his testament:
        'If you provide arms to your enemy,
        You are sure to expedite your demise,

For when your foe decides to use weapons,
He will burden you with a fierce attack.'

"Furthermore, you sent a message to the Caesar,
Calling me a selfish being, accusing me of treason.
You cannot remember important things.
Your words reflect only the lies you have been taught:
That the Caesar has been loyal while I have been unjust.
How could you distinguish between loyalty and iniquity?
Here is my reply, O insensible man,
I shall tell you only what applies to the point.
You concurrently complain and stand witness,
A behavior no intelligent man will concede to.

"When the Caesar washed the dust of misfortune
Off his face, he selected a son-in-law
Of the likes of Parviz because of his valor.
Anyone who tramples the earth with ill intentions
Is surely devoid of wisdom.
Anyone with some remnant of intelligence
Knows that Bahraam Choobineh strapped himself,
Mobilized troops with Iranians united behind him,
And assailed us with a vicious, unprovoked attack
In the hopes of expropriating my royal seat.
He was ultimately defeated by your allies, the Rumis.
Shifting sands cannot be reconnected to the boulder.
Yazdan came to my aid in the struggle,
And through me this mighty host succumbed.
The Iranians heard what happened,
And you must hear it from them in turn.
As for me, the way I treated Niyaatoos
Was out of kindness and humanity
And certainly not in anticipation of a reward.
To this fact, the wise Farrokhzaad can attest.

"One must not look at the world through the eyes of youth.
Goshasp, my treasurer, and the sage
Who was my vizier will tell you as well
That I gave to the Rumis, as a memory of me,
One hundred thousand sacks of gold.
I gave Niyaatoos gold and one thousand stones of ruby
Suitable to be designed into earrings, each of which

Was estimated at a value of one thousand royal mithqals.
I included one hundred freshwater pearls,
Each flawless and worth thirty thousand dirhams.
Finally, I added one hundred magnificent horses,
Selected from my stables, fifty of them with saddles.
The remaining steeds, able to rush across the plain
As rivals of the wind, sported lush brocade covers.
I sent all these to the Caesar with praise and blessings.

"Next you speak of the Messiah's cross,
An old piece of exposed wood in my treasury
That neither served me nor caused me harm
And over which Christians made excessive fanfare.
I was surprised that a man such as the Caesar,
A proud and valiant ruler surrounded by wise men,
Countless intelligent people, and philosophers
Would refer to a man sentenced to death
As a deity and would place high value
On a worthless piece of dry, rotten wood.
If this vile cross was divine, it would have shone
On the head of the moon like Jupiter;
It would have disappeared from my treasury on its own,
Just as the Messiah departed and vanished from earth.

"Next you tell me to ask forgiveness,
To repent, and to seek the path of Yazdan.
Here is my reply: May the tongue and the lips,
The hands and the feet of Ghobaad waste away!
The Creator placed the divine crown upon my head.
I received it with great joy and delight.
When Yazdan reclaimed it, I returned it, and I cannot
Understand why you have a tongue in your mouth.
I declare it by Yazdan and not to a child
Unable to distinguish between good and bad:
I have always approved the actions of Yazdan,
Although I have witnessed much distress and bitterness.
I held on to kingship for thirty-eight years
Without another ruler able to challenge me.
The one who gave me the world will give me another.
I celebrate the glory of royalty. May the world prosper
Under the reign of a just and sage monarch!
With Yazdan as my support and protector,

No one will dare proffer curses at me."

The king turns to Khorraad and says,
"O leader from the lineage of world warriors,
Tell the irritable and ignorant child:
    'You have tarnished our glory,
      And I address to you an eternal farewell.
      I now desire only the company of sages.'
And you, my two respected Persian envoys,
Eloquent and noble, I take leave of you as well.
I implore you to tell him what you have heard.
I bless the entire world, which I never looked
Upon as anything but a temporary dwelling.
Anyone who is born from a mother is meant to die.
Remember the eras from Khosrow to Ghobaad,
From Hooshang and Tahmures to Jamsheed.
They filled the earth with fear and hope.
These worthy rulers obeyed by deevs and wild beasts
Witnessed unfailingly their days come to a final halt.

"The glorious Fereydoon, who freed the world
Of evil, seen and unseen, who tied up the hands
Of the malevolent and bold Zahaak the Taazi,
Could not escape the claws of death.
Aarash, who flung his arrow as far as one farsang;
Ghaaran, victorious warrior and lion vanquisher;
Kay Ghobaad, who emerged from Mount Alborz
And became world master with his army;
Kaavoos the powerful, who conquered the world
With his mighty thoughts and his intentions,
Who traveled to the lofty skies,
Unaware of the wheel of providence.
Kaavoos built the celebrated house of mirrors,
A source of myths and stories, a house ornate
With figures made out of freshwater pearls,
Its door entirely encrusted with shining rubies.
Siaavoosh, a glorious lion, was slain in his youth
By two wicked tigers; he founded the city of Gang-Dej
With such pain and effort, all so futile in the end.
Every single one of these powerful rulers has died.

"What happened to the Tooranian king Afraasiyaab?

I hope that no one like him will exist, not even in dream.
What happened to Rostam, Zaal, and Esfandiar?
The only memory of them lingers in words and stories.
Goodarz and his seventy illustrious sons,
Riders in the arena and lions in battle;
Kay Khosrow, a liberated lion man,
Able to capture beasts in times of war;
Goshtaasp, a king who adopted the true faith
And reigned so gloriously;
What happened to them all?
What happened to Eskandar the renowned,
Who overturned the entire world?
Jaamaasp, an astronomer more brilliant than the sun;
Bahraam the Hunter with no equal
In power and generosity; what happened to them?
What happened to my grandfather,
The illuminated King Anushiravan, who,
After forty-eight years, was forced
To depart and leave his work unattended.
These commanding and learned men, valiant cavaliers,
Literate, each one more worthy than the other,
Who fought for the palm of old age, all left this vast world,
Abandoning their audience halls, arenas, and palaces.

"I did not have an equal among kings,
Although I have not reached the age of some.
I have trampled the earth in joy and sorrow.
Never allowing myself to be burdened my misfortune.
I have weathered many difficult paths,
And have rejected and destroyed many an enemy.
Every land is filled with my treasures.
Everywhere there is water and earth,
One can see the fruits of my labors.
Now that the world ends in this way for me,
All hope for the future of noblemen appears rather dim.
The crown will not remain, not even for my son.
He will lose the throne, and his fortune will perish.

"An angel will come to collect my soul,
And I shall entreat it to take me gently.
Repentance will reassure my earnest heart.

When it is time for me to cross the Bridge of Chinvad,[28]
The ground beneath my feet will be a spread of roses.
I shall lighten my heart with repentance,
And the assurance of my harmless ways
Will function as my protective shield.
Skilled and learned men all say wisely
That when the fortune watching over us declines,
One must anticipate all sorts of terrors.
Foolish is the one who wishes to preserve
And cling onto fading, waning power.
Such is my message to the world, to men, great and small.

"Not much time will pass before the royal troops
And the king destroy each other, kill each other,
And consume the entire stretch of land.
The father dies at the hands of the son,
And, conversely, the son dies at the hands of the father.
The actions of our enemies, their words and deeds,
Their lack of affection, their attempts at diminishing us
Will come under scrutiny and undergo consequences.
They will not have a chance to remain long in this world.
When my kingship ends, so will the rule of Shirooy.
As for you, accept my farewell, my two leaders,
Remain happy, and do not think of me unfavorably."

Oshtaa and the valiant Khorraad, son of Borzeen,
Listen to the heartbreaking message of their master
And cover their faces with their two hands,
Ashamed at having disparaged him.
The two wise men strike their cheeks with their fists,
Shred their clothing on their chests,
And scatter dust over their heads.
They take leave of the king,
Hearts full of sorrow, heads full of grief.

Pained, their faces streaked with tears,
They arrive at the side of Shirooy,

◇◇◇◇◇◇◇◇◇◇◇◇◇
28 Bridge of Chinvad: Or Chinvat, is a bridge in Zoroastrianism to be crossed upon death. It connects the world of the living to the world of the dead. If a person has been wicked, its width is as thin as a strand of hair, its edge as sharp as the blade of a sword. If a person has been virtuous, the bridge is amply wide to allow for crossing.

A king who possesses neither brain nor authority,
And, point by point, they deliver the king's message.

3 | Shirooy Regrets His Actions Toward Khosrow Parviz

Shirooy listens to them, weeping bitterly,
And his heart fears for the crown and throne.
Upon the departure of the two men,
Whose injurious words and their fear of seeing
His father's blood spilled consumed his heart,
Ghobaad climbs down the throne deeply concerned
And places his head between his noble hands.
He abstains from eating and is unable to sleep.
The anguish inspired by Khosrow fills his eyes
With blood tears that flood his face and chest.

Rumors of his distress spread through the troops.
Terrified, they gather together to speak of Khosrow,
Saying that if ever Parviz were to rise to the throne,
The army leaders would perish on the gallows.

As the sun raises its head over the black mountains,
The irritated followers of Shirooy awaken
From their slumber and set out for the palace gates.
Upon hearing the news, Shirooy climbs on the throne.
The proud heroes, members of his family
As well as strangers, enter court
And sit in silence with somber miens.

Keenly aware of the chagrin of the solemn men,
The king says to them, "A man who is not moved
By his father's suffering cannot be considered righteous
And honorable, and deserves to be hung at the gallows.
No one must place his hopes in him, for he is as rotten
As a rotten piece of wood splinter from the willow tree."

The culpable men reply, "Should a man
Admit that he recognizes two rightful kings,
Call him foolish and know that he is nefarious,
No matter how noble he may be."

Shirooy replies, "My father will not find a host,
Since he no longer is in possession of his treasure.
Let us speak softly to him for another month.
Let us avoid the use of harsh words and means.
We may benefit from receiving his instructions,
For this land is full of wealth from border to border."

The army leaders rise and return to their homes.

Shah Shirooy says to his cooks,
"We must not hide anything from Khosrow.
Place before him golden tables,
And offer him the sweetest, most delectable dishes."

The servants take platters to Khosrow,
But he does not touch any of the fare,
Neither the cold nor the warm.
Everything he eats comes from the hand of Shirin,
Who is chagrined to see her ruler so despondent.
She is the only one close to him and the only one
Truly devoted to grieving for his predicament.
She stands by him with a sense of fear and hope,
Her body shivering like the limbs of a willow tree.

One month passes in this way,
With Khosrow suffering night and day.
He recalls his sins and offenses, and the memories
Bar him from enjoying the taste of life.

4 | Baarbad Reacts to the Fate of Khosrow

Forget everything in the world now,
And pay attention to Baarbad's deep wail.
Let us honor his devotion to King Khosrow.

When Baarbad learns that his ruler has abandoned
His throne feeling powerless and irresolute,
That his enemies are plotting his execution,
That the army cannot reach him to imprison him,
He travels from Jahrom to Ctesiphon,
Face flooding with tears, heart swollen with blood.

He finds the king's face, once so brilliant,
As pale as the flower of the fenugreek.
After some time in his presence, he plaintively
Appears at the threshold of the great hall, and there,
Face pallid, heart mournful for the fate of Khosrow
And consumed by the flames' affection,
His eyes become two pools, brimming with tears.
He composes a mournful song with his lute
And sings in the language of Pahlavi.
Khosrow listens to the painful, melancholic song.
The guards watching over him weep,
Their hearts consumed by a burning agony.

Baarbad sings in this way, "Illustrious King,
Glorious and proud monarch, magnanimous hero,
What happened to your majesty, your fortune, your crown?
Where are your lofty rank, your diadem, your glory,
Your bracelets, your power, your throne of ivory?
You once held the world beneath your wings.
Where is the royal hall where singers gathered at night?
Where are the leaders of your citadel and of your court?
Where are the Kaaviani banner and the blue-bladed sword?
What became of your noblemen,
Owners of golden thrones and earrings?
Where is your glorious helmet of steel,
Your golden coat of mail with its bejeweled clasps?
Where is your horse Shabdeez of golden stirrup,
Who shuddered beneath your weight?
Where are your riders of golden reins whose swords
Never had the chance to return to their sheaths?
They all despair of your life.

"Where are your dromedaries, your white elephants,
Your camels of cadenced steps, your golden litters
And your loyal and obliging servants?
Where is your gentle, persuasive speech?
Where is your heart? Where is your shining soul?
Why have you exiled yourself from the world?
Have you ever found in books a day such as this one?
One must not boast of the favors of good fortune,
For it offers one more poison than counter-poison.
You wanted a son so that he may be your friend

And support, but now he is the one responsible
For having you enchained and held captive.
Kings find in their children a certain force,
A shelter against the attacks of providence,
But the King of Kings saw his strength and majesty
Diminish as he watched his son grow up and mature.
Anyone witness to the condition of Khosrow Parviz
Must not place his trust in this transitory world.

"May Iran be in your eyes nothing more
Than a pile of ruins, the lair of lions, the den of leopards!
The leader of Sassanian lineage, the king whose
Power was without equal is on the verge of death,
And it appears that with him Iran will cease to exist.
The hopes of his enemies have triumphed.
No one had a mightier army than this king,
Yet he, in the end, suffered his demise at its hand.
The blame can be directed on the high shepherd
If wolves find their way through the gaps today.
Tell Shirooy,
        'O shameless King,
        This is not the way to treat a glorious sovereign.
        Do not count on the resolve of your army
        When war breaks out on all sides.'

"But you, O Khosrow, may Yazdan protect your soul!
May the heads of slanderers be brought down!
I swear by the Creator, by your royal being,
By Nowruz and Mehregan, by the sunny spring
That should my hands craft another lute,
May my name be deprived of benediction!
I swear to burn all my instruments
So that I may never see one of your sinister enemies
Make his way to sit on your royal throne."

He immediately cuts off four of his fingers,
And, holding up his mutilated hand,
He runs to his residence, lights a great fire,
And burns in it all of his musical instruments.

5 | Mehr Hormozd Kills Khosrow Parviz

Those closest to the noble king
Fear the twists of fate day and night.

Shirooy, as much a coward as he is inexperienced,
Believes his throne to be a trap.
The astrologers understand and sense
That imminent is the day devoted to the powerful.
Criminals, those who contributed keenly
To causing royal damage, rush to the palace and
Appear before Ghobaad recounting their misdeeds.

They say, "We have already told you
And we shall say it again,
Your mind views this affair differently.
When two kings, father and son, sit together,
One on the golden throne, the other on a second seat,
As soon as friendship binds them tightly,
Their subjects' heads fall with one blow.
We cannot consent to such projects,
And you must not mention it to us anymore."

Shirooy is afraid, trembling because he feels
As if he is a powerless slave in their hands.
He replies, "Only a wicked man can trap a lion.
Return to your homes and covertly deliberate.
Find someone in the world to free us from this torment."

Khosrow's enemies engage in a search
For an assassin that could secretly kill him.
Still, no one has the courage to come forward
And volunteer to execute the deed.
No one has the audacity to spill the king's blood
And to burden himself with the weight
Of a crime as heavy as a lofty mountain.

After having searched in every corner,
The conspirators come across a man with blue eyes,
An enraged face, a fleshy and hairy body, and dark lips.
His feet are powdered with dust,
His belly hollow from excessive hunger,

The villain walks around head bare.
No one in the world, neither great nor small,
Is familiar with his name and identity.

The vile man, may he never see paradise,
Goes to Farrokhzaad, and as soon as he is
Aware of the affair, he agrees to commit the act:
"I shall be in charge of this grueling venture
As long as you accept to satisfy my hunger."

Farrokhzaad replies, "Go and catch your prey,
But never open your lips to divulge the secret.
I reserve for you a pouch full of dinars,
And I shall protect you as if you were my own son."

Farrokhzaad gives the murderer a shining
And honed dagger, and he departs in haste,
Heading to meet the king, whom he finds
With a single slave in the first hall of his palace.

At the sight of him, Khosrow senses his end approaching.
He trembles as his tears cross his cheeks.
He says to him, "O odious-looking man,
What is your name, for your mother
Must still weep for having given birth to you?"

The other replies, "They call me Mehr Hormozd.
I am a stranger in this land, without parent or friend."

Khosrow reflects, "My fate is in the hands
Of this wretched being who has devised
The most perverse and sinister scheme.
I see no human trait in his features, and no one
In the world would seek friendship with him."

A young page stands before the king,
To whom Khosrow says, "My loyal servant,
Go and fetch a vase full of water scented with
Musk and aloe, and a beautiful, clean tunic."

The young page moves away to obey,
Unable to decipher the secret within the command.
He soon reappears before the king

With a golden basin and a pitcher full of water.

Khosrow eagerly takes the objects.
At the sight of the barsom, he prays,
For the time for frivolous words is long gone.

After having dressed in the attire,
He murmurs a prayer of repentance
And covers his head with a new veil
To shield him from the assassin's face.

Mehr Hormozd, dagger in hand,
Runs to close the door to the hall, then
He returns to the king's side, removes his tunic,
And plunges the dagger into his royal liver.

Such is the way of this unstable world:
It always hides its mysterious schemes from you.
Everything appears to one hopeless as it spins,
Whether one is prudent and sensible
Or one is presumptuous.
Whether you amass treasures or fatigue and suffering,
You will not remain long in this passing dwelling.
Try to pursue an innocent and loyal life
So that you may acquire a good name.

As soon as word spreads through the marketplace
That Khosrow has perished, his enemies invade
The palace prison detaining more unfortunate people.
The poor souls are the fifteen royal and illustrious sons,
Who, although innocent, are brutally slaughtered
The very day of their father's fatal end.

At the news, Shirooy weeps for a long time,
Then he sends twenty of his guards with the command
To protect the women and children of the deceased.
As for him, the world king, he does not dare
Say anything and forces himself to hide his pain.

Such is the end of Khosrow's reign, the end
Of his vast host, his glory, his courage and power.
No one had ever seen or ever heard of someone
Who enjoyed as much power as he did.

A wise man said it well: "We must not make a case
Of the one who places his trust on the dragon's jaw.
One must consider the world as a cruel beast
Who seizes prey in its claws
To bring to its voracious, grinding teeth."

Such is the end of the reign of Shah Khosrow Parviz.
Such is the downfall of his throne, treasures, and troops.
Placing your hopes in the world is as worthless
As trying to pluck a date from a fruitless willow tree.

Why have you lost your way,
Wandering aimlessly through day and night?
If you do not wish to suffer hardship,
Appreciate anything given to you by the loving dome.
Always think that you may not have enough power,
Even if you find yourself at times in command.
Always attempt to act with justice and generosity,
And fashion your thoughts on a foundation of virtue.
Enjoy life, give dirhams openly if you can,
For everything else is pain and suffering.
The best way to live your life
Is to surround yourself with wise and loyal friends.

6 | Shirooy Pursues Shirin, and She Kills Herself

I come to the conclusion of the story of Khosrow
And shall now turn to the story of Shirooy and Shirin.
Fifty-three days after the murder of the praised king,
Shirooy sends a message to Shirin: "O deceitful witch,
You are skilled in the art of spells and enchantments,
No one is more guilty than you in the land of Iran.
You captivated the king with your evil charms.
You have devious ways able to bring down the moon.
Beware, O criminal, rush to my side this moment
Instead of staying happy and content in your palace."

Affected by the message and the undeserved insults,
Shirin bemoans, "May the one who sheds his father's
Blood be deprived of power, grace, and glory!
I shall never set my sight on someone so guilty,

Not even from a distance,
Neither on days of mourning nor on days of feast."

She summons a scribe full of solicitude
To compose a letter in Pahlavi
In which she dictates her last wishes,
Then estimates her wealth in front of him.

She hides in a box a certain quantity of poison
Unlike any other found in the land.
She hides the bottle beneath her clothes.
She has her servant sew a shroud
To cover her figure, tall as a cypress tree,
Then she sends a reply to Shirooy:
"O King whose glorious forehead is adorned
With the dazzling crown, the words
You attribute to me could never hold
Even the tiniest hint of truth.
Cursed be the heart and the soul of an evil man
Who rejoices for hearing tales of sorcery.

"If King Parviz had been of the character and humor
To taste incantations, if he would have had,
In the women's chambers, a woman magician,
He would have been aware of it.
As for me, he only held me close for pleasure.
At night, when he could not free himself of grief,
He would summon me to the golden harem,
And the sight of me would bring comfort to his soul.
Be ashamed of yourself for uttering such words,
For falsehood does not suit a sovereign.
Reflect on the grandeur of the Justice Giver,
And never speak of this matter to anyone."

Troubled by the language of the innocent woman,
Shirooy replies, "No one in the world
Is found as thirsty for blood as you are.
You have no choice. You may no longer
Avoid or delay your journey to my court.
Come and catch a glimpse of my crown.
If you find me worthy of it, you may praise me."

This command fills Shirin with worry.

PART THIRTY-TWO

She writhes with grief, and her face pales.
She replies, "I shall consent to come to your court
Only in the presence of an assembly
Composed of people whose wisdom, experience,
And eloquent discourse you appreciate."

King Shirooy convenes fifty old men,
Then sends for Shirin: "Rise and come to me.
We have spoken sufficiently."

Shirin dresses in blue and black
And heads toward the royal court.
She goes straight to the hall of feast of Shahdegan,
Where the noble Iranians can speak freely.
There she sits, separated from the king by a curtain,
As it suits a modest and noble woman.

Shirooy says to her, "Two months have passed
Since the death of Khosrow; accept to be my wife
In order to be happy and avoid humiliation.
I shall treat you as did my father, even better,
With a more effusive show of benevolence and affection."

Shirin replies, "Return justice to me first,
And I shall agree to offer you my soul and promise
To never resist your words again or your will,
Or any desire you may have in your blessed heart."

Shirooy consents to her suggestions.
Once the beautiful princess is granted permission,
She raises her voice from behind the curtain and adds,
"O King, may you be victorious and joyous always!
Did you not say that I was an evil woman,
A sorceress, deprived of loyalty and righteousness?"

Shirooy says, "It is true, but generous hearts
Need not be offended by pungent, youthful comments."

Shirin addresses the noble Iranians
Gathered in the Hall of Shahdegan,
"Did you ever witness in my behavior
The slightest blameworthy action, darkness,
Lies, or acts contrary to wisdom and reason?

Queen of Iran for many years, I lent my support
To brave men in every occasion, always seeking
The truth and absconding in the face of falsehoods.
Many governors owe a good portion of their goods
In the world to my intercession on their behalf.
May the one who has seen the shadow of my crown
And of my power speak to reveal the full evidence!"

The noblemen sing the praises of Shirin to the king
And proclaim her status
And splendor unique in the world,
Whether in public circles or in private.

Shirin continues: "O worldly noblemen,
Leaders of the most illustrious exploits,
Three things bring glory to a woman
And make her the adornment of the throne:
In the first place, to ensure her spouse's happiness,
She must be virtuous and rich;
In the second place, she must give birth to a blessed son,
Who will be the pride and joy of his venerated father;
She must be tall, beautiful, and able to always
Conceal her tresses as she does her figure.

"When I became Khosrow's wife,
When I was glorified by the blessed union,
The king was returning from Rum,
Discouraged, saddened, and without shelter.
Yet he was able to soon gain a degree of power
And prosperity such as the world had never seen.
I gave birth to four sons who were his pride and joy:
Nastoor, Shahriar, Foorood, and the youngest,
Mardanesheh, was the crown of the blue firmament.
Neither Jamsheed nor Fereydoon had such a lineage.
May my tongue be mute if I stray from the truth!
All four of them lie now beneath the dust,
Journeying with grace toward paradise."

She says this, draws aside her veil,
Revealing a face as beautiful as the moon
And a mane cascading down her shoulders.
She adds: "In the third place, look into my face,

And if I am lying, raise your hand in accusation!
My honor rests in my covered hair,
Which no one has ever had a chance to perceive.
I reveal to you now the secrets of my charms,
Induced neither by evil spells nor by ruse."

The old sages are stunned, their lips moist
At the sight of her tumbling waves of hair
Never observed or heard of by noblemen.
At the sight of her beauty, Shirooy is stupefied.
Feeling as if his heart has leaped on a passionate flight,
He exclaims "I desire you alone! My only wish
In all of Iran is to make you my life's companion.
I shall agree and pledge to all your requests."

The woman with the exquisite face adds,
"I have not yet made my demands to the King of Iran.
I have two additional requests to address,
Should he permit, may his kingship endure!"

Shirooy replies, "My soul belongs to you,
And all your wishes will be granted."

Shirin replies, "Consent to return to me the wealth
I possess and make it my exclusive property.
Do so in the presence of this illustrious assembly
By attesting, in your own writing in this book,
That you renounce claim to my possessions."
The king immediately gives his consent.

As soon as her requests are acknowledged,
The queen exits the Garden of Shahdegan,
Leaving the leaders and the noblemen,
And returning to her residence.
She frees her slaves, shares with them her wealth,
And distributes the remainder to the poor,
Giving her relatives the most substantial portion.
She makes a donation to the fire temples
For the festivals of Nowruz, Mehregan, and Saddeh,
And another for the restoration of fallen caravansaries
That have converted into lions' lairs.
She makes all these offerings in memory of Khosrow
And to satisfy the soul of the deceased king.

Then she enters the garden, removes her veil,
And sits pale and undone on the ground.
She summons all her servants,
Receives each one with kindness,
And tells them in a rising voice,
"May each of you listen to me with a generous heart.
You will never have a chance to gaze into my face again.
You must fear the Justice Giver,
Creator of the shining stars, of the Moon and the Sun.
Make every effort to always speak the truth;
Falsehoods are not meant for intelligent people.
Since the day I appeared before Khosrow,
Since he admitted me into his golden harem,
Since I became the first princess and the king's pride,
Did I ever appear guilty of a fault in any way?
Guard yourselves to reply with deception.
What good is pretense when it comes to a woman
Who is about to dig her own grave?"

The servants rise and reply in unison,
"Illustrious Queen, you are eloquent and wise
And blessed with a serene heart,
Yazdan is our witness that never
Did anyone catch sight of you
Or heard your voice behind the curtain.
From the time of Hooshang,
No woman has occupied the throne
In a more magnificent and dazzling way."

All the people of her home, servants of ambitious
And vigilant hearts, cry out, "O renowned Queen,
You are celebrated in Chin, Rum, and Taraaz.
Who would dare speak ill of you?
So pure you are, how would you ever commit a sin?"

Shirin replies, "The ill-intentioned Shirooy,
Who will become a source of blame to the celestial sphere,
The one who intended the death of his own father
Only to steal the crown and throne,
May his eyes never witness happiness!
This man who thinks himself exempt from death
Sent me a message that dimmed my soul.

In vain did I answer him that the rest of my life
Will be devoted to the cult of Yazdan, World Creator.
In vain did I reveal to him my behavior.
His malevolence inspired in me renewed concerns:
I fear that after my death, his tongue will slander me.
I pronounce all of you, my slaves, free and liberated."

These words bring her company to shed bitter tears,
And the memory of Parviz consumes their hearts.
When the messengers return to the king
And report what they heard from the mouth
Of the innocent queen, Shirooy tells them
To ask her what other desire her heart may nurture.

Shirin sends a reply, "I have one more wish to express,
One last wish, to open for me the door to the shah's grave,
For I yearn to observe his features one final time."

Shirooy says, "I shall allow it, for you are worthy of it."

The guardians open the door to the tomb.
The virtuous woman sings a mournful lament.
She enters, applies her face against Khosrow's,
And relates to him an account of the developments.
Then she drinks the poison in one shot,
And her sweet existence reaches its end.
She reclines at the side of the king, face veiled,
Her body dressed in a robe drenched in camphor.
In this manner, leaning against the wall,
She expires as someone who leaves behind a good name.

The news deeply afflicts Shirooy.
He fears to witness such a tragic display.
Upon his command, a second tomb is raised,
And she is buried next to her king,
Her head adorned with a crown of musk and camphor.
Then they shut tight the door to Khosrow's crypt.

Not long after, Shirooy is offered a deadly drink,
For the time of kings on earth reaches its end.
Born under disastrous circumstances,
He perishes miserably, leaving the royal crown to his son.
In this way, a prince reigns for seven months,

And on the eighth month, he is forced
To brace himself with a diadem of camphor.
If the throne is the best thing in the world,
A short, ephemeral life is certainly the worst.

I shall now turn to the reign of Shah Ardeshir,
Since he inserts himself inevitably into my story.

PART THIRTY-THREE

The Six-Month Reign
of Ardeshir, Son of Shirooy

The Fifty-Day Reign
of Goraaz, Called Faraaeen

The Six-Month Reign of Boorandokht

The Four-Month Reign of Azarmdokht

The One-Month Reign of Farrokhzaad

The Sixteen-Year Reign of Yazdegerd

I. The Six-Month Reign of Ardeshir, Son of Shirooy

1 | Ardeshir, Son of Shirooy, Ascends the Throne

As King Ardeshir takes possession of the throne,
His subjects, great and small, aging noblemen
And warriors alike, hasten to his court to hear him speak.

The young king declares: "O worldly warriors,
Anyone who occupies the royal throne
Must dip his language in sincerity
And worship Yazdan faithfully.
I shall walk in the footsteps of ancient kings
And obey the dictates of our glorious faith.
May Yazdan, Giver of all that is beneficial to us,
Reside in my mind, and may justice
Direct my thoughts and my actions.
I shall treat men of merit with honor
And righteous servants with kindness,
But, on the other hand, the deeds of malevolent men
Will not go unpunished; blood will be spilled.

"I shall revive the customs of Anushiravan
And fill with joy the souls of noble lords.
I shall surround myself with wise men.
In my care, security will spread across the world,
And the workings of Ahriman will plunge into the dark.
I shall raise my subjects according to merit,
Always rewarding good actions and good deeds.
My gold will bring joy to countless hearts,
And no one will dare devise wicked strategies.
Anyone who places his hopes in me
Need only speak out for his wishes to be granted.
But if, in the army, someone rebels against
My authority and disregards the sworn faith,

He will not be given the chance to escape death:
The only worthy punishment to come from me.
I entrust the army to Firooz Khosrow,
For he respects justice and the glorious king.
With a warrior hero of his stature in Iran,
Your hearts may rest content and in peace,
And you will find that your most cherished desires
Will be within your reach."

2 | Goraaz Urges Firooz to Kill Ardeshir

At the news of the new king, Goraaz, whose
Perfidious actions tormented Khosrow Parviz,
Sends an eloquent messenger to Rum
With a letter and with these words:
"The crown of the vile Shirooy is in the dust.
May his soul be retained in the grips of hell!
May the head of his tomb be overthrown!
The eye and the heart of the world will never
Witness a king of the likes of Khosrow Parviz.
He is the one who gave me principality.
I come from his court to execute his command.
Who would have thought that the tall cypress tree
Would be stifled by grass in the verdant garden?
Who would have believed that providence
Would turn its face suddenly away from him
And would snatch away his part of affection?
Who would have believed that the Sun and Moon
Would deprive him of his power,
That they would seize his throne and crown
And abandon kingship to a man of the likes of Shirooy,
Plunging the land of Iran into the throes of misfortune?

"I was for some time without news of King Parviz.
The smear of the evildoers caused his death.
He perished, and Ardeshir is now master of the crown.
But neither young nor old will be happy with him.
The earth might as well remain without a ruler.
I do not wish for such a man to ascend the throne,
For he desires might and relies on a foreign army.
Even if the affairs of Iran did not lean to our benefit,

I would not allow the wind of Iran to blow over his head.

"I approach now with a vast host,
With leaders from the lands of Rum and Iran.
We shall assess the nature of this new master
Who cultivates hostile ways and ventures.
I shall pluck out his deepest roots
And the question of royalty for him."

After having dismissed the speedy messenger
To ride toward the aging leaders of Iran's army,
He strategizes new plots by writing to Firooz Khosrow:
"The fortune of the Sassanians is fading.
It is time to cinch our waists and seize our weapons.
Perhaps you can devise a plan of action,
Turn your thoughts in every direction,
Unite a great number of companions, young and old,
And liberate the world from the dominion of Ardeshir.
You will obtain in this way
The accomplishment of all your wishes,
And you will enjoy peace and security.
But if you reveal the secret to anyone,
It will be as if you have drenched
Your sword of battle with blood.
I shall bring from Rum such a vast host
As to render the world black before your eyes.
Reflect deeply on my words, and may you not
Disdain the value of these ventures.
You must not fall from your high post
And perish inadvertently into the dust.
When my sword works in the interest of vengeance,
You must not have cause for repentance."

Firooz Khosrow reads the letter and understands
Its origins and the goals established by a vain man.
He contemplates the matter at length
And consults with the noble leaders.
His insightful heart is troubled in his attempts
To find a way to bring harm to Ardeshir.
He is sure that the king will soon suspect him.

The elders reply to Firooz, "O skillful nobleman,

If you eliminate the king, we shall perish as well.
Do not listen to Goraaz's advice.
Try to find a wise and worthy resolution.
Write a letter to him to awaken him from his dream.
Tell him not to stray from Yazdan's path
And to bar the wicked deev from accessing his heart.
Recall the lessons of the way they treated Parviz Shah.
When they brought him down from the royal throne,
It was as if they crushed the lineage of the Sassanians.
When Shirooy sat on the kingly throne
And strapped the Kianian belt around his waist,
His greatest desire was to follow his father's path,
Though he was a most wrathful king.
The world turned in this way, and you know that
He was never able to attain his most desired dreams.
It was as if anything that was good and valuable
Suddenly disappeared from the world.

"But now that Ardeshir replaces Shirooy
And sits on the royal throne, the world rejoices,
And time and space honor his glory.
Why should we stir up this peaceful state
And fill it with chaos and controversy?
Do not pound so hard with your fists on evil's door.
It is not right for an innocent king to be killed.
It is not right for the revolving dome
To annihilate Iran because of a retaliation.
Fear that Yazdan will punish the Iranians
And bring forth more challenging days for us."

After listening to them, Firooz writes
A worthy letter to Goraaz, a man of evil race:
"May the world never see the likes of you."

At the news, it is as if Goraaz's heart has been punched.
Deeply disturbed, he commands the troops
To prepare and dress in armor, to exit the city,
And to begin their journey to the plain.

The news reaches Firooz, and he sends a speedy camel
Instantly to travel to Tokhaar and inform him
Of all the words and the incidents that unfolded.

After the envoy's delivery of the message
And of the hostilities surrounding the royal crown,
Tokhaar sends his reply to Firooz:
"O warrior, do not spill the blood of Iran's noblemen.
Listen to the advice given to you by Goraaz.
Hold off on sending the letter to avoid him
Coming at you with his army and assailing you."

Firooz Khosrow is troubled by the letter.
His heart fills with dread.
How could he ever mistreat or harm the king?

Ardeshir often calls Firooz to his side,
For he is an eloquent and observant man
Who occupies the functions of vizier and treasurer.

During a particularly dark night,
Firooz marches to the palace,
Where he finds wine and gentle words.
Ardeshir is seated in the royal hall
With a few men, young and old.

The appearance of Firooz Khosrow makes the king
Feel as if he has raised his head to the sky in joy.
At the command of Ardeshir, music is played,
And the hall resounds with the sound of song.

After half the night passes,
The leader drinks his wine in a single sip
While the companions of the king are inebriated.
No musician is left to observe the events.

Firooz dismisses all the court's friends,
And, finding himself alone with the king,
The traitor rushes from the curtain,
Suddenly places his hand firmly on the king's mouth,
Smothering him and suffocating him to death.

The palace fills with the swords, bows, and arrows
Of young, ambitious men and old warriors,
Friends of Firooz Khosrow.
The reign of Ardeshir lasted for two and four months,
When he passed away in a most somber manner.

Firooz rushes a messenger on camelback
Toward Goraaz, carrier of a long letter.
Upon receipt, Goraaz's heart shines as bright as the sun.
He exits his land with a host so vast
That neither fly nor ant can pass through.
He rushes as swift as wind to Ctesiphon
With troops avid for carnage.

A number of troops advance on the road to greet him.
No one among them dares to breathe or talk.
They are so numerous they fill up every corner of the city.

II. The Fifty-Day Reign of Goraaz, Called Faraaeen

1 | Goraaz Usurps the Throne

Goraaz invades the city without a vizier or guide.
He holds council at a secret site with famed lords.

Firooz is the first to speak: "O noble warrior,
Who have you in mind to rise to the status of king?
Who have you found worthy of the glorious crown?"

Goraaz the fighter replies, "I wish not to withhold
Anything for Iran. Tomorrow you will witness
The ascension of a new king to the throne.
He will shine as bright as a new moon.
Every man's potential relies on his knowledge.
Avoid the path of ignorance as much as you can.
Speak words based on a foundation of wisdom,
For the one who is endowed with wisdom
Will never encroach upon wicked deeds.
The highest asset for a man is his insight,
And the most worthy path is the way of Yazdan.
An insignificant action need not be remembered,
Even if balanced with great feats,
But with one evil deed you undermine your dignity.
If your head empties of wisdom and your eyes
Are free of shame, your name will be dishonored.
Besides your tainted name,
Your life will lose its meaning.
A man devoid of honor and wisdom has no fear,
Whether he is alive or buried deep in the ground.
In this illusory world,
Extend your hand toward good deeds,
For it does not remain for anyone.
Your intentions must lead to the welfare of humanity

And your religion follow
A warrior's path of righteousness."

Faraaeen (Goraaz) places on his head the Kianian crown
And speaks: "The execution of the kingly occupation,
Sitting happily on the royal throne, has more value
Than spending sixty years redeeming yourself
From bondage and remaining prey to suffering,
Arms hanging by your side like a slave.
My treasure has been depleted, gone to the wind,
And, in my old age, I am ready to reign for many years.
My robes are made of silks and furs.
Upon my departure, my son will ascend the throne
And place upon his head the royal crown.
His rule will mirror his father's,
His nobility will reach even greater heights.
Anyone who makes a display of happiness
Toward us will attain the object of his desires.
At times we shall joyously engage in revelry;
At times we shall surmount our enemies."

His elder son whispers in his ear,
"Tell me, father, which of your sons do you hope
To make the crown-bearer as your successor?
Do not place all your trust in the future.
Advise us on the means of amassing a treasure.
If an offspring of kings were to present himself,
You would not remain here for long.
At that time, you will be plunged into a state of distress."

The youngest son speaks in these terms:
"You are the crown owner and must possess
An imposing host and a treasure worthy of kings.
Your vast wealth will keep you out of trouble.
Did Fereydoon, whose father was Aabteen,
Originate from a kingly lineage?
He divided the world into three sections
And offered a part to each of his blessed sons
As he invested his joy in the act of spreading justice.
Maintain your dominion with your courage and treasury.
No one is born from a mother as a king.
When I am master of power, crown, and throne,

The people will be pleased with me and will enjoy life.
My fortune will shine, and my throne will rise to Saturn."

Goraaz appreciates the words of his youngest son
And urges his elder son to exercise prudence.
He commands the army leader to take his place
In the royal offices and gathers the troops at court.
Day and night, he distributes dinars
And offers gifts of honor to those undeserving.
In two weeks, Ardeshir's wealth is depleted.
Nothing remains, not even an arrow's feather.

When Goraaz enters the garden, he carries eighty
Candles of amber at the front and eighty at the back.
Behind the candles arrive his friends and companions.
He makes use of only gold and silver cups,
And the golden ones are inlaid with fine gems.
He has the custom of passing the entire night in drink,
Filling the hearts of noblemen with disgust.

At the time of sleep, he wanders endlessly
Through the gardens and the public places.
All the people of Iran break their ties to him.
The world becomes increasingly troubled.

Besides eating, drinking, and sleeping,
This petty ruler knows nothing else.
Always in a state of intoxication, he falls asleep
Here and there with his turban under his head.

The army and the people are troubled by him,
And the land is in a state of chaos and disarray.
Faraaeen forgets the idea of giving.
He renounces any attention to justice and generosity.
The people strike their heads with their hands.
His eyes seem solely fixed on the acquisition of gold
While selling the world for a capital of dinars
And spilling the blood of innocent men.

The troops rebel and rise against him.
They speak of him in insolent terms, calling for his death.
They secretly gather and recount his wicked deeds.

During a dark night, Hormozd Shahran,
An elite rider from the city of Estakhr,
Well respected by the land's noblemen,
Speaks at length in a secret assembly.
He says to the Iranians, "O powerful men,
The reign of Faraaeen is tyrannical.
He does not take into account any of the noblemen.
How can your heads and your hearts be so weak?
All eyes fill with tears because of him,
And we are at a loss for a remedy to our ailment.
Faraaeen is not a Sassanian. He does not belong
To the Kianian race. Why should we obey him?
It appears as if your hearts
Have been plucked right out of your chests,
As if courage has decidedly abandoned you."

The warriors reply, "On one hand,
We cannot find a legitimate heir to the throne.
On the other hand, the hatred he inspires
Does not afford him any friends or allies.
We see no one able to snatch this man
Of evil race from the kingly seat.
We are in complete agreement with you.
Tell us what you have learned from honest men
On ways to save Iran-Zamin from this foolish, wicked,
And brainless king. He is incapable of speaking
A kind word or of committing a generous deed.
May he always be deprived of benediction!"

Shahran replies, "The situation in Iran
Has lasted far too long. If you promise to keep me safe
And to behave in the way of free men,
I shall, with the aid of Yazdan, the pure,
Depose him and plunge him into the dust."

The Iranians reply, "May you be guarded from adversity!
Today all the troops are united behind you.
If this venture puts you at risk, we shall be your support."

The hero, a faithful servant of noble sovereigns,
Seeks a means to attack the wretched Goraaz Faraaeen.

2 | Goraaz Faraaeen Dies at the Hand of Hormozd Shahran

One day, the king makes preparations
And exits the city to engage in the hunt.
He is accompanied by an army of Iranians
Composed of men of various ranks.

Faraaeen launches his horse and rushes
Left and right, as swift as Aazargoshasp.
The riders surrounding the king
Charge at the wild beasts to chase after them.

Upon their return to the city, Hormozd Shahran,
The fearless, scrutinizes the miserable king.
He then draws a steel-tipped arrow from his quiver
And launches his black horse,
His army monitoring his every move.
He draws his bow and raises it, fixing the target,
Fluctuating between the king's head and his chest.
It is as if he is playing an instrument,
With an arrow on a string.
When the point protrudes beyond the bow's center,
He releases his thumb at once.
The shot strikes the king, forcing him to drop his whip.
The entire length of the arrow plunges into the flesh
On his back, the tip making an appearance
On the opposite side out of his navel.

Faraaeen falls off his charger, headfirst,
And a torrent of blood spurts out of the wound.
He writhes and, lying on the black dust in pain,
He belts out a single cry of anguish.

The army warriors resort to fight and blows
As dusk descends over the powdery plain.
Throughout the night they hit each other
Without benefiting from the advantage of sight.
Each man receives blows, each man administers blows;
One cursing the outcome, the other lauding the exploits.

As the sun appears like a sheet of yellow brocade,

Speckling the mountain like leopard skin,
Many combatants lie on the ground,
Having been either killed or wounded.
Cavaliers and leaders succumb to fatigue.
This vast army disbands, like a herd of sheep
Scattering at the unexpected sighting of a wolf.

The throne remains vacant of a king
As no one comes to claim it.
In vain do they search for a royal descendant.
No offspring is found of imperial lineage.

III. The Sixth-Month Reign of Boorandokht

There lives a young lady of Sassanian race named
Boorandokht, well-versed in the literature of kings.
Although most believe the affairs of state
Do not evolve smoothly under a woman's control,
They place her on the throne nevertheless,
And noblemen scatter jewels over her person.

Boorandokht speaks as follows:
"I wish for my people to be united as one.
I shall render the poor wealthy, drawing
From my treasury to pull them out of distress.
Heaven forbid a single wretched person
Will suffer, as such a thing would
Poorly reflect on me and my rule.
I shall banish ill-intentioned men from the land
And organize my court according to ancient traditions."

She seeks to track down Firooz, son of Khosrow.
When one of her subjects indicates his whereabouts,
She selects an illustrious man from the army to fetch him.

Once Firooz is present at her court, she says to him,
"O ill-natured man, miserable villain,
You are guilty of crimes and avid for vengeance.
You deserve to receive due punishment.
You will endure the pain of your offenses,
As I shall make torrents of blood flow from your limbs."

At her command, they bring a young,
Untrained, unsaddled horse from the stables,
To which Firooz is attached firmly,
The halter looped around his neck.
The unrestrained horse drags Firooz
And parades him around the public square.
The queen sends a few cavaliers there holding

Their rolled-up nooses around their saddles' hooks,
Charging them to see how the horse handles Firooz
As it dashes about, pounding his body to the ground,
Where he rolls about sadly to the hail of loud cheers.

Finally, the wretched Firooz, his body in shreds,
Blood slowly dripping from his wounds, expires.
How could you depend on justice
When you have yourself committed unjust acts?
You can be sure to suffer, as retribution will be served.

Boorandokht governs the world gently for some time.
The wind blowing from the sky does not stir up the dust.
But as six months of her reign pass,
The circle of her life suddenly deviates to take a turn.
She is taken gravely ill for one week
And dies, taking with her a reputation for kindness.

Such is the law of the revolving skies:
As the master of all things, it leaves you powerless.
Whether you are destitute or wealthy,
Whether you live in abundance or scarcity,
Whether your dreams are fulfilled or unattained,
Whether you have treasure or endure hard labor,
Neither one will remain forever.
Whether you reign for one hundred or one thousand years,
Whether sixty or thirty years, whether ten or four years,
Whether you are young or old, no matter,
For when the time passes, the outcome is the same.
Your only asset and support are your deeds in this world.
May they save you from misery.

Let go of this illusory world,
Look toward the next stage,
Which you will find exceedingly more desirable.
If you strap your belt in service to learning,
Your acquired knowledge
Will raise you above the revolving dome.

IV. The Four-Month Reign of Azarmdokht

There lives another princess named Azarm, who rejoices
To find herself in possession of the lofty crown of power.
She takes a seat on the Kianian throne
To assume governance of the world.

At the beginning of her reign, she proclaims,
"O intelligent, worldly, and noble men,
I shall always conform to justice and custom,
For in the end, our pillow is, inexorably,
A most humble block of cinder.
The one who avows his devotion to me will find in me
A nurturing parent who rewards him with dinars.
If he commits a wrongful act,
I shall be patient with him.
Conversely, should I find a person disloyal,
Who deviates from the rule and the path of reason,
I shall plant his severed head at the gallows,
Whether he is Iranian, Taazi, or Rumi."

The noblemen acclaim her as queen
And scatter jewels over her throne.
The people of Iran are happy and grateful
To have her rule, and not a single enemy remains.
She receives presents and homage
From the lands of Turks, Rum, India, and Chin.

She occupies the throne for four months,
But upon the fifth month, her power is shattered.
Fortune withdraws its favors, and
The star that once guided her loses its luster.
The queen dies, and the throne, deprived of a ruler,
Is abandoned to the ambition of wicked enemies.

Such is the law of the turning skies:
It pursues with distaste those it once favored.

V. The One-Month Reign of Farrokhzaad

They summon Farrokhzaad from the city of Jahrom
To assume a seat on the kingly throne.

His heart pure, he addresses homage to the Creator:
"As the son of mighty kings,
I desire only peace on earth.
If someone seeks the path of evil,
He will not attain power for long under my rule.
On the other hand, the one who cultivates righteousness
In his heart will be as dear to me as my own life.
I shall never cause harm to those who are upright.
Anyone who works devotedly for king and crown
Will be rewarded for his efforts with wealth.
Embrace all my friends and allies, as noblemen
Will have the means to elevate themselves.
My inferiors will obtain safety by my side,
Whether they hold affection for me or hostility."

The army is united in paying homage to his term:
"May Earth and Time never be deprived of you!"

But after one month of his reign, the king's power
And good fortune are plunged into the dust.
He has a noble slave of cypress stature, of handsome
And gracious demeanor, whose name is Siah Chashm.
May the wheel of sky never produce such a being!

The king also has a slave whom he loves passionately.
One day, she passes in front of Siah Chashm by chance,
And the latter gives her the following message:
"If you agree to grant me a meeting,
I shall offer you innumerable presents,
And I shall adorn your diadem with jewels."

The female slave listens to him without responding,

But she reports the strange exchange to Farrokhzaad.
The king is indignant to learn of this adventure.
Grief causes him to lose his appetite and his sleep.
He asks for Siah Chashm's feet to be bound
And assigns him the dungeon for dwelling.

But after some time, after many people
Intercede in his behalf, the just king caves in
And commands that the sinful man be freed.

Siah Chashm, a most wicked person,
Resumes his service at court, but his desire
For vengeance curtails the days for his master.
Profiting from a moment of royal rest,
Siah Chashm mixes poison with wine.
The king drinks the fatal tonic
And survives just one week.

All those who hear of the incident weep.
His dominion comes to an abrupt end.
His enemies take advantage of his death
To advance their malicious schemes.
The fortune of the Sassanian throne
Is overturned by the Iranians' evil action.

Such is the working of this versatile destiny.
Attempt to draw profit from it if you can.
Enjoy your possessions and do not leave
Anything for the next day, as tomorrow,
Who knows what the inconstant world will bring?
Its nature is to vacillate and bound around randomly.
It will strip your assets to hand to another,
On whose head it will rest the Kianian crown.

VI. The Twenty-Year Reign of Yazdegerd

1 | The Rise of Yazdegerd

After the death of Farrokhzaad,
Yazdegerd rises as king
On the twenty-fifth day of the month of Esfand.
What did he say, the eloquent and brave man
Who is wary of the revolutions of days:
"Alas, my mother had to give birth to me!
Alas, the sublime skies have spun over my head!
What shall I say of the narrow circle of life
Traced between the two celestial orbs?
Long days remain for neither the one in power
Nor the one in great distress.
It is best to always maintain silence.
Upon careful consideration, life is but an instant.
Since it is so, do not enter into conflict with it.
Set the table, empty the cup, and let us
Not mention the concerns of this world.
Even if providence, so unpredictable,
Were to launch your horse by the bridle,
Ultimately your head is sure
To find a cinder block to rest upon.
When you assume the positiion of king,
What is the conclusion?
It begins with the ascent to the throne,
But what is to be the outcome?
Do not attach your heart to inconsequential fears.
Have trust in the sublime sphere,
Yet do not rest too assured at the same time.
Fate amuses itself with lions and elephants,
And it does so out of playfulness, not out of need.

"It is inevitable that you will die one day,
And destiny will continue its trajectory.
The story is drawn out;

You best avoid ceding to arrogance.
You are not more powerful than Fereydoon.
You cannot be compared to the mighty Parviz,
Who was the master of throne and crown,
Or to Jamsheed, who dominated the deevs.
Your soul did not rise up to the firmament
Like the illustrious Kay Kaavoos.
Reflect well, and observe the way
The seven skies deal with Yazdegerd."

Once he sits happily on the royal throne
And adorns his head with the crown of power,
He declares,
"By the revolutions of the spinning sphere,
I am the pure descendant of Anushiravan.
From father to son, I am in direct line of kingship.
The Sun, monarchy, and the house of Pisces favor me.
I shall give power to noblemen
And never bring harm to the humble.
I shall seek glory and wisdom, courage and valor,
For the days of good fortune, treasury,
Crown, and throne do not remain for anyone.
One must hope to leave behind
An enduring name and a shining reputation.
Renounce joy and glorify your name.
This is the way a man acquires immortality
After his body has been buried in the dust.
The most important thing for a king
Is to proceed and rule with justice and faith.
Everyone praises his name and his person.
I wish to remain alive long enough to eradicate
The roots of evil proliferating in the world."

The noblemen pay homage to Yazdegerd
And proclaim him world king.
For two times eight years, Sun and Moon
Turn over him, and this king, who governs
The world guided by ancient customs,
Brings joy to the land of Iran.

2 | Saad, Son of Vaghas, Attacks Iran, and Rostam's Letter to His Brother

There lives an illustrious and noble Arab
Named Saad, son of Vaghas,
Who converts day to night with his blade.

Omar, the leader of the Muslims,
Highly praises Saad and offers him an army
To wage war on King Yazdegerd.

At the time when the fortune of the Arabs
Conquers the fortune of the Iranians,
The Sassanians' streak of luck decidedly dims.
The empire of kings falls, its cup spills,
Gold vanishes, and worthless currency
Makes an appearance to overtake all others.
Evil becomes desirable, and virtue turns to evil.
It is as if the road to hell passes through paradise.
The face of the revolving dome assumes new features.
It severs its bond of affection with the Iranians.
The servants of faith must willfully accept
Anything handed out by the World Creator.
No one can withstand or argue with divine resolve.
Besides Yazdan, there exists no being
Able to craft the human face and infuse it with life.

As soon as he is informed,
Yazdegerd musters troops from all corners
And commands one of the sons of Hormozd, Rostam,
To lead the army as it marches off.
Rostam is an aware, prudent, intelligent, brave man,
Quite capable of governing the world.
He possesses knowledge of astrology,
Vast wisdom, and heeds the discourse of wise men.

As soon as Rostam hears of the Arab invasion,
He goes to the king of serene heart, kisses the ground,
Summons divine honor on his majesty,
And holds himself at his side for a long time.

Yazdegerd showers him with praise and says,

"O descendant of Kianians,
Warrior of elephant stature and lion claws,
You vanquish the raging whale.
When you seize your sword on the day of battle,
You overturn the proudest heads.
I learn that innumerable Taazian troops,
Their faces black as tar,
Have crossed our borders to wage war,
Although they possess neither treasure nor king.
Their leader is Saad, son of Vaghas,
A man most avid for power and wealth.
I am entrusting you, O devoted warrior,
With the empire's banner, a treasury, and an army.
Enroll the troops, prepare for war without delay.
When you march off.
Wjem the armies come face to face,
Observe the Taazian and reflect on all the strategies
That could be either advantageous or harmful to us."

Rostam replies, "I am your servant.
I stand before you, attentive to your instructions.
I shall cut off the heads of the king's enemies.
I shall capture and enchain the minds of evildoers."
Then he bows down to kiss the ground
And takes his leave to spend the night in thought.

As the shining sun climbs over the horizon,
Rostam, avid for vengeance, departs in haste,
Taking under his command the most noble warriors
And all those who exhibit prudence and valor.

Thirty days pass in this way.
Once he is ready to engage in battle in Kadesia,[29]
Rostam, a learned, benevolent and just astrologer,
Understands the danger they are in and says,
"A battle here is not a wise or timely course of action.
The river of kings must not flow through this riverbed."

He brings an astrolabe and, after observing the stars

◇◇◇◇◇◇◇◇◇◇◇◇◇
29 Kadesia: A region on the Arabian Peninsula, site of the battle between the
Arabs and the Iranians at the time of the Arab conquest.

And seeing a calamitous day ahead,
He brings his hands to his face despondently.
In his grief, he writes a letter to his brother
In which he recounts the unfolding developments.
After having celebrated the praises of the Creator,
Giver of days of both prosperity and misfortune,
He continues: "The seeker has cause to worry
About the future revolutions of destiny.
I am the most culpable man of this era,
And Ahriman has captured me in his noose,
As I see it, the royal family is condemned
To lose the throne, as our days of victory
And splendor are about to come to an abrupt end.

"At the moment the sun rises
To the crest of the fourth sky,
Noblemen must hasten to battle.
We are left with no choice but to proceed.
Misfortune swiftly marches toward us.
Mars and Venus are unfavorable to us.
We cannot evade the sublime wheel of sky.
Mercury, seated in the house of Gemini,
And Saturn are to be positioned side by side.
Such is the situation: A mighty challenge rises
Before us, and our hearts will be weary of life.
We can see into the future, we can decipher
Its mysteries, but we must keep silent.
I weep bitter tears over the fate of the Iranians,
And I am consumed by the blaze of suffering
At the thought of the Sassanian family.
Alas, this head, this crown, this throne!
Alas, this power, this glory, this illustrious dynasty!
It will all be shattered by a Taazian conquest.
The stars will spin only to further our detriment.
For the duration of four hundred years,
No heir of our race will rise to be world master!

"An Arab envoy has come to my side
To discuss various subjects with our assembly.
He said,
          'We shall surrender to the king
          All the lands between Kadesia and the river's edge.

But we shall open a path from the other bank
To one of your cities with a marketplace
So that we may open the way to trade.
We shall not ask for anything more.
We shall pay a costly tribute
Without setting our sights on the crown.
We shall obey the King of Kings,
And if he demands hostages from us, we shall oblige.'

"But these are merely words and not actions.
All this comes from the stars that have digressed.
A great war will arise
Where hundreds of intrepid lions will perish.
The noblemen who fight at my side
Choose to ignore these propositions:
Golbooy from Tabaristan and Armani are fighting
Against promoters of the faith of Ahriman,
Maahooy Soori and chiefs armed with weapons
And heavy maces raise their heads and exclaim:
    'Who are these people?
    What right do they have
    To enter the lands of Iran and Mazandaran?
    The invasion of our borders and roads,
    Our rise and fall,
    Everything will be decided by mace and saber.
    We shall fight as men
    And reduce the enemy to the breaking point
    By constricting the world for them.'
No one is privy to the secrets of the unstable skies,
Which appear to have altered their treatment of us.

"After you read this letter,
Work and act in concert with the empire's noblemen.
Assemble all there is in terms
Of wealth, slaves, and precious furnishing,
And drive your army in haste to Azerbaijan,
To the leaders and illustrious Iranians.
Hand over all your possessions of horses
To the treasurer of Aazargoshasp.
If troops arrive from Zabolestan and Iran
To fall under your protection, welcome them,
Dress them, and treat them with affection.

Beware of the revolutions of the spinning skies
That give you moments of joy and pain,
That raise you at a whim or bring you down abruptly.
Relate to my mother the contents of this letter,
For she will never again set her sight on me.
Relate to her my farewell, lavish her with advice,
So that she may avoid a blow of misfortune.

"If you receive sad news on my account,
Do not mourn in excess.
Do not forget that someone else
Will enjoy the treasures you have amassed
With great effort in this perishable dwelling.
Once you are gone, they are worthless penalties
That will fall into a void to the benefit of another.
Why then spend so much effort to nurse your greed?
Always remain a loyal Yazdan worshipper,
And banish from your heart
The worries of this fleeting world.

"Misfortune will pursue us,
And the king will never catch a glimpse of me.
You and all the offspring of our lineage, young and old,
Pay homage to the World Creator at night.
Know that my army and I are prey
To weariness, worry, and adversity
As I stand in a state of distress here with my troops.
At the end of all this, there is no salvation for us.
Alas, the gentle breeze drifting over Iran-Zamin!
Destiny overwhelms and constricts the king.
Do not think of your wealth, your body, or your life,
For the noble King Yazdegerd is all that we have left
Of this illustrious and blessed race.

"Never bring weakness to any of your ventures.
We only have this protector left on earth,
The only surviving Sassanian ruler, and after him,
You will never find another heir of his blood and lineage.
Alas, his crown, his generosity, his sense of justice!
It will all drift away with the wind.
May you live happy and powerful!
Devote yourself to defending the king, day and night!

If danger menaces him, place yourself before him
And, eager to battle, protect him with your sword.

"Once the pulpit rises before the throne,
All the names will be Abu Bakr and Omar,
Our fortune will be on the decline
For a long period of time.
The question of throne, crown, and city
Will become absolutely meaningless.
The stars revolve in favor of the Taazian
And will hand over it all to them.
Day will succeed day, the decline of our power
Will ensue, and they will enjoy a life free of need.
Among the strangers, many will dress in black[30]
And style their heads with silken tiaras.
There will no longer be either throne or crown,
Golden ankle boots or jewels, diadem
Or golden banner floating over heads.
To some the fatigue, to others the pleasures.
People will come to brush aside
And disregard justice and generosity.

"Favored by night, a watchful enemy
Will invade the homes of the ones who hide.
A stranger will become master of day and night.
He will cinch his royal waist and wear a headdress.
Neither faith nor the oath of loyalty will be respected.
Falsehoods and lies will assume a place of honor.
True warriors will turn into infantrymen,
And liars and frauds will form the new army.
The bold farmer will, unawares, grow keen on war.
Birth and race will cease to bear weight or bear fruit.
This one will rob the other, and vice versa.
No longer will there exist a distinction
Between blasphemy and benediction,
And deceit will prevail over tolerance.
And, at an accelerating speed,
The hearts of men will toughen as hard as granite.

"The father will harbor ill thoughts for his son,

◇◇◇◇◇◇◇◇◇◇◇◇◇
30 Perhaps an allusion to the Abbasid dynasty for which black was the official color.

433

And the son will detest his father.
A vile slave will rise to a status of dominance.
Neither birth nor grandeur will matter.
The world will no longer know honor and loyalty,
As injustice will invade people's hearts and lips.
A mixed race will emerge
Of Iranians, Turks, and Taazian.
Poet bards will join the race of the extinct.
Discussions will resemble banter.
Each person will bury his treasure,
And, upon his death, his enemy
Will inherit the fruits of his labors.
Sorrow, suffering, and divisions
Will rule supreme in measure
To the joy reigning in the time of Bahraam Goor.
Feast and revelry will be banished, as well as
Music and song, jewels and dreams fulfilled.

"Everywhere ruse, deception, and traps will prevail.
People will have no qualms about hurting each other.
Each will seek his own profit to the detriment of others,
Every act in the name of religion.
Spring will no longer succeed winter.
Wine will be absent in times of celebration.
With so many yearning to reach superior ranks,
Yearning to possess more and more,
People will be left to consume bread and curdled milk
And dress in coarse hawker's coats.
A long time will pass, and no one
Will gaze in the direction of Iran.
Abundant blood will be spilled for the acquisition
Of wealth, and ominous days will be upon us.

"My heart swells with blood, my face pales,
My mouth is parched, my lips are blue with sighs
To think that since I emerged as an indomitable
Iranian leader, the fortune of the Sassanians has dimmed.
This fickle, inconstant sphere will betray us,
Persecute us, and withdraw its affection.
My spear and javelin, once able to pierce
A mountain of steel, somehow fall powerless
Against the bare bodies of my rivals.

The tip of my sword, once so sharp it easily
Slashed through the necks of lions and elephants,
Now falls blunt against Taazian skin.
Science has brought me hindrance upon hindrance.
I wish I never had the sort of insight
That brings to light future days of sorrow!
The leaders who followed me to Kadesia
Are coarse warriors, determined enemies of the Taazian.
They hope to bring an end to the struggle soon,
Spread torrents of blood,
Convert the land into the River Jayhoon.
Not one of them knows the mysteries of the skies.
Not one of them is aware that pain and suffering
Are to last a long, long time.

"Once a family's days come to an end,
How will hostilities, strain, and battle benefit us?
As for you, O dear brother, may you live in health
With the purpose to comfort the heart of the King of Iran!
The land of Kadesia is to be my tomb,
My armor my shroud, and a crown of blood my helmet.
Such are the mysteries of the sublime dome of sky.
Do not link your heart to a brother's agony.
Keep your eyes on the world king to safeguard him
And sacrifice your life on the battlefield for him.
The days of Ahriman rush forward,
With the spinning sphere playing the role of enemy."

After having sealed the letter with affection,
He adds to the envoy, "May the sky's benedictions
Escort you and the missive to my brother,
And may you adequately relate the subject discussed."

3 | Rostam's Letter to Saad, Son of Vaghas

Rostam immediately dispatches his messenger,
Who travels as swift as lightning and thunder to Saad.
The letter, written on white silk, is full of hope and fear:
"On the part of the son of Shah Hormozd,
The charitable, the vengeful world warrior Rostam;
To Saad, son of Vaghas, battle-seeker,

Knowledgeable, thoughtful, and patient."

The letter begins: "Let us not reject the fear
And the respect due the pure Creator,
Whose sovereignty, founded on love and justice,
Steers the ever-moving sphere;
May divine blessings rest upon our eminent king,
Worthy of crown, throne, and seal,
Glory of majesty, grandeur, victory, and power,
Master of the sword and the sublime throne,
Whose supremacy holds Ahriman in manacles!
An odious affair arises that is sure to bring
Suffering and futile battles.
Tell me, who is your king?
Tell me, what kind of a man are you?
What religion or cult do you adhere to?
How do you intend to pursue fame and glory?

"You and your troops are short of weapons.
You are dying of hunger,
And a bit of bread would satisfy you.
You have neither elephant nor throne,
Neither provisions nor wealth.
Why not come here and settle in the land of Iran?
The king of royal lineage possesses crown and seal.
He is master of elephants, treasures, throne, and glory.
His stature is so striking not even the moon compares.
The earth has never witnessed a greater sovereign.
When he sits in feast, happy and exhibiting a smile,
He distributes gifts more valuable
Than all the Taazian heads put together.
He does so without draining his treasury.
He possesses ten plus two thousand
Dogs, cheetahs, and falcons
Decked with bells and golden pendants.

"During the year, from one end of the plain
Of spear-riders to the other, Taazian nomads
Are unable to subsist off of game.
The chase belongs to the king
Who seizes the wild animals
With his sprightly dogs and cheetahs.

All you have to consume
Is camel milk and alligator meat.
And now you are bold enough to confront us,
Setting your sights on the throne of Iran?
I spit on the wind and on the revolving dome.

"You must be deprived of any sense of modesty.
Your level of wisdom is familiar
With neither respect nor affection.
How could you, with your faces, your origins,
Your customs, dare aspire to Iran's kingship?
If you yearn for power according to your merits,
If your words are not spoken in jest, send me
An eloquent messenger, experienced,
Valiant, and learned, so that I may understand
The goal you pursue and who is guiding you
Toward aspiring to usurp the Kianian throne.

"I shall rush a rider to the king
And urge him to accept your demands.
But do not seek to battle a sovereign
Endowed with such power,
For the outcome would be fatal to you.
He is the grandson of world master Anushiravan,
Whose justice renewed the hearts of old men.
He is the rightful heir to kings from father to son
And a rightful king himself,
With no equal in this century.
A sage and equitable man has no right to covet
The Kianian seat if not issued from royal blood.
Do not make yourself an object of horror to the world.
Do not be responsible for people cursing you.
Do not be the enemy of your faith and beliefs.
Pay attention to the sage advice in this letter
Without enchaining your wisdom's eyes and ears."

After affixing the seal to the letter,
He hands it over to the noble Pirooz, son of Shahpoor,
Who immediately takes it to Saad, son of Vaghas,
Accompanied by noble Iranians of serene souls
Equipped with silver armor, shields, and golden belts.

4 | Saad's Reply to Rostam's Letter

Saad, informed of the arrival of the illustrious Pirooz,
Marches as swift as dust to meet him with his host.
After driving him into his tent,
The leader questions him on the subject
Of the army and the warrior hero,
On the king, his vizier, his troops,
His vigilant army general, and his provinces.

He throws a cloak under Pirooz's feet and says,
"We are equipped with javelins and sabers.
Intrepid warriors do not speak of silk, gold,
And silver, or food, rest, and sleep.
You resemble women with beauty, color, and scent,
And lack the virtues that belong to valiant fighters.
Your greatest asset is flaunting silken robes
And drawing pretty pictures on ceilings and doors."

After speaking, Pirooz hands him the letter
And relates to him Rostam's words.

Saad listens and reads the letter written in Pahlavi.
He is deeply surprised by the message.
Immediately he composes a reply in Arabic,
In which he discusses strengths and weaknesses.
He begins in the name of the Creator,
And in the name of Muhammad, divine messenger,
Who guides you on the path to truth.
He brings up the nature of jinn,[31] fairies, and humans.
He mentions the words uttered by Hashemi[32] prophets,
The dogma of unity, the Koran, promises and menaces,
The future of the world, and the new religion.
He describes hell with its burning river of tar,
Its flames, and its dreadful, punishing cold.
He describes paradise with its streams of milk,
Its widespread camphor, its gushing pure springs,
Its heavenly tree, and its fountains of wine and honey.

◇◇◇◇◇◇◇◇◇◇◇◇◇◇◇
31 Jinn: Supernatural beings or spirits able to take on various shapes; common in
myths and stories.
32 Hashemi: Arab descendants of the Prophet Muhammad.

Then he adds, "If the king were to embrace
The true religion, kingship and happiness
Would belong to him in both worlds.
Furthermore, he would obtain earrings and crown,
And all his years would be enriched
With color, scent, and beauty.
He would receive pardon for all his sins
With the intercession of Muhammad,
And his body would be as pure as distilled rosewater.
When the promised reward is paradise, one must not
Sow seeds of hatred in the field of misfortune.

"The person of Yazdegerd, the vast earth,
Palaces opening to lush gardens, audience halls
And courts, the royal throne, feast and festivals
Are not worth one hair of Houri.[33]
Your eyes are fixed on this perishable journey,
And for that reason, you seek crown and treasure.
You take a seat, content on the ivory throne
With your fortune, your seal and crown,
But this world, valued at merely a sip of cold syrup,
Is not worth the worry it stirs up in your heart?
Anyone who comes to me to engage in war
Will encounter either hell or a narrow grave.
It is best for you to relinquish these illusions
And not stray from the path of religion.
Should the king accept,
Paradise will be his dwelling as he deserves it.
Allow him to reflect well on the next course of action.
Everything is in a constant state of change.
Any wise man knows this to be true."

Saad places the seal of the Arabs on the parchment
And adds blessings in honor of Muhammad.
Then he singles out Shohbeh Moghaira among warriors
As envoy to make his way to the hero Rostam.

At the same time, an illustrious Iranian informs
The army leader: "An old emissary arrives.
He has neither horse nor armor nor proper attire.

◇◇◇◇◇◇◇◇◇◇◇◇◇
33 Houri: A beautiful maiden who welcomes the devout Muslim into paradise.

His body is bent over. He hides a narrow blade,
Its handle poking through his tunic's tears."

At these words, Rostam sets up a tent of brocade,
Adorned with cushions of Chini silk.
The troops, as numerous as ants and locusts,
Fall into formation. A golden seat is fetched
On which the army hero takes his place.
One hundred and sixty Iranian riders, lions in battle,
Dressed in headdresses and robes of golden brocade,
Fitted in golden boots, necks and ears adorned
With jewels, line up around the luxurious royal tent.

Shohbeh arrives at the threshold,
And, avoiding stepping on the carpets,
He walks modestly on the dust,
Using his sword as a cane.
Then he sits on the floor without glancing at anyone
Or raising his eyes toward the army leader.

Rostam says to him, "Be happy, and may learning
Maintain your soul and body in good health!"

Shohbeh replies, "O renowned man,
If you accept the true religion, may salvation be yours!"

These words displease Rostam, who furrows his brow.
He receives the letter from Shohbeh and hears him out,
Then hands it to his scribe to read.

After the deed is done, Rostam replies in these terms:
"Tell your master on my part:
        'You are neither king nor heir to the throne,
        But your fortune appeared dim to you
        And your heart coveted the royal seat.
        Such speech is not insignificant in the eyes
        Of experienced people, and you show a lack
        Of prudence by entertaining the idea of a bold venture.
        If Saad were to bear the Sassanian crown,
        I would be allowed to take part in his wars and feasts.
        But the fault belongs to the malevolent stars.
        What more can I say? We live in times of hardship.
        If Muhammad were my guide, if I left my ancient

Religion for a new faith, everything would be
Overturned beneath the hunchbacked vault of sky.
Everything would surely be a challenge for me.'

"As for you, O messenger, return in peace.
There is no reason to discuss further
When the time has arrived to prepare for war.
Tell Saad that I prefer to perish bravely on the battlefield
Than to live to witness the triumph of my enemy."

Shohbeh takes leave of the camp
And departs in tandem with the speed of wind.

5 | The Battle of Rostam With Saad, and Rostam's Death

Soon after Shohbeh's departure,
Rostam commands the army to prepare for war.
He asks for the blare of clarions,
And the troops rush to form ranks.
From the midst of dust clouds, cries rise so loud
They have the power to pierce the most exercised ear.

On his side, as soon as Shohbeh returns,
Bearer of words as menacing as thunder,
The valiant Saad commands his troops
To march to battle with the ardor of lions.

The two armies advance with a firm stride
And fall upon each other in the arena.
The glimmer of blades pierces through the dust
Like stars in the indigo sky.
The pounding of spears on helmets of steel multiplies.
The struggle continues in this way for three days.
The Iranians are in need of water, overwhelmed
Beneath the weight of their heavy armor.
They have to sustain the assault of the enemy.
Severe thirst exhausts and weakens the heroes
And displaces the steeds of noble race.

Rostam finds himself with parched lips

As thirst lacerates his tongue.
So grave is the distress of the warriors and horses
So lacking are they in provisions, that they can only
Find a measure of relief by ingesting wet clay.

Rostam casts a glance on the battlefield.
Seeing many of his illustrious chiefs slain,
He roars like a great stroke of thunder.

Saad and Rostam come face to face.
They emerge from their army center simultaneously
And meet outside the brawl, isolated from troops.
The two vengeful leaders ride off to the mountain base.

Rostam shouts a thunderous cry
And strikes the head of Saad's charger with his sword.
The battle beast's head rolls in the dust,
And the valiant Saad is unhorsed.

Rostam brandishes his sharp blade again to administer
A mortal blow and sever the head of his adversary.
But the dark dust renders the combatants
Imperceptible to each other.

Rostam climbs down his saddle of leopard skin
And attaches the ends of the bridle to his belt,
But then a flow of dust rushes into his face
Rendering him momentarily blind.

Immediately Saad lunges at him,
Assails his opponent's helmet with his sword's blow,
And splits his skull, inundating his face with blood
And decidedly rendering his vision black as night.

The ambitious Arab claims victory.
One more time he strikes the head of the hero warrior
And sends his valiant body to roll in the dust.

The two armies remain without news of their leaders.
They rush in search of them
And charge upon the scene of the fight.

At the sight of Rostam from afar soiled

With dust and blood, his body split right through,
The Iranians surrender and quickly take flight.
Many of them, the most illustrious, are killed.
Many others perish on the saddle, tormented by thirst,
And in this sad way, the dynasty of kings comes to an end.

The Iranian troops take a detour, and, seeing the plains
And the roads strewn with corpses of their own,
They ride night and day to return to the King of Iran.
The Muslim troops rush after them like wild lions.

Yazdegerd is in Baghdad
When the troops arrive and flock around him.
They relay the news that Rostam has passed away,
And it is as if, from the grief,
Rivers and seas have drained of water.

After killing more Iranians, the Arabs return,
Victors from the battlefield, and stop in Karkh.

Farrokhzaad, son of Hormozd, furious and weeping,
Crosses the Arvand River, enters Karkh, and delivers
A fierce assault eradicating the army of spear-riders.

The troops exit Baghdad and seek battle on the plain.

6 | Yazdegerd Holds Counsel With the Iranians

As soon as the dust of the fight dissipates,
The Iranians take flight, with Farrokhzaad at the lead.
They retrace their steps and return to Yazdegerd,
Covered in dust and dressed in war gear.

Farrokhzaad dismounts in front of the king,
Bows low, and summons divine blessings on him,
Eyes full of blood and heart burning with rage,
He asks, "O King, why are you so wistful?
Do you wish to wash the Kianian throne with tears?
After you, we find no descendants of your race
In the line of succession worthy of the throne and crown.
You are the only one, and your enemies

Are more than one hundred thousand.
How could I still battle across the world?
March to the Forest of Naarvan,
Where the people will gather around you.
From there, like Fereydoon the warrior,
You can renew your fortune."

The King of Kings reflects on new thoughts.
The next day, he sits on his throne with majesty
And places on his head the Kianian crown.
Then gathering all the sages, nobles, and wise men,
He asks, "What do you think of this affair?
What memory can you invoke of times gone by?
Farrokhzaad advised me as follows:
> 'March with an escort to the Forest of Naarvan.
> Amol and Sari abound with your subjects.
> When you have mustered a vast army,
> Return to battle and glorify your name.'

Now, illustrious army leaders,
What observations have you for me?
Does this suggestion meet with your approval?"

They all cry out, "Yes, it is quite suitable."

Yazdegerd adds, "No, this course of action cannot be.
My heart has devised a different strategy.
What do you mean, I would leave Iran's noblemen,
An army so vast, an empire so great, the throne
And crown, only to save myself and take flight?
Such a cowardly behavior would not conform
To kingly grandeur, courage, and wisdom.
I prefer to fight with my enemies than be disgraced,
For the leopard once gave advice on the matter:
> 'Do not turn your back on your rivals
> When fortune has its back on you.'

Just as subjects owe obeisance to the king
In good and bad circumstances,
A king must make use of his wealth
To guard his subjects from falling prey to peril."

The noblemen acclaim him and say,
"Such is the custom of kings, guardians of faith.

Tell us now what is your command.
What do you need from us?
What oath do you ask us to pledge?"

The king replies, "These thoughts will lead
My heart to drift onto the road of perdition.
The best course of action is for all of us
To ride to Khorasan and take shelter from an attack.
We have there a vast host of bold warriors.
The great men of the land of Turks
And the Emperor of Chin will come to pay us homage.
I shall marry the daughter of the Tarkhan
And thereby draw to our side an alliance
And an intrepid army of noble Tooranian warriors.
Maahooy, the powerful border guard of Marv,
Is rich in troops, elephants, and all sorts of goods.
I raised his status to chief border guard
And chief shepherd because he was a seeker,
An eloquent poet, and a warrior who grew up in the fields.
Though he is of humble origins,
I gave him elephants, a province, a border, troops,
And he was able to serve my court well.
I have heard the wise men cite this sentence
Drawn from ancient words:
    'Watch out for the man you mistreat and punish unjustly.
    Place your trust in the one you elevated with kindness.
    And since I never caused Maahooy any harm,
    He will be the one now to battle against my enemies.'"

Farrokhzaad strikes his two hands together and cries,
"O King, O Yazdan worshipper, do not trust evil men.
In accordance to a new story:
No matter how much you try to change
Or elevate the nature of a person,
All your efforts will be in vain.
The creator made him this way, and you will
Never obtain the key to divine secrets."

The king replies, "O intrepid lion, the venture
I wish to undertake cannot put me at risk."

Night passes. The next day at dawn,

The illustrious men take to the road.
They depart from Baghdad in the direction
Of Khorasan, holding on to the belief
That the hardships ahead would be endurable.

The Iranian noblemen, deeply aggrieved,
Accompany the king, acclaim him, and exclaim,
"May time and space never be deprived of your presence!"

A cry of anguish emerges from the camp
When they learn of the king's departure.
Iranian landowners, descendants of warriors,
Moan and lament on the trail of their sovereign,
Their eyes pools of tears as they plead with him,
"O King, we all stand as your slaves,
Our bodies and souls beat with affection for you.
How could our hearts be at peace without our ruler?
We shall abandon everything, our flourishing nation,
Our families and our wealth, to partake in your suffering.
We never wish this world to be deprived of your throne.
May your fortune never be shaken or overturned!
We shall walk with you to determine what kind
Of a game the revolving dome is playing on us
At a time when we have to engage in fight."

The most eloquent Iranians bow low to the dust
And cry, "We have left our land for your sake,
Considering you the refuge of the world.
Now you wish to go heartbroken to the Emperor of Chin?
You wish to abandon the land of Iran for the land of Tooran?"

The king sheds copious tears and says with sadness,
"Glorify and celebrate Yazdan in unison!
Perhaps I will set my sight on you again,
At a time when our hardships are behind us.
Perhaps the success of the Arabs will be short-lived.
You are all my purest supporters, my father's legacy.
I shall not allow you to suffer,
Nor shall I allow you to share in my perils.
Let us determine in whose favor the wheel of sky spins.
Resign yourselves to its supreme power,
Since we cannot escape its will and its whims."

Then he addresses the merchants of Chin:
"Do not remain long in Iran-Zamin,
For the Taazian will impair your affairs."

They take leave of the king, weeping and moaning,
Hearts full of grief and anguish.

Farrokhzaad takes command of the army
After calling to his side skilled men of Iran.
Worried and saddened, the king departs,
Preceded by the leader and his troops.

From station to station, they arrive in Rey,
Rest there for some time in the midst of feast and music.
Then Yazdegerd travels to Gorgan, as swift as wind,
Where he remains for seven days,
At times in joy and at times in sorrow.
In the end, he takes the road to Bost
With a worried mien and a shattered heart.

7 | Yazdegerd's Letter to Maahooy Soori

As the world master makes his way to Marv
And to its governor, Maahooy Soori,
He addresses him a letter full of emotion,
His heart full of hope, eyes bathed in tears.
He summons a skillful scribe and gives
Free run to the sorrow stirring in his heart.

After glorifying the Creator, wise and benevolent
Sovereign who imprints the motions of Mars and Sun,
Who reigns over the elephant and the ant,
Who draws things out of the void without need for a model,
He continues in these terms, "Misfortune plagued us.
Our kingdom has lost its force and its splendor.
Grief has constricted the world for us
Since the moment Rostam perished on the battlefield
At the hands of Saad, son of Vaghas,
A man lacking land, family, wisdom, and power.

"At a time when the Arab army is at the gates of Ctesiphon

And the forests and valleys separate us,
Prepare your troops and march to battle.
Prepare to rally the people to my cause.
As for me, I shall remain no more than seven days
In Nishapur and will face much suffering and pain.
I shall travel to Marv and send an envoy
To the Emperor of Chin and the ruler of Tooran-Zamin.
I shall request a vast host to end our misfortune.
I shall follow this letter closely behind and shall arrive,
As swift as wind, at your side, O son of pure race."

8 | Yazdegerd's Letter to the Border Guards of Tous

Yazdegerd selects another messenger,
A man of intelligence and good counsel.
His heart swollen with blood,
His face as pale as sandarac,
He writes another letter to the border of Tous:
"Glory and praise be to the sovereign Judge
Who gives power, fortune, and virtue,
Master of victory, majesty, throne, and royal crown!
Everything from an insect's foot
To the swift-beating eagle's wing,
From the elephant on the ground
To the whale in the water,
Everything submits to divine will and divine laws,
And every breath drawn is by divine permission.

"This letter is composed by the world king,
Yazdegerd the great, son of an illustrious father,
Powerful monarch, victorious leader of Iran's armies,
World sovereign and world arbiter,
Offspring of a glorious race, loyal to Yazdan's faith
And grateful to be bestowed the royal crown;
A descendant of a lineage that has made
The world prosper and has brought
Dazzle to the crown, throne, and royal seal,
This letter is addressed to the border guards
Who rule gloriously and according to justice,
Owners of grace, glory, crown, and army:

On the lands and the peoples of Shemiran,[34] Rooendej,[35]
Zavehkooh,[36] and Kalaat, among others.
May the Creator be your support
And protect you from the reaches of fate!

"It is a well-known fact among illustrious leaders,
A fact celebrated across the world,
That our hearts have always reflected
Solicitude, benevolence, and a sense of justice
For military might and high birth.
I attest to your pure nobility,
For kings have exerted upon you more hardship
Than rewarded you with treasure and wealth.
When Bahraam Choobineh rebelled
Against the king's power and crown,
He caused you to quickly abandon your city-states,
Your gardens, your squares and palaces.
You spent your days in deep valleys and mountain crests
To escape the reach of the wretched man.

"If the Creator gives us power, if fortune favors
Our hearts' desires, we shall generously recognize
Your actions and reward any and all services rendered.
You have been informed that the stars have unleashed
Against us vile serpents, men resembling Ahrimans,
Devoid of knowledge, intelligence, name, or honor,
Who propose to abandon the world to destruction.
It appears our kingship is coming to an end.
Such is the decree of the sublime sky:
Our dynasty will be eradicated by dark-skinned men.
They barrel hungrily toward us
To capture our royal throne.

"Treasures and jewels have been scattered,
And the tomb's crater is filled with many skulls.
The kingdom has been abandoned to the wretched Arabs.
Anushiravan had a vision in his dreams
Of the declining royal splendor

◇◇◇◇◇◇◇◇◇◇◇◇◇
34 Shemiran: The present-day capital of Shimiranat County, in Tehran Province.
35 Rooendej: A region in Iran.
36 Zavehkooh: A village in Iran, in today's Azerbaijan Province.

As one hundred thousand Taazian charging on drunken,
Unrestrained camels crossed the Arvand River.
He saw black smoke climb to the sphere of Saturn
As the enemy unraveled our land's rich warp and weft.
He saw harvests destroyed in Iran and Babel.
He saw the world on the verge of annihilation,
Flames being extinguished in pyres, the luster
Of Nowruz and the feast of Saddeh smothered.
Ultimately, the kings' battlements
Shattered and collapsed into the main square.

"The fulfillment of this dream is manifest today.
The unstable firmament is withdrawing its support.
Those who were once illustrious have been humiliated,
And the destiny of common men has been elevated.
Crimes multiply everywhere in the world.
Misery is more and more prevalent; joy has vanished.
Every land witnesses the emergence of a tyrant,
A malevolent, hideous demon.
Signs of an imminent deep, dark night emerge,
Snuffing out the bright light of hope.

"As for us, with the aid of our allies,
Hero warriors of pure intelligence,
We shall march toward Khorasan,
To the warlike border guards.
We shall determine the decision made by destiny.
To this end, we have gathered our elephants
And our drums for the ruler of Tous.
We have strapped our waists in preparation
To fight with the belligerent Taazian.
Farrokhzaad, our intimate friend and relative
Whose devotion never wavers, has left for Altoonieh[37]
In search of battle and to measure himself against our foes.
Kashamgan, his son, has arrived to find us in our camp.
He spoke with us respectfully, as it suits a loyal servant.
I have heard his account of the situation
In these regions, valleys, mountains, and caves.
Emissaries left in every direction
To seek additional help from auxiliaries.

◇◇◇◇◇◇◇◇◇◇◇◇◇◇
37 Altoonieh: Unclear of the location.

PART THIRTY-THREE

Still, an army as vast as ours
Cannot hold garrison in these narrow fortresses.
In consequence, the centers of Fort Gombadan
And Fort Lajevardeen, all the way to Germaneh,[38]
Will serve as depots for our provisions."

"The loads of the vast army will not fit
In the small forts of Aal, Fakhrum, and Dashtgol.[39]
We convened the leaders and held counsel.
Following a long deliberation on various subjects,
We came to an agreement on the following:
Along with crown, throne, seal, and royal ring,
We shall transport tunics from Rum,
Valuables from Cashmere and Chin,
Products from Ghebchaagh[40] and Yerevan,[41]
Such as golden brocade and bolts of fabric.
We shall take anything else worth taking
As well as the necessary provisions for days of distress.
Forty thousand buffalos harnessed to carts
Will carry a sufficient load of wheat in sheaves,
To which we shall add twelve thousand loads of rice.
A wise man will bring millet, pistachios, and pomegranates.

"While we wait for the sublime dome to reveal its wishes,
We shall place a heavy load of salt on buffalo carts;
One thousand lambskins full of lard;
One thousand loads of dates and one thousand of sugar;
Twelve thousand loads of honeycombs.
Our servants will gather forty thousand slices
Of salted meat to take to the forts.
Three hundred camel loads of black naphtha
Will arrive in the space of two months.
A wise man with an escort will travel
From Shemiran and Zavehkooh.
So numerous are the old men, sages, and lords
That the border guards appear insignificant next to them.
We shall draw two records of the inventory

◇◇◇◇◇◇◇◇◇◇◇◇◇
38 Fort Gombadan, Fort Lajevardeen, and Germaneh: Appear to be insignificant sites.
39 Aal, Fakhrum, and Dashtgol: Appear to be small forts.
40 Ghebchaagh: A village in northwestern Iran near Lake Urmia.
41 Yerevan: A city north of Iran, which is today the capital of Armenia.

Of the provisions taken to the fortresses,
One of which is to be handed to my treasurer,
And the other, O noblemen of my counsel,
To hold in your possession.

"The Turks and Taazian will not find access to them.
In these difficult times, you can provide us great service.
Our sage and eloquent vizier will instruct our treasurer
To distribute five tunics of Persian cloth
And a gold-embroidered turban to any warrior
Who has braved danger in times of war.

"In these dark and disastrous days,
Each of those who serve our cause loyally
Will receive, in addition to his service pay,
One of those royal coins valued at sixty dirhams.
From the sixty, some receive six dongs[42]
And others four dongs.
Each dirham will have an inscription to be read out loud.
On one side:
        'In the name of Yazdan, the pure,
        Source of our hopes and fears!'
On the opposite side will be my crowned portrait
With the inscription:
        'The earth flourishes with our love.'

"All this will be arranged during Nowruz and Mehregan,
Two festivals full of solemnity and magnificence.
May Yazdan, World Protector, bless men
Of noble race who will remain loyal to our crown!"

After a stamp is affixed to the letter,
The king sends it to his army chief.
An illustrious cavalier born under an auspicious star
Presents himself before him, royal letter in hand.

◇◇◇◇◇◇◇◇◇◇◇◇◇◇
42 Dong: Six parts of a piece of real estate that can be divided and apportioned.

9 | Yazdegerd Arrives in Tous, Where He Is Received by Maahooy Soori

The king calls for the drum of timpani
To signal departure from Nishabur to Tous.

Maahooy Soori, aware of the royal army reaching
The territory of Tous, marches toward Dahestan,
Advancing on the road with a vast escort
Dressed in armor and armed with spears.

As soon as the king appears in the majesty of his cortege,
Beneath the royal standard, surrounded by warriors,
Maahooy dismounts and exhibits marks of respect
And obeisance, as suits a loyal and humble subject.

Slowly he advances on the warm soil,
His eyes filling with tears of emotion.
He kisses the ground,
Honors the king with divine blessings,
And remains a long time standing in his presence.
His troops acclaim the king, and in succession
Lower their foreheads to the dust.

Farrokhzaad, as soon as he sees Maahooy,
Organizes his army in methodical formation.
He rejoices in his heart at the behavior of Maahooy,
Offers him wise recommendations and adds,
"I place under your protection
This descendant of noble Kianians.
You may seize weapons in his defense.
Watch over him, guard him from the slightest gust of wind
Or from being indebted to others for favors rendered.
As for me, my duty calls me to the land of Rey.
I know not when I shall ever see the royal crown again,
For many of my armed companions have perished
In battle against the vengeful, spear-wielding warriors.
My brother Rostam had no equal in the world as a rider.
No one had ever heard of a fighter of his mien and stature,
Yet he fell beneath the blows of a crow-faced fighter,
And the day of his death was a day of calamity for us.
May Yazdan place the hero among the elected,

And may Yazdan punish the sinister crows
With justifiable torture at arrow's point!"

Maahooy replies, "Assure yourself,
O brave hero, that the king is as dear to me
As my own eyes and as my own life.
I accept your demand for defense.
I take under my protection your fortune and your king."

Farrokhzaad, son of Hormozd, departs
On the road to Rey, as dictated by the king's command.
But soon after, the perfidious Maahooy
Rejects his benevolent dispositions
And fails to send warriors to fight the Taazian.
The turquoise dome of sky revolves in favor of the enemy.
The face of the Iranian king pales with grief
As his heart grows wary of the enemy's actions.

Maahooy, seeing the fortune of the king dim,
Covets the throne in the silence of the night.
Effecting a complete change in tone and behavior,
He feigns illness and neglects to pay proper homage.

10 | Maahooy Soori Incites Bijan to Wage War on Yazdegerd

There lives a warrior hero with far-reaching power,
A descendant of the Tarkhan, whose name is Bijan.
He resides on the border of Samarkand
And has a great number of allies in this land.

The baneful Maahooy, who seeks independence,
Writes the following letter to Bijan:
"O son of a warrior, your fortune is beyond reach.
An expedition presents itself to your advantage:
The world king is here in Marv without his host.
Come and claim his crown and throne, troops and treasure.
Inspire yourself with your ancestor's sense of hate,
And exercise vengeance on the royal family."

Bijan reads the letter, thinks about it,

And seeing that the world surrenders
To Maahooy's ambitions, he asks his vizier:
"You are my chief counselor,
What are your thoughts on this affair?
If I drive my army to Maahooy's rescue,
It may put an end to my power.
The king will mock me and will consider me
A man full of deception, a man lacking integrity.
Or perhaps the rumor will spread
That I never go to war for fear of losing."

The vizier replies, "O man of lion heart,
Warrior avid for battle, it would be a shame for you
To lend a hand to Maahooy Soori and return here.
If you engage in war at his instigation,
Serious men will accuse you of foolishness.
You must entrust Barsaam with the care
Of leading an auxiliary army to Maahooy's aid."

Bijan says, "You give me sound advice.
As for me, it does not suit me to move away."

He commands Barsaam to lead ten thousand
Elite riders armed with daggers to Marv,
Entrusting him with the direction of the war
In the hope of conquering the throne of Iran.
This brilliant army of pheasant wing
Marches from Bukhara to Marv in one week.
In the dark night, at the hour of the cockcrow,
The sound of timpani resounds over the plains.

King Yazdegerd is unaware of Maahooy Soori's
Perfidious designs when someone rushes to him to say,
"Maahooy affirms that an army of Turks advances swiftly.
What is the king's command?
Their leader is the Faghfoor of Chin,
And the earth is far too narrow for his vast host."

The king, deeply troubled, dresses in armor,
And the two parties march one against the other.
After organizing the right and left wings,
Yazdegerd leads his troops forward in one line
And places himself in its center, spear in hand.

Clouds of dust obscure the world.
The king, at the sight of the Turks' force and rashness,
Takes his hand to his belt, draws his sword,
And charges like an elephant to the battle front.
Flows of blood make the earth roll like the River Nile.
He assails the enemy like a tiger
From the very first assault on the Turks,
But he finds himself abandoned by his own warriors.
They all turn their backs on their master,
Leaving him in the midst of the enemy.

Once Maahooy recedes, the world king
Understands the secret cunning ploy against him.
He sees that Maahooy's goal was
To place him in harm's way.

In vain, the King of Kings deploys his courage,
Exhibits wonders of valor and boldness,
Killing singlehandedly many renowned leaders.
In the end, in light of his weak position, he takes flight.
He rides away, as swift as lightning shredding a cloud,
A Kabuli sword gripped in his hand,
With Turkish troops tightly closing in on him.

At the sight of a windmill on the shore of the River Zargh,[43]
He dismounts and seeks a place of refuge
Away from the furor of his enemies.

The Turks persevere in their chase,
And the region of Zargh falls into a state of turmoil.
The king abandons his horse of golden strappings,
His mass of weapons and his saber of golden sheath.
As the Turks, keen on their search, fall upon his horse
And his arms, the king flees to the windmill,
Enters and settles himself on a heap of hay.

Such is the law of the deceitful world:
Once we climb the mountain and reach the top,
We face, on the other side, a steep slope.
As long as the king was protected by fortune,

◇◇◇◇◇◇◇◇◇◇◇◇◇
43 River Zargh: A river near Marv.

His throne rose above the dome of sky.
But he finds himself now seeking shelter in a windmill,
And, in lieu of honey, he is forced to ingest poison.

If you were wise, you would not attach your heart
To this scheming realm where the signal of departure
Tirelessly strikes your ears,
Where you are sure to meet a dreadful end.
When you wish to touch it gently,
It is as soft and pliable as a snake
Yet may infuse you with warm poison.
Why attach yourself to this passing world,
Where your ears constantly echo: "Prepare yourself.
The grave's slab is the only throne reserved for you."

Exhausted from hunger, eyes full of tears,
The king remains in this state until sunrise.

At that moment, the miller opens the door,
Carrying a load of forage on his shoulders.
This common man named Khosrow possesses
Neither wealth nor fame, neither wisdom nor aspiration.
He lives off the product of his windmill
And does not exercise any other profession.

At the sight of the warrior of cypress stature,
Seated humbly upon the ground,
His head adorned with a crown,
His body wrapped in Chini brocade;
At the sight of his deer-like eyes and lion neck,
His golden boots, his tunic woven
With golden threads, embedded with pearls,
The miller finds himself unable to peel his gaze off of him.

In a state of surprise and admiration,
He invokes the name of Yazdan and says,
"O young man, your face shines as bright as the sun.
How did you find your way into my windmill?
Is a mill full of grain, forage, and dust worthy of you?
Who are you? For your stature and face
Bear a majesty such as the world has never seen?"

The king replies, "I am an Iranian

457

Who has evaded and fled the army of Tooran.
If you can spare some food to nourish my body,
I would be most grateful, O Yazdan worshipper."

The miller says in a timid tone,
"Poverty and misery are my sole companions.
If you can be content with a slice of barley bread
And some simple watercress from the riverbed,
I shall happily offer you a meal.
I'm afraid it is all that I possess.
Wretched, poor men are reduced to lament."

During his three days of battle,
The king experienced neither nourishment nor sleep.
He says to the miller, "Bring me whatever you have.
I shall be happy, as long as I have the Barsom."

The poor miller places watercress and barley bread
On a woven tray and runs to the oratory
To inform the chief of Zargh of the request.

Meanwhile, Maahooy sends emissaries
Everywhere in pursuit of the king.
The village chief, addressing the miller, says:
"Brave man, why do you make such a request?
For whom do you seek the Barsom?"

The miller replies, "A warrior entered my windmill
And sits there on the grass, his stature as majestic
As a cypress tree, his face as glorious as the sun.
Beneath the arch of his eyebrows, his eyes
Hold the imprint of sadness, his lips exhale sighs,
And sorrow seems to deeply oppress his soul.
I served him a simple ration of barley bread,
But he requested the Barsom for prayer.
All this must decidedly excite your curiosity!"

The chief replies, "Depart right away, and
Reveal this information to Maahooy Soori,
For fear that the vile man of impure birth
May manifest his perverse essence
Should he be told by someone else."

He quickly entrusts the miller to an illustrious man
Who takes him to Maahooy Soori.
The latter says to the unresourceful artisan,
"Tell me the truth, who requested the Barsom?"

The miller shakily replies,
"I was returning to my mill with my load,
When, upon opening the door,
A vision of light as bright as the sun flooded my eyes.
Before me was a man whose eyes
Resembled those of a frightened deer,
Whose hair was as black as night.
The air drifted with the scent of musk.
His face is certainly worthy of the crown.
My mill shines like the sun with his presence.
Seated on forage, he ate some dry bread.
May anyone who has not gleamed
Into divine majesty take my key to experience it.
A diadem of pearls adorned his forehead;
A tunic of Chini brocade enveloped his chest.
He appeared like spring in paradise.
Never has a farmer planted a more stately cypress tree."

11 | Maahooy Soori Sends the Miller to Behead Yazdegerd

Maahooy Soori reflects on these words,
Surmising that the miller is referring to Yazdegerd.
He retorts, "Swiftly go and cut off the head of this man
Or else I will behead you and your relatives."

The leaders and vigilant noblemen hear this exchange.
They are driven into a state of fury.
Words rush to their lips, tears roll down their cheeks.
One of the wise men, named Raadooy, whose heart
Listens to the yoke of reason, speaks in these terms:
"O man of criminal intentions, the deev has blinded you.
Know that kingship and prophecy are two pearls
Implanted in the same ring. To break one of them
Is to trample wisdom and life beneath one's feet.

Observe what you are about to do, and put an end to it.
Do not offend the World Creator,
For you will be the first one to be punished.
You will leave behind for your sons a harvest
That will produce bloody leaves and bitter fruit.
Your forehead will soon bear the imprint of shame.
Your wicked act will be exposed to the world,
And your children will collect the seeds you sow.
Your crime targets the cult of Yazdan.
The curse of throne and crown will be yours."

In the assembly there is a pious Yazdan worshipper
Whose hand never dipped in acts of injustice.
His name is Hormozd, son of Khorraad.
He addresses Maahooy: "O unjust man, beware,
For you will abandon the path of the pure Creator.
I see darkness pervading your heart and your mind.
I see destiny leading you to espouse a dusty grave.
You are endowed with stature and force
But lack intelligence, and your soul is feeble.
You yearn to capture the smoke in the fire.
It is as if you aspire to be the dishonor of the world.
It is as if you rush with ardor and greed to your end.
You will be dragged into a miserable existence,
And after your death you will dwell in hell."

Hormozd takes a seat, and Shahrooy rises to speak:
"Why would you dare engage in such a bold feat?
Why would you seek battle with the King of Kings
And seal alliances with the Tarkhan and the Faghfoor?
We have seen many a royal heir in need of allies,
But never did any of them attempt to spill royal blood.
If you are a subject, refrain from killing,
For curses will chase you until the day of Resurrection."

Shahrooy speaks in this way, then sits down moaning,
Heart swollen with blood, eyes filled with tears.

After he takes his place, Mehrnoosh rises, and, overcome
With grief and outrage, addresses Maahooy Soori:
"O evil man of evil race, you obey neither reason nor justice!
Even the whale would be horrified with royal bloodshed,

And the leopard would dare not tear at their limbs.
Are you more ruthless and cruel than a wild beast
As you covet the throne of the King of Kings?

"How did Zahaak's fortune benefit
From the act of killing Jamsheed?
Zahaak once held the earth under his dominion,
But Aabteen appeared, gave birth to the illustrious
Fereydoon, and the world took on a new face.
You have heard the wretched fate the tyrant
Endured and the punishment he drew onto himself.
More than one thousand years passed
Before he was seized by the avenging Fereydoon.
Furthermore, Toor, an arrogant man pining for Iran,
Killed the pure Iraj and sent his head to the valiant
Fereydoon, plunging the world into a state of sorrow.
But Manoochehr, of royal birth, appeared
And triumphantly severed the knots of iniquity.

"In the third place, during the time of Siaavoosh,
Afraasiyaab, following Garsivaz's advice,
Violated the laws of wisdom and heart
By beheading the noble son of the King of Iran,
The world was horrified by the murder of the young prince.
Kay Khosrow, conqueror and descendant of both Siaavoosh
And Afraasiyaab, emerged and filled the world with tumult.
Armed with a dagger, he pierced his grandfather's body,
Splitting it and spreading terror through his enemies' hearts.

"In the fourth place, remember the retribution
Endured by Arjaasp for the murder of Lohraasp?
Esfandiar declared war on him and did not allow
Much time to pass over his unpunished crime.
In the fifth place, I shall cite Esfandiar's vengeance
And Rostam, who severed his head on the battlefield.

"The sixth vengeance belongs to King Firooz,
Who perished under the blows of Khoshnavaz.
Soofraay armed himself to avenge the king's death.
He trampled beneath his feet the head of the murderer.
The seventh vengeance is the one on King Hormozd
When Khosrow Parviz was at the heights of power,

He treated Bandooy and Gostaham as you know,
For the sublime sphere never stops its revolutions.
Master of power, Parviz ended the lives of the two traitors.
Do not consider vengeance a thing to be scorned.
Khosrow Parviz, so keen on avenging his father's blood,
Overlooked all the services they had rendered him.
When his power reached its zenith,
He quickly ordered their execution.
You must never underestimate the door of hate.
The day will come when you will regret
The illicit thoughts you nurture today.
Your sons will collect the seeds you sow,
And destiny will never remain in a slumber
When it comes to the cause of hatred.

"Abstain from reaching out
And yearning for royal treasure
And a crown that are not meant for you.
You turn your head at the instigation of the deev
Forcing your heart to stray from the path of Yazdan.
You cannot see that the deev is seducing you
With the bait of something that is not destined to be yours.
Do not surrender your body and soul to blazing flames.
Do not dull the gleam of the world-illuminating crown!
Gather your scattered troops,
And swiftly retract your wicked plans.
Excuse yourself in the presence of the king.
Renew your homage to him as a vassal.
Prepare everything to fight his enemies, and
Do not act in any way contrary to wisdom and respect.
You will wither in this world and in the other
If you close your ear to the speech of wise men.

"Should you leave for tomorrow today's work,
You will suffer severe consequences.
Your behavior toward King Yazdegerd is more
Relentless than the evil Turks against their enemies.
Yazdegerd, a battle lion, master of the throne,
Who shines as bright as the full moon,
Is the sole heir to the Sassanian Dynasty.
No rider arms himself with as much ardor for war.
Since Anushiravan until the era of Ardeshir,

His ancestors were all noble and wise.
Born of Ardeshir by eight generations,
He is world sovereign and heir to the crown of Sassan.
He has received the royal diadem from Yazdan,
And all his ancestors boast illustrious roots.

"Men more powerful than you have lived in the world,
And never did any of them aspire to such designs.
Your actions are akin to those of Bahraam Choobineh,
Who had three hundred thousand loyal riders at his side.
As soon as he shot one arrow toward the king,
His supporters fled and abandoned the battlefield.
As soon as he avowed his hatred for the royal race,
His shining star was quick to be eclipsed.
Faraaeen (Goraaz), who yearned for the throne,
Though he was not worthy of it, and who dipped
His hand in crime, also succumbed to a miserable death.
The world does not tolerate falsehoods and lies.

"You must fear Yazdan, World Creator,
Creator of throne, crown, and royal seal.
Do not surrender yourself blindly to shame,
For this venture will soon turn against you.
Anyone who does not tell you the truth is,
Without a doubt, your adversary. You are the patient,
And I am the physician who spills tears of blood.
Since your rank is inferior
To the rank of the most humble slave,
Do not nurture in your heart ambitious thoughts,
Sacrifice your hatred for Yazdan,
And ask for power only in measure to your merit."

But the simple shepherd's son has an ambitious heart,
And the advice of the wise men weighs heavy on him.
It is not surprising for things to unfold in this manner,
For the whims of fortune are varied and limitless.
It exalts one to the lofty sphere of the firmament
While it plunges another into poverty, scorn, and pain
Without holding affection for the former
Or hostility toward the latter.
Neither shame nor knowledge, neither grace nor faith
Will allow you to glean divine mysteries.

The wise men continue to lavish Maahooy with advice
Until the moon supplants the sun
And a velvety cloak of ebony enfolds the earth.
But their counsel has no effect on him
As hatred feeds his determination.

At nightfall, Maahooy says to them,
"O intelligent men, it is time to retire.
I wish to deliberate tonight on this matter
With my son and with men of knowledge.
To that end, I shall convene twenty worldly leaders.
There will be no cause to shed tears."

The prudent wise men withdraw,
And the warriors arrive on their trail.
Maahooy sits with his confidants and asks,
"What course of action shall we take?
If Yazdegerd is still alive, troops will soon
Arrive from everywhere to rescue him.
Everyone, great and small, will discover my plans.
The king's retribution will be my downfall,
And I shall at once lose my body, life, and power."

A wise man replies to Maahooy Soori,
"On principle, your behavior was not warranted.
If the King of Iran desires to fight with you,
You can be sure to suffer grave consequences.
If your hand spills his blood, you can be sure
That Yazdan will pay retributions.
On every side, I see only torment and affliction.
Decide what is to be your course of action."

Maahooy's son says, "O my blessed father,
Since you have identified him as your enemy,
It is best to get rid of him promptly.
Otherwise he will attack us with all the power
Of Chin and Maachin and constrict the world for us.
Do not consider this affair as insignificant.
Since you are at an advantage today,
Arrive resolutely to the end of your goals.
If the king's allies create a royal banner of his tunic,
Their troops will chase you from this world."

12 | Yazdegerd Is Beheaded By the Miller

The perfidious Maahooy hears his son out
And turns to the miller to speak:
"Take with you a number of cavaliers
And spill the blood of my enemy, for he would
Escape me forever if this secret were to be known."

The miller takes in the command without fully
Understanding the extend of the action demanded.
He leaves Maahooy's court and residence,
His eyes full of tears, his heart swollen with blood,
At the time when the moon rises to sit on its throne,
He returns to the windmill and to the king.

Maahooy sends on his trail riders of speed and says,
"The crown, the earrings, the seal, and the king's tunic
Must not be stained with blood. Undress him first."

Meanwhile, the miller marches on,
Face pale and awash with tears, lamenting,
"O Creator, you are above the wheel of destiny,
Abandon the heart and soul of the one who gave me
Such a cruel and barbaric command!"

He arrives at the side of the king, heart full of shame
And fear, face flooding with tears, mouth parched.
He approaches with care as if he is about to tell him
A secret, then he plunges a dagger into the royal waist.
Fatally wounded, the king exhales a sigh, his head
And crown fall to the ground next to the barley bread.

May the one able to find an exit escape the dome of sky.
Devoid of wisdom, one can explain
Nether its hatred nor its favors.
By avoiding your gaze to fall upon the world,
You will not witness its affection and its wrath.
The seven realms are wary of those they protect
And abandon to death innocent men like Yazdegerd.
Never did a king perish in this fashion,
Where none of his warriors suffered injury or death.

The riders of the evil Maahooy find the king
Lying on the ground like a glorious tree,
Far from the throne and the battlefield.
They approach him to examine his features.
Then they unfasten his purple tunic,
His crown, his torque, his golden boots.
Leaving the lifeless body lying on the floor's dust,
Stained in blood, waist torn by the blade gaping,
They take the road uttering this curse:
"May Maahooy's corpse lie on the ground,
Bathing in its own blood in a similar fashion."

They inform Maahooy that throne, war, and possessions
Are meaningless now for the noble monarch.
Maahooy orders the corpse to be tossed
Into the waters at the hour of rest.
Two cruel servants drag the bloody king's body
And, without knowing the victim's identity,
Hurl it into the bend of the River Zargh.
There it floats away on the surface,
At times facing up, at times facing down.

As night succeeds day and men emerge from
Their homes, two distinguished, Christian characters
Devoted to penitence arrive at the site.
One of them approaches the river's edge
And notices the bare body floating in the water.
Seized by a sense of dread,
He retraces his steps to the monastery.
He recounts to the monks what he witnessed:
The king of the century lying naked in the river's flows.

Right away, the abbots and the monks
Rush out, and a cry of pain rises:
"O illustrious king of noble race,
Who has ever seen a ruler in such a dismal state?
Who has ever heard of a disloyal subject, a villain,
A wretched dog, who, after cajoling his master,
Viciously tears him to shreds in an act of treason?
Maahooy deserves to be damned!
O King, alas, your body, your majestic stature,
Your hand, your mace, your heart,

Your wisdom, your sense of reason!
Alas, the last offspring of Ardeshir!
Alas, the glorious and illustrious rider warrior!
Let us shed tears for the Sassanian throne,
For power, glory, and the crown of the kings!

"Not long ago you lived full of fervor and wisdom.
You will now carry the news to Anushiravan.
You will tell him that you, a sovereign,
Born to the crown and to kingship,
With a face as handsome as the moon,
Have been destroyed by a dagger in a windmill,
Your naked body cast away at the bottom of an abyss!
Even the dust, to the depths of its soul,
Will weep at the heart-wrenching news.
Even the dust of Ardeshir's grave will holler in grief,
For no king ever was allotted water as a burial place.
Look at this body, bloody and exposed, thus cast away."

Four of the monks strip and enter into the river.
They take the naked body of the noble monarch,
Grandson of Anushiravan, onto dry land.
Everyone, young and old, sings a mournful song.
A tomb is raised in the enclosure, as high as the clouds.

After having treated the king's wound,
They apply myrrh, camphor, and musk,
Then dress him in a tunic of yellow brocade.
They place a fine linen cloth beneath his corpse
And cover him with a silken fabric the color of lapis lazuli.
Then the priests scatter wine, myrrh, camphor, musk,
And rosewater at the bottom of the sepulcher.

Once the noble cypress-like body is buried,
A venerable poet from Marv utters these words:
"Happy is the man who, thanks to his generosity,
Exits the world in a state of peace!"

Another says, "Even when a man has a smile
On his lips, he must know that he is a mere pawn
In the game of the unstable sphere that shows him
In turn its climbs, in turn its descents."

Another adds, "Do not assign the name of sage
To the one who cares for his body but neglects
His soul, who searches for wealth at the price
Of a poor reputation, without fear of destiny."

Another adds, "The king's lips are sealed.
He will never again see his crown and throne,
His armor, his courtesans and diadem,
His kingdom, his glory, and power.
Since none of these are helpful as we pass,
Then what is the point of exerting ourselves ?"

Another adds, "To celebrate a good reputation,
I cannot find enough praise worthy of him.
He planted a cypress tree in the garden of paradise,
And his soul will see the tree that owes its birth to him."

Another adds, "Yazdan collected your soul
And surrendered your body to religious men.
Death will be your soul's salvation,
And, for your cruel enemy, his damnation.
The king resides gloriously in paradise
While the soul of his murderer is on its way to hell."

Another continues, "O learned King,
Sage descendant of the race of Ardeshir,
You collected the fruits you sowed in the orchards.
The royal torch shines in all its glory."

Another adds, "O generous monarch, you sleep,
But your soul is aware and awake.
Your lips are mute, your life escaped moaning,
And your body has been abandoned here.
But if this body is lifeless, your soul is active,
And your enemy's head is to be fixed at the gallows.
If your mouth is closed, your soul speaks.
If your body is injured, your soul is purified.
If your hands have released the reins,
Your soul has recaptured the spear."

Another adds, "O renowned warrior,
You left guided by your good deeds
To occupy your heavenly throne

468

PART THIRTY-THREE

And to leave this afflicted earth in the hands of another."

Another adds, "The daring man who killed you
Is sure to experience a destiny of hardship and misery."

The bishop rises to speak: "We are your servants.
The eulogists of your pure soul.
May this grave be for you a garden of tulips,
Your shroud a verdant and happy meadow!"

They speak, then carry the casket across the plain
To deposit inside the sepulcher.
The ill-fated king is taken to his final resting place,
For he no longer possesses throne and crown.

O eloquent, worldly speaker,
Do not choose the path of greed
But rather the path leading to the truth.
We demand justice for Yazdegerd.
We demand vengeance against the seven planets.
The revolving dome does not discriminate
One way or another, for hatred or for justice.
So the philosophers have no way of explaining
Its machinations. And even if they were
To offer me some sort of clarification,
It would be enfolded in layers of mystery
And would always remain so forever.

O holy man, since wealth has little meaning in this life,
Enrich your heart and do not depend on tomorrow.
The world is fleeting. Time counts our every breath.
Exercise frugality on your soul, and sow seeds
Rooted in virtue for as long as you live in your body.

Take care not to give into gluttony.
You will not leave anything behind
Besides joy and a good name.
Guard yourself from acts of cruelty
To evade punishment.

As for me, if my resources equaled my expenses,
Fortune would have treated me as a brother.
But this year, hail assailed me like death.

Death would have been a more desirable outcome
For me than this unendurable plague.
My supply of wood, wheat, and herd depleted,
The sublime sphere of sky has closed the door to profit.

Cupbearer, bring me some wine; this day is short-lived.
Such is this world's eternal law, where no one remains.
Since the injustice of men burdens us, the wise thing
To do is to drink without resigning to complaint.

13 | Maahooy Soori Climbs on the Throne

Someone presents himself to Maahooy Soori and says,
"The grave closed on the world king.
The Rumi abbots, priests, and monks,
Young and old, sang a mournful song
As they pulled the king's body out of the river
And raised for him a superb burial place
In the orchard, its top reaching the hillcrest."

The perverse, nefarious Maahooy cries out,
"Never until today has Iran
Forged a successful alliance with Rum!"

He commands all those involved in raising the tomb
And rendering the last rites to the king to be slain
And their lands forsaken to devastation.
Such is the will of Maahooy Soori;
Such is the extent of his viciousness.

Then his gaze wanders across the world
And determines the absence of a kingly heir.
With the royal crown and ring in his possession,
The son of a shepherd covets the imperial throne.

He summons his confidants
And communicates at length his projects.
Addressing his vizier, he says,
"O worldly man, the day of quarrel and fight is here.
Deprived as I am of treasury, glory, and birth,
I am exposed to mortal threats.

The name of Yazdegerd is engraved in the seal.
My sword did not subjugate the land to my authority.
All the people of Iran remain loyal subjects of Yazdegerd,
Whether they are related to him or not.
No intelligent man wishes to give me the title of king,
And my seal does not inspire trust in the troops.
I was faced with other courses of action.
Why did I have to spill royal blood?
Why did I have to annihilate the leader of nobility?
All my nights are now spent in a state of fear,
And Yazdan, World Master, has divined my situation."

His vizier replies, "The deed is accomplished
And has filled the world with disputes.
Care for your affairs, since you have clipped your holy belt.
Yazdegerd now lies at the bottom of a grave,
And the dust of the crypt has bound his wounds.
Convene the world's most skilled men, and may
Your tongue pronounce gentle, eloquent words
In a declaration to the effect of:
        'This crown and this seal were offered
        To me by the king at a time when
        The Taazian army was approaching.
        He summoned me in the middle of the night and said,
                "The winds of war are stirring,
                And no one knows who will be the victor.
                Keep the crown and seal,
                Perhaps they will serve you one day.
                I only have one daughter in the world,
                And I have hidden her from the Arabs.
                Now it is your place to defend my throne
                And to follow my path in the exercise of power."
        I hold this crown as inheritance from the king,
        And I sit upon the throne by virtue of his will.'
By this means, you will establish your authority.
Besides, who will know if you speak the truth or not?"

Maahooy listens to him and replies, "It is a perfect plan.
You are my wisest counselor, and no one is above you."

He convenes the army leaders and addresses them
With the words following the agreed convention.

The chiefs are fully aware of his network of lies
And believe he deserves
To pay with his head for his impudence.

One of the leaders exclaims, "Whether your words
Are true or false, this is your affair."

Maahooy swiftly positions himself on the throne
And, with his deceitful methods, brings down
The land of Khorasan to fall under his dominion.
He attributes governance to principal leaders
And says, "I possess the seal, and I am world king!"

He usurps kingship and excites the stunned stars
By distributing various lands openly.
He gives Balkh and Herat to his eldest son,
Sends troops in every direction,
And, conforming to his evil nature,
He places villains in positions of power.
Everywhere he endorses wicked men
With his wicked nature and forces good men
To bend their heads in shame.
Truth is humiliated, and falsehood rears its ugly head.

This perverse man gathers a vast host and treasury.
His heart rejoicing, he lavishes the troops with dirhams
And favors, for he contemplates waging war on Bijan.
Men from his lineage rise, their heads full of wind.
He marches away with host and sentinels.

A noble, worldly warrior named Garsioon departs
With a valiant escort toward the city of Bukhara.
The troops are well equipped and full of ardor.

Garsioon says,
"Samarkand and Chaadj must submit to this crown
And seal according to the will of world king Yazdegerd,
A monarch who was obeyed by the seven realms.
I come with my sword for Bijan to be avenged,
For he is to blame for the dimming fortune of the great king."

14 | Bijan Learns of the Death of Yazdegerd

Such is the situation when Bijan is informed
That Maahooy Soori has seized kingship
And that, spreading everywhere
His orders adorned with royal seal,
He causes the world to fall under his dominion.
He learns that the usurper is heading
Toward the Jayhoon River
To fight at the head of a valiant host.

Curious to find out how Maahooy
Obtained the royal seal, Bijan asks around,
And Barsaam, an eloquent man, recounts,
"As soon as you reached Farab, nothing more
Was said on the unfolding of destiny,
Whether good or bad. Squadrons departed
From here toward Maahooy's host,
Full of riders avid for fame.
He told you,
        'I shall send you the crown
        Of the King of Kings once you dispatch your host.
        With it will be the golden throne
        And rings adorned with precious stones,
        For you are the only one worthy of them.'

"When your troops arrived in Marv,
They found the king, whom they encircled.
The Iranian warriors turned their backs and fled.
Once left alone, the wise king, in fear of his own host,
Marched off and sought refuge in a windmill.
As soon as he found out Yazdegerd's location,
Maahooy Soori sent someone to kill his master
And to seize the royal seal and crown.
Two parts of the shame and humiliation belong to you
For having sent your host to fight the king."

Barsaam continues, "O prince,
I did not take many riders from Chaadj.
I simply hauled provisions and equipment,
Leaving Yazdegerd alone in Marv.
He had mentioned that he would send to you

His golden crown, throne, his cache of jewels.
You are to be the owner of kingly possessions.
I fought in Marv for three days.
On the fourth day, as the sun spread its light,
Exhausted from the long battle, I continued to fight
While the perfidious Maahooy turned his back on me.
The Shah of Iran, concerned to find himself alone,
Appeared like a wild lion in front of our host
And killed a great number of our illustrious warriors.
Abandoned by his men, he took flight.

"I cannot understand how Maahooy
Was able to successfully execute the king.
A ruler's murderer knows not the meaning of loyalty.
Maahooy seized his masters' treasures effortlessly.
As soon as this evildoer was surrounded by royal wealth,
It was as if he no longer recognized me.
During the two months that our army spent in Marv,
He never cast our way a benevolent glance.
He is the one who secretly killed his master,
The great king, light of the world,
A rider who, in the midst of his host,
Raised his head above the sphere of the moon.
The Turks dared not approach his mace;
He sent fright into the hearts of the bravest men.
I have never seen a rider with his stature and his might,
Never one with his shield, coat of mail, hand, and mace.

"Maahooy, master of royal treasures,
Usurped kingship, and he did so
By means of the most odious crimes.
Now scouts announce the approach of his troops.
They must not find a path to reach us.
When your enemy rests its head on a pillow,
You must not linger. May weeds find not
A way to sprout in the kingly garden,
For should they invade, the garden will be destroyed!"

Bijan is deeply disturbed by these words.
He feels responsible for the king's downfall.
He unites the troops of rider Turks skilled
In the art of war and departs from Ghajghaarbaashi

In a bout of fury and without a moment's waste.

Approaching the city of Bukhara, he deploys
The troops in the plain and says to his officers,
"Let us not make haste today.
Allow the enemy to cross the river and engage in war.
Then I shall be able to avenge the king."

Bijan then asks, "Has the illustrious king, world master,
Not left any child behind we may benefit from?
Has he any known brothers?
In the absence of a son, is there perhaps
A daughter that we could bring forth
And use to our advantage to triumph over Maahooy?"

Barsaam replies, "O renowned prince,
The royal family has reached the end of its lineage.
The Taazian have seized all the lands,
Leaving neither king nor fire worshipper."

Bijan, fearing the vicissitudes of fate,
Places his hands over his head.
Sentinels warn him that the enemy is approaching
And will soon launch an assault on Paykand.
An army disembarks from a boat,
Stirring the dust and obscuring the sun.
The leader takes his position at the vanguard
To better direct the action.

As soon as Maahooy Soori spots Bijan's vast host,
It is as if his soul is about to take flight
So numerous are the armor, helmets, and Chini shields,
So dense is the forest of spears, maces, and Chaadji axes.
Consumed with worry, he nonetheless faces the enemy.
The light is obscured, and the earth disappears
Beneath the number of combatants.

15 | The Battle of Bijan and Maahooy Soori

After putting order to his army,
Bijan prepares to launch an attack on the Iranians.
Maahooy, positioned at the center,
Foresees this strategy and withdraws hollering.

Bijan spots his floating banner in retreat.
He directs a command to Barsaam:
"Advance your troops from the center.
We must not allow Maahooy Soori to reject a fight
And to take shelter by the Jayhoon River.
Go with speed. Do not lose sight of him,
And act in a way as to grant us victory."

The Chini Barsaam fixes his gaze on Maahooy's banner,
Sets his army into motion, and drives it swiftly
To the edge of the city of Farab,
His features drawn in anger, his mouth full of curses.
He finds Maahooy in the sands of Farab.
Pressing firmly into his stirrups, Barsaam gallops,
Jumps right at Maahooy, and, instead of striking him
With his sword, he acts with even more boldness:
He seizes his belt, removes him from the saddle,
And flings him to the ground effortlessly.
Then he climbs off his horse, ties up Maahooy's hands,
And, back on his saddle, has him walk before him.

At that moment, Barsaam's companions arrive,
Filling the plain with tumult.
They exhort their chief to not take Maahooy away
But instead cut off his head with a blow of an ax.

Barsaam replies, "It is not right to proceed
Since Bijan is not yet informed of his capture."

At that moment, news reaches Bijan
That his faithless slave has been captured,
The ambitious Maahooy of perverse mind,
An evil, ruthless man who killed his master.
Delighted, Bijan smiles and banishes further concerns.
He shouts like a lion, and a number of Turks go to him.

After deliberations, they decide
To expedite Maahooy Soori's execution.
They slay a great number of subjects at Maahooy's court.
They plunder all his belongings and provisions
And drag him bare and on foot to Bijan.

The wicked man spots Bijan,
And reason abandons his mind.
Struck with terror, he picks up rocks from the ground
To scatter over his head,
As if his soul has left his body.

Bijan says to him, "O infamous man,
I shall never wish a slave like you on anyone.
Why did you rush to fling a just king to his death?
He was the master of throne and victory,
The son of kings, a king himself,
And the last living offspring of Anushiravan!"

Maahooy Soori replies, "What can you expect
From a malevolent man but murder and blame?
To expiate for the crime I committed,
Take my head and toss it before the army."

Bijan retorts, "I wish to inflict punitive measures
That would satisfy my heart's wrath
And banish the hate I harbor from it since,
Devoid of courage, wisdom, sense,
And character as you are,
You coveted the crown of the King of Kings."

And with a blow of his saber, he cuts off his hand,
Saying, "This hand never had an equal in crime."
Then he has his two feet severed to keep him still.
Next his ears and nose are cut off as well.

Bijan climbs on his horse, instructing his men
To allow him to remain on the burning sand
Until he expires from shame and humiliation.

They bring rope and tie Maahooy Soori from head to toe.
The sound of clarions rises.

A herald makes the rounds of the camp,
Passing on the threshold of every tent to proclaim,
"O slaves and assassins of your masters,
Do not surrender your minds to foolish hopes.
May the one who does not spare the king's life
Endure the same fate as Maahooy Soori,
And may he never gain any power whatsoever!"

A nobleman named Goraaz,
Who was promoted by Maahooy Soori,
Is the border guard of Marv.
When he learns of the fate of his master,
He sets up a crown of power
For the elder son of Maahooy.

From every side, troops arrive in Marv.
The city stirs with tumult and battle.
Goraaz is killed in the brawl,
And the fortune of his entire family dims.
His three sons, warriors in the army, own throne and diadem.
A great pyre is lit, and the three are burned with their father.
No one remains of their race, or if some offspring survives,
All those who encounter him would chase him away.

The noblemen torment this family
And pursue its members with hatred
Because of the murder of the king.
They say, "May this family be cursed,
And may there always be men to scorn them."

Bijan was at fault in this affair,
And a time comes when his life's cup overflows.
He loses his mind and ultimately kills himself.
Praise be to the hunchback revolving dome.
Such is the outcome of crimes:
Anyone who commits them is ultimately punished.

The era of Omar takes root:
It brings a new religion
And replaces the throne with the pulpit.

16 | Date of the Completion of The Shahnameh

Sixty-five years have passed over my head;
My mind is overwhelmed by sorrow and grief.
The more I searched for the story of kings,
The more my star of fortune slowed its pace.
Noble characters, distinguished by their wisdom
And their birth, many renowned and learned men
Owe their reputations to this book, copying it freely
While I sit idly on the side, watching them from afar.
It is as if they have offered me compensation,
Though all I have received from them is praise.
Their accolades have depleted my valor
And have drained me of my vigor.
My heart has been much afflicted in finding
The venerable, ancient pouches tightly sealed.

Nevertheless, among the illustrious townspeople,
Ali Abu Dolas from Deylam treated me with kindness.
He was an honest man of shining soul.
An Iranian lord, Hoyay, son of Khotaibeh,
Did not receive my verses without rewarding me.
He offered me food, clothing, gold and silver,
And furnished me with the means to earn power.
I did not have reason to worry about expenses,
And my days unfolded surrounded by abundance.
Had the king not been tightfisted,
I would have found myself sitting proudly on a throne.

As I attained seventy-one years,
The wheel of sky was humbled by my poem.
For thirty-five years spent in this perishing world,
I exerted my efforts for some reward.
But these efforts have been sterile, cast to the wind,
And these thirty-five years have produced little.
Today my life reaches its eightieth year,
And my hopes have vanished with the wind.
All at once, I finish the story of Yazdegerd
On the twenty-fifth day of the month of Esfand,[44]

◇◇◇◇◇◇◇◇◇◇◇◇◇
44 Twenty-fifth day of Esfand: March 16.

Five times eighty years after Hijrah,[45]
I complete the valuable book of kings.

May the throne of King Mahmud flourish!
May he live in health, may his head remain young
And his heart dwell in eternal joy!
The praise that I lavish upon him
Will remain in the world in perpetuum.
Though I have received much acclaim from him,
The compliments I address him are far more numerous.
May this sage monarch live eternally,
And may his desires be fulfilled through his actions!
I bestow upon him as a memory this poem
That comprises six times ten thousand distiches.

My life comes to an end; my youth turns to old age.
Here it is, completed, this noble, glorious poem!
The gleam of my glory will light up the world!
Echoes of my name will rebound across the land.
I shall not die, immortal through my name,
For, with my words, I have sown the seeds of wisdom.
Any intelligent, judicious, and virtuous man
Will bless my memory long after I am gone.

The SHAHNAMEH by Ferdowsi
A native of Tous.

End of Volume Five

◇◇◇◇◇◇◇◇◇◇◇◇◇
45 Hijrah: Refers to Muhammad and his followers' departure from Mecca and their journey to Medina in the year 622.

APPENDIX

Glossary of Names

Aabteen: Fereydoon's father; killed and served as a meal to Zahaak's snakes. (Vol. 1)

Aarash: Iranian warrior in the army of Kay Khosrow and father of warrior Manoochehr from Khorasan. (Vol. 3)

Aarash: Seventh Ashkanian king. (Vol. 4)

Aarash: Border guard and warrior under the rule of Yazdegerd. (Vol. 4)

Aarash Kamangir: Ancestor of Gorgeen, Milaad, and Bahraam Choobineh. Not a character in The Shahnameh but famous in legends for having settled the border between Iran and Tooran with the launch of his arrow. The arrow traveled for two days from Iran before landing on the other side of the Jayhoon River.

Aarezooy: Daughter of Sarv, king of Yemen, and wife of Salm; son of Fereydoon. (Vol. 1)

Aaveh: Son of Samkanan and descendant of Fereydoon; ally of Kay Khosrow in the great battle with Afraasiyaab. (Vol. 3)

Aayaas: Of Chin, warrior ally of King Arjaasp. (Vol. 3)

Aazaad Sarv: Lives during Ferdowsi's time in Marv, owns the Khoday Nameh, one of the sources for The Shahnameh, and is a man who can trace his origins to Saam, son of Nariman. (Vol. 3)

Aazaad Sarv: A nobleman in the service of King Kesra Anushiravan. (Vol. 4)

Aazaadeh: Lute player and one of the wives of Bahraam (son of Yazdegerd). Killed by her husband, Bahraam. (Vol. 4)

Aazarafrooz: Son of Esfandiar whose brothers are Bahman, Mehrnoosh, and Nooshaazar. (Vol. 3)

Aazargoshasp: Warrior in the army of Khosrow Parviz in the war against Bahraam Choobineh. (Vol. 5)

Abbas: Taazian commander leading a host against King Hormoz, son of Kesra Anushiravan. (Vol. 4)

Abol-Fazl: Also Abul-Fazl al-Bal'ami; the vizier of Amir Nasr, died in 940. (Vol. 4)

Afraasiyaab: King of Tooran-Zamin and son of Pashang (son of Zaadsham). Father of Karookhan, Sorkheh, Jahn, Shiddeh, Gurch, Afraasiyaab, Faranguis, and Manijeh. Killed by Kay Khosrow. (Vols. 1-3)

Afraasiyaab: Son of Afraasiyaab; Tooranian warrior. (Vol. 3)

Aghriras: Brother of Afraasiyaab and Garsivaz, and son of Pashang. Killed by Afraasiyaab. (Vol. 1)

Aghriras: Tooranian leader who fights in the great war (not to be confused with Afraasiyaab's brother). (Vol. 3)

Ahran: Rumi nobleman who weds the third daughter of the Caesar. (Vol. 3)

Ahriman: Dark spirit whose goal is to promote division and chaos.

Ajnaas: Tooranian warrior in Afraasiyaab's army. (Vols. 1-2)

Akhvaast: Tooranian warrior. Killed by Zangueh in the battle of the heroes. (Vols. 2-3)

Akvan Deev: A threatening creature that resembles a deev with a black stripe down its back. Killed by Rostam. (Vols. 2-3)

Alkoos: Tooranian warrior in Afraasiyaab's army. Killed by Rostam. (Vol. 1)

Alvaah: Zaboli warrior in Rostam's retinue. Killed by Kaamoos. (Vols. 1-3)

Amr: Taazian commander leading a host against King Hormoz, son of

Kesra Anushiravan. (Vol. 4)

Andariman: Tooranian warrior and brother of Afraasiyaab. Killed by Gorgeen in the battle of the heroes. (Vols. 2-3)

Andariman: Brother of King Arjaasp, Biderafsh, and Kohram. Killed by Esfandiar. (Vol. 3)

Andian: Devoted and wise leader under the rule of King Khosrow Parviz who becomes governor of Kerman. (Vol. 5)

Andman: King of Rey under the reign of Bahraam the Hunter. (Vol. 4)

Anushiravan: Or Khosrow I, Kesra Anushiravan, son of Ghobaad; Sassanian king who rules for forty-eight years, from 531 to 579. (Vols. 3-4)

Arastalis: Aristotle, whom Ferdowsi places in the land of Rum; advisor to Eskandar. Historically, Aristotle was Alexander the Great's tutor up to the time he ascended to the throne in 336 BCE. (Vol. 3)

Ardavan: Also called Ardavan the Great. Descendant of Aarash, he was the ninth Ashkanian king. He has four sons. He is wounded in battle and executed at the order of Ardeshir Babakan. (Vol. 4)

Ardeshir: Bijan's son and Giv's grandson; Iranian warrior in the army of Lohraasp. (Vol. 3)

Ardeshir: Prince, with brother Shiddasp, sons of King Goshtaasp. Killed by Arjaasp troops. (Vol. 3)

Ardeshir: Tooranian warrior in the army of Arjaasp. (Vol. 3)

Ardeshir: Name given by King Goshtaasp to Bahman, son of Esfandiar. (Vol. 3)

Ardeshir: The younger brother of King Shahpoor who is regent and rules for ten years. He is referred to as Nikookaar, or the Benevolent. Dies naturally and leaves the throne to his son Shahpoor. (Vol. 4)

Ardeshir: Grand wise master under the rule of Pirooz and his son. (Vol. 4)

Ardeshir: Son of King Shirooy and a Sassanian king who reigns for six months. (Vol. 5)

Ardeshir Babakan: Descendant of Esfandiar and son of Sassan and Babak's unnamed daughter. First Sassanian king, who reigns for forty years and two months. He weds Golnaar and Ardavan's daughter, who gives him a child named Shahpoor. Dies at the age of seventy-eight. (Vol. 4)

Arezoo: A jeweler's daughter and lute player who marries Bahraam the Hunter. (Vol. 4)

Arjaasp: King of Tooran; his parentage is somewhat unclear but most likely is the son of Garsivaz (son of Pashang). Killed by Esfandiar in the impregnable castle. (Vol. 3)

Arjang: Deev and army commander in Mazandaran. Killed by Rostam. (Vol. 1)

Arjang: Son of Zerreh and brother of Garooy; Tooranian warrior in the army of Tajov. Killed by Tous. (Vol. 2)

Arjasp: Tooranian leader in the army of Afraasiyaab. (Vols. 1-2)

Armail: With brother Garmail, saves intended victims of Zahaak's serpents. (Vol. 1)

Armani: Iranian leader in the army of Rostam under the rule of the last Sassanian ruler, King Yazdegerd. (Vol. 5)

Arnavaaz: Daughter or sister of Jamsheed; concubine of Zahaak, then wife of Fereydoon and mother of Iraj. (Vol. 1)

Ashk: First Ashkanian king and a descendant of Ghobaad. (Vol. 4)

Ashkanian: The Ashkanian Empire, also known as the Parthian Empire or Arsacid Empire, was a political and culture power from 247 BCE to 284 CE in what is now northeastern Iran.

Ashkeboos: Ally of Afraasiyaab from Kushan who fights Rohaam and Rostam. Killed by Rostam. (Vol. 2)

Ashkesh: Of the family of Ghobaad and leader in the Iranian army under the rules of Kay Kaavoos and Kay Khosrow. (Vols. 1-3)

Aspanooy: Slave under the command of Tajov, Afraasiyaab's son-in-law. (Vol. 2)

Ayeen Goshasp: One of King Hormozd's ministers. Killed by a wicked fellow citizen. (Vol. 5)

Azar Goshasp: Warrior in the army of King Hormozd led by Bahraam Choobineh and supporter of Bahraam when he rebels against the king. (Vols. 5)

Azar Mahan: Father of Farrokhzaad during the rule of Khosrow Parviz. (Vol. 5)

Azarmdokht: Rules as queen for four months. (Vol. 5)

Baabooy: Warrior in the army of Bahraam Choobineh in the fight against Khosrow Parviz. (Vol. 5)

Baanoogoshasp: Rostam's daughter and Giv's wife. (Vol. 2)

Baarbad: Musician and singer at the court of Khosrow Parviz. (Vol. 5)

Baarmaan: Tooranian warrior, son of Viseh (son of Zaadsham). (Vols. 1-3) Killed by Ghaaran. (Vol. 1)

Baarmaan: Tooranian warrior killed by Rohaam in the battle of the heroes. (Vols. 2-3)

Baateroon: Rumi army commander. (Vol. 4)

Baazoor: Tooranian sorcerer. (Vol. 2)

Babak: Governor of Estakhr appointed by Ashkanian king Ardavan and father-in-law of Sassan (son of Dara and father of Ardeshir Babakan). (Vol. 4)

Babak: Wise man in service to the Sassanian King Kesra Anushiravan. (Vol. 4)

Babak's daughter: Unnamed wife of Sassan and mother of Ardeshir Babakan. (Vol. 4)

Bahman/Ardeshir: Esfandiar's son and King of Iran; his grandfather Goshtaasp also calls him Ardeshir (some Persian editions of The

Shahnameh refer to him as Ardeshir); marries his daughter Homay/ Chehrzaad. (Vol. 3)

Bahman: Son of Ardavan, the ninth Ashkanian king. Killed in battle. (Vol. 4)

Bahman: Wise man at the court of Kesra Anushiravan. (Vol. 4)

Bahraam: Son of Goodarz and Iranian warrior under the rules of Kay Kaavoos, Kay Khosrow, and King Lohraasp. (Vols. 1-3)

Bahraam: Eighth Ashkanian king. (Vol. 4)

Bahraam: Son of Ormazd (son of King Shahpoor) who rules as Sassanian king for three years and three months. Father of Bahraam. (Vol. 4)

Bahraam: Son of Bahraam (son of King Ormazd) who rules as Sassanian king for nineteen years. Father of Bahraam Bahraamian. (Vol. 4)

Bahraam: Only son of Shahpoor (son of Shahpoor); he rules as a Sassanian king for fourteen years. He has a brother named Yazdegerd and a daughter. (Vol. 4)

Bahraam: Descendant of Siaavoosh and important Iranian warrior in the army of King Hormozd led by Bahraam Choobineh; ultimately he is killed by Choobineh. (Vols. 5)

Bahraam: Warrior in the army of Khosrow Parviz in the war against Bahraam Choobineh. (Vol. 5)

Bahraam Azarmahan: Friend of Simah Borzeen who deceives him at King Hormozd's command and is executed. (Vol. 5)

Bahraam Bahraamian: Son of Bahraam (son of Bahraam); Sassanian king for four months. Recognized as the King of Kerman. Father of Nersi. (Vol. 4)

Bahraam Choobineh: Son of Goshasp, brother of Gordieh and Gordooy; powerful warrior hero in the service of King Hormozd (son of Kesra Anushiravan) who overcomes King Saaveh in battle, then challenges Khosrow Parviz for the throne of Iran. He is killed by Gholoon at the instigation of Khorraad, son of Borzeen. (Vols. 5)

Bahraam of Pirooz: Son of Bahraamian; leader under the reign of Bahraam the Hunter. (Vol. 4)

Bahraam the Hunter: Son of Yazdegerd; Sassanian king who rules for sixty-three years. (Vol. 4)

Balaash: Youngest son of King Pirooz and brother of Ghobaad and Jaamaasp; rules as Sassanian king for five years and two months. (Vol. 4)

Balooy: Leader under the rule of Khosrow Parviz who is rewarded with the governance of the land of Chaadj. (Vol. 5)

Bandooy: With Gostaham, maternal uncles of Khosrow Parviz; wise man and hero during the rule King Hormozd who is imprisoned by the king. He and Gostaham rebel against the crown and blind King Hormozd. Killed at the order of Khosrow Parviz. (Vols. 4-5)

Barsaam: Chini warrior in Bijan's army. (Vol. 5)

Barteh: Iranian warrior and leader of the family of Tavaabeh under the rule of Kay Khosrow. (Vols. 1-3)

Barzeen: Wealthy landowner with three daughters: a lute player, a singer, and a dancer. The three marry Bahraam the Hunter. (Vol. 4)

Bastaam: Name of Gostaham, Khosrow Parviz's maternal uncle who is killed by the king. (Vol. 5)

Beed: Deev in the army of Mazandaran. Killed by Rostam. (Vol. 1)

Behaafarid: Daughter of King Goshtaasp; sister of Homay and Esfandiar. (Vol. 3)

Behrooz: Son of Hoor, horseman in the company of Bahraam the Hunter. (Vol. 4)

Behzaad: Siaavosh's horse, then mastered by Kay Khosrow. (Vol. 2)

Behzaad: King Goshtaasp's stallion. (Vol. 3)

Behzaad: Son of Barzeen; warrior from the lineage of Rostam during the reign of Yazdegerd. (Vol. 4)

Bendah: Sindhi leader. (Vol. 3)

Beraham: A tightfisted, wealthy man who lives under the rule of Bahraam the Hunter. (Vol. 4)

Bezanoosh: Rumi leader and descendant of the Caesars; he drives his army against King Shahpoor and later ascends to the Rumi throne. (Vol. 4)

Biderafsh: Powerful Chini/Tooranian leader in the army of King Arjaasp and his brother. Killed by Esfandiar, son of Goshtaasp. (Vol. 3)

Bijan: Son of Giv and Baanoogoshasp, Rostam's daughter; Iranian warrior under the rule of Kay Khosrow. Loses his life in the blizzard after Kay Khosrow disappears. (Vols. 1-3)

Bijan: Fourth Ashkanian king. (Vol. 4)

Bijan: Descendant of the Tarkhan and resident of Samarkand; as a warrior in Yazdegerd's army, incited by Maahooy Soori to wage war on the king. (Vol. 5)

Bitghoon: Eskandar's vizier who disguises himself as the Caesar. (Vol. 3)

Bivard: Ruler of Kaat and ally of Afraasiyaab. (Vol. 2)

Bivard: Warrior under the rule of Yazdegerd. (Vol. 4)

Booraab: A Rumi blacksmith. (Vol. 3)

Boorandokht: Rules as queen for six months. (Vol. 5)

Boossepaas: Father of Kooh; Hoomaan pretends to be him when he meets Rostam. (Vol. 2)

Borzeen: Iranian warrior and son of Garshaasp. (Vols. 1-2)

Borzmehr: Iranian wise man and emissary under the rule of Bahraam the Hunter. (Vol. 4)

Borzmehr: One of three scribes or viziers under the rule of Anushiravan who is sentenced to death by Hormozd Shah. (Vol. 4)

Borzmehr: Vizier and scribe during the reign of Khosrow Parviz. (Vol. 5)

Borzooy: Name adopted by Bahraam the Hunter to hide his identity from King Shangal of India. (Vol. 4)

Borzooy: Eloquent physician at Kesra Anushiravan's court. (Vol. 4)

Borzvila: Ally of Afraasiyaab in the last great battle during the reign of Kay Khosrow. (Vol. 3)

Bozorgmehr: Learned and wise youth who serves at the court of Kesra Anushiravan. (Vol. 4)

Brahmin: Guide and teacher of the Hindu caste. (Vol. 3)

Caesar of Rum: Title assigned to various Rumi rulers who are often allies of Tooran and Chin. (Vols. 1-4)

Changgesh: Ally of Afraasiyaab who fights Rostam and is killed by him. (Vol. 2)

Chegel: Name of a Turkish tribe famous for the beauty of its people.

Chief of Zargh: Village chief during the reign of King Yazdegerd, last Sassanian king. (Vol. 5)

Chinooy: Noble warrior in the army of the Emperor of Chin during the reign of Khosrow Parviz. (Vol. 5)

Daad Barzeen: Warrior under the reign of Bahraam the Hunter. (Vol. 4)

Daaraab: Son of Homay and Bahman who is raised by the laundryman and his wife; husband of Nahid of Rum and father of Eskandar and Dara. (Vol. 3)

Damoor: Tooranian warrior who lends a hand in the slaying of Siaavosh. (Vols. 2-3)

Dara: Son of Daaraab and half-brother of Eskandar. (Vol. 3)

Dara Panah: Army leader loyal to Bahraam Choobineh during the reign of Khosrow Parviz. (Vol. 5)

Deev: Child of Ahriman, also referred to as Eblis; represents the material or physical embodiment of Ahriman; a fragment of the dark spirit.

Delafrooz: Descendant of Kay Ghobaad and Iranian warrior in the army of Kay Khosrow. (Vol. 3)

Delafrooz: Lumberjack in a village who helps Bahraam the Hunter. (Vol. 4)

Delafroozeh Farrokhpay: Rumi maiden who rescues King Shahpoor and frees him of the donkey skin. (Vol. 4)

Delarai: Wife of King Dara and mother of Roshanak, Eskandar's wife. (Vol. 3)

Eblis: Name synonymous with Ahriman and deev. Eblis is one of the many physical manifestations of Ahriman.

Elias: Son of Mehraas, King of Khazaria. Defeated by Goshtaasp, son of Lohraasp. (Vol. 3)

Emir: A nobleman who attempts to deceive Haftvaad and is met with death. (Vol. 4)

Emperor of Chin: Or Faghfoor of Chin, title given to the rulers of Chin or China, allies of Afraasiyaab and, later, descendants of Arjaasp and Afraasiyaab. (Vols. 2-4)

Esfandiar: Son of Goshtaasp and Katayoon, and brother of Pashootan, Behaafarid, Shiroo, Nivezaar, Shiddasp, and Farshidvard; his sons are Bahman, Mehrnoosh, Aazarafrooz, and Nooshaazar. Calls himself Khorraad at the impregnable castle. Killed by Rostam. (Vol. 3)

Eskandar: Persian equivalent to Alexander; son of King Daaraab and Nahid of Rum, and half-brother of Dara; marries Roshanak, daughter of Dara. (Vol. 3)

Faghanish: King of Chaghan and relative of Bahraam the Hunter. (Vol. 4)

Faghfoor: Title assigned to the Emperor of Chin, or China, who governs under the authority of Tooran-Zamin. (Vols. 1-4)

Fanj: Commander of the host of the Emperor of Chin. (Vol. 4)

Faraaeen: A wise man, follower of Kesra during the rule of Sassanian King Ghobaad. (Vol. 4)

Faraaeen: Also called Goraaz, reigns as king for fifty days. Killed by Hormozd Shahran. (Vol. 5)

Faraamarz: Rostam's son and Iranian warrior under the rules of Kay Kaavoos, Kay Khosrow, King Lohraasp, and King Goshtaasp. Killed in vengeance by King Bahman. (Vols. 1-3)

Faraanak: Fereydoon's mother and Aabteen's wife. (Vol. 1)

Faraanak: Second daughter of the wealthy Barzeen; sister of Maah-Aafareed and Shambeleed; skilled lute player. The three sisters wed Bahraam the Hunter. (Vol. 4)

Faranguis: Afraasiyaab's daughter, wife of Siaavosh, and mother of Kay Khosrow who later marries Fariborz, son of Kaavoos. (Vol. 2)

Farfoorius: Leader of the Caesar's host in the war against Kesra Anushiravan. (Vol. 4)

Farghaar: Skillful warrior who defends Afraasiyaab. (Vol. 2)

Farhaad: Grandson of Goodarz; Iranian warrior under the rules of Kay Kaavoos and Kay Khosrow. (Vols. 1-3)

Farhaad: Leads the left wing of Kesra Anushiravan's host in the war against Rum. (Vol. 4)

Fariborz: Son of Kaavoos and brother of Siaavosh. Loses his life in the blizzard after Kay Khosrow disappears. (Vols. 1-3)

Farrokh: Commander of Nimrooz loyal to Khosrow Parviz. (Vol. 5)

Farrokhzaad: Adoptive name of Goshtaasp, son of Lohraasp, during his stay in Rum. (Vol. 3)

Farrokhzaad: Son of Azar Mahan; illustrious lord and head of King Hormozd's stables (son of Kesra Anushiravan); warrior in the Iranian army of Khosrow Parviz. (Vols. 4-5)

Farrokhzaad: Rules as Sassanian king for one month; poisoned by his servant Siah Chashm; father of Kashamgan. (Vol. 5)

Farrokhzaad: Son of Hormozd and leader of the Iranian army in the fight against the Taazian under the rule of Yazdegerd. (Vol. 5)

Farshidvard: Tooranian warrior and leader in Afraasiyaab's army; son of Viseh (son of Zaadsham). He and his brother Lahaak are killed by Gostaham, son of Gojdaham. (Vols. 1-3)

Farshidvard: Son of King Goshtaasp and Esfandiar's brother. Killed by Kohram. (Vol. 3)

Farshidvard: A wealthy villager, owner of sheep and cattle, who refuses to offer Bahraam the Hunter shelter for the night because of his extreme parsimony. (Vol. 4)

Fartoos: Ruler of Chaghan and ally of Afraasiyaab. Killed by Fariborz, son of Kaavoos, in the great war. (Vols. 2-3)

Fazl: Son of Ahmad, or Abbas Fazl bin Ahmad; minister of Sultan Mahmoud during the time of Ferdowsi. (Vol. 3)

Fereydoon: Sixth king and son of Aabteen and Faraanak; father of Salm, Toor, and Iraj; great-grandfather of Manoochehr. Dies of old age. (Vol. 1)

Filghoos: Caesar of Rum and father of Nahid, who weds King Daaraab. (Vol. 3)

Firooz Khosrow: Son of Khosrow Parviz and chief leader in the army of Ardeshir (son of Shirooy). Killed by Queen Boorandokht. (Vol. 5)

Five Chambermaids: Rudaabeh's servants. (Vol. 1)

Foor: Leader of the Indian army of Sindh. (Vol. 3)

Foorood: Son of Siaavosh and Jarireh (Piran's daughter). Killed by Bijan. (Vol. 2)

Foorood: Son of Khosrow Parviz and Shirin. Killed by his father's enemies. (Vol. 5)

Fooroohal: Iranian warrior in Kay Khosrow's army. (Vol. 3)

Gao: Son of the Indian ruler Jemhoor. (Vol. 4)

APPENDIX

Gargooy: Iranian warrior in King Goshtaasp's army. (Vol. 3)

Garmail: With brother Armail, a cook in Zahaak's kitchen. (Vol. 1)

Garooy: Son of Zerreh, descendant of Toor, and Tooranian warrior responsible for Siaavosh's death. Killed at the order of Kay Khosrow. (Vols. 2-3)

Garshaasp: Son of Zu and tenth King of Iran who rules for nine years. (Vol. 1)

Garshaasp: Son of Nariman and father of Saam and Borzeen; warrior in Manoochehr's army. (Vol. 2)

Garshaasp: Warrior in King Shahpoor's army. (Vol. 4)

Garsioon: Warrior in the army of King Yazdegerd, last Sassanian ruler. (Vol. 5)

Garsivan: Tooranian warrior. (Vol. 3)

Garsivaz: Pashang's son and Afraasiyaab's brother, responsible for Siaavosh's death; father of Andariman, Arjaasp, Biderafsh, and Kohram. Killed at the order of Kay Khosrow. (Vols. 1-3)

Garukhan: A family that supports Kay Khosrow in his great battle against Afraasiyaab. (Vol. 3)

Garzam: Tooranian warrior in Afraasiyaab's army. Killed by Giv. (Vol. 1)

Ghaaloos: Rumi emissary and advisor of the Caesar. (Vol. 3)

Ghaaran: Son of Kaveh; brother of Kashvaad; Iranian warrior and chief. (Vols. 1-3)

Ghaaran: Ruler of eastern lands and ally of Kay Khosrow in the great battle against Afraasiyaab. (Vol. 3)

Ghaaran: Son of Goshasp, warrior under the rule of Yazdegerd. (Vol. 4)

Ghaaran: Son of Borzmehr warrior under the reign of Bahraam the Hunter. (Vol. 4)

Ghabtoon: King of Egypt during the time of Eskandar. (Vol. 3)

Gharakhan: Tooranian warrior who serves Afraasiyaab. (Vol. 3)

Gharakhan: Army commander under the rule of Kesra Anushiravan. (Vol. 4)

Ghatfar: Hephthalite king. (Vol. 4)

Gheys: Son of Haress and leader of free Arabs. (Vol. 5)

Gheyssian: Or Ghassanids; Arab tribe that resided in Yemen. (Vol. 4)

Ghobaad: Son of Kashvaad (son of Kaaveh); Iranian warrior in Manoochehr's army; not to be confused with Kay Ghobaad. Killed by Baarmaan. (Vol. 1)

Ghobaad: Son of King Pirooz and brother of Balaash and Jaamaasp; he rules for forty years after his brother Balaash is cast aside by Soofraay. (Vol. 4)

Ghobaad: Also known as Shirooy, is the son of Khosrow Parviz and Mariam (daughter of the Caesar), and father of King Ardeshir; Sassanian king who rules for seven months. Poisoned by enemies. (Vol. 5)

Gholoon: Tooranian warrior in the army of Afraasiyaab. Killed by Rostam. (Vol. 1)

Gholoon: A Turk who mourns the death of his relative of Maghaatooreh and kills Bahraam Choobineh in retribution and at the insistence of Khorraad Borzeen. Killed at the order of the Emperor of Chin. (Vol. 5)

Ghool: Name meaning giant; witch defeated by Esfandiar in the fourth stage of his quest. (Vol. 3)

Ghorcheh: Tooranian warrior in the army of Afraasiyaab. (Vol. 2)

Giv: Son of Goodarz, grandson of Kashvaad, husband of Baanoogoshasp, and father of Bijan and Goraazeh; Iranian leader and warrior who serves under Kay Kaavoos and Kay Khosrow. Loses his life in the blizzard after Kay Khosrow disappears. (Vols. 1-3)

Gojdaham: Iranian warrior, defender of the White Castle, and father of Gostaham, Gordaafareed, and Hojir's wife. (Vols. 1-3)

Golbaad: Tooranian warrior killed by Zaal. (Vol. 1)

Golbaad: Tooranian warrior and leader in the army of Afraasiyaab. (Vol. 2-3)

Golbooy: Iranian leader from Tabaristan in the army of Rostam under the rule of the last Sassanian ruler, King Yazdegerd. (Vol. 5)

Golgoon: Goodarz's horse. (Vol. 2)

Golgoon: Lohraasp's horse. (Vol. 3)

Golgoon: Bahraam the Hunter's horse. (Vol. 4)

Golinoosh: Shirooy's advisor in Ctesiphon who is charged with the guard of Khosrow Parviz. (Vol. 5)

Golnaar: Advisor and treasurer of King Ardavan who falls in love with Ardeshir Babakan. (Vol. 4)

Golrang: Fereydoon's horse. (Vol. 1)

Golrang: Fariborz's horse. (Vol. 2)

Golshahr: Piran's wife and mother of Jarireh. (Vol. 2)

Goodarz: Iranian leader who serves under Kay Kaavoos, Kay Khosrow, and Lohraasp; son of Kashvaad (son of Kaaveh); has 78 sons and grandsons. (Vols. 1-3)

Goodarz: Third Ashkanian king. (Vol. 4)

Gooshbastar: Strange and hairy man Eskandar encounters on his way to Babel. (Vol. 3)

Goraaz: Also called Faraaeen, is a deev-like servant who betrays Khosrow Parviz; later, he returns to Iran and plots the murder of King Ardeshir. Rules as king for fifty days. Killed by Hormozd Shahran. (Vol. 5)

Goraaz: Nobleman in Maahooy Soori's host and border guard of Marv who is killed in battle. (Vol. 5)

Goraazeh: Son of Giv (son of Goodarz); Iranian warrior under the rules of Kay Kaavoos and Kay Khosrow. (Vols. 1-3)

Gorazm: Iranian warrior of Kianian lineage in the army of Goshtaasp. Killed by King Arjaasp's troops. (Vol. 3)

Gord: The Armenian; warrior in the army of Bahraam Choobineh in the fight against Khosrow Parviz. (Vol. 5)

Gordaafareed: Iranian female warrior who fights with Sohraab; daughter of Gojdaham (of the family of Goodarz). (Vol. 1)

Gordieh: The wise sister of Bahraam Choobineh and Gordooy. (Vol. 5)

Gordooy: Son of Goshasp and brother of Bahraam Choobineh and Gordieh; wise leader and trusted vizier of King Khosrow Parviz. (Vol. 5)

Gorgeen: Son of Milaad and Iranian warrior in the armies of Kay Kaavoos and Kay Khosrow; from the lineage of Aarash Kamangir. (Vols. 1-3, 5)

Gorgsaar: Commander of King Arjaasp's host. Captured and later killed by Esfandiar. (Vol. 3)

Goshasp: Wise man and scribe under the rule of Yazdegerd and Bahraam the Hunter; father of Ghaaran. (Vol. 4)

Goshasp: Warrior in Kesra Anushiravan's host and father of Bahraam Choobineh and Gordooy. (Vol. 4)

Goshasp: Khosrow Parviz's treasurer. (Vol. 5)

Goshtaasp: Son of Lohraasp, King of Iran; marries Katayoon, daughter of the Rumi Caesar; father of Esfandiar, Shiroo, Nivezaar, Shiddasp, Farshidvard, and Behaafarid; conceals his identity behind the name Farrokhzaad in Rum. (Vol. 3)

Gostaham: Son of Nozar; brother of Tous (different from Gostaham, son of Gojdaham). (Vols. 1-3)

Gostaham: Young son of Gojdaham and brother of Gordaafareed (different from the son of Nozar). (Vols. 1-3)

Gostaham: Iranian warrior under the reigns of Yazdegerd and Khosrow and vizier to Bahraam the Hunter. (Vol. 4)

Gostaham: With Bandooy, maternal uncles of Khosrow Parviz; wise man and hero during the rule King Hormozd who is imprisoned by the king. He and Bandooy rebel against the crown and blind King Hormozd; Gostaham is the vizier of Khosrow Parviz who also has the name of Bastaam. Killed at the order of Khosrow Parviz. (Vols. 4-5)

Gueraami: Son of Jaamaasp, Goshtaasp's minister. Killed by Arjaasp's troops. (Vol. 3)

Gurch: Afraasiyaab's fifth son and Tooranian leader. (Vol. 3)

Haaroot: Angel who along with the fairy Maaroot comes to earth to teach spells. They lose access to heaven because of their sins and are imprisoned in Babel. (Vol. 2)

Haftvaad: A resident of Kojaran who has seven sons and one daughter. Killed by Ardeshir. (Vol. 4)

Haftvaad's daughter: Discovers the worm that helps her spin more threads. (Vol. 4)

Haftvaad's worm: Magical worm. Killed by Ardeshir. (Vol. 4)

Hamdan Goshasp: Grand scribe and warrior in charge of the vanguard in the army of King Hormozd led by Bahraam Choobineh. (Vol. 5)

Hashemi: Arab descendants of the Prophet Mohammad. (Vol. 5)

Hephthalites: Residents of a region in central Asia during the fifth to the eighth centuries CE. (Vol. 4)

Hermit: An insightful old man Khosrow Parviz encounters in Rum. (Vol. 5)

Heshoo: Rumi guardian of the shores. (Vol. 3)

Hirbad: Sudaabeh's servant. (Vol. 2)

Hojir: Son of Goodarz; Iranian warrior and Gojdaham's son-in-law. (Vols. 1-3)

Homa: Large and powerful bird in Persian mythology, symbol of happiness; similar to the griffin or the phoenix. (Vols. 1-3)

Homay: King Bahman's daughter, sister of Ardeshir/Sassan, also called Chehrzaad; marries her father, Bahman, and they have a son, Daaraab; upon Bahman's death, she rules as queen for thirty-two years. (Vol. 3)

Homay: A wise emissary who takes a letter to the Tarkhan of Chin under the rule of Bahraam the Hunter. (Vol. 4)

Hoom: A devout descendant of Fereydoon who lives humbly as a hermit in a mountainous cave. (Vol. 3)

Hoomaan: Tooranian leader, son of Viseh (son of Zaadsham). Killed by Bijan. (Vols. 1-3)

Hooshang: Second King of Iran and son of Siaamak who rules for forty years. (Vol. 1)

Hooshdeev: Malicious Tooranian warrior under the command of King Arjaasp. (Vol. 3)

Hormoz: Son of Yazdegerd (son of Bahraam the Hunter) and brother of Pirooz; Sassanian king who rules for one year. Falls into a ditch and dies. (Vol. 4)

Hormozd: Son of Khorraad and warrior in the army of Kesra Anushiravan. (Vol. 4)

Hormozd: Son of King Kesra Anushiravan; Sassanian king who rules for twelve years; father of Khosrow Parviz; father of two sons, one of them Rostam, a leader in the army of Yazdegerd, the last Sassanian king. Killed by men from his court: Gostaham and Bandooy. (Vols. 4-5)

Hormozd Shahran: An elite rider from the city of Estakhr. (Vol. 5)

Hormozd: Son of Khorraad; wise man who advises Maahooy Soori to refrain from killing King Yazdegerd, the last Sassanian king. (Vol. 5)

Hoshyar: Wise man from Pars and astrologer at the court of Yazdegerd. (Vol. 4)

Houri: A beautiful maiden who welcomes the devout Muslim into paradise. (Vol. 5)

Illa: Unclear whether he is Afraasiyaab's son or grandson; Tooranian warrior. (Vol. 3)

Iraj: Youngest son of Fereydoon and Arnavaaz; brother of Salm and Toor; grandfather of Manoochehr. Killed by his brothers. (Vol. 1)

Iraj: Ruler of Kabol and ally of Kay Khosrow in the great battle against Afraasiyaab. (Vol. 3)

Israfil: One of the four angels equivalent to Raphael of Uriel; angel of music. (Vol. 3)

Izad Goshasp: One of three scribes or leaders under the rule of Anushiravan and Hormozd Shah and a supporter of Bahraam Choobineh when he rebels against the king. (Vols. 5)

Jaamaasp: Astrologer and guide to Goshtaasp. (Vol. 3)

Jaamaasp: Younger brother of Sassanian King Ghobaad. (Vol. 4)

Jahn: Tooranian warrior and Afraasiyaab's son and advisor. Overthrown by Rostam in Gang but survives and is offered the rulership of Tooran-Zamin by Kay Khosrow, who forgives him. (Vols. 2-3)

Jahn: Son of Barzeen and builder of King Fereydoon's throne; appointed as governor of Sari and Amol by the king. (Vol. 5)

Jamsheed: Son of Tahmures and fourth King of Iran who rules for 700 years. Killed by Zahaak. (Vol. 1)

Jandal: A wise envoy sent by Fereydoon to find three sisters to marry Toor, Salm, and Iraj. (Vol. 1)

Janfoorooz: Warrior in the army of Bahraam Choobineh. (Vol. 5)

Janoosyar: Vizier and treasurer of King Dara who conspires with Maahiar to kill the king. Killed by Eskandar. (Vol. 3)

Janus: Brother of the Caesar during King Shahpoor's rule. Defeated in war by Shahpoor. (Vol. 4)

Jaranjas: Tooranian leader who fights for Afraasiyaab in the great war. (Vol. 3)

Jarireh: Siaavosh's wife and Foorood's mother; eldest daughter of Piran. (Vol. 2)

Javanooy: Persian emissary and Bahraam the Hunter's treasurer. (Vol. 4)

Jemhoor: Indian ruler under the reign of Kesra Anushiravan and father of Gao. (Vol. 4)

Jinn: Supernatural beings or spirits able to take on various shapes; common in myths and stories. (Vol. 5)

Jooyaa: A warrior leader in the army of the King of Mazandaran. Killed by Rostam. (Vol. 1)

Kaafoor: "Man-eater" Tooranian who dwells in the city of Bidaad. Killed by Rostam. (Vol. 2)

Kaakooy: Descendant of Zahaak who battles Manoochehr. Killed by Manoochehr. (Vol. 1)

Kaaloo: Tooranian warrior in the army of Afraasiyaab. (Vol. 2)

Kaamoos: Ruler of Kushan and Afraasiyaab's ally in war. Killed by Rostam. (Vol. 2)

Kaakooleh: Descendant of Toor and Tooranian warrior. (Vol. 3)

Kaaveh: Father of Kashvaad and Ghaaran; blacksmith who leads the rebellion against Zahaak. (Vol. 1)

Kaboodeh: Servant of Tajov, ruler of Gorooguerd. Killed by Bahraam. (Vol. 2)

Kahaar: From Kahan, an ally of Afraasiyaab. Killed by Rostam. (Vol. 2)

Kahtan: Conqueror of the land of Yemen. (Vol. 3)

Kalaahoor: Warrior rider in the army of the King of Mazandaran. (Vol. 1)

Kappi: A strange and wild beast or dragon who dwells in the mountains of Chin and devours the residents, including the emperor's daughter. Killed by Bahraam Choobineh. (Vol. 5)

Karkoo: Warrior and ally of Afraasiyaab. (Vol. 2)

Karkooy: Salm's grandson and a relative of Zahaak on his mother's side. Killed by Saam. (Vol. 1)

Karookhan: Tooranian warrior in Afraasiyaab's army and relative of Viseh; Afraasiyaab's minister. (Vol. 1)

Karookhan: Afraasiyaab's eldest son and Tooranian leader. (Vol. 3)

Kashamgan: Son of Farrokhzaad (son of Hormozd) and warrior in the army of King Yazdegerd under the leadership of his father. (Vol. 5)

Kashvaad: Son of Kaaveh and brother of Ghaaran; father of Ghobaad, Garshaasp and Goodarz; Iranian warrior and soldier. (Vols. 1-2)

Katayoon: Daughter of the Rumi Caesar; marries Goshtaasp, future King of Iran, and gives birth to their son, Esfandiar. (Vol. 3)

Katib: Father of Nasr, ruler of Mecca at the time of Eskandar's visit. (Vol. 3)

Kay Aarash: Son of Kay Ghobaad. (Vols. 1-2)

Kay Aarmin: Son of Kay Ghobaad. (Vol. 1)

Kay Ghobaad: Descendant of Fereydoon and eleventh King of Iran who rules for one hundred years; father to four sons: Kay Kaavoos, Kay Aarash, Kay Pashin, and Kay Aarmin. (Vol. 1)

Kay Kaavoos: Son of Kay Ghobaad and twelfth King of Iran who rules for 150 years. (Vols. 1-3)

Kay Khosrow: Son of Siaavosh and Faranguis, and grandson of Kay Kaavoos and Afraasiyaab; thirteenth King of Iran. (Vols. 1-3)

Kay Pashin: Son of Kay Ghobaad. (Vols. 1-2)

Kayvan: A learned man in charge of the accounts under the rule of Bahraam the Hunter. (Vol. 4)

Kebord: Tooranian warrior. (Vol. 3)

Kebrooy: A heavy drinker of wine under the rule of Bahraam the Hunter. Killed by a crow. (Vol. 4)

Kehila: Tooranian warrior. Killed by Manoochehr in the great war. (Vol. 3)

Keid: Indian King of Ghennooj. (Vols. 3-4)

Kesra Anushiravan: Son of Sassanian King Ghobaad and the daughter of a landowner, descendant of Fereydoon. He is named Anushiravan upon his ascent to the throne and rules for forty-eight years. (Vol. 4)

Ketmaareh: Iranian warrior and son of Ghaaran. (Vol. 3)

Keydafeh: Queen of Andalusia. (Vol. 3)

Keydroosh: Son of Keydafeh and son-in-law of King Faryan; brother of Teynoosh. (Vol. 3)

Khanegi: Rumi leader at the Caesar's court during the time of Khosrow Parviz. (Vol. 5)

Khashaash: Important warrior in King Arjaasp's army. (Vol. 3)

Khazar: Semi-nomadic person from the land of Khazaria. (Vol. 3)

Khazarvan: Tooranian warrior in the army of Afraasiyaab. Killed by Zaal. (Vol. 1)

Khazarvan: Leader under the reign of Bahraam the Hunter. (Vol. 4)

Khezr: Believed to have been a messenger and prophet, guardian of the sea. (Vol. 3)

Khojabr: Tooranian warrior in the army of Afraasiyaab. (Vol. 1)

Khonjast: From Oman, support of Khosrow Parviz. (Vol. 4)

Khorraad: Iranian warrior in the army of Kay Kaavoos. (Vols. 1-3)

Khorraad: Old man at the court of Ardeshir. (Vol. 4)

Khorraad: Son of Borzeen and descendant of Ardeshir; commander in the army of King Hormozd who overcomes the Khazars in battle; later he supports Hormozd's son, Khosrow Parviz. (Vols. 5)

Khorsheed: Son of Khorraad (son of Borzeen) and Iranian leader under the rule of Khosrow Parviz. (Vol. 5)

Khoshnavaz: Son of the Tarkhan under the rule of King Pirooz. (Vol. 4)

Khosrow: Descendant of Kay Pashin; placed on the Sassanian throne as king after the death of Yazdegerd. (Vol. 4)

Khosrow: Leader of the land of Khazaria and ally of Bahraam Choobineh. (Vol. 5)

Khosrow: A common miller who finds King Yazdegerd taking shelter in his windmill; he kills the king at the command of Maahooy Soori. (Vol. 5)

Khosrow Parviz: Son of Hormozd (son of Kesra Anushiravan). He ascends the Sassanian throne when his father is blinded by his uncles Bandooy and Gostaham. He rules for thirty-eight years and marries Mariam, Gordieh, and Shirin. Father of Shirooy (Ghobaad) and fifteen other sons. Killed by the villainous Mehr Hormozd. (Vols. 4-5)

Khosrow Khazarvan: Leader of the land of Khazars. (Vol. 5)

Khozaa: Descendant of Abraham and leader of Mecca; Eskandar executes him and his entire family. (Vol. 3)

Khuzan: Ruler of the land of Pars and Iranian warrior leader who fights alongside Kay Khosrow. (Vol. 3)

Kiaanoosh: Fereydoon's brother. (Vol. 1)

King Faryan: Ruler of a fortified city on some border between Egypt and Spain, and father-in-law of Keydroosh, Keydafeh's son. (Vol. 3)

King Firooz: Descendant of Kay Ghobaad and ruler of Gharchehgan; ally of Kay Khosrow in the great battle against Afraasiyaab. (Vol. 3)

King of Alaanan: Ruler of a region in northwestern Iran. (Vol. 4)

King of Cashmere: Ally of Shangal, King of India. (Vol. 4)

King of Chaghan: Refers to the King of Hephthalites. (Vol. 4)

King of Chegel: Warrior leader in King Arjaasp's army. (Vol. 3)

King of Egypt: Ally of the King of Haamaavaran. Killed by Zavaareh in the battle with the three nations. (Vol. 1)

King of Guran: Ally of Kay Khosrow in the great battle against Afraasiyaab. (Vol. 3)

King of Haamaavaran: Father of Sudaabeh, wife of Kay Kaavoos. Killed by Rostam to save Kay Kaavoos. (Vol. 2)

King of Jandal: Ally of Shangal, King of India. (Vol. 4)

King of Kabol: Father-in-law of Shaghaad, Zaal's son. Killed by Faraamarz, Rostam's son. (Vol. 3)

King of Kabol: Ally of Shangal, King of India. (Vol. 4)

King of Kerman: Ally of Kay Khosrow in the great battle against Afraasiyaab. (Vol. 3)

King of Khotan: Afraasiyaab's ally in war. (Vol. 3)

King of Khuzan: Ally of Kay Khosrow in the great battle against Afraasiyaab. (Vol. 3)

King of Mazandaran: Ruler of a kingdom of deevs who captures Kay Kaavoos and is then killed in Rostam's epic seven-stage quest. (Vol. 1)

King of Mokran: Afraasiyaab's ally in the great war. Killed by Tokhaar and Tous. (Vol. 3)

King of Moulton: Ally of Shangal, King of India. (Vol. 4)

King of Rus: King of Russia. (Vol. 3)

King of Sandal: Ally of Shangal, King of India. (Vol. 4)

King of Shaam: King of Syria and ally of the King of Haamaavaran. Captured by Rostam in the battle with three nations (Vol. 1)

King of Sindh: Ally of Afraasiyaab. (Vol. 2)

King of Sindh: Ally of Shangal, King of India. (Vol. 4)

Kiumars: First King of Iran, who rules from a mountaintop for fifty years. (Vol. 1)

Kohram: Tooranian warrior. Killed by Barteh in the battle of the heroes. (Vols. 2-3)

Kohram: Brother of King Arjaasp, Andariman, and Biderafsh. Killed by Shiddasp, son of Goshtaasp. (Vol. 3)

Kohram: King Arjaasp's eldest son. Killed by Esfandiar. (Vol. 3)

Kolbaad: Son of Viseh; Tooranian warrior. Killed by Fariborz, son of Kaavoos, in the battle of the heroes. (Vol. 3)

Konaarang Deev: Guardian of a rocky, desolate place on the way to the White Deev's dwelling. (Vol. 1)

Konda Goshasp: Warrior in charge of the rearguard in the army of King Hormozd led by Bahraam Choobineh. (Vol. 5)

Kondor: From the land of Saghlaab and an ally of Afraasiyaab in war; warrior in the army of King Arjaasp. (Vols. 2-3)

Kooh: Assumed name used by Hoomaan to trick Rostam; son of Boossepaas. (Vol. 2)

Koot: Rumi army leader who fights to save Khosrow Parviz. Killed by Bahraam Choobineh. (Vol. 5)

Kundrow: Zahaak's minister. (Vol. 1)

Lahaak: Son of Viseh (son of Zaadsham); Tooranian warrior and leader in the army of Afraasiyaab. He and his brother Farshidvard are killed by Gostaham. (Vols. 2-3)

Lambak: Water carrier and kind man who lives under the rule of Bahraam the Hunter. (Vol. 4)

Laundryman: Finds Daaraab, son of Homay and Bahman, floating in a box on the river and raises him with his wife. (Vol. 3)

Lohraasp: Iranian warrior in Kay Khosrow's army who is named King of Iran by Kay Khosrow; son of Arvand Shah (descendant of Kay Pashin, descendant of Kay Ghobaad), and father of Goshtaasp and Zarir. Killed by Arjaasp's troops. (Vol. 3)

Maah Aafareed: One of Iraj's wives and Manoochehr's grandmother. (Vol. 1)

Maah Aafareed: First daughter of the wealthy Barzeen; sister of Faraanak and Shambeleed; skilled singer. The three sisters wed Bahraam the Hunter. (Vol. 4)

Maah Azar: One of three scribes or viziers under the rule of Anushiravan who is sentenced to death by Hormozd Shah. (Vol. 5)

Maah-e Aazaadeh Khooy: Daughter of Sarv, King of Yemen, and wife of Toor, son of Fereydoon. (Vol. 1)

Maahiar: Vizier and advisor of King Dara who conspires with Janoosyar to kill the king. Killed by Eskandar. (Vol. 3)

Maahiar: An older nobleman at the court of Bahraam the Hunter. (Vol. 4)

Maahiar: A jeweler whose daughter, Arezoo, marries Bahraam the Hunter. (Vol. 4)

Maakh: A border guard living in Herat during the time of Fereydoon with knowledge of the reign of Hormozd, son of Kesra Anushiravan. (Vol. 4)

Maay: Brother of the Indian ruler Jemhoor who resides in Dambar. He succeeds his late brother on the throne and marries Jemhoor's widow. They have a son named Talhand. (Vol. 4)

Maghaatooreh: Leader in the army of the Emperor of Chin during the reign of Khosrow Parviz. Killed by Bahraam Choobineh. (Vol. 5)

Mahbood: Kesra Anushiravan's vizier; father of two sons. His wife and two sons are responsible for the king's meals. His entire family is killed after they are falsely accused of attempting to poison the king. (Vol. 4)

Mahrooy: Warrior in the army of Bahraam Choobineh. (Vol. 5)

Maahooy Soori: Iranian leader in the army of Rostam under the rule of the last Sassanian ruler, King Yazdegerd. Bijan cuts off his hands, feet, ears, and nose. (Vol. 5)

Malekeh: Daughter of Nooshah, Nersi's daughter, and the Arab Taaer. (Vol. 4)

Mamoon: Or al-Mamun (786-833); the seventh Abbasid caliph.

Mani: Iranian prophet who wrote the holy book of Manichaeism, Arjang, also known as The Book of Pictures. He preached through-out the land of Persia in the third century BCE. He appears at King Shahpoor's court. Historical accounts vary on the timeline of his life and on the circumstances of his death, but in The Shahnameh, he is skinned and killed at the order of King Shahpoor. (Vols. 3-4)

Manijeh: Afraasiyaab's daughter and Bijan's wife. (Vol. 1)

Manoochehr: Seventh King of Iran and grandson of Iraj, who rules for 120 years; son of Pashang and Nameless. (Vol. 1)

Manoochehr: Son of Aarash and warrior from Khorasan; ally of Kay Khosrow. (Vol. 3)

Manooshan: Ruler of the land of Pars and Iranian warrior leader who fights alongside Kay Khosrow. (Vol. 3)

Manshoor: Ruler of Chin and ally of Afraasiyaab. (Vol. 2)

Mardaas: Zahaak's father, ruler in Mesopotamia. Killed by Eblis. (Vol. 1)

Mardanesheh: Son of Khosrow Parviz and Shirin. Killed at the hand of his father's enemies. (Vol. 5)

Mardooy: Tooranian warrior in the army of Tajov. (Vol. 2)

Mardooy: The treasurer of Kesra Anushiravan. (Vol. 4)

Mardooy: Gardener and guardian at the court of Khosrow Parviz. (Vol. 5)

Mariam: Daughter of the Caesar of Rum, wife of Khosrow Parviz (other wives are Gordieh and Shirin), and mother of Shirooy. Poisoned by Shirin. (Vol. 5)

Mazdak: Physician under the rule of Sassanian King Ghobaad who becomes the royal vizier and imposes his own beliefs on the king and his subjects. Hanged by Kesra, son of Ghobaad, along with all his followers. (Vol. 4)

Mehraab: Ruler of Kabol and father of Rudaabeh; descendant of Zahaak. (Vols. 1-2)

Mehraas: King of Khazaria. (Vol. 3)

Mehraas: Envoy serving the Rumi Caesar and intermediary with Kesra Anushiravan. (Vol. 4)

Mehrak: Son of Nooshzaad. Killed by Ardeshir. (Vol. 4)

Mehrak's daughter: Marries Shahpoor, son of Ardeshir. They have a son named Ormazd. (Vol. 4)

Mehran: Wise man with deep foresight who advises the Indian Keid. (Vol. 3)

Mehran: The treasurer of King Yazdegerd, father of Bahraam. (Vol. 4)

Mehran: Warrior in the army of Kesra Anushiravan. (Vol. 4)

Mehran: Scribe in the service of King Hormozd who accompanies Bahraam Choobineh to war against King Saaveh. (Vol. 4)

Mehran Setaad: An old and wise nobleman and envoy of Anushiravan who selects one of the daughters of the Emperor of Chin to wed to the king. (Vol. 4)

Mehran Setaad: Merchant from Kaarzi who encounters Khosrow Parviz on the road to Rum and shares his provisions with him. (Vol. 5)

Mehrbandad: A farmer under the rule of Bahraam the Hunter. (Vol. 4)

Mehr Aazar: Resident of Pars and supporter of Kesra under the rule of Sassanian King Ghobaad. (Vol. 4)

Mehr Barzeen: Son of Khorraad; leader under the reign of Bahraam the Hunter. (Vol. 4)

Mehr Hormozd: A villain who volunteers to kill Khosrow Parviz. (Vol. 5)

Mehrnoosh: Son of Esfandiar and brother of Bahman, Aazarafrooz, and Nooshaazar. Killed by Faraamarz. (Vol. 3)

Mehrnoosh: Wise man who advises Maahooy Soori to refrain from killing King Yazdegerd, the last Sassanian king. (Vol. 5)

Mehr Pirooz: Son of Behzaad; leader under the reign of Bahraam the Hunter. (Vol. 4)

Milaad: Father of Gorgeen and Iranian hero in the army of Kay Kaavoos and Kay Khosrow; from the lineage of Aarash Kamangir; ancestor of Bahraam Choobineh. (Vols. 1-2, 5)

Milaad: Warrior under the rule of Yazdegerd. (Vol. 4)

Mirin: Wealthy Rumi descendant of Salm who marries the second daughter of the Caesar. (Vol. 3)

Monzer: King of Yemen and father of Noman; comes from the land of Arabia to teach King Yazdegerd's son, Bahraam. (Vol. 4)

Moolookeh Tavayef: Meaning "King of Tribes"; name assigned to any minor ruler. They held power for a period of two hundred years after the death of Eskandar. (Vols. 3-4)

Moshkenek: One of the four miller's daughters who are wedded to Bahraam the Hunter; name meaning partridge. (Vol. 4)

Moshknaz: One of the four miller's daughters who are wedded to Bahraam the Hunter; name meaning pure musk. (Vol. 4)

Moossil: The Armenian, ally of Khosrow Parviz who comes to the aid of Bandooy. (Vol. 5)

Mother of Siaavosh: Descendant of Fereydoon and granddaughter of Garsivaz. (Vol. 2)

Muhammad: Founder of the religion of Islam and considered by Muslims as their divinely appointed prophet.

Nahel: Tooranian warrior. (Vol. 2)

Nahid: Daughter of Filghoos, Caesar of Rum; wife of King Daaraab and mother of Eskandar. (Vol. 3)

Nameless: Daughter of Maah Aafareed and Iraj; granddaughter of Fereydoon; wife of Pashang, mother of Manoochehr. Ferdowsi does not assign her a name. (Vol. 1)

Namkhaast: Evil sorcerer at the court of King Arjaasp. (Vol. 3)

Nariman: Great Iranian warrior in the army of Manoochehr; Saam's father and Zaal's grandfather. (Vols. 1-2)

Nasr: Son of Katib; ruler of Mecca at the time of Eskandar's visit; he is a descendant of Abraham. (Vol. 3)

Nasr, Amir: Samanid King who ruled from 865 to 892. (Vol. 4)

Nastaar: Guardian of the Rumi Caesar's stables. (Vol. 3)

Nastihan: Tooranian warrior; son of Viseh (son of Zaadsham) and brother of Piran, Pilsam, Hoomaan, Baarmaan, and Kolbaad. Killed by Bijan. (Vols. 2-3)

Nastooh: Son of Goodarz and an Iranian warrior. (Vols. 2-3)

Nastooh: Tooranian commander who fights for Afraasiyaab in the great war. (Vol. 3)

Nastooh: Son of Mehran Setaad; servant of Sassanian King Hormozd (son of Kesra Anushiravan); supporter of King Khosrow Parviz. (Vols. 5)

Nastoor: Son of Zarir, son of Lohraasp; King Goshtaasp grants him his daughter's hand. (Vol. 3)

Nastoor: Son of Khosrow Parviz and Shirin. Killed by his father's enemies. (Vol. 5)

Nazyab: One of the four miller's daughters who are wedded to Bahraam the Hunter; name meaning flirtatious. (Vol. 4)

Nersi: Son of Bahraam Bahraamian; a Sassanian king who rules for seventy years, then dies, surrendering the throne to his son Ormazd. (Vol. 4)

Nersi: Bahraam the Hunter's brother from the lineage of Pashin; Bahraam offers him the land of Khorasan to rule. (Vol. 4)

Nivezaar: Son of King Goshtaasp. Killed by Arjaasp's troops. (Vol. 3)

Niyaatoos: Brother of the Caesar during the time of Khosrow Parviz; Rumi army leader. (Vol. 5)

Nooshaazar: Esfandiar's son; his brothers are Bahman, Mehrnoosh, and Aazarafrooz. Killed by Zavaareh. (Vol. 3)

Nooshah: The daughter of Nersi who is abducted by Taaer. The two have a daughter he names Malekeh. (Vol. 4)

Nooshzaad: Of Kianian lineage and father of Mehrak. (Vol. 4)

Nooshzaad: Son of Kesra Anushiravan and his Christian wife. Killed in a battle to usurp his father's throne. (Vol. 4)

Nozar: Son of Manoochehr and eighth King of Iran who rules for seven years; father of Tous and Gostaham. Beheaded by Afraasiyaab. (Vol. 1)

Noman: Son of Monzer, King of Yemen; comes from the land of Arabia with his father to teach King Yazdegerd's son, Bahraam. (Vol. 4)

Omar: Ibn al-Khattab, father-in-law of the Prophet Muhammad and Arab leader under the rule of Yazdegerd, the last Sassanian king, one of four caliphs. Under his rule, the Arab conquest of Iran led to the end of the Sassanian Dynasty. (Vol. 5)

Ormazd: Or Hormozd, Avesta name for Ahura Mazda, meaning creator. In the ancient Persian solar calendar, each day had the name of a deity instead of a number. Ormazd represented the first day of the month. Each name evoked a concept. The division then was not based on a seven-day week but on a thirty-day month.

Ormazd: Sixth Ashkanian king. (Vol. 4)

Ormazd: Son of Shahpoor and Mehrak's daughter; third Sassanian king. (Vol. 4)

Ormazd: Son of Nersi (son of Bahraam Bahraamian) and Sassanian king who rules for nine years. Father of Shahpoor. (Vol. 4)

Ormazd: Bahraam the Hunter's vizier and counselor. (Vol. 4)

Ormazd: Warrior in the army of Khosrow Parviz in the war against Bahraam Choobineh. (Vol. 5)

Oshtaa: Son of Pirooz and warrior in the army of Khosrow Parviz in the war against Bahraam Choobineh. (Vol. 5)

Oshtaa: Son of Goshasp and wise man under Khosrow Parviz and King Shirooy. (Vol. 5)

Ostaad: Son of Barzeen and leader of Kesra Anushiravan's right wing. (Vol. 4)

Ostaay: From Gorgan, supporter of Khosrow Parviz. (Vol. 4)

Ostaghila: Ally of Afraasiyaab in the great battle. (Vol. 3)

Palaashan: Tooranian warrior and Afraasiyaab's army leader. Killed by Bijan. (Vol. 2)

Parmoodeh: Emperor of Chin and son of King Saaveh who asks protection from Bahraam Choobineh, leader of the Iranian army of King Hormozd. (Vol. 5)

Pashang: Iranian warrior from the seed of Jamsheed; Fereydoon's nephew (his brother's son), selected by Fereydoon to marry Fereydoon's Nameless granddaughter; father of Manoochehr. (Vol. 1)

Pashang: Son of Zaadsham and father of Aghriras, Afraasiyaab, Garsivaz, Andariman, Sepahram, and Kohram. (Vols. 1-3)

Pashootan: Son of Goshtaasp and Katayoon, and brother and advisor of Esfandiar. King Bahman's vizier. (Vol. 3)

Philosopher: One of the wonders of the Indian Keid who is given to Eskandar as a tribute. (Vol. 3)

Physician: One of the wonders of the Indian Keid who is given to Eskandar. (Vol. 3)

Pilsam: Son of Viseh (son of Zaadsham) and brother of Piran; Tooranian army leader. Killed by Rostam. (Vols. 1-2)

Piran: Son of Viseh (son of Zaadsham) and brother of Pilsam, Hoomaan, Nastihan, Baarmaan, and Kolbaad; Tooranian army leader. Killed by Goodarz in the battle of the heroes. (Vols. 1-3)

Pirooz: Rider from Gorzban and warrior under the rule of Yazdegerd. (Vol. 4)

Pirooz: Son of Yazdegerd (son of Bahraam the Hunter) and brother of Hormoz; father of Balaash, Ghobaad, Jaamaasp, and Oshtaa; Sassanian king for eleven years. Falls into a ditch and dies in the battle with Khoshnavaz. (Vol. 4)

Pirooz: From Kerman, supporter of Khosrow Parviz. (Vol. 4)

Pirooz: Son of Shahpoor and messenger leader in service to the last Sassanian king, Yazdegerd. (Vol. 5)

Plato: Ancient Greek philosopher (fourth century BCE) and student of Socrates. His contribution greatly influenced Western philosophy.

Poolaad: Of Ghondi; ruler deev in the army of Mazandaran with hooves as feet. Killed by Rostam. (Vol. 1)

Poolaad: Tooranian warrior. (Vols. 2)

Poolaadvand: Fierce Tooranian warrior who dwells in the mountains of Chin. Killed by Rostam. (Vol. 2)

Pormaye: Cow that nurses Fereydoon. (Vol. 1)

Pormaye: Fereydoon's brother; same name as the cow that nursed Fereydoon. (Vol. 1)

Raadman: Leader of Armenia under the rule of King Khosrow Parviz. (Vol. 5)

Raadooy: A wise man who advises Maahooy Soori to refrain from killing King Yazdegerd, the last Sassanian king. (Vol. 5)

Raam: Warrior in the army of Bahraam Choobineh along with Yalan Sineh and Izad Goshasp. (Vol. 5)

Raam Barzeen: Governor of Zabolestan under the reign of Bahraam the Hunter and governor of Mada'in under the rule of Kesra Anushiravan; governor of Daaraab-Gerd and Estakhr during the reign of Khosrow Parviz. (Vols. 4-5)

Rajah: Title for an Indian king, prince, or local ruler. (Vol. 4)

Rakhsh: Rostam's horse. Killed by Shaghaad, Rostam's brother. (Vols. 1-3)

Rashnavaad: Warrior leader in the army of Queen Homay. (Vol. 3)

Rezvan: Keeper of paradise. (Vol. 2)

Rivniz: Tous's son-in-law and brother-in-law to Zarasp; Iranian warrior who has forty beautiful sisters. Killed by Foorood. (Vol. 2)

Rivniz: Son of Fariborz and grandson of Kaavoos. Killed by the Tooranians under Kaavoos's reign. (Vol. 2)

Rivniz: Son of Zarasp and Iranian warrior, "worshipper of Aazargoshasp." (Vols. 2-3)

Rohaam: Son of Goodarz and brother of Giv, Bahraam, Hojir, and Shiddush; Iranian warrior under the rule of Kay Kaavoos and Kay Khosrow. (Vols. 1-3)

Rohaam: King of Gilan under the reign of Bahraam the Hunter. (Vol. 4)

Rooeen: Son of Piran (son of Viseh) and Tooranian warrior. Killed by Bijan in the battle of the heroes. (Vols. 1-3)

Roozbeh: King Bahraam the Hunter's grand wise master. (Vol. 4)

Roozbeh: Khosrow Parviz's scribe. (Vol. 5)

Roshanak: Daughter of King Dara and Delarai, and wife of Eskandar; name of Eskandar's wife in Ferdowsi's legend; historically one of Alexander's wives was Roxana, a Bactrian princess, while his Persian wives were Stateira II, daughter of Stateira I and Darius III of Persia, and Parysatis II, daughter of Artaxerxes III of Persia. (Vol. 3)

Rostam: Iranian world hero and son of Zaal and Rudaabeh; marries Shahrbaanoo; father of Faraamarz and Baanoogoshasp. Killed by his brother Shaghaad. (Vols. 1-3)

Rostam: Son of Hormozd (son of Kesra Anushiravan) and leader in the army of Yazdegerd. Killed by Saad, son of Vaghas. (Vol. 5)

Rudaabeh: Daughter of Mehraab and Sindokht; wife of Zaal and mother of Rostam. (Vols. 1-3)

Rudaki: Abu Abd Allah Ja'far ibn Muhammad Rudaki (859-940), the first great poet of the Persian language. (Vol. 4)

Saabeh: Wise man at the court of Kesra Anushiravan. (Vol. 4)

Saad: Son of Vaghas, companion of Mohammad, and conquering Arab. He overthrows King Yazdegerd and the Sassanian Dynasty. (Vol. 5)

Saam: Iranian warrior and head of Manoochehr's army; Nariman's son and Zaal's father. (Vol. 1)

Saam: Nobleman and warrior after the death of Yazdegerd; a descendant of Kay Ghobaad. (Vol. 4)

Saam: From Shiraz, supporter of Khosrow Parviz. (Vol. 4)

Saaveh: Relative of Kaamoos and warrior ally of Afraasiyaab. Killed by Rostam. (Vol. 2)

Saaveh: Warrior in Esfandiar's army. (Vol. 3)

Saaveh, King: Ruler who advances with an army of Turks to challenge Sassanian
King Hormozd and his host led by Bahraam Choobineh; father of the Emperor of Chin. Killed by Bahraam Choobineh. (Vol. 4)

Sabbaah: King of Yemen and ally of Kay Khosrow in the great battle against Afraasiyaab. (Vol. 3)

Saghil: Rumi prince, son of the Caesar, and brother of Katayoon. (Vol. 3)

Sahi: Daughter of Sarv, King of Yemen, and wife of Iraj, son of Fereydoon. (Vol. 1)

Salm: Son of Fereydoon and Shahrnaaz; brother of Toor and Iraj. (Vol. 1)

Samanid Dynasty: Ruled Iran from 819 to 999. (Vol. 3)

Samkanan: Warrior in the army of Kay Khosrow in the great battle; father of Aaveh. (Vol. 3)

Sanjeh: One of the deevs in the service of Mazandaran; guard of the mountain on the path to the White Deev. (Vol. 1)

Sarguis: Rumi army leader during the reign of Khosrow Parviz. (Vol. 5)

Sarkesh: Musician and singer at the court of Khosrow Parviz. (Vol. 5)

Sarv: King of Yemen and father of the three maidens who marry Fereydoon's sons Toor, Salm, and Iraj. (Vol. 1)

Sassan: Named Ardeshir, son of King Bahman and brother of Homay/Chehrzaad; father of Sassan. (Vol. 3)

Sassan: Son of Sassan (son of Bahman). (Vol. 3)

Sassan: Son of Dara, flees Iran and goes to India, where he dies. He leaves behind a son named Sassan. (Vols. 3-4)

Sassan: Son of Sassan and descendant of Bahman/Ardeshir; becomes one of Babak's shepherds and marries Babak's daughter. They have a son named Ardeshir Babakan. (Vol. 4)

Sassanian Dynasty: Ruled Iran from 224 to 651. (Vols. 3-4)

Sepahram: Brother of Afraasiyaab and Tooranian leader. Killed by Hojir. (Vols. 2-3)

Sepansaar: Army warrior in the army of Khosrow Parviz in the fight against Bahraam Choobineh. (Vol. 5)

Sepinood: Daughter of Shangal, King of India, who weds Bahraam the Hunter when he travels disguised as an emissary. (Vol. 4)

Sevorg: Indian leader assigned to rule by Eskandar. (Vol. 3)

Shaavaran: Father of Zangueh. (Vols. 1-3)

Shabaahang: Farhaad's white horse. (Vol. 2)

Shabaahang: Bijan's horse. (Vol. 3)

Shabdeez: Mehraab's horse (Vol. 1)

Shabdeez: Ghobaad's horse (Vol. 1); Giv's horse (Vols. 1-2).

Shabdeez: Bahraam the Hunter's horse. (Vol. 4)

Shabrang: Bijan's horse. (Vol. 2)

Shadan: Son of Barzeen. (Vol. 4)

Shaghaad: Rostam's brother, born from Zaal and a musically inclined slave. Killed by Rostam. (Vol. 3)

Shahan Goraaz: Warrior in the army of Bahraam Choobineh. (Vol. 5)

Shahooy: Haftvaad's eldest son. Killed in the battle with Ardeshir. (Vol. 4)

Shahpoor: Iranian warrior who serves the kings from Fereydoon to Lohraasp. (Vols. 1-3)

Shahpoor: Second Ashkanian king. (Vol. 4)

Shahpoor: The son of Ardeshir and Ardavan's daughter; second Sassanian king; weds Mehrak's daughter with whom he has a son named Ormazd. (Vol. 4)

Shahpoor: Son of Ormazd, son of Nersi, and Sassanian king who rules for seventy years. The Arabs call him Zolaktaaf because he pierces his captives' shoulder blades. He marries his cousin, Malekeh, the daughter of Taaer the Arab, and his aunt Nooshah. (Vol. 4)

Shahpoor: Son of King Shahpoor who is too young to rule so his uncle Ardeshir is made regent of the Sassanian Dynasty. Once he matures, he rules for five years and four months. Killed by a canopy pole during a windstorm. (Vol. 4)

Shahpoor: Descendant of Mehrak and enemy of Soofraay under the rule of Ghobaad (son of Pirooz). (Vol. 4)

Shahpoor: Wise leader under the rule of King Khosrow Parviz; father of Pirooz. (Vol. 5)

Shahrbaanoo: Giv's sister and Rostam's wife; mother of Faraamarz. (Vol. 2)

Shahrguir: Warrior who takes Keydroosh and his wife captive near Spain. (Vol. 3)

Shahrnaaz: Daughter or sister of Jamsheed; concubine of Zahaak before she weds Fereydoon and gives birth to Salm and Toor. (Vol. 1)

Shahrguir: Commander of Ardeshir's army. (Vol. 4)

Shahriar: Son of Khosrow Parviz and Shirin. Killed by his father's enemies. (Vol. 5)

Shahrooy: Wise man and servant of the crown who governs the world while Shahpoor, son of Ormazd, matures. (Vol. 4)

Shahrooy: Wise man who advises Maahooy Soori to refrain from killing King Yazdegerd, the last Sassanian king. (Vol. 5)

Shaknan: Iranian nobleman and warrior under the rule of Yazdegerd. (Vol. 4)

Shamaasaas: Tooranian warrior in the army of Afraasiyaab. Killed in battle by Ghaaran. (Vol. 1)

Shambeleed: Third daughter of the wealthy Barzeen; sister of Maah-Aafareed and Faraanak; skilled dancer. The three sisters wed Bahraam the Hunter. (Vol. 4)

Shammaakh: Ruler of Syria and ally of Kay Khosrow in the great battle against Afraasiyaab. (Vol. 3)

Shamiran: From Shakni, an ally of Afraasiyaab. (Vol. 2)

Shammas: Commander of the army of Nooshzaad, son of Kesra Anushiravan. (Vol. 4)

Shangal: From India, an ally of Afraasiyaab. Killed by Rostam. (Vol. 2)

Shangal: King of India and enemy of Bahraam the Hunter. (Vol. 4)

Shayban: A tribe that resided in Iraq and the Persian Gulf region in pre-Islamic times. (Vol. 4)

Shemiran Shah: Ancestor of the Sassanians and of Bahraam the Hunter. (Vol. 4)

Shiddasp: Minister under the rule of Tahmures. (Vol. 1)

Shiddasp: Son of King Goshtaasp and brother of Ardeshir. Killed by Arjaasp's warrior. (Vol. 3)

Shiddeh: Also referred to as Pashang. Afraasiyaab's son and Tooranian leader who fights in the great war. Killed by Kay Khosrow. (Vols. 2-3)

Shiddush: Son of Goodarz (son of Kashvaad) and an Iranian warrior serving the kings from Manoochehr to Kay Khosrow. (Vols. 1-3)

Shirezil: Warrior in the army of Khosrow Parviz in the war against Bahraam Choobineh. (Vol. 5)

Shirkhoon: Guide of Zabolestan in Zaal's retinue. (Vol. 3)

Shirin: One of Khosrow Parviz's favorite wives (with Mariam and Gordieh); together they have four sons: Nastoor, Shahriar, Foorood, and Mardanesheh. Kills herself after the death of Khosrow Parviz. (Vol. 5)

Shiroo: Son of King Goshtaasp. Killed by Arjaasp's troops. (Vol. 3)

Shirooy: Son of Bahraam and commander in the army of Kesra Anushiravan. (Vol. 4)

Shirooy: Also known as Ghobaad, is the son of Khosrow Parviz and Mariam (daughter of the Caesar) and father of Ardeshir; Sassanian king who rules for seven months. Poisoned by his enemies. (Vol. 5)

Shirui: Warrior in Toor's army. (Vol. 1)

Shiruye: Iranian warrior and general in Manoochehr's army. (Vol. 1)

Shiruye: Iranian warrior in Lohraasp's army and grandson of Giv. (Vol. 3)

Shirzad: Herald who serves Kesra Anushiravan. (Vol. 4)

Shitarakh: Tooranian warrior. (Vol. 2)

Shoaib: Taazian leader from the Arabian Peninsula from the lineage of Ghotaib. Killed by Daaraab's troops. (Vol. 3)

Shohbeh Moghaira: An Arab warrior and envoy in service to Saad. (Vol. 5)

Shohreh: Warrior in Bahraam the Hunter's army who is appointed King of Tooran. (Vol. 4)

Siaamak: Son of Kiumars; father of Hooshang. Killed by the deev. (Vol. 1)

Siaamak: Tooranian warrior. Killed by Goraazeh in the battle of the heroes. (Vol. 3)

Siaavosh: Son of Iranian Kay Kaavoos and descendant of Tooranian Garsivaz. (Vol. 2)

Siah Chashm: Servant of King Farrokhzaad who betrays him and kills him. (Vol. 5)

Simah Borzeen: Friend of Bahraam Azarmahan who is deceived by him at the king's command. (Vol. 4)

Simorgh: Bird of knowledge that rescues and raises Zaal. (Vol. 2)

Sindokht: Mother of Rudaabeh and wife of Mehraab. (Vol. 1)

Sohraab: Son of Rostam and Tahmineh. Killed by Rostam. (Vol. 1)

Sombaaz: Noble leader in the army of Bahraam Choobineh. (Vol. 5)

Soofraay: Descendant of Ghaaran, from Shiraz; governor of Kabolestan, Bost, Ghaznein, and Zabolestan, who becomes the vizier of Balaash (youngest son of King Pirooz); father of Zarmehr. Executed at the order of King Ghobaad. (Vol. 4)

Sooroosh: Archangel able to hear and relay divine messages. (Vols. 1-3)

Sooroosh: Indian mystic and astrologer at the court of Yazdegerd. (Vol. 4)

Soossanek: One of the four miller's daughters who are wedded to

Bahraam the Hunter; name meaning small lily. (Vol. 4)

Sootooh: Sorcerer in the service of King Arjaasp. (Vol. 3)

Sorkheh: Afraasiyaab's son and Tooranian leader. Killed at the order of Zavaareh. (Vol. 2)

Sudaabeh: Daughter of the King of Haamaavaran; wife of Kay Kaavoos. (Vols. 1-2)

Sultan Mahmoud, Abul Ghassem: Ghaznavid ruler of Iran (999-1030) during Ferdowsi's later years.

Taaer: Ghassanian king and Arab warrior from Syria who invades Iran and abducts Nooshah, Nersi's daughter. They have a daughter he names Malekeh. Killed by Shahpoor. (Vol. 4)

Taazi/Taazian: Bedouins or tribes living in the land of Arabia or Mesopotamia (between the Tigris and the Euphrates), also "field of warriors" or "field of spear-riders"; worshippers of the Black Stone or Kaaba, as given by the Prophet Mohammad; symbolic rather than cultural, national, or geographical.

Tabah: Tooranian warrior in King Arjaasp's host. (Vol. 3)

Tabaak: Ruler of the city of Jahrom and ally of Ardeshir; father to seven sons. (Vol. 4)

Tahmineh: Wife of Rostam and mother of Sohraab; daughter of the king of Samangan. (Vol. 1)

Tahmures: Son of Hooshang and third King of Iran; deev-binder who rules for thirty years. (Vol. 1)

Tajov: Ruler of Gorooguerd, a province of Tooran-Zamin; of Iranian lineage but also Afraasiyaab's son-in-law. (Vol. 2)

Talhand: Son of Maay, Indian ruler, and half-brother of Gao. (Vol. 4)

Taliman: Iranian warrior in Nozar's army (Vol. 1); ally of Kay Khosrow (Vol. 3).

Tarkhan of Chin: Title assigned to rulers of Chin, allies of Tooran-Zamin. (Vols. 2-4)

Tavaabeh: Name of a family of warriors loyal to Kay Khosrow, led by Barteh. (Vol. 2)

Tevorg: Sentinel who watches over Afraasiyaab's city. (Vol. 2)

Tevorg: Chini warrior in the army of the Emperor of Chin. Killed by Gordieh, Bahraam Choobineh's sister. (Vol. 5)

Teynoosh: The Rumi, was the Caesar's ambassador during the reign of Yazdegerd. (Vol. 4)

Teynoosh: Son of Keydafeh and brother of Keydroosh. (Vol. 3)

Toghrol: A black bird offered to King Bahraam by the Emperor of Chin to assist in the hunt. (Vol. 4)

Tokhaar: Warrior in Foorood's army and Foorood's advisor. (Vol. 2)

Tokhaar: Ruler of Dahestan and leader in Kay Khosrow's army from the noble race of Vashmeh. (Vol. 3)

Tokhaar: Warrior in the time of Sassanian King Ardeshir. (Vol. 5)

Tokhaareh: Warrior in the army of Khosrow Parviz in the war against Bahraam Choobineh. (Vol. 5)

Toor: Son of Fereydoon and Shahrnaaz; brother of Salm and Iraj. Killed by Manoochehr. (Vol. 1)

Tous: Son of Nozar, brother of Gostaham, and commander of troops under Kay Khosrow; bearer of the Kaaviani banner and the golden boots. Loses his life in the blizzard after Kay Khosrow disappears. (Vols. 1-3)

Turks: The Turks of The Shahnameh are nomadic tribes moving through the lands east of Iran with no relation to today's Turkey, which sits west of Iran and which was established in the eleventh century upon the conquest of the Turks by the Byzantines. (Vols. 1-3)

Turkish boy: Servant of Zaal during his courtship with Rudaabeh. (Vol. 1)

Tuvarg: Tooranian warrior. (Vol. 3)

Ulaad: Landowner in the fifth stage of Rostam's epic quest. Ultimately, Rostam makes him ruler of Mazandaran. (Vol. 1)

Ulaad's guardian: Unnamed guardian of the field owned by Ulaad. (Vol. 1)

Varaazaad: King of Sepijaab and warrior who fights for Afraasiyaab. Killed by Faraamarz. (Vol. 2)

Vashmeh: Name of a family, led by Tokhaar, ruler of Dahestan, ally of Kay Khosrow in the great battle. (Vol. 3)

Viseh: Father of Piran, Pilsam, Nastihan, Kolbaad, Baarmaan, and Hoomaan; Tooranian army leader and Afraasiyaab's minister. (Vols. 1-2)

White Deev: Leader in Mazandaran. Killed by Rostam. (Vol. 1)

Wife of the laundryman: Raises Daaraab, son of Homay and Bahman, with her husband. (Vol. 3)

Witch: Woman who conspires with Sudaabeh to avow her innocence. (Vol. 2)

Yajooj and Majooj: Two tribes residing in Manchuria and causing mayhem across the neighboring lands.

Yalan Sineh: Warrior in the army of King Hormozd and supporter of Bahraam Choobineh when he rebels against the king. (Vols. 5)

Yazdan: Plural of Yzad (divine), encompasses all of divinity, Creator of all that is manifested, unmanifested, and all that is yet to come into existence.

Yazdegerd: Brother of Sassanian King Bahraam who rises to kingship and rules for thirty years; is referred to as Yazdegerd the Wicked. Killed by the white hippopotamus. (Vol. 4)

Yazdegerd: Son of Bahraam the Hunter, who reigns for eighteen years; father of Hormoz and Pirooz. (Vol. 4)

Yazdegerd: A scribe under the rule of Kesra Anushiravan. (Vol. 4)

Yazdegerd: Grandson of Kesra Anushiravan who rules as Sassanian king for sixteen years. (Vol. 5)

Yazdegerd: Descendant of Kesra Anushiravan; the last Sassanian king, who rules for twenty years. Killed at the order of Maahooy Soori by the miller Khosrow. (Vol. 5)

Yzad: Singular of Yazdan, Divine Creator.

Zaadsham: Afraasiyaab's grandfather and Pashang's father. (Vols. 1-3)

Zaal: Saam's son; Rudaabeh's husband and Rostam's father; also called Dastan-e Zand by Simorgh and Zaal-e Zar by Saam; father of Shaghaad. (Vols. 1-3)

Zahaak: Son of Mardaas and fifth King of Iran, who rules for one thousand years. Captured by Fereydoon. (Vol. 1)

Zangaleh: Tooranian warrior. Killed by Fooroohal. (Vol. 3)

Zangueh: Son of Shaavaran; Iranian warrior under the rules of Kay Kaavoos and Kay Khosrow. (Vols. 1-3)

Zangooy: Warrior in the army of Khosrow Parviz in the war against Bahraam Choobineh. (Vol. 5)

Zangooy: Chini warrior in the army of the Emperor of Chin during the reign of Khosrow Parviz. (Vol. 5)

Zarasp: Son of King Manoochehr and brother of Nozar; Kay Khosrow's treasurer. (Vols. 1-3)

Zarasp: Son of Tous (son of Nozar) and brother-in-law of Rivniz. A warrior under the rule of Kay Khosrow. Killed at the hands of Foorood. (Vol. 2)

Zarir: Son of Lohraasp; brother of Goshtaasp. Killed by Biderafsh, Arjaasp's brother. (Vol. 3)

Zarmehr: Son of Soofraay who forgives Ghobaad for having killed his father. (Vol. 4)

Zartosht: Zoroaster or Zarathustra, Iranian prophet who lived in the sixth century BCE. (Vol. 3)

Zartosht: Grand wise master under the rule of Kesra Anushiravan who is poisoned by Hormozd Shah. (Vol. 5)

Zarvan: King Kesra Anushiravan's chamberlain and enemy of Mahbood. Killed after the king discovers that he conspired against Mahbood. (Vol. 4)

Zavaareh: Rostam's brother. Killed by Shaghaad. (Vols. 1-3)

Zerreh: Father of Garooy and Arjang; Tooranian warrior. (Vol. 2)

Zhendehrazm: Son of the King of Samangan and brother of Tahmineh; uncle of Sohraab. Killed by Rostam. (Vol. 1)

Zirak: A wise man who interprets Zahaak's dream of Fereydoon. (Vol. 1)

Zohir: Iranian warrior in the army of Kay Khosrow. (Vol. 3)

Zu: Son of Tahmaasp, descendant of Fereydoon; and ninth King of Iran, who rules for five years and dies at the age of 86. (Vol. 1)

THE KIANIAN KINGS: LINE OF SUCCESSION
From Kiumars to Kay Kaavoos

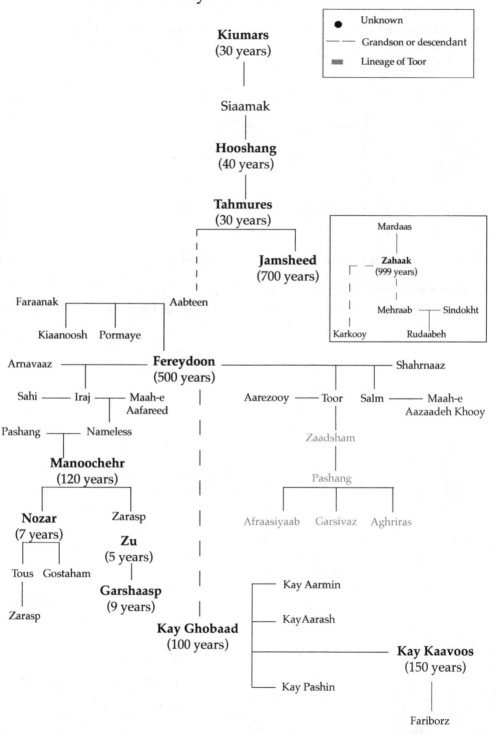

THE KIANIAN KINGS: LINE OF SUCCESSION
From Kay Khosrow to Eskandar

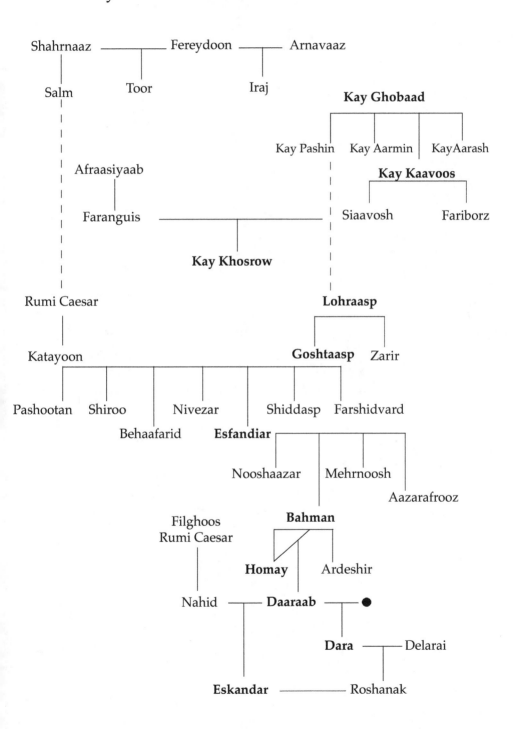

THE ASHKANIAN KINGS: LINE OF SUCCESSION
According to Ferdowsi

Moolookeh Tavayef

Ghobaad
|
|
|
|

Ashk

Shahpoor

Goodarz

Bijan

Nersi

Ormazd

Aarash

Bahraam

Ardavan
|
|
Bahman

THE SASSANIAN KINGS: LINE OF SUCCESSION
From Ardeshir Babakan to Yazdegerd the Wicked

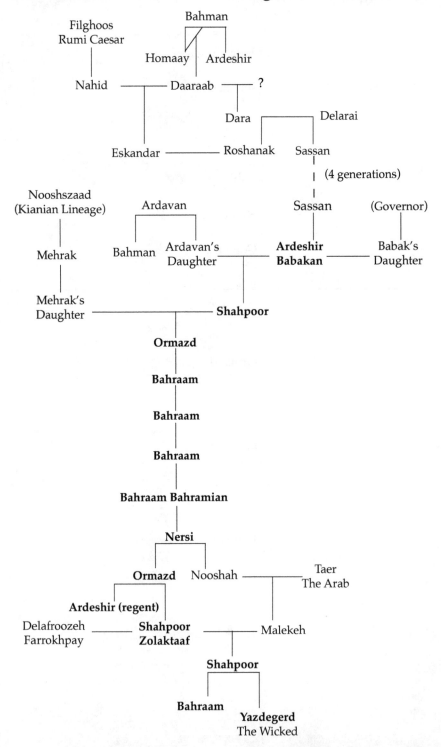

THE SASSANIAN KINGS: LINE OF SUCCESSION
From Yazdegerd the Wicked to Yazdegerd

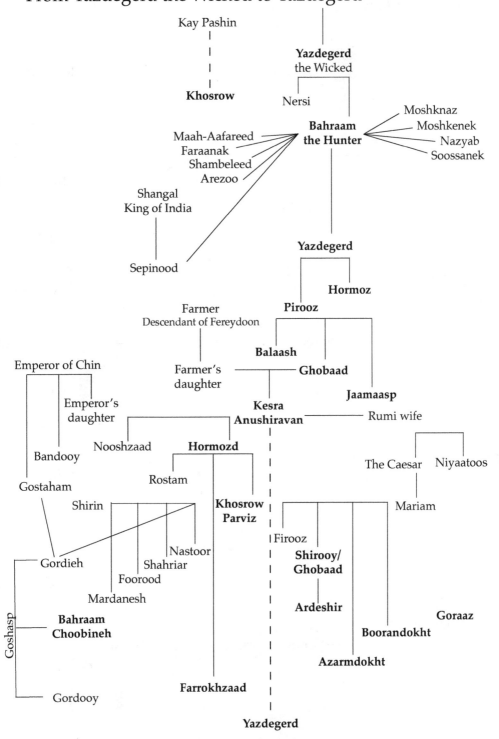

THE IRANIAN HEROES: LINE OF SUCCESSION
Kianian Period

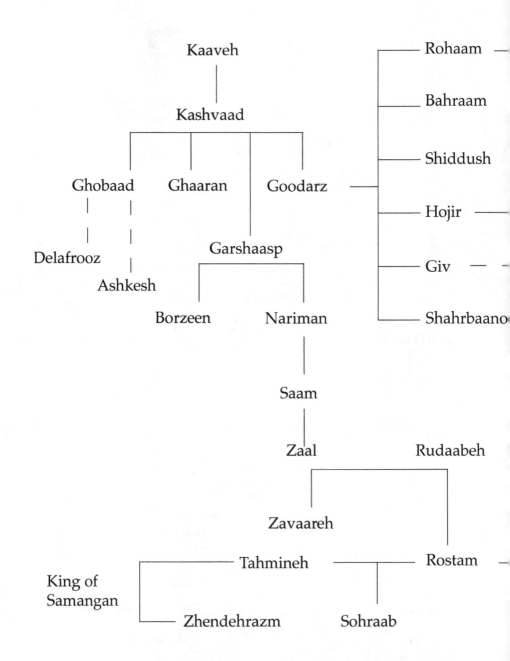

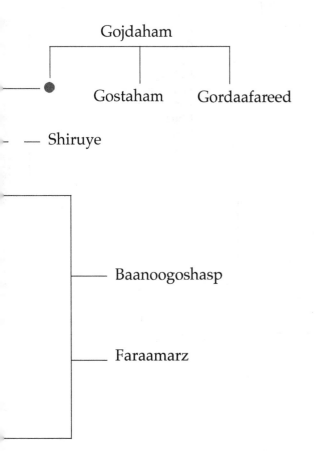

Farhaad

Gojdaham

Gostaham   Gordaafareed

Shiruye

Baanoogoshasp

Faraamarz

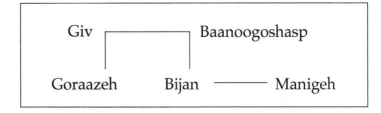

Giv   Baanoogoshasp

Goraazeh   Bijan   Manigeh

The Iranian Warriors
Manoochehr-Kay Khosrow

Aarash
Aaveh
Borzeen
Delafrooz
Farhaad
Fooroohal
Gargooy
Goraazeh
Gorazm
Gorgeen
Ketmareh
Khorraad
Manooshan
Milaad
Rashnavaad
Rohaam
Saaveh
Samkanan
Shaavaran
Shahpoor
Shiddush
Taliman
Tokhaar
Zangueh
Zohir

The Iranian Warriors
Lohraasp-Esfandiar

Aarash
Ardeshir
Bitghoon
Delafrooz
Esfandiar
Gargooy
Garukhan
Ghaaran
Gorazm
Gueraami
Iraj
Jaamaasp
Janoosyar
Ketmaareh
Khuzan
Maahiar
Rashnavaad

The Iranian Warriors and Wise Men
Sassanian Period

Aarash
Aazaad Sarv
Andian
Andman
Armani
Azar Goshasp
Aazargoshasp
Baabooy
Babak
Bahraam
Bahraam
Bahraam Choobineh
Bahraam of Pirooz
Balooy
Bandooy
Barsam
Behzaad
Behzaad of Barzeen
Bijan Bivard
Bozorgmehr
Daad Barzeen
Dara Panah
Faraaeen
Farhaad
Farrokhzaad
Farrokhzaad
Garshaasp
Garsioon
Ghaaran
Ghaaran, son of Borzmehr
Gharakhan
Golbooy
Gord
Gordooy
Gostaham
Goshasp
Hamdam Goshasp
Hormozd Shahran
Hormozd son of Khorraad
Izad Goshasp
Janfoorooz
Khazarvan
Khonjast
Khorraad

Khorraad
Khorraad Borzeen
Khorsheed
Khosrow Khazarvan
King of Alaan Mahbood
Konda Goshasp
Koot
Maahooy Soori
Mehr Barzeen, son of Khorraad
Mehr Pirooz, son of Behzaad
Mehran
Mehran Setaad
MilaadOstaad (son of Barzeen)
Nastooh
Ormazd
Oshtaa, son of Pirooz
Ostaay
Pirooz
Pirooz
Pirooz son of Shahpoor
Raadman
Raam Barzeen
Randooy
Rohaam
Rostam son of Hormozd Saam
Saam, son of Esfandiar
Sarguis
Sepansaar
Shahpoor
Shahpoor
Shaknan
Shammaas
Shirezil
Shirooy
Sombaaz
Soofraay
Shohreh
Tokhaar
Tokhaareh
Yalan Sineh
Yazdegerd
Zangooy
Zarmehr

THE TOORANIAN KINGS AND WARRIORS:
LINE OF SUCCESSION Kianian Period

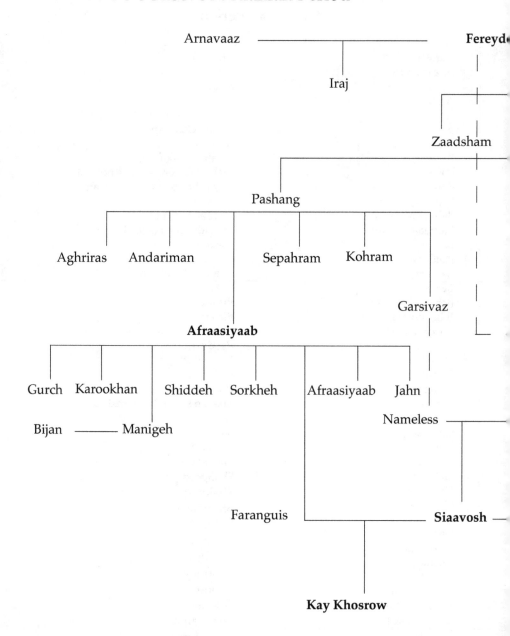

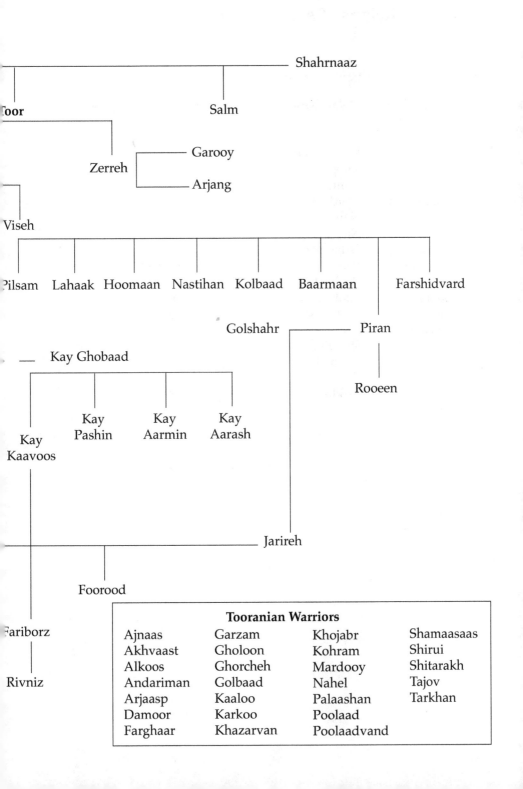

Shahrnaaz

Toor

Salm

Zerreh

Garooy

Arjang

Viseh

Pilsam   Lahaak   Hoomaan   Nastihan   Kolbaad   Baarmaan   Farshidvard

Golshahr ———— Piran

Kay Ghobaad

Rooeen

Kay
Pashin

Kay
Aarmin

Kay
Aarash

Kay
Kaavoos

Jarireh

Foorood

Fariborz

Rivniz

Tooranian Warriors

Ajnaas	Garzam	Khojabr	Shamaasaas
Akhvaast	Gholoon	Kohram	Shirui
Alkoos	Ghorcheh	Mardooy	Shitarakh
Andariman	Golbaad	Nahel	Tajov
Arjaasp	Kaaloo	Palaashan	Tarkhan
Damoor	Karkoo	Poolaad	
Farghaar	Khazarvan	Poolaadvand	

THE TOORANIAN HEROES:
Under the Reigns of Afraasiyaab and Arjaasp

Afraasiyaab's Warriors

Aghriras	Kebord
Ajnaas	Khazarvan
Akhvaast	Khojabr
Alkoos	Kohram
Andariman	Mardooy
Arjaasp	Nahel
Borzvilla	Nastooh
Damoor	Ostaghilaa
Farghaar	Palaashan
Garzam	Poolaad
Gholoon	Poolaadvand
Ghorcheh	Shamaasaas
Golbaad	Shirui
Illa	Shitarakh
Jaranjas	Siaamak
Kaakooleh	Tajov
Kaaloo	Tarkhan
Karkoo	

Arjaasp's Warriors

Ayaas
Ardeshir
Biderafsh
Garsivan
Gorgsaar
Hooshdeev
Khashaash
Kohram
Sootooh
Tabah
Tuvarg
Zangaleh

Glossary of Geographical Markers

Aal, Fort: A small fort in Iran.

Aarayesheh Rum: Rumi fort captured by Kesra Anushiravan; name meaning the ornament of Rum.

Aarman-Zamin: On the border of Tooran-Zamin and Iran-Zamin.

Aavaazeh, Castle of: Property of Parmoodeh, Emperor of Chin and son of King Saaveh.

Aazar Abadegan: Refers to today's Azerbaijan.

Aden: An ancient port city in Yemen that is today the temporary capital.

Ahvaz: A city in southwest Iran; capital of the province of Khuzestan.

Alaanan: Region in northwest Iran, north of the Aras River; a part of the Caucasus.

Alborz, Mount: Regarded as a holy mountain in myths and legends. In geographical terms, it stands in northern Iran.

Almas River: Perhaps beyond the borders of Tooran-Zamin.

Altoonieh: Unclear of the location.

Amol: A city in Iran where Fereydoon resides before taking residence in his capital city of Tammisheh. Situated in the Mazandaran Province, near the Alborz mountains.

Amol, Mount: Perhaps another name for Alborz.

Amoorieh: A Rumi city that no longer exists but would be in present-day Turkey.

Amoy: A city that appears to be somewhere in Chin.

Amu: A city near Amu Darya (Jayhoon River).

Andalusia: Southern region of Spain.

Andaraab: A city in present-day Afghanistan.

Andiv: An ancient city. Unclear of the location.

Antioch: An ancient Greek city that would be in today's Turkey, near the city of Antakya.

Ardabil: An ancient city in northwestern Iran; it was founded by Sassanian King Pirooz and previously named Baadan-Pirooz.

Arman or Arman-Zamin: On the border of Tooran-Zamin and Iran-Zamin.

Armenia: Armenia.

Arvand: A river also known as the Shatt al-Arab River. It begins at the confluence of the Tigris and Euphrates rivers.

Asprooz, Mount: Perhaps a mythical mountain on the way to Mazandaran where Kaavoos is blinded by the deevs.

Assyria: Mesopotamia.

Azerbaijan: A region in northwestern Iran.

Baadan-Pirooz: A city founded by Pirooz, Sassanian king, along with the city of Pirooz-Ram; its name was later changed to Ardabil.

Baamian: A city in present-day Afghanistan.

Babel: Or Babylon, ancient city in Babylonia that is situated in today's Iraq.

Badakhshan: In today's northeast Afghanistan and southeast Tajikistan.

Baghdad: Capital of Iraq.

Baheleh: Perhaps a reference to Deir al-Balah, an ancient city that would be located in the Gaza Strip.

Bahraam, Mount: The name for the heap of heads severed in the battle between Bahraam Choobineh and the Emperor of Chin, Parmood-eh.

Bahraamcheed: Meaning "the killings of Bahraam," it is the name of the heap of corpses left by Bahraam Choobineh in the battle with Khosrow Parviz.

Bahrain: A country on the Persian Gulf, once part of the Persian Empire.

Baikand: Must be a fictional region on the border of Iran.

Bait-Al Moghaddas: Jerusalem; meaning pure city.

Balkh: A city in Iran-Zamin, situated in today's Afghanistan.

Balkh Bami: Bami is the old name for Balkh, a city in ancient Iran, today situated in Afghanistan, south of the Jayhoon River (Amu Darya).

Baluchistan: A province in today's Iran bordering Pakistan and Afghanistan.

Barda: A city in present-day Azerbaijan that once was the capital of Caucasian Albania.

Barein: A city in Iran-Zamin.

Barghoveh: With Jaz, perhaps a village under the rule of Bahraam the Hunter.

Barkeh-yeh Ardeshir: A city founded by King Ardeshir.

Bastam: A city in the province of Semnan, in north-central Iran.

Bidaad: Meaning unjust, also referred to as "city of battle"; a city built by Toor with spells and magic in Tooran-Zamin and populated by man-eaters.

Bost: A city and river east of Sistan; situated in today's Afghanistan and now named Lashkargah.

Borz: Another name for Mount Alborz.

Bozgoosh: Area on the way to the dwelling of the White Deev.

Bukhara: A town in Tooran-Zamin; ancient city situated in today's Uzbekistan.

Chaadj: A city near in Tooran-Zamin; near today's Tashkent in Uzbekistan.

Chagal: A city in Tooran-Zamin, in today's Turkestan region.

Chaghan: Or Chaghaniyan, land independent of Iran-Zamin or Tooran-Zamin; a region in Afghanistan north of the Jayhoon River; ruled by an ally of Afraasiyaab.

Chaghvan: A city in the Far East, perhaps Changwon in South Korea.

Chalus: A seaside town on the Caspian Sea; may refer to Mount Koos or Caucasus.

Chichast: Same as Lake Urmia in northwestern Iran in Azerbaijan.

Chin: China; generally refers to lands to the east of Iran, as Rum represents the lands to the west. In later stories, Chin is part of Tooran-Zamin.

Chinvad, Bridge: Or Chinvat, is a bridge in Zoroastrianism to be crossed upon death. It connects the world of the living to the world of the dead. If a person has been wicked, its width is that of a strand of hair. Its edge is as sharp as the blade of a sword. If a person has been virtuous, the bridge is amply wide to cross.

Constantinople: Once Byzantium, this city and capital of the Byzantine and Ottoman empires was renamed by Constantine the Great in 324. In the early 20th century, the name of Istanbul was adopted as the capital of modern Turkey.

Coshmaihan: A region around the city of Marv, near the Jayhoon River.

Ctesiphon: An ancient city near the Tigris River and southeast of Baghdad; the royal capital of the Persian Empire during Parthian and Sassanian times over a period of eight hundred years.

Daaraab-Guerd: A city founded by King Daaraab.

Daghooy: Hunting plains near the border of Tooran-Zamin.

Dahestan: Presently located in Turkmenistan and northern Iran.

Dahr: Land outside the borders of Iran-Zamin or Tooran-Zamin.

Dajleh: Arabic for Tigris River.

Damavand, Mount: The highest peak on the Alborz mountain range.

Dambar: A place in today's eastern Afghanistan.

Damghan: A city east of Tehran.

Dashtgol: A small fort in Iran.

Deylam: A city in the Gilan Province of Iran, near the Caspian Sea.

Djaz: Name of a region in ancient Rum.

Dook: Somewhere on the way to Aazar Abadegan.

Eram: A Persian garden in Shiraz, Iran; also a heavenly garden in the desert; it is said to appear to the traveler like a mirage.

Eskandarieh: Or Alexandria, an ancient Egyptian city founded in 331 BCE by Eskandar (Alexander the Great).

Estakhr: An ancient city in southern Iran in the Pars Province, north of Persepolis; seat of Kashvaad's palace.

Euphrates River: River in Mesopotamia. It flows from Syria to Iraq and into the Tigris River.

Faariaab: A city in present-day Afghanistan.

Faarghin: An ancient Rumi city situated in today's Turkey.

Fakhrum: A small fort in Iran.

Farab: An ancient city on the Silk Road in present-day Kazakhstan.

Fasghoon, Forest of: A forest in Rum (perhaps fictional) where a fierce wolf "with the body of a dragon and the strength of a whale" dwells.

Fort Bahman: A fortress on the border of Iran-Zamin and Tooran-Zamin.

Gang: May be an ancient city on the edge of the Sayhoon River (Syr Darya); seat of Afraasiyaab for some time.

Gang-Behesht: Same as Gang-Dej, the city built by Siaavosh.

Gang-Dej: A fort city built by Siaavosh past the Sea of Chin.

Germaneh: Unknown location.

Ghaaf, Mount: A mythical mountain often depicted in images as encircling the world.

Ghaaran, Mount: Perhaps a fictional mountain somewhere in Iran.

Ghabchaagh: A region in Tooran-Zamin.

Ghajghaarbaashi: A town in Tooran-Zamin, situated in today's Turkey.

Ghalinus, Fort: Rumi castle captured by Kesra Anushiravan.

Gharcheh: A city in Iran-Zamin.

Gharchehgan: Land around Gharcheh in Iran-Zamin.

Ghatan: A city located in present-day Afghanistan.

Ghaznein: A city in Iran-Zamin, in present-day Afghanistan.

Ghebchaagh: A village in northwestern Iran near Lake Urmia.

Ghennooj: A city near or in India.

Ghobaad: A city built by King Ghobaad between Ahvaz and Pars that the Arabs called Awan, situated in present-day western Iran.

Gholoo, Mountain of: Unclear of the location but in Tooran-Zamin.

Gholzom, Sea of: The Red Sea, between Egypt, Saudi Arabia, Sudan, and Yemen.

Ghom: Or Qom, a city between Tehran and Isfahan.

Ghoor: A province in Afghanistan.

Ghoz: A city in Iran-Zamin.

Gilan: A province in today's northwestern Iran bordering the Caspian Sea; Iranian warrior shields often come from this region.

Gilan, Sea of: Caspian Sea.

Golzarioon: A fictional river in Tooran-Zamin.

Gombadan, Fortress of: A castle in Iran where Esfandiar is locked up for some time at his father's order.

Goor: Or Khorreh-yeh Ardeshir; the city of Firozabad in the Pars province of Iran.

Goozganan: A city in present-day Afghanistan.

Gorgan: A city in northern Iran; capital of the Golestan Province.

Gorganj: Land in the region of Khaarazm.

Gorgsaaran: Meaning "land of the wolf," marks the border separating Iran-Zamin from Mazandaran.

Gorooguerd: A province of Tooran-Zamin.

Gorzban: Unclear location.

Green Sea: Probably a sea in the Far East, perhaps the Sea of Japan.

Gundeh Shahpoor: Or Gundeh Shahpur, is a city built by King Ardeshir for his son Shahpoor; it is situated in southwestern Iran and is the literary center of the Sassanian Dynasty in the province of Khuzestan.

Guraabeh: Burial site of Saam, the hero.

Guran: In today's Lorestan Province of Iran.

Haamaavaran: Perhaps a fictional land; perhaps a reference to Yemen.

Habash: Or al-Habash, an ancient part of eastern Africa situated in present-day Ethiopia.

Halab: Equivalent to the city of Aleppo in today's Syria; once part of the Persian Empire during the Achaemenid period.

Hamaavan, Mount: A site of retreat for Iranian warriors in Tooran-Zamin.

Hamedan: A city and a province in western Iran.

Haraah: A region ruled by an ally of Afraasiyaab; perhaps al-Harrah in today's western Saudi Arabia, near Jordan.

Haroom: A fictional city of women where each resident has a male breast and a female breast.

Hejaz: A western region on the Arabian Peninsula including the cities of Mecca and Medina.

Hendia: An ancient Rumi city that is Diyarbakir in present-day Turkey.

Herat: Or Hari, a city in Iran-Zamin, situated in today's Afghanistan.

Hirmand: On the border of Iran and Afghanistan.

Hirmand River: Flowing through Sistan and through today's Afghanistan.

House of Goshtaasp: A fire temple founded by King Goshtaasp.

Impregnable castle: The residence of Arjaasp in the land of Chin.

Iran-Zamin: Land of Iran.

Isfahan: A city in Iran, south of Tehran; seat of the hero Giv, where he receives Kay Khosrow upon his arrival in Iran-Zamin.

Jahrom: A city in the Iranian province of Fars.

Jaram: A city situated in today's Afghanistan.

Jayhoon River: Also known as the Oxus River (in Greek and Roman texts) and Amu Darya; located in present-day Afghanistan.

Jaz: With Barghoveh, perhaps a village or hunting plains under the rule of Bahraam the Hunter.

Jeddah: A port city on the Arabian Peninsula by the Red Sea.

Kaaba: Meaning "cube" in Arabic, in pre-Islamic times, it was a holy site of pilgrimage for Taazian Bedouin tribes and idol worshippers in Mecca, an important city and a center for trade. After Islam, it became a shrine at the center of the Great Mosque. Muslims everywhere face its direction at the time of their prayers; some believe that it was built by Abraham and his son Ismail.

Kaasseh Rood: Perhaps a fictional river in Tooran-Zamin.

Kaat: Capital of Khaarazm, or Chorasmia, in ancient times, situated in west-central Asia, south of the Aral Sea.

Kaarzi: A region of Pars near Shiraz.

Kabol: A city in today's Afghanistan.

Kadesia: A region on the Arabian Peninsula, site of the battle between the Arabs and the Iranians at the time of the Arab conquest.

Kahan: Land independent of Iran or Tooran; its ruler is Kahaar, ally of Afraasiyaab.

Kalaat: A city in present-day Afghanistan.

Kandahar: A city in today's southern Afghanistan.

Karkh: Name for the ancient western section of Baghdad.

Karsan: Perhaps a city in ancient Rum.

Kashaf: A city in northeastern Iran.

Keemaak, Sea of: Most likely refers to the Caspian Sea.

Kerman: A city southeast of Tehran.

Khaarazm: Or Chorasmia; in present-day Tajikistan and Afghanistan, south of the Aral Sea.

Khalkh: Region in present-day Mongolia.

Khalokh: A town in the land of Tooran.

Khargaah: A border town or area near the Jayhoon River and part of Tooran-Zamin.

Khataah: A city near Chin.

Khatl: Unknown location; perhaps in southern Iran.

Khazar Sea: Caspian Sea.

Khazaria: Land northeast of the Caspian Sea occupying today's Uzbekistan.

Khoonehye Asiran: A city in the district of Ahvaz built by King Shahpoor to house Rumi prisoners; meaning "the dwelling of prisoners."

Khorasan: Region in today's northeastern Iran.

Khorm: Perhaps refers to Khorma, a village in today's northern Iran.

Khorraad: Iranian fire temple.

Khorram Abad: A city built by King Shahpoor in Khuzestan, northwestern Iran.

Khorreh-yeh Ardeshir: A city founded by King Ardeshir in the province of Pars after his victory over Ardavan. It is also referred to as Goor or Firuzabad.

Khotan: A town on the southern side of the Silk Road between China and the west; situated in Tooran-Zamin and ruled for some time by Piran.

Khotlan: A city in Maavaronhar.

Khuzan: A small village in today's Alborz Province of Iran.

Kimaak, Sea of: Kimaak was the name of a Turkic tribe long ago; may refer to the Ural River, which discharges into the Caspian Sea.

Kohan-Dej: A castle in Nishapur built by King Shahpoor that houses the royal administrative offices for some time.

Kojaran: A city on the Persian Gulf.

Konaabad: A city in Tooran-Zamin.

Konaabad, Mount: A mountain in Tooran-Zamin

Kondaz: Pahlavi name for the city of Paykand near today's Bukhara.

Kooch and Baluch: Kooch is a village in today's Iran; Kooch and Baluch are two tribes near Baluchistan, Iran.

Koos: Caucasus.

Kufah: A city in Iran-Zamin on the banks of the Euphrates River.

Kushan: A mountainous region in today's China.

Laadan: In present-day Ukraine; site of a battle where the Iranians lost heavily to the Tooranians under Kay Khosrow.

Lajevardeen, Fortress of: A small fort in Iran.

Maachin: Comprises greater China.

Maavaranhar: An area near the Jayhoon River and part of Tooran-Zamin.

Mada'in: An ancient city on the Tigris River between Ctesiphon and Seleucia.

Mai: An area in today's eastern Afghanistan or Indian subcontinent.

Maimargh: A village in the region of Bukhara.

Manooy: Perhaps an ancient city in Rum.

Margh: A city in today's south Khorasan Province of Iran.

Maroosepend: Palace and the residence of Golinoosh, who guards Khosrow Parviz.

Marv: A city in Iran, situated in today's Afghanistan.

Mayam: A fictional river or sea.

Mazandaran: Residence of the deevs and the White Deev in The Shahnameh including Gorgsaaran; a non-geographical realm that in no way references the present-day province in northern Iran bordering the Caspian Sea.

Mehr Borzeen: Iranian fire temple established by Goshtaasp Shah.

Milad: Also Malad; appears to be a region in India, north of today's Mumbai.

Milad Castle: Residence of the Indian Keid.

Mokran: In Iran-Zamin and in the coastal region of today's Baluchistan, in southern Iran.

Naarvan: An area in northern Iran, perhaps in present-day Mazandaran.

Naarvan, Forest of: Must be somewhere in Mazandaran Province.

Nahravan: A village in northwestern Iran.

Nahravan, Forest of: In northwestern Iran.

Nahravan, River: A reference to the Nahrawan Canal near Ctesiphon and in present-day central Iraq.

Nassibin: A city in northern Iraq.

Navand: A village in northwestern Iran where shines the flame of Barzeen.

Nessa: A city in ancient Khorasan Province.

Nile River: A river in northeastern Africa.

Nimrooz: Capital of Zabolestan or Sistan; served as the prime meridian until Europe gained strength and made the switch to Greenwich, England.

Nishabur: A city in Iran-Zamin, situated in today's Afghanistan.

Nohbahaar: Buddhist temple in Balkh.

Oorigh: Perhaps an ancient city in Rum.

Ormazd-Ardeshir: A city founded by King Ardeshir in Khuzestan.

Paloyeneh: Unclear location, but in the land of Rum.

Pars: A province in southern Iran with Persepolis as its capital.

Pashan: Perhaps in present-day India; site of a battle where the Iranians heavily lost to the Tooranians under the reign of Kay Khosrow.

Paykand: Or Baykand; a city in Tooran-Zamin, near today's Bukhara (Uzbekistan).

Pirooz-Shahpoor: A city in Syria built by King Shahpoor.

Pirooz-Ram: City founded by Pirooz, Sassanian king.

Raibad: A city in Tooran-Zamin

Raam: An Iranian fire temple.

Raameh-Ardeshir: A city founded by King Ardeshir on the way to Pars.

Rey: The oldest city in the province of Tehran; today it is part of the capital city.

Rooendej: A region in Iran.

Rum: Name of regions west of Iran; Byzantium, eastern Roman Empire.

Rumi: Adjective meaning from Byzantium.

Rus: Ancient name for Russia.

Saghilaa, Mount: Appears to be a fictional mountain in Rum.

Saghilaa, Fort: A castle in Rum.

Saghlaab: Land outside of Iran-Zamin and Tooran-Zamin; land of the Slavic people; ruled by Kondor, ally of Afraasiyaab.

Sagsaar: East of Afghanistan.

Sagsaaran: Or Sistan, is in today's eastern Iran and southern Afghanistan, near Baluchistan; also named Sakastan.

Samangan: Land in ancient times and a province in present-day Afghanistan.

Samarkand: A city in Tooran-Zamin, a destination on the Silk Road and in present-day Uzbekistan.

Sari: A town in present-day Mazandaran; once the capital of Iran.

Saroj, Desert of: Region in Iran; unclear of the location.

Sea of Chin: Reference to a body of water in the Far East.

Sea of Sindh: May refer to the Gulf of Oman, south of the Sindh Province, or perhaps the Sindhu (Indus) River.

Sendal: A village in northwestern India.

Sepad, Mount: Appears to be a fictional mountain in Kalaat.

Sepand, Mount: Meaning sacred, holy.

Sepijaab: Area in Tooran-Zamin close to the Jayhoon River.

Shaam: Syria.

Shahd, Mount: Unclear location, perhaps in India.

Shahd River: May be a reference to the Arvand River, also known as the Shatt al-Arab; in today's southern Iraq.

Shahdegan: Name of the hall of feast at the court of King Shirooy.

Shaheh: A city in today's Khuzestan Province of Iran.

Shahpoor: A city built by King Shahpoor.

Shahrzoor: Region in today's Iraq.

Shakni: Land outside of Iran-Zamin and Tooran-Zamin ruled by Shamira.

Shangan: A city around the border between Iran-Zamin and Tooran-Zamin.

Shemiran: The present-day capital of Shimiranat County, in Tehran Province.

Shirkhan: An area in Damavand in western Iran.

Shooraab: A city in northwestern Iran.

Shushtar: An ancient fortress city in the province of Khuzestan where King Shahpoor has a bridge built by the Rumi Bezanoosh.

Siaavosh-Guerd: A city built by Siaavosh in Tooran-Zamin on land given to him by Afraasiyaab.

Sindh: A province in the southeastern part of India.

Sindhu River: Indus River in India.

Sistan: A province in today's eastern Iran and southern Afghanistan, part of Baluchistan; same as Zabolestan.

Soghdi: A region in Tooran-Zamin.

Sorsan: Or Shorsan, a village in central India.

Sughd: A town in Tooran-Zamin; perhaps in northern Mongolia, near the Chinese border.

Sursan: A city founded by Kesra Anushiravan on the way to Rum; no longer in existence.

Taakhdis, Throne of: A multi-level throne raised by Khosrow Parviz in the hippodrome created out of fragments that date back to the time of Iraj, son of Fereydoon. It has one seat for poet bards and landowners; one seat for warriors; a turquoise seat for the vizier/treasurer, closest to the king; and the royal throne.

Tabaristan: Ancient name for the coastal Caspian region of today's province of Mazandaran in northern Iran.

Taleghan: A city in the Alborz mountain range.

Tammisheh: Fereydoon's capital in northern Iran; in Mount Koos (meaning Caucasus).

Taraaz: Or Taraz, a city in Turkestan famous for its beautiful women; also a river in today's Kazakhstan.

Tarmaz: A town on the edge of the Jayhoon River, on the border between Iran-Zamin and Tooran-Zamin; ancient city in northern Afghanistan.

Tartar: Situated in Tooran-Zamin, in today's Azerbaijan.

Tehran: Present-day capital of Iran since 1786.

Terek River: A major river north of Iran that flows into the Caspian Sea.

Tooran-Zamin: Land of Toor and his descendants Pashang and Afraasiyaab; also referred to as Turkestan.

Tous: An ancient city in the province of Khorasan in Iran; also the city where Ferdowsi lived and worked.

Transoxiana: Also referred to as Maavaran-nahr (Arabic). It is in the land of Tooran beyond the Jayhoon (Oxus) River and covers the region in today's Uzbekistan and Tajikistan, and parts of Kyrgyzstan and Kazakhstan.

Turkestan: Land of Turks east of Iran; also referred to as Tooran-Zamin.

Urmia, Lake of: A saltwater lake in the northwestern part of Iran.

Viseh-Guerd: A city in Tooran-Zamin named after Piran's father, Viseh; ancient city in northern Afghanistan.

White Castle: A castle defended by Gojdaham and his children in Iran-Zamin, near Tooran's border.

Yerevan: A city north of Iran that is today the capital of Armenia.

Zaabeh, Mount: Perhaps a mythical mountain in the Alborz mountain range.

Zavehkooh: A village in Iran, in today's Azerbaijan Province.

Zabol: Capital of Sistan, or Zabolestan; a province in today's eastern Iran, part of Baluchistan.

Zabolestan: Also Sistan; land ruled by the hero Nariman and his descendants Saam, Zaal, and Rostam; in today's southern Afghanistan.

Zam: A city on the border between Iran-Zamin and Tooran-Zamin.

Zargh: A village near Marv.

Zargh, River: A river near Marv.

Zarnoosh: A city built by King Dara in the region of Ahvaz, in south-western Iran.

Zerreh, Sea of: Situated in southwestern Afghanistan.

Zibeh Khosrow: A city founded by Kesra Anushiravan to house the Rumi prisoners, built after the ancient city of Antioch.

The World
of
Ferdowsi's *Shahnameh*

Ural River

KHAZARIA

Terek River

*Caucasus
Mountains*

Black Sea

Koos

**Caspian
Sea
Sea of
Gilan**

Konaabad

Dahestan

Yerevan

Tartar

Gorganj

RUM
Byzantium/
Constantinople

ARMENIA

AZERBAIJAN

Amoorieh

Nassibin

Nahravan

Barda

Tammisheh

Khorm

Naarvan

Bastam

Nishab

GILAN

Navand

Halab

Ghebchaagh

Deylam

Shooraab

Ardabil

Gorgan

HAMEDAN

Mount Zaabeh

Chalus

GOLESTAN
GORGSAAR

*Tigris River/
Dajleh*

Khuzan

*Mount
Alborz*

Mount

Amol

Sari

Euphrates River

LORESTAN

Rey

MAZANDARAN

Mount Damavand

Damgha

Taleghan

Bozgoos

Jerusalem

Guran

Tehran

Shemiran

Mount Asprooz

Karkh

Baghdad

Shirkhan

Margh

Kufah

Ctesiphon

Khorram Abad

Ghom

Babylon

Mada'in

*Arvand River/
Shatt al-Arab*

IRAN-ZAMIN

MESOPOTAMIA
ASSYRIA

Shushtar

Ahvaz

Isfahan

Zargh

Land of Taazian
Haamaavaran
Egypt
Nile River

Ghobaad/Awan

Estakhr

Kerman

Shiraz

KAARZI

Mokran

Bahrein

PARS

Jahrom

Zarnoosh

YEMEN

Kojaran

Persian Gulf

*The markings on this map are mere reference points to
the story and may not be historically accurate*

RUS/RUSSIA

Dambar

Mazandaran
Residence of the deevs and the White Deev
in *The Shahnameh* including Gorgsaaran;
a non-geographical realm which in no way
references the present-day province in northern Iran
bordering the Caspian Sea.

*Syr Darya/
Sayhoon River*

Khalkh

**Aral
Sea**

Khotlan

Farab

MAAVARANHAR

SOGHDI

Soghd

Kaat   Paykand   Samarkand

Bukhara

Mai   Khargaah   Chagal   Taraaz   *Kushan Mountains*

*Amu Darya
Jayhoon/Oxus*   Chaadj

T O O R A N - Z A M I N

Maimargh   Khataah

ARMAN-ZAMIN
COSHMAIHAN   CHIN/CHINA   Amoy

Ghabchaagh

Marv   Bukhara   Samangan

Tous   Tarmaz   Andaraab   Khotan

Balkh

Kashaf   Baamian   Dambar

Faariaab   **GHOOR**   Kabol

KHORASAN   Ghaznein

Ghatan

Herat/Hari   Jaram   Zam

Hirmand   Chaghan

Nimrooz

Zabol   Bost

ZABOLESTAN   Kalat

SISTAN   Kandahar   Firozabad

River Hirmand

Sorsan

BALUCHISTAN

*Sindhu River/
Indus River*   INDIA

Ghennooj   Sendal

SINDH

Milad

Sea of Sindh

Glossary of Persian Words

Aab: From aaberoo, meaning honor, nobility, and integrity; code of honor.

Aaban: Eighth month of the solar year.

Aazar: Ninth month of the solar year and ninth day of the month.

Aazar Borzeen: Fire temple founded by Lohraasp.

Aazargoshasp: Divine, holy, eternal flame of the Zoroastrians; a revered fire temple for kings and warriors during the Sassanian times in Azerbaijan.

Andisheh: Thought.

Ard: The twenty-ninth day of any month is the day of Ard in ancient Iran.

Arrash: Unit of measurement corresponding to the length of the forearm, from fingertip to elbow.

Aroos: Meaning bride, is the name for the treasure Kay Khosrow collects in the city of Tous.

Aroos: Meaning bride, is the name for the treasure Khosrow Parviz forms from tributes collected from Chin, Bulgaria, Rum, and Russia.

Ayeen: Divine principle or code of human life; path and purpose that reflects all that encompasses the divine, free of barriers set by culture, geography, dogma, or religion.

Baad: Meaning wind; name of the eight treasure Khosrow Parviz forms.

Baadaavar: Meaning windblown, is the name of the second treasure

Khosrow Parviz forms.

Babreh Bayan: Armor that is worn only by Rostam. Uncertain about its meaning. Literally refers to leopard skin. Other interpretations refer to beaver skin or dragon skin. It is meant to be waterproof and impenetrable.

Bahman: Name of the second day of the month and the eleventh month of the solar year.

Bahraam: Mars.

Barsom: Sacred twigs from the pomegranate tree used in ancient Zoroastrian prayers and ceremonies.

Barzeen: Zoroastrian fire temple with an ever-burning flame situated in Khorasan, in northeastern Iran.

Bidaad: Meaning unjust.

Daad: Infinite justice; justice that is non-judgmental and unchangeable for it is divine, constant, eternal; different from human justice that is encompassed by a strict set of laws.

Dehghan: Farmer; keeper of land and crops, of rain and sun, and all that grows; keeper of ancient wisdom, poet, and bard.

Dibah Khosravi: Meaning royal silk; name of the third treasure Khosrow Parviz forms.

Dinar: Gold coin.

Dirham: Silver coin.

Dong: Six parts of a piece of real estate that can be divided and apportioned.

Esfand: Twelfth month of the Persian solar calendar; begins in February and ends in March; also the name of the plant and herb rue; also meaning sacred or holy, as in Sepand.

Esfand: Rue; meaning sacred or holy, as in Sepand; also twelfth month of the Persian solar calendar; begins in February and ends in March.

Farr: Divine grace; state of consciousness holding infinite grace of light and life.

Farsang: Ancient unit of measure equivalent to 6.24 kilometers or 3.88 miles.

Gohar: Essence.

Haft Cheshmeh: Meaning Seven Sources; a jewel given by Fereydoon to his son Iraj.

Hejrat: Or solar Hijri, refers to the calendar adopted in Iran after the Muslim invasion; it dates to the time the Prophet Muhammad traveled from Mecca to Medina in the Gregorian year 622. The calendar year begins on the first day of spring, on Nowruz, at the time of the spring equinox. It is somewhat different from the Hijri Islamic lunar calendar: though journey from Mecca to Medina also mars the starting date, the new year falls in the month of July.

Hoor, day of: The eleventh day of every month, the day of the Sun.

Jaan: Life force, soul, spirit.

Kaavian: Belonging to Kaaveh, the blacksmith, who leads the opposition against Zahaak. The Kaaviani banner is made of the cloth of blacksmiths with the colors red, yellow, and purple representing the two ends of the color spectrum as well as the center color.

Kalileh and Demneh: An ancient collection of animal stories originally written in Sanskrit but subsequently translated into Arabic and Persian.

Kamand: Ancient unit of measure.

Kay: King.

Kharvaar: A unit of measure equivalent to about 300 kilograms.

Khazraa: Meaning green; name of the sixth treasure formed by Khosrow Parviz out of freshwater pearls.

Kherrad: Wisdom; Eternal Wisdom; absolute, pure consciousness.

Khodaay Nameh: Translates as The Book of Kings. It is one of the sources, written in prose and in the language of Pahlavi, used by Ferdowsi for his work.

Kianian: Royal; from kian, meaning royalty.

Kiblah: Or Qiblah, is the direction of the Sacred Mosque in Mecca and the direction of prayer.

Kushti: A sacred belt or girdle worn by Zoroastrians around their waists; it has 72 interwoven white strands of sheep's wool representing seventy-two chapters of a part of The Avesta.

Laajevard: Lapis lazuli; name of the middle seat on the throne of Taakhdis.

Mahn: Reference to a form of weight measurement in the ancient Middle East, around 3 kilograms or 6.6 pounds; so 600 mahns is equivalent to 1,800 kilograms or 3,968 pounds.

Mehr: Complex word that includes deep eternal love, affection, compassion, mercy; also the seventh month of the Iranian calendar.

Mehregan: A festival and memorial to Fereydoon, still celebrated today on the Mehr day of the Mehr month of the year. Iranian fall festival during the month of October.

Mishsar: Ram's head; name of the lower seat on the throne of Taakhdis.

Mithqal: Unit of measuring weight equivalent to 4.25 grams; often used to weigh precious metal.

Naam: Divine essence, what is contained in space; also defined as "name."

Nowruz: New Day, the Persian New Year, still observed by Iranians of all religions during the spring equinox on or around March 21.

Pahlavan: Noble hero, paladin, warrior, fighter for the cause of mehr; guardian of crown and throne, soldier of light.

Pahlavi: Or middle Persian; literary language during the Sassanian rule until the advent of the modern Persian language.

Pandavsi: A Pahlavi currency, each coin equivalent to five dinars.

Pishdaadian: Meaning the era prior to the rule of law. The dynasty comprises the first Persian kings: Kiumars, Hooshang, and Tahmures.

Quintal: An historical unit of mass; 0.01 quintal is equivalent to 1 kilogram or around 2 pounds.

Raai: Will or thought (andisheh); intellect or knowing that works in favor of universal time, not human or chronological time.

Ratal: A measure of weight equivalent to 12 to 16 ounces.

Saddeh: Festival to celebrate Hooshang's discovery of fire in The Shahnameh; meaning one hundred, it marks one hundred days before the start of spring, or Nowruz; it is a celebration of overcoming darkness. Also referred to as the Feast of Bahman.

Sepand: Same as esfand, meaning sacred or holy.

Sepandarmaz: The fifth day of any month on the solar calendar.

Sitir: Form of measure equivalent to 75 grams.

Shaadvard: Meaning giver of joy; name of the seventh treasure formed by Khosrow Parviz.

Shavaal: Tenth month of the Islamic calendar.

Sokhan: Divine Word, ultimate truth.

Sookhteh: Meaning burnt; name of the fifth treasure formed by Khosrow Parviz.

Tammuz: Tenth month of the Hebrew calendar and the modern Assyrian calendar; corresponds to July in the Gregorian calendar.

Teer: Mercury.

Yazdan: Creator of all that is manifested, unmanifested, and all that is yet to come into existence. Plural of Yzad (divine) encompasses all of divinity.

Zamin: Land of; for instance, Iran-Zamin means land of Iran.

Zand Avesta: Avesta is the Zoroastrian holy scripture; Zand is the interpretation of it.

The Persian Calendar

Based on the solar calendar, the months are named after twelve divinities and correspond to nature's cycles and the signs of the zodiac:

Spring:
Farvardin – Aries; the first month of the year begins with Nowruz, the first day of spring and the spring equinox.
Ordibehesht – Taurus; spans the months of April and May.
Khordaad – Gemini; third month of the year.

Summer:
Teer – Cancer; Mercury; the fourth month begins with the summer solstice.
Mordaad – Leo; fifth month of the year.
Shahrivar – Virgo; sixth month of the solar year.

Fall:
Mehr – Libra; the seventh month begins with the fall equinox or Mehregan.
Aaban – Scorpio; eighth month of the year.
Aazar – Sagittarius; ninth month of the year, ends with the winter solstice or Yalda.

Winter:
Dey – Capricorn; tenth month of the year.
Bahman – Aquarius; eleventh month of the solar year.
Esfand – Pisces; twelfth month of the year.

Printed in the USA
CPSIA information can be obtained
at www.ICGtesting.com
LVHW041624041123
762611LV00007B/8